"*Murmuring against Moses* is a fascinating book that combines in a unique way an overview of dissident Pentateuchal research in the last 150 years, a revelation of the major shortcomings of Pentateuch models (especially the very obvious absence of any Zion theology in the Pentateuch that urgently asks for a convincing explanation), and a research history on Pentateuchal research from antiquity to the classic formulation of the documentary hypothesis by Julius Wellhausen. Students and colleagues will benefit greatly from it and will be encouraged to break new ground in their own Pentateuchal studies."

—BENJAMIN KILCHÖR
Staatsunabhängige Theologische Hochschule, Switzerland

"*Murmuring against Moses: The Contentious History and Contested Future of Pentateuchal Studies* by John S. Bergsma and Jeffrey L. Morrow is a thoroughly researched and well-argued presentation of the widely accepted scholarly construct which has rejected the Mosaic authorship of the Pentateuch in favor of its composition from four late documents (J, E, D, and P), as most memorably set forth by Julius Wellhausen in the late nineteenth century. The authors point out anti-Semitic and anti-Catholic elements embraced by Wellhausen and his predecessors. They note the improbability of his assumption of the Prophets coming before the Law, and highlight problems posed to his construction by the Samaritan Pentateuch. They also detail the objections to the Documentary Hypothesis raised by Jewish scholars such as Umberto Cassuto and Cyrus H. Gordon and by Egyptologists such as Kenneth A. Kitchen and James K. Hoffmeier. If the authors are correct, which I believe they are, then there should be no 'future' to this long-lived hypothesis in Pentateuchal studies."

—EDWIN M. YAMAUCHI
Miami University

MURMURING AGAINST

MOSES

MURMURING
AGAINST
MOSES

The Contentious History and Contested
Future of Pentateuchal Studies

John S. Bergsma *&* Jeffrey L. Morrow

EMMAUS
ACADEMIC

Steubenville, Ohio

EMMAUS
ACADEMIC

Steubenville, Ohio
www.emmausacademic.com

A Division of The St. Paul Center for Biblical Theology
Editor-in-Chief: Scott Hahn
1468 Parkview Circle
Steubenville, Ohio 43952

Library of Congress Cataloging-in-Publication Data applied for
ISBNs: 978-1-64585-149-3 hardcover / 978-1-64585-150-9 paperback / 978-1-64585-151-6 ebook

Many of the Scripture quotations have been translated into English from the original Hebrew by the authors. All rights reserved.

Excerpts from the Catechism of the Catholic Church, second edition, copyright © 2000, Libreria Editrice Vaticana—United States Conference of Catholic Bishops, Washington, D.C. Noted as "CCC" in the text.

Cover design by Emily Demary and Emma Nagle.
Layout by Allison Merrick.
Cover image: *The Adoration of the Golden Calf* by Nicolas Poussin

CONTENTS

INTRODUCTION

In 1998, David Clines published the humorous essay, "New Directions in Pooh Studies: Überlieferungs- und religionsgeschichtliche Studien zum Pu-Buch," which pointed out how silly and arbitrary so much of literary source criticism can prove to be.[1] For anyone familiar with A. A. Milne's classic works on Winnie the Pooh, Clines's piece is quite enjoyable. Familiarity with source critical theories like the Documentary Hypothesis of Pentateuchal composition—which is clearly the paradigm for the essay—makes Clines's satire spot on. As an example, Clines mentions the various ways to which Winnie the Pooh is referred throughout the Pooh corpus: Pooh, Winnie the Pooh, Bear, Edward Bear, Pooh-Bear, etc. He points out, tongue firmly planted in cheek, that "We observe the oscillation between various *names* for Pooh, an unerring pointer to diversity of authorship."[2] He proceeds to examine doublets and other stylistic criteria found in other source critical theories. The first example is worth sharing:

> An excellent example of the redactor's method of intertwining his sources may be seen in the account of Pooh's being stuck in the entrance to Rabbit's house . . . When Pooh realizes he is stuck, according to the first source:
> "'Oh, help!' said Pooh. 'I'd better go back.'"
> But according to the second source:
> "'Oh, bother!' said Pooh. 'I shall have to go on.'"
> The redactor has simply set down these two contradictory statements side by side, and then has attempted to harmonize them by his own conflation:
> "'I can't do either!', said Pooh. 'Oh, help and bother!'"[3]

---

[1] David J. A. Clines, *On the Way to the Postmodern: Old Testament Essays, 1967–1998*, (Sheffield, UK: Sheffield Academic Press, 1998), 2:830–39.

[2] Clines, *On the Way*, 2:830.

[3] Clines, *On the Way*, 2:831–32.

The classic example of source criticism within biblical studies is the Documentary Hypothesis for the composition of the Pentateuch, the Bible's first five books. Indeed, the question of the Pentateuch's origins lies at the heart of the modern historical critical study of the Bible. Its core principles focus on double names and double narratives. These two literary features formed the very basis for the historical critical method, first in source criticism, and became fundamental to modern biblical studies as a scholarly discipline.[4] What we hope to do in this present volume is contribute to the conversation within Pentateuchal studies that seeks to break new ground and shift the reigning scholarly paradigm.[5] In doing this we are joining a growing group of scholars who are unsatisfied with traditional source critical approaches to the Pentateuch precisely because of the many ways such approaches—for all their benefits—fail to account for the growing data from diverse disciplines bearing on the Pentateuch's origin.[6]

What we are not doing in this book: We are not going to argue that Moses is the author of the Pentateuch. In fact, we are not going to come to a conclusion on who is responsible for the Pentateuch in its final form. We are not even going to come to a conclusion as to precisely when the Pentateuch was written or finalized. What our work hopes to accomplish is to challenge the hegemony of standard source critical approaches to the composition of the Pentateuch and to highlight new evidence for the Pentateuch's antiquity, at least prior to the Babylonian Exile. We do this by first reviewing the vast amount of scholarly literature composed over more than a century that challenges the Documentary Hypothesis, supporting both the unity and historical reliability of the Pentateuch. These arguments against the Documentary Hypothesis come from scholars representing a wide range of religious traditions—Jewish, Catholic, and Protestant, including orthodox and more secular scholars—and scholarly disciplines: biblical studies, archaeology, Egyptology, and ancient Near Eastern studies.

In this book we do not endorse any of the particular scholars we survey here—and they often hold contradictory positions among themselves. We are simply providing an overview of the history of scholarly challenges to the Documentary Hypothesis. We believe this will be useful because the

---

[4] See the important study on this by Aulikki Nahkola, *Double Narratives in the Old Testament: The Foundations of Method in Biblical Criticism* (Berlin: Walter de Gruyter, 2001).

[5] The notion of paradigm shifting is indebted to Thomas S. Kuhn's philosophical classic, *The Structure of Scientific Revolutions* (Chicago: University of Chicago Press, 1962).

[6] See, e.g., the important contributions in Matthias Armgardt, Benjamin Kilchör, and Markus Zehnder, ed., *Paradigm Change in Pentateuchal Research* (Wiesbaden: Harrassowitz, 2019); and Daniel I. Block and Richard L. Schultz, ed., *Sepher Torath Mosheh: Studies in the Composition and Interpretation of Deuteronomy* (Peabody, MA: Hendrickson, 2017).

Documentary Hypothesis is often presented in the classroom as the starting assumption—and as unassailable—for approaching the Pentateuch.

Our book is divided into three parts, with each part composed of three chapters. Our first part reviews and exposits these various positions challenging the Documentary Hypothesis. In so doing, we have provided a useful resource for those interested in the history of scholarship pointing out the many flaws of the foundation of biblical source criticism. These first chapters have a wide application outside of Pentateuchal studies into the source critical studies of other parts of the Bible.

After surveying the history of scholarly challenges to Pentateuchal source criticism, we come to the second part of our volume, where we present new evidence from the Samaritan Pentateuch as well as from the Prophets demonstrating the antiquity of the Pentateuch. Whereas scholars have argued (and assumed) that the final form of the Pentateuch—including much of the material in Exodus through Numbers ("Priestly" and "Holiness" traditions, or "P" and "H") and also Deuteronomy ("Deuteronomic" traditions or "D")—was composed or heavily edited after the Babylonian Exile (c. 587–537 BCE), we show that this is no longer tenable in light of the evidence of quotation or allusion to all of the supposed sources of the Pentateuch in the pre-exilic or exilic Prophets, as well the absence of any focus on Jerusalem in the Pentateuch, which is difficult to explain in the post-exilic period in the face of the rise of Samaritanism and the Samaritan embrace of the Pentateuch.

The third and final part of our volume concludes with a history of Pentateuchal source criticism from its earliest stages in late antiquity through its zenith in Julius Wellhausen's classic formulation of the Documentary Hypothesis at the end of the nineteenth century. These chapters show the development of literary source criticism as somewhat arbitrary and haphazard, forged in religious polemics as well as the particular politics of specific exegetes. We also note how Muslim polemicists played an important role early in the medieval period in attempting to discredit the Pentateuch in its present form as divine revelation.

These criticisms were picked up again in the seventeenth century by skeptics attempting to subvert religious authority structures and elevate the status of individual scholars over and against more traditional religious interpretive authorities. In the Enlightenment period, ever more secular academic institutions created an environment at the same time increasingly hostile to particularistic faith traditions and hospitable to the flourishing of nonreligious readings of the Bible and of its history (and history of composition) that fit the politics of the day. This is the historical and social context in which scholars developed the methods that would lead to the dissection of Scripture along hypothetical lines. The Bible would thus be dismembered into fragments allegedly representing original hypothetical sources. This hermeneutical trend served secular political ends.

Now that we have given an overview of the sections of our present work, it is worthwhile to look more specifically at what each chapter will discuss. Our first chapter surveys the history of challenges to the Documentary Hypothesis for approximately the first half of the twentieth century, primarily coming from literary analysis. The second and third chapters pick up where the first left off and continue the survey for the remainder of the twentieth century into the twenty-first, primarily from the perspective of the disciplines of archaeology and ancient Near Eastern studies. Chapter four closely examines important verbal parallels that indicate that the Prophets knew the texts of Leviticus and Deuteronomy. This is significant because it runs counter to how biblical scholars have been conditioned to understand the relationship. Scholars typically view Leviticus and Deuteronomy ("P/H" and "D") as influenced by the Prophets, being written or edited after the Prophets, and not the other way around. The evidence examined in this chapter supports the view that both Leviticus and Deuteronomy were written prior to the exilic prophets, mainly Ezekiel and Jeremiah.

Chapter five highlights the complete absence of Zion theology from the Torah. The Pentateuch as we have it makes no sense if Jerusalem was already the center of Judaism. There is no mention of Jerusalem anywhere in the Pentateuch, nor is there any mention of the Temple, nor of the Davidic kingdom. Moreover, the Pentateuch, even the Masoretic Text, has a much more northern tone to it than is usually recognized. Such a northern focus favors the Samaritans in ways that do not make sense if much of this was the product of the southern Kingdom of Judah, or of priests in Jerusalem attempting to weaponize Israelite tradition with a Southern-focused text after the Exile. The sixth chapter continues this discussion, focusing in more detail on the presence of Zion theology in all the other parts of the Hebrew Bible *except* the Pentateuch.

The remaining three chapters look at the history of how questions about the Pentateuch's origins led first to the denial of its Mosaic authorship and origin and eventually to the development of source criticism. Chapter seven surveys the challenges to the Pentateuch's Mosaic authorship from early Gnostic and Roman anti-Christian polemics through the medieval Muslim period, showing how these arguments survived in the medieval Latin Christian West. Chapter eight examines the Renaissance through the early Enlightenment period (the seventeenth century). The focus is on the early modern skeptics who begin to speculate on late dating the Pentateuch to the period after the Babylonian Exile and, relying on previous arguments from the medieval period, begin to challenge the Pentateuch's Mosaic authorship based on stylistic criteria and on apparent anachronisms in the text.

The final chapter examines how eighteenth- and nineteenth-century scholars built upon this skeptical textual foundation with literary theories designed to identify distinct sources underlying the Pentateuch. In each of these three chapters we show how philosophical, theological, and political factors played a far stronger role in developing these source critical theories than did any purely objective attempt to get at a real history behind the texts. Indeed, we can see how Joseph Blenkinsopp can conclude that "it must be acknowledged that [Wellhausen's] presentation of early Judaism stands within a long tradition of denigration which, greatly reinforced by the clarity and persuasiveness of his own work, made its modest contribution in due course to the 'final solution' of the Jewish problem under the Third Reich."[7] Wellhausen's opinions on Judaism were the context for his Documentary Hypothesis. This is why Solomon Schechter entitled his famous essay critiquing Wellhausen's views "Higher Criticism—Higher Anti-Semitism."[8]

Our hope is that this volume will help show that the assured results of more than a century of the historical critical method are anything but assured. The time is ripe for a paradigm shift in biblical studies that continues to take history seriously but refuses to rest on the past scholarly tradition without a willingness to challenge those assumptions. We believe, and we think this volume shows, that the Pentateuch as a primarily unified pre-exilic document has greater explanatory power than the standard source critical approaches.

---

[7] Joseph Blenkinsopp, *Prophecy and Canon: A Contribution to the Study of Jewish Origins* (Notre Dame, IN: University of Notre Dame Press, 1977), 20. For more on the implicit anti-Judaism in Wellhausen's work see Moshe Weinfeld, *Normative and Sectarian Judaism in the Second Temple Period* (London: T & T Clark, 2005), 289–90.

[8] Solomon Schechter, "Higher Criticism—Higher Anti-Semitism," in *Seminary Address and Other Papers* (Cincinnati, OH: Ark Publishers, 1915), 35–39.

PART 1

MOSES AND THE SOURCES:
A SURVEY OF CHALLENGES TO THE
DOCUMENTARY HYPOTHESIS

CHAPTER 1

STYLISTIC UNITY:

THE FIRST FIFTY YEARS OF LITERARY CHALLENGES TO THE DOCUMENTARY HYPOTHESIS

It is often forgotten that challenges to various aspects of the Documentary Hypothesis came immediately, and have continued fairly unabated, for more than a century. Perhaps the most famous was August Dillmann, who argued that P, the Priestly Source, was much older than Wellhausen would allow, reaching back before the Assyrian Exile sometime between 800 and 700 BCE.[1] Julius Wellhausen's own friend and colleague in classical studies at both Geifswald and Göttingen, Ulrich von Wilamowitz-Moellendorff, criticized him for his staunch refusal to incorporate ancient Near Eastern findings in his biblical studies.[2] In this chapter, we take a look at some of the lesser-known, but important, challenges to the Documentary Hypothesis from early in the first half of the twentieth century.

---

[1] Dillmann was an important Semitic philologist, noted especially for his work on Ethiopic in addition to his Old Testament studies. See, e.g., Messay Kebede, "Eurocentrism and Ethiopian Historiography: Deconstructing Semitization," *International Journal of Ethiopian Studies* 1, no. 1 (2003): 1; Jack Fellman, "Founders of Ethiopic Studies: Job Ludolf (1624–1704) and August Dillmann (1823–1894)," *Ancient Near Eastern Studies* 39 (2002): 207–11. Among Dillmann's main contributions to the conversation on the Documentary Hypothesis were his *Die Genesis*, 5th ed. (Leipzig: Hirzel, 1886); and especially *Die Bücher Numeri, Deuteronomium und Josue* (Leipzig: Hirzel, 1886).

[2] Ulrich von Wilamowitz-Moellendorff, *Erinnerungen, 1814–1914*, 2nd ed. (Leipzig: Koehler, 1928), 189–90; and *Letter 31* (1918), in *The Preserved Letters of Ulrich von Wilamowitz-Moellendorff to Eduard Schwartz*, ed. William M. Calder III and Robert L. Fowler (Munich: Verlag der Bayerischen Akademie der Wissenschaften, 1986), 32.

We begin with a look at the momentous challenge the very existence of the Samaritan Pentateuch posed. After this, we focus on a few Jewish, Catholic, and Protestant scholars who concentrated on the literary analysis of the Pentateuch. They argue, each in their different ways, that the case for literary unity is stronger than the case supporting the Documentary Hypothesis. Some of these scholars also argue for the antiquity of the Pentateuch, against Wellhausen's later dating of the Pentateuchal sources.

THE PROBLEM OF THE SAMARITAN PENTATEUCH

In 1911, one of the earliest robust challenges to the Documentary Hypothesis was published by J. Iverach Munro, a minister of the United Free Church.[3] Although dated, Munro's work remains full of important insights that would continue to pose a serious challenge to Wellhausenian Documentary-type hypotheses—at least regarding the late dating of sources to the Babylonian Exile or afterward. That is, it would continue to pose such a challenge were it not almost completely ignored by contemporary scholars. We will attempt to revive Munro's important work by updating some of his arguments in our chapter on the Samaritans.

The existence of the Samaritan Pentateuch had long been an obstacle to late dating of Pentateuchal material. Although the Samaritans had been reading the Pentateuch in their own language and textual tradition for centuries, Western Europe didn't really encounter the Samaritan Pentateuch until the sixteenth century, the time of the Protestant Reformation. It appears that Guillaume Postel may have been the first intellectual in Western Europe to obtain Samaritan manuscripts, and although he may not have had the Pentateuch, he at least knew about its existence in the Samaritan language. The famous Joseph Scaliger, who had befriended Postel, attempted to obtain a copy of the it by contacting various Samaritans living in Egypt and Palestine but had no success. Early in the seventeenth century, Pietro della Valle was able to secure a manuscript that ended up in the Oratory of Paris's library, and this was followed by successive European acquisitions of Samaritan Pentateuch manuscripts. Jean Morin was the key figure placing Samaritan studies on the map in Europe, amassing manuscripts and producing studies of this unique form of the Pentateuch.[4]

---

[3] J. Iverach Munro, *The Samaritan Pentateuch and Modern Criticism* (London: James Nisbet & Co., 1911).

[4] Scott Mandelbrote, "The Old Testament and Its Ancient Versions in Manuscript and Print in the West, from c. 1480 to c. 1780," in *The New Cambridge History of the Bible*, vol. 3, *From 1450 to 1750*, ed. Euan Cameron (Cambridge, UK: Cambridge University Press, 2016), 82–109 at 102–3; and Alastair Hamilton, "Scaliger the Orientalist," in *"All My*

The main problem the Samaritan Pentateuch would pose for a late dating of any portion of the Pentateuch is that the two Pentateuchs, Samaritan and Masoretic, were almost identical in content. Up through the work of Wilhelm Martin Leberecht de Wette (1780–1849), one of the founding professors of the University of Berlin, scholars recognized that the Pentateuch must date from prior to the schism between Northern Israel and Judah, long before the Babylonian Exile. Why would northern Israelites like the Samaritans use the same portions of the Pentateuch as southern Judeans if those texts were written in the South after their schism? It only makes sense that they shared the text in common because it was formed prior to their separation. De Wette fabricated a narrative that would account for the Samaritans continually borrowing from their enemies to the south as they put together their own Pentateuch. He asserted that the North had an unbroken relationship with the South and thus updated their Pentateuch accordingly to match, in most instances, what was being composed and redacted in the South. De Wette imagines a priest from the South bringing the proto-Masoretic Pentateuch to the North at the founding of Mount Gerizim, accounting for the Samaritan Pentateuch.[5] He was not the first to do this, but his narrative became the most influential, and it is the most elaborate to date.[6] After de Wette cleared the way for a late Pentateuch, dated to after the northern Israelite separation from the south, later scholars were able to go back and embellish claims about the differences between the two Pentateuchs.

Heinrich Friedrich Wilhelm Gesenius, a biblical scholar and author of a famous Hebrew grammar,[7] was one of the main perpetrators of this embellishment in his attack of the Samaritan Pentateuch. J. Iverach Munro's main target in his challenge to the Documentary Hypothesis was not de Wette but Gesenius. Since there was no historical foundation for de Wette's imaginative assertions about the Samaritans borrowing from the South, no one

---

Books in Foreign Tongues": Scaliger's Oriental Legacy in Leiden, ed. Arnoud Vrolijk and Kasper van Ommen (Leiden, NL: Leiden University Library, 2009), 10–17.

5   Wilhelm Martin Leberecht de Wette, *Beiträge zur Einleitung in das Alte Testament*, vol. 1, *Kritischer Versuch über die Glaubwürdigkeit der Bücher der Chronik mit Hinsicht auf die Geschichte der Mosaischen Bücher und Gesetzgebung* (Halle: Schimmelpfennig, 1806), 188–223.

6   On de Wette's importance here, see Scott W. Hahn and Jeffrey L. Morrow, *Modern Biblical Criticism as a Tool of Statecraft (1700–1900)* (Steubenville, OH: Emmaus Academic, 2020), 140–42; and John W. Rogerson, *W. M. L. de Wette, Founder of Modern Biblical Criticism: An Intellectual Biography* (Sheffield, UK: Journal for the Study of the Old Testament Press, 1992), 59.

7   The specific text under question appears to be Gulielmi Gesenii, *De Pentateuchi Samaritani origine Indole et Auctoritate: Commentario Philologica-Critica* (Halle: Libreria Rengerianae, 1815).

really questioned the similarities between the two versions of the Pentateuch after his theories gained traction. When questions did arise in the nineteenth century, Gesenius and others exaggerated the differences between the two. Thus, Munro's work is an attempt to show that, in fact, the two Pentateuchs are remarkably similar, containing all of the various portions attributed by Wellhausen to different documentary sources. The main point his work makes is that, had the Jewish Pentateuch been a patchwork of documentary sources, coming together long after the split between North and South—in fact after the Babylonian Exile, sometime in the fourth century—the Samaritans would be expected only to have the Pentateuchal portion commonly ascribed to Northern Israel, namely the Elohistic narratives ("E"). And yet they have the entire Pentateuch, with only minor variations—notably the early central sanctuary for Israel being located at Mt. Gerizim instead of Mt. Ebal (Deut 27:3).

Munro goes further than this, however, in showing the problems with the common source critical assumption that Deuteronomy, the alleged product of the Deuteronomist, emerged from no earlier than the time of King Josiah and supported the policies of the South. If that were the case, Munro underscores, then why would the Jewish version of the Pentateuch agree with the Samaritan Pentateuch in identifying the central sanctuary and location of the Mosaic promulgation of Deuteronomy in the North, in the region of Shechem, albeit at Ebal and not Gerizim?

> The unanimity of the Hebrew-Samaritan and Hebrew Pentateuch in bearing witness to the Shechem district having been selected by Moses for the promulgation of the Law is a fact of outstanding importance—one of the controlling factors in settling the problem. This fact when truly realised practically destroys that current view of the origin of the Pentateuch which places it either in or after the time of the Exile. It seems also to reduce the theory, that Deuteronomy was first written in the time of Josiah, to an impossibility. This fact can be weighed aright by asking, Where is Jerusalem in Deuteronomy? The answer is, Nowhere; the very name is absent. From the point of view of criticism, then, the fact that both Hebrew and Hebrew-Samaritan Pentateuchs *unite* in signally honouring the district of Shechem, a part of Northern Israel embracing both Ebal and Gerizim, reduces the question between Ebal and Gerizim to nothing. Where is Jerusalem? Ephraim is much in evidence. Where is the city of David? A central sanctuary, advocated in Josiah's time without reference to Jerusalem, is a glaring anachronism; such a central sanctuary emphasizing the claims of Ephraim, as is here done by both Jew and Samaritan, completely

ignoring Jerusalem, is, on any sound principles of historical criticism, so improbable as to amount to an impossibility.[8]

As we shall see later in our volume, Munro's basic arguments regarding the antiquity of the Pentateuch have become increasingly persuasive in light of recent evidence of the antiquity of the Samaritan cult.

THE NAMES OF GOD IN THE QUR'AN

Another important figure, and American contemporary of the British Munro, was Robert Dick Wilson (1856–1930). Wilson's work is all but ignored now, and would likely be regarded as "fundamentalist" by contemporary scholars. "Fundamentalist" has become a term of contempt used to dismiss devout religious adherents of whatever tradition, but was originally a self-identification of a group of scholars at Princeton Theological Seminary.[9] Wilson was among this group that eventually left the institution. These "Fundamentalists" were not, contrary to popular imagination, ignorant or unlearned folk. Wilson, for example, had studied more than forty languages. He read the German source critics to whom he responded in their original languages, and he read the Bible and ancillary ancient literature in their original languages as well. In 1919, Wilson wrote an important article that challenged just one aspect of the Wellhausenian Documentary Hypothesis, namely the division of J (Yahwist) and E (Elohist) sources based on the use of different names for God (*Yahweh* for J, and *Elohim* for E), based upon Wilson's study of the names for God in the Muslim Qur'an.[10]

At the outset of his article, Wilson summarizes the great Old Testament scholar Samuel Rolles Driver (of the famous *Brown-Driver-Briggs Hebrew and English Lexicon*) to show that "the main objective reason why the unity of authorship in the case of the so-called Jehovistic and Elohistic documents of the Pentateuch is denied lies in the fact that in some chapters and sections the word *Elohim* (God) is used and in others Jehovah."[11] He then turns to the study of the uses of two Arabic words used for God in the Qur'an, *Allah* and *Rab*, with detailed tables showing their occurrences within the Quranic *suras*. In his conclusion, he explains that "The above tables show every kind

---

[8] Munro, *Samaritan Pentateuch*, 59–60.

[9] See, e.g., William L. Portier, "Fundamentalism in North America: A Modern Anti-Modernism," *Communio* 28, no. 3 (2001): 581–98; and George M. Marsden, *Fundamentalism and American Culture* (Oxford, UK: Oxford University Press, 2006).

[10] R. D. Wilson, "The Use of 'God' and 'Lord' in the Koran," *Princeton Theological Review* 17 (1919): 644–50.

[11] Wilson, "Use of 'God,'" 644.

of variation in the use of the designations of the Deity that is met within the Pentateuch. In the case of the Koran the unity of authorship is undeniable. Why then should it be thought" that in the case of the Pentatateuch, multiple authors are required?[12]

REV. ARTHUR HENRY FINN ON THE PENTATEUCH'S UNITY

Rev. Arthur Henry Finn, who spent time as a missionary in Burma and India, also had been a lecturer in Hebrew at Leeds Clergy School and published a number of works on the Bible. For our purposes, his most significant is his massive (556 pages) *The Unity of the Pentateuch*, which, although no date is given, was likely written around 1924.[13] Finn divides his work into two major halves. The first half examines the evidence for source critical divisions of the Pentateuch,[14] beginning with the narratives[15] and followed by the laws.[16] The second half challenges the dominant Pentateuchal source critical paradigm,[17] first critiquing the methods[18] and followed by the specific results.[19]

---

[12] Wilson, "Use of 'God,'" 650. Wilson wrote a number of other texts that challenged other aspects of the Documentary Hypothesis, but they are perhaps less significant, certainly less unique, than his article on the Qur'an. See, e.g., "Scientific Biblical Criticism," *Princeton Theological Review* 17 (1919): 190–240 (notably, he praises Munro's book as an "able criticism of the work of Gesenius" on 224n63); and *A Scientific Investigation of the Old Testament* (Philadelphia, PA: The Sunday School Times Company, 1926).

[13] A. H. Finn, *The Unity of the Pentateuch: An Examination of the Higher Critical Theory as to the Composite Nature of the Pentateuch* (London: Marshall Brothers, n.d.). In his lecture notes, Kenneth Kitchen dates Finn's work to 1924. See his citations throughout in Kenneth A. Kitchen, *Pentateuchal Criticism and Interpretation: Notes of Three Lectures Given at the Annual Conference of the Theological Students' Fellowship, Held at the Hayes, Swanwick, Derbyshire from December 27 to 31, 1965* (Leicester, UK: Theological Students' Fellowship, 1965), which is where we first found out about Finn's work. We know that Finn's book was published after 1911 because he cites the eleventh edition of the Encyclopaedia Britannica, which was published in 1910–1911, as "the latest" edition. The so-called twelfth edition was merely the eleventh edition with a supplement attached to it in 1922, so it is not clear if Finn had this edition in mind. The thirteenth edition involved another supplemental addition, which was published in 1926. It was not until the fourteenth edition of 1929 that there was a major revision and departure from what had been published in the eleventh edition.

[14] Finn, *Unity of the Pentateuch*, 1–328.

[15] Finn, *Unity of the Pentateuch*, 3–145.

[16] Finn, *Unity of the Pentateuch*, 147–328.

[17] Finn, *Unity of the Pentateuch*, 329–495.

[18] Finn, *Unity of the Pentateuch*, 331–412.

[19] Finn, *Unity of the Pentateuch*, 413–95. The volume concludes with a brief conclusion and three appendices on Bacon, P, and the historical criticism of the New Testament.

At the very outset of his work, Finn shows himself to be a more careful reader of the source critical discussions than many of his contemporaries, even more than the textbook versions, which limit the discussion to the J, E, D, and P sources. Finn analyzes the redactional activity that Wellhausen and others posited, including, for example, the various hypothetical stages of J.[20] He also walks through the discussion of the relationship of P and H.[21] He traces the history of these source identifications back to Jean Astruc and the division of the text based on different names for God.[22] He proceeds to discuss duplicate narratives,[23] and all of the other major criteria assessed in the Documentary Hypothesis, all the while linking each attribute of the theory with concrete examples from the biblical text. He does this so that readers can see the merit of the source critical position while at the same time raising challenges as he goes. His main source critical interlocutor is S. R. Driver. Interestingly, throughout his analysis he includes a few footnotes challenging source critical scholars who ignore textual critical issues involving examples in Hebrew, Greek, Samaritan, Syriac, etc., showing that Finn is an astute reader of the text, the scholarship, and the textual traditions.[24]

The bulk of Finn's work is devoted to providing textual and historical explanations as to why the Pentateuch appears as it does and contains certain information that can be explained on historical grounds and on the basis of the narratives as we have them without need for the Documentary Hypothesis. After covering some philosophical arguments of varying strength posing some challenges for the Documentary Hypothesis, Finn writes that "The critical theory, based on internal evidence, rests primarily on what are believed to be variations in style. . . . It is only after the work has been thus analyzed by the test of style that other criteria . . . are brought in to confirm the conclusions arrived at."[25] Throughout his work, he points out how subjective such evaluations of literary style are, almost by necessity. He further observes how many of the arguments put forward in defense of the Documentary Hypothesis are arguments from silence, or else only a very few verses, and then how inconsistent the criteria are. For example, he

---

[20] See, e.g., Finn, *Unity of the Pentateuch*, 3–4.

[21] Finn, *Unity of the Pentateuch*, 200–207.

[22] Finn, *Unity of the Pentateuch*, 6. His discussion of the "Jehovist" and "Elohist" are on pp. 6–16.

[23] Finn, *Unity of the Pentateuch*, 17–31.

[24] As just one example, consider the solitary note on Finn, *Unity of the Pentateuch*, 45, where he remarks, "Dr. Driver, on the word 'God' in this verse [Gen 7:9], notes . . . 'Sam. Targ. Vulg. Jehovah; no doubt rightly,' for that would suit the contention that this is a J passage. He does not mention that 2 of De Rossi's Heb: MSS, the Samaritan, Syriac, and lxx read Elohim for Jehovah in vii. 1 . . . That would not suit his theory."

[25] Finn, *Unity of the Pentateuch*, 333.

notes that "Remarkable words and phrases alleged to be peculiar to P are also found in passages ascribed to JE. It is taken for granted that these have been interpolated from P, but that begs the question whether these are really distinctive of P, or are common to both sets of passages."[26] Finn clarifies that the main point of his analysis is not to disprove the Documentary Hypothesis but rather to show that the traditional unified view of the Pentateuch makes at least as much sense as the Documentary Hypothesis and should probably be preferred.[27]

CATHOLIC RESPONSE

In 1928, the Jesuit biblical scholar Augustin Bea[28] published an important work on the Pentateuch, which defended it against the by-then-common source critical approach.[29] Bea had always shown a facility with languages—he had studied Oriental (i.e., ancient Near Eastern and biblical) languages at the predominantly Protestant University of Berlin, where he had such giant historical critics as Eduard Meyer and Hermann Strack for teachers.[30] Bea began teaching Sacred Scripture at the Pontifical Gregorian University and Old Testament at the Pontifical Biblical Institute in 1924, and he would become the rector of the Biblical Institute as well as its academic dean. Eventually, he would be the personal confessor to Pope Pius XII and would play a very important role at the Second Vatican Council, both in helping draft *Nostra Aetate* but also as president of the mixed commission responsible for *Dei Verbum*, the Council's Dogmatic Constitution on Divine

---

26 Finn, *Unity of the Pentateuch*, 353.

27 See his comments in, e.g., Finn, *Unity of the Pentateuch*, 501.

28 On Bea see, e.g., Jeffrey L. Morrow, "Bea, Augustin Cardinal (1881–1968)," in *The Encyclopedia of Christian Civilization*, vol. 1, ed. George Thomas Kurian (Oxford, UK: Wiley-Blackwell, 2011), 217–18; Jerome-Michael Vereb, *"Because He Was a German!": Cardinal Bea and the Origins of Roman Catholic Engagement in the Ecumenical Movement* (Grand Rapids: Eerdmans, 2006); and Stjepan Schmidt, *Augustin Bea: The Cardinal of Unity* (New Rochelle, NY: New City Press, 1992).

29 Augustinus Bea, *Institutiones biblicae scholis accommodatae*, vol. 2, *De Libris Veteris Testamenti. I. De Pentateucho* (Rome: Pontifical Biblical Institute, 1933 [1928]). For a critical review of Bea's arguments, situating it within its context, see Jean-Louis Ska, "L'Institut Biblique et l'hypothèse documantaire: un dialogue difficile. À propos du Pentateuque," in *Biblical Exegesis in Progress: Old and New Testament Essays*, ed. J. N. Aletti and J. L. Ska (Rome: Editrice Pontificio Istituto Biblico, 2009), 1–32.

30 Maurice Gilbert, *The Pontifical Biblical Institute: A Century of History (1909–2009)* (Rome: Pontifical Biblical Institute, 2009), 67.

Revelation, after which he would write a very important commentary on that document.[31]

In his volume *De Pentateucho*, Bea addresses contemporary questions surrounding the Pentateuch, spending the bulk of his time defending its Mosaic authorship and then responding to a number of exegetical and historical questions concerning portions of it.[32] His arguments fit within what was accepted at the time by the Church's Magisterium, as stated in the Pontifical Biblical Commission's 1906 statement on the Mosaic authorship of the Pentateuch.[33] Bea begins with the evidence found in Scripture itself, where it hints that Moses was the Pentateuch's author, or where it attributes certain passages to Moses.[34] Bea proceeds to amass evidence for the Mosaic authorship of the Pentateuch from within the Catholic tradition.[35] He then looks at internal evidence that supports Moses as the Pentateuch's author.[36]

After this initial defense of the traditional view of Mosaic authorship, Bea briefly traces the history, as he understands it, of the development of the Documentary Hypothesis, beginning with Jean Astruc in 1753 and continuing to Julius Wellhausen's classic formulation in 1883.[37] He spends some time explaining Wellhausen's formulation[38] as well as Catholic engagement with the Documentary Hypothesis.[39] His first major critique of such documentary source criticism is philosophical.[40] He maintains that the entire theory is grounded in theories of evolution, including and especially Hegel's philosophy.[41] After this philosophical critique, Bea challenges the fundamental tenets of Wellhausen's theory,[42] providing what he believes to be a faithful Catholic response. Just as the major arguments of Wellhausen and the other source critics of the time were mainly internal and literary, so too were Bea's responses, wherein he showed how different uses of terms for God, as well as the other literary devices and narratives that Wellhausen et al.

[31] Augustin Bea, *La Parola di Dio e l'umanità. La dottrina del concilio sulla rivelazione* (Assisi: Cittadella, 1967).

[32] Bea, *De Pentateucho*, 11–133; 134–218.

[33] Pontifical Biblical Commission, "De mosaica authentia Pentateuchi," Acta Sanctae Sedis 39 (1906): 377–78.

[34] Bea, *De Pentateucho*, 13–19.

[35] Bea, *De Pentateucho*, 19–21.

[36] Bea, *De Pentateucho*, 21–24.

[37] Bea, *De Pentateucho*, 29.

[38] Bea, *De Pentateucho*, 30–33.

[39] Bea, *De Pentateucho*, 33–36.

[40] Bea, *De Pentateucho*, 38–43.

[41] Bea, *De Pentateucho*, 38–39.

[42] Bea, *De Pentateucho*, 43–85.

identified as indications of multiple authorship, could be in fact the result of a single author.[43]

QUESTIONING GENESIS: EVIDENCE OF LITERARY UNITY

Umberto Cassuto was the chief rabbi of Florence, Italy for more than a decade, after which he taught Hebrew at the University of Florence and then La Sapienza University of Rome. Eventually, late in the 1930s, he moved to Israel and became one of the early professors at Hebrew University in Jerusalem.[44] Unlike earlier Protestant Fundamentalist scholars (e.g. Wilson), and unlike some of the later evangelical Protestant scholars whose arguments we will explore below, Cassuto did not believe the Pentateuch to date from Moses's time, but much later, from the time of Ezra. A number of his important and yet neglected works, however, posed a robust challenge to the Documentary Hypothesis on the question of multiple authorship, on which the hypothesis is grounded. Cassuto deftly showed how the Pentateuch can be accounted for as a work of a single author.

In 1934, while still teaching in Italy, Cassuto published *La questione della Genesi*,[45] which laid the foundation for his later more popular *The Documentary Hypothesis*.[46] *La questione della Genesi* emerged out of Cassuto's courses on the Hebrew text of Genesis that he taught at the University of Florence beginning in 1925, and he utilized an incredibly wide array of scholarly sources in a number of languages, including Bea's work.[47] Cassuto begins his important volume with an almost one-hundred-page chapter dedicated to the question of distinguishing sources based on the use of different names for God.[48] Cassuto begins his history of the distinctions between authors based on such stylistic observations with a discussion

---

[43] An exception to this is when Bea addresses historical and archaeological evidence used to push the Pentateuch later than the time of Moses, and Bea's response to these lines of evidence in Bea, *De Pentateucho*, 85–120.

[44] On Cassuto see, e.g., Angelo M. Piattelli, "Umberto Cassuto: dalla formazione al Collegio Rabbinico Italiano alla polemica con Alfonso Pacifici," *La Rassegna Mensile di Israel* 82 (2016): 27–89; Gabriele Rigano, "Umberto Cassuto all'Università di Roma," *La Rassegna Mensile di Israel* 82 (2016): 117–36; Ariel Viterbo, "'Maestro di Bibbia nel paese della Bibbia': Umberto Cassuto in Eretz Israel," *La Rassegna Mensile di Israel* 82 (2016): 137–62; and Pier Francesco Fumagalli, "Umberto Cassuto, peritissimus rerum hebraicarum magister," *La Rassegna Mensile di Israel* 82 (2016): 285–94.

[45] Umberto Cassuto, *La questione della Genesi* (Florence: Felice Le Monnier, 1934).

[46] Umberto Cassuto, *The Documentary Hypothesis and the Composition of the Pentateuch: Eight Lectures* (Jerusalem: Shalem Press, 2006 [1941]).

[47] He uses Bea's *De Pentateucho*. See, e.g., Cassuto, *La questione*, 100n2, 118n1, and 311n1.

[48] Cassuto, *La questione*, 1–92.

of the early eighteenth-century work of Henning Bernhard Witter, whom very few scholars—from Cassuto's time, earlier, or even now—reference, perhaps because his work was not influential.[49] After Witter, Cassuto turns to the work of the French physician Jean Astruc, who attempted to isolate sources Moses may have used in composing Genesis.[50] He proceeds to discuss other, lesser-known figures who attempted to deal with the distinction in divine names found in Genesis and the rest of the Pentateuch. This is significant, because the distinction of divine names was the foundation of the Documentary Hypothesis, and the remaining theoretical architecture was built on this methodological foundation.

When Cassuto begins his own analysis of the names, he takes a broad look at the ancient Semitic evidence for cognate words, including in the Ugaritic literature then coming to the fore; Cassuto was actually a pioneering figure in early Ugaritic studies.[51] In part, Cassuto explains:

> This is what we reason explains the promiscuous use of Yhwh and Elohim in the narrative literature: when it relates to the traditions, memories, and documents belonging to the national Israelite environment it uses the name Yhwh; insofar as it uses and reproduces international material, it derives from the nature of the argument, or from the custom and cultures of non-Israelite sources, it uses the name Elohim.[52]

Significantly, as Cassuto mentions but too many scholars ignore: "El is common Semitic vocabulary for 'god.'"[53] YHWH, in contrast, is God's personal name revealed to the nation of Israel. Thus, the distinction of names has more to do with *Elohim* (God) being used for God as generic divinity,

---

[49] Cassuto, *La questione*, 1–2. The work referenced is Henning Bernhard Witter, *Jura israe-litarum in Palaestinam Terram Chananaeam Commentatione in Genesin Perpetua sic demonstrate ut idiomatis authentici nativus sensus fideliter detegatur, Mosis autoris pri-maeva intentio sollicite desiniatur, adeoque corpus doctrinae et juris Cum antiquissimum, tum consumatissimum tandem eruatur; accedit in paginarum fronte ipse textus Hebraeus cum versione Latina* (Hildesheim: Schröder, 1711).

[50] Cassuto, *La questione*, 2–5. The work referenced is Jean Astruc, *Conjectures sur les mem-oires originaux dont il paroit que Moyse s'est servi pour composer le Livre de la Genèse. Avec des Remarques, qui appuient ou qui éclaircissent ces Conjectures* (Brussels [Paris]: Fricx, 1753). Astruc's book listed Brussels as its place of publication, but he in fact had it pub-lished in Paris.

[51] Mark S. Smith, *Untold Stories: The Bible and Ugaritic Studies in the Twentieth Century* (Peabody, MA: Hendrickson, 2001), 7, 16, 21–22, 64.

[52] Cassuto, *La questione*, 33 (our own translation).

[53] Cassuto, *La questione*, 60 (our own translation).

relatable to all the nations—thus international—whereas YHWH is the personal name of the national God of Israel.[54]

The genius of Cassuto's work is that, in contrast to most of the prior critiques of Wellhausenian source criticism, he argues for a fairly comprehensive alternative understanding of the distinctions used as markers of "sources." Based on his exhaustive readings of Hebrew literature, other literature in multiple languages, and ancient Near Eastern documents (including Ugaritic) in their original languages, Cassuto identifies the various distinctive names and apparent doublets as part of a literary style that a single author would use. He tackles not only the different names for God[55] but also contrasts in language and style,[56] as well as apparent internal contradictions,[57] double narratives,[58] and apparent composite texts.[59]

Seven years later, from his new home in Jerusalem, Cassuto published a series of eight lectures intended for school teachers that summarized his findings from *La questione della Genesi* for non-specialists. He entitled it *The Documentary Hypothesis and the Composition of the Pentateuch*.[60] Most of the arguments here are the same as in his prior work, but his introductory material makes an important and insightful connection regarding the history of source criticism—the first of its kind that we have been able to identify. Cassuto links the developments in Pentateuchal source criticism with parallel developments happening at roughly the same time in Homeric criticism.[61] These parallels will later be noted by other scholars, some of whom at least followed Cassuto's insights.[62] His extensive comments are

---

[54] Cassuto, *La questione*, 92.

[55] Cassuto, *La questione*, 1–92. He covers this topic in a briefer and more accessible way in Cassuto, *Documentary Hypothesis*, 18–49.

[56] Cassuto, *La questione*, 93–178. Also in Cassuto, *Documentary Hypothesis*, 50–65.

[57] Cassuto, *La questione*, 179–253. Also in Cassuto, *Documentary Hypothesis*, 66–82.

[58] Cassuto, *La questione*, 255–318. Also in Cassuto, *Documentary Hypothesis*, 83–100.

[59] Cassuto, *La questione*, 319–91. Also in Cassuto, *Documentary Hypothesis*, 101–16.

[60] Cassuto, *Documentary Hypothesis*.

[61] Cassuto, *Documentary Hypothesis*, 11–16.

[62] E.g., Edwin Yamauchi, *Composition and Corroboration in Classical and Biblical Studies* (Philadelphia, PA: Presbyterian and Reformed, 1966), 13–19 and 27–29; Guy G. Stroumsa, "Homeros Hebraios: Homère et la Bible aux origines de la culture européenne (17e–18e siècles)," in *L'Orient dans l'histoire religieuse de l'Europe: L'invention des origines*, ed. Mohammad Ali Amir-Moezzi and John Scheid (Turnhout, BE: Brepols, 2000), 87–100; Jean-Louis Ska, "The Yahwist, a Hero with a Thousand Faces: A Chapter in the History of Modern Exegesis," in *Abschied vom Jahwisten: Die Komposition des Hexateuch in der jüngsten Diskussion*, ed. Jan Christian Gertz, Konrad Schmid, and Markus Witte (Berlin: Walter de Gruyter, 2002), 5 and 11–12; John Van Seters, *The Edited Bible: The Curious History of the "Editor" in Biblical Criticism* (Winona Lake, IN: Eisenbrauns, 2006), 133–243; and Hahn and Morrow, *Modern Biblical Criticism*, 106–15.

worth quoting at length, and we will return to look at this history in more detail in a later chapter:

> My purpose is only to indicate briefly the relationship between the course taken by research with respect to our problem and that followed by scholarship relative to the analogous question in Greek literature concerning the works of Homer, to wit, the origin of the two poems, the *Iliad* and *Odyssey*, which are attributed to him. . . .
>
> The relationship between the history of the Homeric problem and that of the biblical problem has not yet been adequately investigated. But even at this stage, one may state that there is a surprising parallelism between the evolution of views and theories in the two fields of inquiry; in every generation similar concepts and hypotheses prevail at the same time in regard to the Homeric and biblical problems.
>
> In each case, after sporadic doubts had been expressed earlier, systematic criticism began to be voiced in the seventeenth century. . . . The work of the French physician Astruc . . . appeared . . . in 1753 under the title *Conjectures sur les mémoires originaux don't il paroit que Moyse s'est servi pour composer le livre de la Génèse*. . . . Similarly in the case of Homer's writings, the earliest foundations of the new concepts were laid by a French dilettante, Abbé d'Aubignac. . . . In his book *Conjectures accadémiques ou dissertations sur l'Iliade*, which was published posthumously in 1715, he, too, expressed the opinion that Homer's poems are not unitary compositions. . . .
>
> The French amateur was followed in each subject by a German professional scholar who transformed the Frenchman's opinions into a completely systematized theory: on the one side, Eichhorn, who published the first edition of his work *Einleitung ins Alte Testament* between the years 1780–83, and on the other, Wolf, whose treatise *Prolegomena ad Homerum* appeared in 1795. In this instance too, the names of the two works correspond to one another, each being an "Introduction." Also in the present case, the similarity in the names of the books is not a mere coincidence: it is indicative of a like textual approach and similar methods of research. The parallelism of approach and method resulted in analogous conclusions: in regard to the Pentateuch as well as the Homeric poems it was postulated that independent source-documents served as

their basis. . . . there arose in biblical exegesis a new thesis called the "Theory of Fragments," . . .

In the early thirties of the nineteenth century, yet another theory, the "Supplement Hypothesis," was advanced. . . . It was precisely at this time that K. F. Hermann put forward a similar view with reference to Homer. . . .

This doctrine did not endure long in regard to either the Pentateuch or Homer's poems. . . . Lachmann validated once more the views concerning the documents from which the epic [Homer] was composed, and in order to reconstruct these source documents, he developed the analytical method, which was continued and perfected by his successors, until it reached its consummation under Wilamowitz. In like manner, Hupfeld succeeded, a few years after the publication of Lachmann's researches, in renewing and consolidating the documentary hypothesis . . . with the help of the analytical method . . . which was amplified by Graf and attained its highest perfection through the labors of Wellhausen, the colleague and friend of Wilamowitz.[63]

As we shall see, Cassuto's instincts here are keen and his history is fundamentally correct. Nor were these parallels random. They were shaped by interpersonal relationships and shared academic cultural pressures.

"THESE ARE THE GENERATIONS"

Two years after Cassuto published *La questione della Genesi*, a non-academic, P. J. Wiseman, published a small amateur volume on Genesis, creatively challenging the Documentary Hypothesis. He initially entitled that volume *New Discoveries in Babylonia About Genesis*, but the title was later changed to *Ancient Records and the Structure of Genesis*.[64] Wiseman is less well known than his son, Donald J. Wiseman, formerly Professor of Assyriology at the University of London, who would become a premier scholar of Assyriology and of the Old Testament.[65] P. J. Wiseman hypothesizes that "The book of

---

[63] Cassuto, *Documentary Hypothesis*, 11–14.

[64] P. J. Wiseman, *Ancient Records and the Structure of Genesis: A Case for Literary Unity* (Nashville, TN: Thomas Nelson, 1985 [1936]).

[65] On Donald Wiseman, see his self-published memoirs, Donald John Wiseman, *Life Above and Below: Memoirs* (n.p.: privately published, 2003); and Alan R. Millard, "Donald John Wiseman 1918–2010," *Proceedings of the British Academy* 172 (2011): 379–93.

Genesis was originally written on tablets in the ancient script of the time by the patriarchs who were intimately concerned with the events related, and whose names are clearly stated."[66]

After Wiseman's preliminary chapters covering the history of archaeology of the ancient Near East, he has a helpful chapter on the work of ancient Near Eastern scribes.[67] This is important because for most of source criticism's history up to that point, little or no reference was made to ancient Near Eastern writing practices, in part because archaeology was a relatively young discipline and the relevant languages were still being deciphered. It is toward the end of this chapter that Wiseman makes his grand discovery, which he then applies to Genesis. He explains:

> When, however, the lengthy nature of the writing required more than one tablet, it was just as necessary then as it is today (with the pages of letters or books) to adopt means to preserve their proper sequence, especially when a considerable number of tablets were required to complete the series. This was achieved by the use of "titles," "catch-lines," and "numbering." *The title was taken from the first words of the first tablet, these were repeated at the end of each subsequent tablet, followed by the serial number of that tablet.*[68]

This becomes "the key to the structure of Genesis," which is what he entitles his next chapter.[69] Wiseman believes "that the master key to the method of compilation that underlies the structure of the book of Genesis is to be found in an understanding of the phrase 'These are the generations of.'..."[70] He then goes through the key places where we find these divisions:

2:4	These are the generations of the heavens and the earth.
5:1	This is the book of the generations of Adam.
6:9	These are the generations of Noah.
10:1	These are the generations of the sons of Noah.
11:10	These are the generations of Shem.
11:27	These are the generations of Terah.
25:12	These are the generations of Ishmael.
25:19	These are the generations of Isaac.

---

[66] Wiseman, *Ancient Records*, 20. He attributes to Moses the role of "compiler and editor" (20). Italics have been removed from the quotation (Wiseman italicized all of the words quoted here).

[67] Wiseman, *Ancient Records*, 47–58.

[68] Wiseman, *Ancient Records*, 56–57.

[69] Wiseman, *Ancient Records*, 59.

[70] Wiseman, *Ancient Records*, 59.

36:1   These are the generations of Esau.
36:9   These are the generations of Esau.
37:2   These are the generations of Jacob.[71]

In comparing Genesis here with similar ancient Near Eastern literature, Wiseman remarks, "In the early days of Babylonia, the most treasured tablets were those containing the record of ancestors and the appropriate place for such a genealogical list is at the *beginning* of a tablet."[72] After these discussions, Wiseman proceeded to summarize some of the challenges others had posed already to the Documentary Hypothesis and walk through the biblical traditions associating the Pentateuch with Moses. His most significant contribution to the debate, however, was his argument concerning the *toledot* ("these are the generations") divisions. Although not a scholar himself, his son Donald Wiseman, an eminent ancient Near Eastern and biblical scholar, makes the following comments in the foreword to the 1985 edition of his father's text:

> My father's interest as a Bible student was quickened by his residence in the Middle East, especially during 1923–25 and 1931–33 when in Iraq. He read extensively and took the opportunity of visiting the principal excavations. . . . He had many discussions with . . . scholars there. . . . While he himself did not read the cuneiform scripts and had a limited knowledge of classical Hebrew, he carefully checked his theories with competent scholars. . . . P. J. Wiseman's theory is a simple one. . . . He takes the Genesis narratives as they stand and relates them to well-attested ancient literary methods. . . . Since this book was first written there have been many more colophons discovered among the cuneiform texts which have been found in Babylonia. . . . These substantiate the references to this scribal device which is the "key" to the elucidation of the documents which were composed in Genesis. Recent discoveries of Semitic literature from Syria and Mesopotamia . . . show the continuity in tradition both of scribal education and literary practices. In many instances tablets show them to have continued virtually unchanged for a further two millenniums.[73]

---

[71] Wiseman, *Ancient Records*, 60. This is also one of the divisions followed in John Bergsma and Brant Pitre, *A Catholic Introduction to the Bible*, vol. 1, *The Old Testament* (San Francisco: Ignatius Press, 2018), 94.

[72] Wiseman, *Ancient Records*, 65.

[73] Wiseman's foreword to *Ancient Records*, 8–9.

THE RELIGION OF ISRAEL AND THE ANTIQUITY OF P

From 1937 to 1956 Yehezkel Kaufmann published a massive eight-volume work in Hebrew on the history of ancient Israel's religion.[74] Despite the length of this project, it was never really completed. A heavily abridged single-volume edition (of the first seven volumes) exists in English, translated by the eminent twentieth-century Israeli Bible scholar Moshe Greenberg, with the title *The Religion of Israel*.[75] Kaufmann was born in a Russian Jewish family in Ukraine. After studying at the famous Yavneh yeshivah in Odessa, he furthered his education at the Academy for Jewish and Oriental Studies in St. Petersburg, followed by the University of Bern in Switzerland. He then lived and studied in Berlin until 1928, when the rampant anti-Semitism made the environment too hostile. As Cassuto would later do, Kaufmann emigrated to the Holy Land, and initially taught in Haifa before eventually joining Cassuto on faculty at Hebrew University in Jerusalem.

Kaufmann is an especially interesting critic of Wellhausen and the Documentary Hypothesis not only because, like Cassuto, he is a Jewish scholar and dates the final form of the Pentateuch late (i.e. after the Exile) but also because he accepts the basic literary divisions of the Documentary Hypothesis. As Cassuto himself comments: "Even a scholar like Yehezkel Kaufman, who stands outside this school of interpretation and successfully opposes a given portion of its concepts, as he does in his valuable studies on the history of the Israelite religion, still accepts the fundamental principle of

---

[74] On Kaufmann see, e.g., Thomas M. Krapf, "Yehezkel Kaufman: An Outline of his Life and Work," in *Yehezkel Kaufmann and the Reinvention of Jewish Biblical Scholarship*, ed. Job Y. Jindo, Benjamin D. Sommer, and Thomas Staubli (Fribourg: Academic Press; Göttingen: Vandenhoeck & Ruprecht, 2017), 3–44; Job Y. Jindo, "Recontextualizing Yehezkel Kaufmann: His Empirical Conception of the Bible and Its Significance in Jewish Intellectual History," *Journal of Jewish Thought and Philosophy* 19, no. 2 (2011): 95–129; and Job Y. Jindo, "Revisiting Kaufmann: Fundamental Problems in Modern Biblical Scholarship," *Journal of the Interdisciplinary Study of Monotheistic Religions* 3 (2007): 41–77.

[75] Yehezkel Kaufmann, *The Religion of Israel: From Its Beginnings to the Babylonian Exile*, trans. and abridged by Moshe Greenberg (Chicago: University of Chicago Press, 1960). This edition is heavily abridged and reorganized. Greenberg lays out the reorganization and abridgement structure in his preface to the volume. The following shows the relationship between the chapters and the original version by indicating the chapter in the present volume = taken from volume and chapter of the original, where 1.1 would indicate volume one, chapter one in the original: ch. 1 = 2.10; ch. 2 = 2.11; ch. 3 = 2.12; ch. 4 = 3.13, 15; ch. 5 = 1; ch. 6 = 3.17, 4.1–3; ch. 7 = 3.14, 4.4–5; ch. 8 = 3.16, 4.6–9; ch. 9 = 5; ch. 10 = 6.1; ch. 11 = 6.2–3; ch. 12 = 6.4, 6, 7.10; ch. 13 = 7.11–13; epilogue = 6.5 (and also adapted from another of his works). In our chapter, we quote and cite from this abridged English edition.

the customary division of the text according to sources, and bases his views thereon."[76]

Indeed, Kaufmann's *Religion of Israel* concedes the basic literary divisions into JE, P, and D sources, as he writes, "such of its [criticism's] findings as the analysis of three chief sources in the Torah (JE, P, and D) have stood the test of inquiry and may be considered established."[77] Later, in fact, he will explain, "Several of the conclusions of this theory [of Wellhausen's] may be considered assured. To this category belongs the analysis of the three primary sources—JE, P, and D—with their laws and narrative framework."[78] Nevertheless, at the outset of his volume he remarks, "This study is a fundamental critique of classical criticism."[79] Kaufmann's primary criticism, and the one most significant as a contribution to challenging the Documentary Hypothesis, is his dating of the so-called Priestly material (P) early, long before the Exile:

> Its [criticism's] basic postulate—that the priestly stratum of the Torah was composed in the Babylonian exile, and that the literature of the Torah was still being written and revised in and after the Exile—is untenable. The Torah . . . is the literary product of the earliest stages of Israelite religion, the stage prior to literary prophecy . . . its sources are demonstrably ancient—not in part, not in their general content, but in their entirety, even to their language and formulation.[80]

Kaufmann is one of Wellhausen's early critics to challenge the philosophically Hegelian developmental approach undergirding the theory, within the context of the evolution-mania running through the post-Darwin intellectual world of the nineteenth century. He notes, "The evolutionary doctrine that changed the face of all sciences during the nineteenth

---

[76] Cassuto, *Documentary Hypothesis*, 9–10.

[77] Kaufmann, *Religion of Israel*, 1. Further in his volume, Kaufmann will add, "A second established conclusion of classical criticism is that the present Torah book was not in pre-exilic times canonical and binding upon the nation. The literature that was to become incorporated in the Torah existed in various documents and versions; a single book had not yet been crystallized. Before the book, there was an extended period of literary creation by priests and religious writers. Third, there are sufficient grounds . . . for maintaining that Deuteronomy was promulgated in the reign of Josiah, and that the Torah, as a whole, was promulgated and fixed in the times of Ezra-Nehemiah" (157).

[78] Kaufmann, *Religion of Israel*, 156. He elaborates on the same page, "The source JE is manifestly composed of parallel accounts, even though their unraveling cannot always be accomplished with certainty. The tripartite separation is clearest in the legal material."

[79] Kaufmann, *Religion of Israel*, 1.

[80] Kaufmann, *Religion of Israel*, 1–2.

century left its mark on the history of religion as well."[81] In the context of Wellhausen's theory, where the Priestly Source is a late post-exilic development of the work of the Deuteronomist, Kaufmann has the following to say: "P cannot . . . be considered a revision or adaptation of D. Each of the three codes of the Torah is to be regarded as an independent crystallization of Israel's ancient juristic-moral literature. The evolutionary sequence and literary dependence assumed by Wellhausen has no foundation."[82] In a parenthetical aside, Kaufmann drives home one of the problems so prevalent in modern criticism, namely, that "The habit of developing far-reaching theories from a novel exegesis of an isolated passage—usually an obscure one at that—and of reaching large conclusions literally from jots and tittles, is deeply ingrained in biblical scholarship."[83]

Kaufmann identifies, quite correctly, "The revolutionary concept of the Wellhausenian view in its classic formulation was that prophecy was the fountainhead of Israelite monotheism. . . . the Torah is but the later popular-priestly formulation of prophetic teaching."[84] And yet, as he points out, "The several early law codes that have come to light since the laws of Hammurabi were discovered in 1902 testify to the rich legal tradition of the ancient Near East."[85] Kaufmann argues extensively and persuasively for the antiquity of P.[86] He likewise argues for the antiquity of what he identifies as "the Torah literature."[87]

One of the many trenchant points Kaufmann makes is that the later prophetic literature underscores the absolute horror of the Babylonian Exile, whereas "The Torah knows nothing of all this. . . . The image of exile in the Torah must, therefore, be an ancient one, antedating the historical experience of destruction and exile."[88] He underscores how "It is incredible that a priestly law which evolved at this time should pass over this dominant idea [of centralization] in silence . . . there is no trace whatever of D's

---

[81] Kaufmann, *Religion of Israel*, 153.

[82] Kaufmann, *Religion of Israel*, 170.

[83] Kaufmann, *Religion of Israel*, 3.

[84] Kaufmann, *Religion of Israel*, 157.

[85] Kaufmann, *Religion of Israel*, 170. Writing further on the same page, Kaufmann explains, "Israel's obligation to this ancient, common tradition is evident from the patent relationship between the Covenant Code and Hammurabi's laws . . . the advanced state of Hammurabi's laws, relative to those of the Covenant Code, precludes the possibility of the biblical code having borrowed from the Babylonian. The Covenant Code is to be considered rather an early formulation and crystallization of the common Near Eastern law of which Hammurabi's laws are a more advanced development."

[86] Kaufmann, *Religion of Israel*, 175–200.

[87] Kaufmann, *Religion of Israel*, 200–208.

[88] Kaufmann, *Religion of Israel*, 205.

centralization idea in P; P must, therefore, have been composed before the age of Hezekiah."[89]

Writing further in a footnote, Kaufmann points out how "Only the fact that the Torah shows no knowledge whatever of later historical conditions fixes the date of its sources between termini different entirely from those postulated by the prevailing view."[90] Likewise, buried in a footnote, Kaufmann drives home how "All supposed tokens of P's lateness are overshadowed by this monumental fact. Wellhausen's idea that the early religion of Israel was spontaneous and rite-free is persuasive only so long as the cuneiform literature (that already in his time was being studied with reference to the religion of Israel) is not taken into account."[91] These are among the arguments that lead Kaufmann to affirm that, "In every detail, P betrays its antiquity"[92] since, for example, "P is ignorant of Jerusalem's significance."[93] This then is Kaufmann's enduring legacy of critiquing the Documentary Hypothesis, in some sense from within the system, since he accepted the basic literary division of sources. He challenged the late dating of P, highlighting the evidence for P's antiquity, and his challenge of the evolutionary model employed, which denigrated the priesthood as a late corruption.

Names for God in the Bible

We will end this chapter with a brief look at M. H. Segal's 1955 article on the names for God in the Pentateuch.[94] Segal's article focuses on the use of the names for God in other parts of the Bible, and is fairly exhaustive. He notes the problem with how the Documentary Hypothesis assigns the use of Yahweh and Elohim to various sources, showing how doing so does not fit how the rest of the Bible employs them, and thus underscores how artificial and arbitrary such stylistic criteria are. He notes further that "The greater abundance of Elohim in the Pentateuchal narratives as compared with the historical books must be explained by the greater antiquity of the Pentateuchal narratives when the name Elohim was more frequent in the spoken language than in the post-Mosaic ages."[95]

---

[89] Kaufmann, *Religion of Israel*, 205.

[90] Kaufmann, *Religion of Israel*, 205n15.

[91] Kaufmann, *Religion of Israel*, 205n16.

[92] Kaufmann, *Religion of Israel*, 206.

[93] Kaufmann, *Religion of Israel*, 206.

[94] M. H. Segal, "El, Elohim, and Yhwh in the Bible," *Jewish Quarterly Review* 46, no. 2 (1955): 89–115.

[95] Segal, "El, Elohim, and Yhwh," 112. In reference to the use of the divine names in the narrative of creation in Genesis, Segal writes, "As for the exclusive use of Elohim in certain

The Documentary Hypothesis is primarily an internal literary analysis based upon style and vocabulary. Thus, it should not come as a surprise that many of the challenges to the Documentary Hypothesis likewise involved forms of such literary analysis. In this chapter we reviewed primarily these literary arguments from the first fifty years or so of the twentieth century. In the next chapter, we will look at the challenges to the Documentary Hypothesis that came from the massive studies of archaeological evidence, beginning in the 1940s. Two of the towering figures here were William Foxwell Albright and Cyrus H. Gordon, and the "schools" they formed composed of their many doctoral students.

---

passages in Genesis, this may be due to a variety of causes. Thus in the story of the creation which opens the Torah (Gen. 1–2.3) the creator is designated by the name Elohim, by which name the deity was generally known in the Hebrew speaking world, but in the immediately following story of the detailed creation of man and of his fall (2.4–3.24) the deity is described as Yhwh Elohim in order to indicate the identity of Elohim, the creator, with Yhwh, the God of Israel . . ." (113).

CHAPTER 2

THE PENTATEUCH, MOSES, AND ANCIENT HISTORY:

THE INITIAL VIEW FROM ANCIENT NEAR EASTERN STUDIES AND ARCHAEOLOGY

This chapter examines the growing archaeological landscape that began really to blossom after the Second World War. The archaeological finds helped create a climate of positive appreciation for the ways in which the Pentateuch clearly fit an early second millennium BCE context, the time period in which its recorded events took place. This optimistic view would last until the beginning of the 1970s. The variety of challenges to the Documentary Hypothesis that would emerge from the 1950s to today, however, in many ways built upon the challenges that were leveled against aspects of the theory in the first half of the twentieth century. We begin by looking at the work of the figures who helped shape the discipline of the study of archaeology and the ancient Near East in the twentieth century, and we conclude with two of the leading archaeologists and ancient historians who have defended the historical reliability of the Pentateuch during the latter half of the twentieth and into the twenty-first century.

ANCIENT NEAR EASTERN STUDIES AND ARCHAEOLOGY

Wellhausen's work, and the work of his predecessors in formulating the Documentary Hypothesis, was basically conducted in a vacuum, without recourse to the study of the ancient Near Eastern world that formed the context in which the Pentateuch was written. Two of the towering twentieth-century scholars involved in helping challenge the Documentary Hypothesis were experts first of all in the study of the ancient Near East: William Foxwell Albright and Cyrus Gordon.

W. F. ALBRIGHT: THE DEAN OF AMERICAN OLD TESTAMENT STUDIES

Albright, the senior of the two, shaped an entire generation of scholars.[1] At one point, most of the major Old Testament scholars in the United States—including virtually everyone in Old Testament, archaeology, and ancient Near Eastern Studies at Harvard—were Albright's former students. He had well over one thousand publications and directed fifty-seven doctoral dissertations. Hailing from a Methodist background, Albright was self-taught in Akkadian, the language of the Babylonians and Assyrians, as well as in Hebrew. He earned his doctorate at Johns Hopkins University (where he then taught for his entire career) under Paul Haupt, and mastered source critical methods (like the Documentary Hypothesis), as well as the recent methods of archaeology and the study of all of the major ancient Near-eastern languages.

A number of Albright's works contributed to the massive challenge that the Documentary Hypothesis—and nineteenth-century-style historical

---

[1] On Albright see, e.g., Peter Douglas Feinman, *William Foxwell Albright: And the Origins of Biblical Archaeology* (Berrien Springs, MI: Andrews University Press, 2000); Mark S. Smith, "W. F. Albright and His 'Household': The Cases of C. H. Gordon, M. H. Pope, and F. M. Cross," in *"A Wise and Discerning Mind": Essays in Honor of Burke O. Long*, ed. Saul M. Olyan and Robert C. Culley (Providence: Brown University Press, 2000), 221–44; Peter Machinist, "William Foxwell Albright: The Man and His Work," in *The Study of the Ancient Near East in the Twenty-First Century: The William Foxwell Albright Centennial Conference*, ed. Jerrold S. Cooper and Glenn M. Schwartz (Winona Lake, IN: Eisenbrauns, 1996), 385–403; Jack M. Sasson, "Albright as an Orientalist," *Biblical Archaeologist* 56, no. 1 (1993): 3–7; William G. Dever, "What Remains of the House That Albright Built?" *Biblical Archaeologist* 56, no. 1 (1993): 25–35; Burke O. Long, "Mythic Trope in the Autobiography of William Foxwell Albright," *Biblical Archaeologist* 56, no. 1 (1993): 36–45; Gus W. Van Beek, "William Foxwell Albright: A Short Biography," in *The Scholarship of William Foxwell Albright: An Appraisal: Papers Delivered at the Symposium "Homage to William Foxwell Albright," The* American *Friends of the Israel Exploration Society, Rockville, Maryland, 1984*, ed. Gus W. Van Beek (Atlanta, GA: Scholars Press, 1989), 7–15; Frank Moore Cross, "The Contributions of W. F. Albright to Semitic Epigraphy and Palaeography," in *Scholarship of William Foxwell Albright*, 17–31; Delbert R. Hillers, "William F. Albright as a Philologian," in *Scholarship of William Foxwell Albright*, 45–59; Gus W. Van Beek, "W. F. Albright's Contribution to Archaeology," in *Scholarship of William Foxwell Albright*, 61–73; and Leona Glidden Running and David Noel Freedman, William Foxwell Albright: A Twentieth-Century Genius (New York: Morgan Press, 1975).

criticism as a whole—was undergoing in the mid-twentieth century.[2] Like Kaufmann, however, Albright accepted the basic source divisions of the Documentary Hypothesis. Yet, as a seasoned ancient Near Eastern scholar, Albright took up the question of Homeric authorship, which had followed a similar trajectory to the question of Mosaic authorship of the Pentateuch.[3] His comments on this subject could apply equally well to biblical critical theories:

> The Orientalist counters by pointing out that much of ancient Eastern literature is composed in a somewhat similar synthetic "dialect," which may be described as a literary language containing archaizing deposits from various periods and literary "dialects." For example, the prologue and epilogue to the Code of Hammurabi were written about 1690 BC, according to the minimal Babylonian chronology. Much of them is unquestionably in poetic language, and both style and language contrast strikingly with the classical Old Babylonian of the code of law itself. There are a great many grammatical forms and literary phrases which go back to the Dynasty of Accad in the 24th–23rd centuries BC; other elements reflect the so-called hymnal-epic dialect, really the language of the court of the Third Dynasty of Ur, in the 21st and 20th centuries; still more extensive passages and expressions reflect contemporary or nearly contemporary usage. The triumphal poems of Ramesses III, celebrating his victories over Sea Peoples and Libyans in the early twelfth century BC, generally imitate literary Middle Egyptian (the court language of the Twelfth Dynasty, cir. 2000–1800 BC), but contain archaisms from other periods and are full of Late Egyptian neologisms. The Assyrian royal inscriptions of the ninth century BC try to reflect Middle Babylonian (properly the literary

---

[2] Just a very few include: William Foxwell Albright, *Archaeology and the Religion of Israel* (Louisville, KY: Westminster John Knox Press, 2006 [1942]); William Foxwell Albright, *From the Stone Age to Christianity: Monotheism and the Historical Process* (Baltimore, MD: The Johns Hopkins University Press, 1946); William Foxwell Albright, *The Archaeology of Palestine* (New York: Penguin, 1949); William Foxwell Albright, *The Biblical Period from Abraham to Ezra* (San Francisco: Harper & Row, 1963 [1950]); William Foxwell Albright, *Archaeology, Historical Analogy, and Early Biblical Tradition* (Baton Rouge, LA: Louisiana State University Press, 1966); William Foxwell Albright, *Yahweh and the Gods of Canaan: A Historical Analysis of Two Contrasting Faiths* (Winona Lake, IN: Eisenbrauns, 1994 [1968]); and W. F. Albright, "Moses in Historical and Theological Perspective," in *Magnalia Dei: The Mighty Acts of God*, ed. Frank M. Cross, Werner F. Lemke, and Patrick D. Miller (Garden City, NY: Doubleday, 1976), 120–31.

[3] W. F. Albright, "Some Oriental Glosses on the Homeric Problem," *American Journal of Archaeology* 54, no. 3 (1950): 162–76.

language of Cossaean Babylonia), but they swarm with Babylonian and especially with Assyrian neologisms; they also contain numerous echoes of Old Assyrian, transmitted through Middle Assyrian channels.[4]

Albright concludes from this that "Under such circumstances, it is quite impossible to infer anything about authorship from composite language."[5]

The area in which the Documentary Hypothesis received its most devastating critique from Albright, however, was in the late dating of source material. Albright's work, and that of many of his students, helped fill out a picture of the Bible in light of its ancient Near Eastern background, showing how the various content fit very well, overall, within the ancient Near Eastern historical and cultural context in which each portion allegedly originated. Albright and his students at Johns Hopkins University did this through their engagement with archaeology and study of the documents in their original languages, emerging from archaeological excavations in the twentieth century, something to which the eighteenth- and nineteenth-century pioneering historical critics either had no access or else ignored. Albright was conscious of this shift and its implications. He wrote:

Practically all important forward steps in the historical criticism of the OT since 1840 fall in the generation from 1850 to 1880, that is, at a time when the interpretation of Egyptian, Mesopotamian, and South-Arabian documents was still in its first stage, and before there was either sufficient material or philological foundations strong enough to bear a reliable synthesis of any kind. The greatest Semitic philologian of modern times, Theodor Nöldeke, stubbornly disregarded the young field of Assyriology, though after he passed his sixtieth year he expressed regret that he had not mastered it. For all his profound control of Arabic, Ethiopic, Hebrew, and the Aramaic dialects, he was helpless, as he candidly confessed, in the terrain of Assyrian, Egyptian, and Sabaean. What was true of Nöldeke was true *a fortiori* of the great founders of modern OT science. . . . No less a man than Wellhausen, great Semitist though he was, neglected the new material from the ancient Orient with a disdain as arrogant as it was complete.[6]

---

[4] Albright, "Some Oriental Glosses," 163.
[5] Albright, "Some Oriental Glosses," 163.
[6] W. F. Albright, "The Ancient Near East and the Religion of Israel," *Journal of Biblical Literature* 59, no. 2 (1940): 91–92.

As one of the most renowned and prolific archaeologists and philologists in history, Albright and his students shaped the field for several scholarly generations, from about 1945 to about 1972, roughly speaking.

CYRUS H. GORDON: MORE THAN SEVENTY YEARS OF ANCIENT MEDITERRANEAN STUDIES

Cyrus Gordon is another important figure to mention at this point.[7] Gordon was a secular Jewish scholar who taught primarily in ancient Near Eastern studies and what he called "Mediterranean Studies" (which combined biblical studies, classical antiquity, and the study of the ancient Near East). Like Albright, Gordon was a master linguist with competence in more than forty languages. He was a pioneer with Ugaritic, and his grammar of that language has proven to be one of the most significant.[8] Gordon taught at a number of institutions, mostly at Brandeis University, but also at Dropsie College and New York University, and ended up directing more doctoral dissertations than Albright (over 60). Although James Montgomery of the University of Pennsylvania directed Gordon's doctoral dissertation, and Gordon also studied with Albright while engaged in archaeological excavations in the Holy Land, perhaps his most influential teacher, whose courses he merely audited, was Max Margolis, often described as the first Jewish modern biblical scholar.[9] Gordon's work, and that of many of his students,

---

[7] On Gordon see, e.g., Gary A. Rendsburg, "Cyrus H. Gordon (1908–2001): A Giant Among Scholars," *Jewish Quarterly Review* 92 (2001): 137–43; Cyrus H. Gordon, *A Scholar's Odyssey* (Atlanta, GA: Society of Biblical Literature, 2000); Meir Lubetski and Claire Gottlieb, "'Forever Gordon': Portrait of a Master Scholar with a Global Perspective," *Biblical Archaeologist* 59, no. 1 (1996): 2–12; Howard Marblestone, "A 'Mediterranean Synthesis': Professor Cyrus H. Gordon's Contributions to the Classics," *Biblical Archaeologist* 59, no. 1 (1996): 22–30; Martha A. Morrison, "A Continuing Adventure: Cyrus Gordon and Mesopotamia," *Biblical Archaeologist* 59, no. 1 (1996): 31–35; Gary A. Rendsburg, "'Someone Will Succeed in Deciphering Minoan': Cyrus H. Gordon and Minoan Linear A," *Biblical Archaeologist* 59, no. 1 (1996): 36–43; David Toshio Tsumura, "The Father of Ugaritic Studies," *Biblical Archaeologist* 59, no. 1 (1996): 44–50; and Edwin M. Yamauchi, "Magic Bowls: Cyrus H. Gordon and the Ubiquity of Magic in the Pre-Modern World," *Biblical Archaeologist* 59, no. 1 (1996): 51–55.

[8] It was first published as Cyrus H. Gordon, *Ugaritic Grammar* (Rome: Pontifical Biblical Institute, 1940), then revised as *Ugaritic Handbooks* (Rome: Pontifical Biblical Institute, 1947), revised again as *Ugaritic Manual* (Rome: Pontifical Biblical Institute, 1955), and finally revised again as *Ugaritic Textbook* (Rome: Pontifical Biblical Institute, 1965). This final edition was further revised and reprinted (in 1967 and 1998).

[9] On Margolis see especially Leonard Greenspoon, "On the Jewishness of Modern Jewish Biblical Scholarship: The Case of Max L. Margolis," *Judaism* 39 (1990): 82–92; Leonard Greenspoon, *Max Leopold Margolis: A Scholar's Scholar* (Atlanta: Scholars Press, 1987);

contributed along with the "Albright School" to a greater confidence in the historical reliability and authentic antiquity of the Old Testament.[10]

As with Albright, Gordon pointed out the ways in which source criticism developed in a vacuum cut off from ancient Near Eastern material: "It is well to remember that Higher Criticism is a legacy from a period before the age of archaeological and epigraphical discovery."[11] Unlike Albright, however, Gordon was less sanguine about the accuracy and even utility of the hypothetical (and he thought somewhat arbitrary) literary divisions source critics invented, especially the Documentary Hypothesis. He explains this in his memoirs:

> While at Dropsie [College] I reread the description of Utnapishtim's ark in the Gilgamesh Epic and observed similar concern with detailed specifications. If this feature obliged us to attribute the Genesis account to P of the fifth century, it must, I reasoned, do the same for the Babylonian account, which is absurd. I also found other absurdities in the so-called higher criticism of the Establishment. If *Yahweh-Elohim* owed its origin to the combination

---

Leonard Greenspoon, "Max Leopold Margolis: A Scholar's Scholar (A BA Portrait)," *Biblical Archaeologist* 48 (1985): 103–6; Robert Gordis, "The Life of Professor Max Leopold Margolis: An Appreciation," in *Max Leopold Margolis: Scholar and Teacher*, ed. Robert Gordis (New York: Bloch, 1952), 1–16; Frank Zimmermann, "The Contributions of M. L. Margolis to the Fields of Bible and Rabbinics," in *Max Leopold Margolis*, 17–26; Ephraim A. Speiser, "The Contribution of Max Leopold Margolis to Semitic Linguistics," in *Max Leopold Margolis*, 27–33; Harry M. Orlinsky, "Margolis' Work in the Septuagint," in *Max Leopold Margolis*, 35–44; and Joshua Bloch, "Max L. Margolis' Contribution to the History and Philosophy of Judaism," in *Max Leopold Margolis*, 45–59.

10 A sample of Gordon's works that helped here include Cyrus H. Gordon, *Introduction to Old Testament Times* (Ventnor, NJ: Ventnor, 1953); Cyrus H. Gordon, *New Horizons in Old Testament Literature* (Ventnor, NJ: Ventnor, 1960); Cyrus H. Gordon, "The Story of Jacob and Laban in the Light of the Nuzi Tablets," *Bulletin of the American Schools of Oriental Research* 66 (1937): 25–27; Cyrus H. Gordon, "Biblical Customs and the Nuzu Tablets," *Biblical Archaeologist* 3 (1940): 1–12; Cyrus H. Gordon, "The Patriarchal Age," *Journal of Bible and Religion* 21 (1953): 238–43; Cyrus H. Gordon, "The Patriarchal Narratives," *Journal of Near Eastern Studies* 13 (1954): 56–59; Cyrus H. Gordon, "Abraham and the Merchants of Ura," *Journal of Near Eastern Studies* 17, no. 1 (1958): 28–31; Cyrus H. Gordon, "Higher Critics and Forbidden Fruit," *Christianity Today* 4 (23 November 1959): 3–6; Cyrus H. Gordon, "Ancient Israel and Egypt," *New York University Education Quarterly* 12 (1981): 9–13; and Cyrus H. Gordon, "Ebla and Genesis 11," in *A Spectrum of Thought: Essays in Honor of Dennis F. Kinlaw*, ed. Michael L. Peterson (Wilmore: Asbury College Press, 1982), 125–34.

11 Cyrus H. Gordon, "Homer and the Bible: The Origin and Character of East Mediterranean Literature," *Hebrew Union College Annual* 26 (1955): 49. In this text, Gordon brings up a few challenges to the Documentary Hypothesis, using the work of Kaufmann, among others, to show the antiquity of P.

of God's name in J (*Jehovah* is the mistaken reading of *Yahweh*) with his name in E (*Elohim*), then every Egyptian inscription mentioning the god Amon-Re must have derived the name from an A-document combined with an R-document. One might also argue the same for Ugaritic documents, which abound with divine names composed of two elements.[12]

Gordon's work on Ugaritic was especially important for solidifying his views. He writes elsewhere:

> The bearing of Ugaritic literature on the higher criticism of the Bible is considerable. The criterion of variant names (specifically for God) as an indication for differences of authorship must be drastically discounted in the light of Ugarit. In one and the same poem, Baal may be called Baal, Aliyn Baal, Dagan's Son, Rider of Clouds, etc. If it be argued that these are not different names but simply a name and its epithets, this cannot be said of the alternation of Baal and Hadd. . . . Indeed the parallelistic nature of the poetry calls for such variant names. *Per se*, Elohim and Yahwe need not simply imply dual authorship in a chapter of the Bible any more than Baal and Hadd do in a Ugaritic myth.[13]

From the 1940s to the beginning of the 1970s, the archaeological discoveries, and their main interpretations influenced by the "Albright School" and the "Gordon School," made it seem as though the academy would likely have to abandon the skepticism of the Wellhausen school in the near future. This was the context for Edwin Yamauchi's (one of Gordon's students) publication of *The Stones and the Scriptures* in 1972.[14] Things began to change around 1973, thus causing the collapse of what had been the growing confidence in the historical trustworthiness of the Old Testament thanks to Albright and Gordon—many would add Ephraim Speiser to this list—as well as their students. Less than a decade after publishing *The Stones and the Scriptures*, Yamauchi reflects on what happened in Old Testament scholarship:

---

[12] Gordon, *Scholar's Odyssey*, 80.

[13] Cyrus H. Gordon, *Ugaritic Literature: A Comprehensive Translation of the Poetic and Prose Texts* (Rome: Pontifical Biblical Institute, 1949), 6. See 6–7 for further arguments and evidence.

[14] Edwin M. Yamauchi, *The Stones and the Scriptures: An Introduction to Biblical Archaeology* (Philadelphia, PA: Lippincott, 1972).

Now in the eight years since I published *The Stones and the Scriptures* the trends have not all been positive in confirming the Scriptures as I had anticipated. There has been a very strong negative reaction to some of the syntheses which were accepted then. . . . In the 1970s we have seen the passing away of a great host of giants in the field of archaeology. Most of these were at an advanced age. . . . In 1971 three giants in the field of biblical archaeology passed away: the greatest of them all, W. F. Albright, was followed by his disciple, Nelson Glueck . . . and then by Roland de Vaux. . . . In 1974 G. Ernest Wright of Harvard passed away. In 1976 Yohanan Aharoni of Tel Aviv University died. . . . These discoveries [at Mari and Nuzi] were interpreted in a positive manner. . . . This then was the climate of the scholarly consensus on the patriarchs when I wrote *The Stones and the Scriptures* in 1972. . . . there was general agreement on the antiquity and authenticity of the patriarchal stories. . . . In the years immediately following 1972, there were published two very strong challenges to the historicity and authenticity of the patriarchal narratives.[15] . . . These two writers [Thomas Thompson and John Van Seters] have reverted essentially to the radical view of Wellhausen.[16]

As Yamauchi and many others concede, however, the synthesis forged by the "schools" of Albright, Speiser, and Gordon went too far in some of their assertions based on the evidence. The tendency since then, though, has been to throw out the proverbial baby with the bathwater. A number of scholars in the generation after Albright, Speiser, and Gordon, who came of age professionally during this earlier optimistic period, made important contributions to the field of Old Testament studies and the study of the Pentateuch.

MOSHE WEINFELD AND THE CONTINUATION OF THE WORK OF CASSUTO AND KAUFMANN

In 1979, Moshe Weinfeld published an important but completely neglected study on Wellhausen's Documentary Hypothesis as a forty-seven-page

---

[15] Yamauchi refers here to Thomas L. Thompson, *The Historicity of the Patriarchal Narratives: The Quest for the Historical Abraham* (Berlin: Walter de Gruyter, 1974); and John Van Seters, *Abraham in History and Tradition* (New Haven, CT: Yale University Press, 1975).

[16] Edwin M. Yamauchi, *The Scriptures and Archaeology: Abraham to Daniel* (Portland, OR: Western Conservative Baptist Seminary, 1980), 1 and 3.

booklet.[17] Weinfeld had been a student of both Cassuto and Kaufmann at Hebrew University.[18] He summarizes Wellhausen at the outset: "Wellhausen's revolutionary aim in the *Prolegomena* was to prove that the main legal sections of the Pentateuch ... are in fact a reflection of post exilic Judaism and must therefore be considered a turning away from the prophetic religion which preceded."[19] Weinfeld then remarked at how amazing it was that Wellhausen's views became so widely accepted, and so quickly, among his contemporaries, including Theodor Nöldeke who, Weinfeld notes, originally resisted the hypothesis, and Samuel Rolles Driver, who, Weinfeld notes, "rarely allowed himself to become unquestioningly convinced by attractive theories, preferring at all times to weigh matters independently."[20]

Weinfeld's short study is in part an attempt to unmask the bias inherent in Wellhausen's theory. He points out how Wellhausen understood so much of the ritual laws of Judaism as rooted not merely in the Torah but particularly in those portions identified as the Priestly Code. He then notes both how Wellhausen viewed this portion of the Law as culminating in the Pharisees of the Second Temple period and also how, not by mere coincidence, Wellhausen's first serious scholarly foray into history was a study on the Pharisees.[21] Weinfeld asserts that the link Wellhausen made between the Priestly Code and the "theocracy" of the Second Temple period "became the foundation of Wellhausen's theory—that the Priestly Code is a product of Second Temple times."[22] In other words, "The Priestly Torah, according to his view, is not the Torah of Israel, not the ideal Torah from which the prophetic message and the Christian gospel derive, but the Torah of *Judaism* (Judentum)."[23]

---

[17] Moshe Weinfeld, *Getting at the Roots of Wellhausen's Understanding of the Law of Israel on the 100th Anniversary of the Prolegomena* (Jerusalem: Institute for Advanced Studies, Hebrew University, 1979).

[18] On Weinfeld see, e.g., Chaim Cohen, Avi Hurvitz, and Shalom Paul, "Prof. Moshe Weinfeld: A Professional Profile," in *Sefer Moshe: The Moshe Weinfeld Jubilee Volume: Studies in the Bible and the Ancient Near East, Qumran, and Post-Biblical Judaism*, ed. Chaim Cohen, Avi M. Hurvitz, and Shalom M. Paul (Winona Lake, IN: Eisenbrauns, 2004), ix–xi; and Zeev Weisman, "Prof. Moshe Weinfeld's Contribution to Biblical Scholarship: An Appreciation," in *Sefer Moshe*, xii–xviii.

[19] Weinfeld, *Getting at the Roots*, 1.

[20] Weinfeld, *Getting at the Roots*, 1. For Nöldeke's embracing the Documentary Hypothesis see, e.g., Theodor Nöldeke, *Untersuchungen zur Kritik des Alten Testaments* (Kiel: Schwers, 1869). For Driver's adoption of the Documentary Hypothesis see, e.g., S. R. Driver, "On Some Alleged Linguistic Affinities of the Elohist," *Journal of Philology* 11 (1882): 201–36.

[21] Weinfeld, *Getting at the Roots*, 3. He is referring to J. Wellhausen, *Die Pharisäer und die Sadducäer. Eine Untersuchung zur innern jüdischen Geschichte* (Greifswald: Bamberg, 1874).

[22] Weinfeld, *Getting at the Roots*, 3.

[23] Weinfeld, *Getting at the Roots*, 3–4.

Weinfeld thus examines Wellhausen's views on the Pharisees and on rabbinic Judaism in order to show how they shaped his understanding of the origin of the Torah.[24] He explains how for Wellhausen the Priestly Code is "a manifestation of the 'decline and decay' of Judaism which began in the exile and which paved the way for the subsequent Pharisaic theocracy. This theocracy, whose establishment is attributed by the Priestly document to Moses, is but a fictional retrojection of exilic and post-exilic realities, fabricated of the imaginings of Second Temple scribes who wished to portray the Priestly ideology of Second Temple times."[25] Weinfeld links such a conclusion as natural for a "liberal Protestant who abhors ceremony and ritual."[26]

Weinfeld then proceeds to challenge the specifics of Wellhausen's source criticism.[27] Here he sounds very much like his mentor Kaufmann, whom he cites and summarizes at length.[28] Weinfeld identifies "five pillars" of Wellhausen's theory pertaining to the tabernacle, sacrificial rituals, ritual feasts, priests and Levites, and the clerical endowment. After challenging Wellhausen's views and the late dating of each of these "pillars," Weinfeld concludes that in the end there is no foundation for Wellhausen's assumptions about the creation of these pillars of the Priestly Code in the Second Temple period. Weinfeld proceeds with an examination of external evidence from the ancient Near East, evidence that Wellhausen did not have available.[29] He closes his discussion with some brief remarks about Wellhausen's methodological problems.[30]

EVANGELICAL ANCIENT NEAR EASTERN SCHOLARSHIP

For the remainder of this chapter, we begin to look at how critics of the Documentary Hypothesis from biblical studies, Egyptology, and ancient Near Eastern studies built upon all of this prior work we have thus far covered. This examination will continue into the next chapter, concluding the first part of this present volume. The period with which we begin, in the 1950s, is in the context of the scholarly outlook Albright, Speiser, and Gordon—and their many students—built over the decades. That period of

---

[24] Weinfeld, *Getting at the Roots*, 3–15.

[25] Weinfeld, *Getting at the Roots*, 15.

[26] Weinfeld, *Getting at the Roots*, 15.

[27] Weinfeld, *Getting at the Roots*, 16–27.

[28] Weinfeld, *Getting at the Roots*, 20–25.

[29] Weinfeld, *Getting at the Roots*, 27–38. Among other examples, he points to early evidence from Mesopotamia, Canaan, and the Hittites for elaborate temple rituals, the sort of rituals Wellhausen thought had to be late.

[30] Weinfeld, *Getting at the Roots*, 38–40.

time, which was heavily influenced by the discipline of archaeology, lasted roughly from 1945 to 1972.

In addition to the students of Albright, Speiser, and Gordon, evangelical Protestant scholars (some of whom were students of Gordon) became some of the most outspoken critics of the Documentary Hypothesis. Unlike most of the adherents of the Documentary Hypothesis, who hailed from biblical studies, however, many of these evangelical scholars were trained primarily in Egyptology, Assyriology, or ancient Mediterranean Studies. Thus, they were trained to read the Bible in a similar fashion to how other ancient texts were being studied.

One of the towering figures in the study of the ancient Near East during the twentieth century was the great Assyriologist and Sumerologist of Yale University, William Hallo.[31] Like Weinfeld, Gordon, and Cassuto, Hallo was a Jewish scholar who spent time studying the Bible, but he was most famous for his work in Sumerology and Assyriology, studying ancient Mesopotamia. An expert on how ancient scribes worked and on ancient Near Eastern historiography, he was well placed to comment on the study of the Bible in its ancient historical context. Hallo wrote about limits that must be imposed on skepticism.[32] Hallo explained the absence of a developed literary criticism (like the historical critical method in biblical studies) within the discipline of Assyriology. He argued that the textual sources—both for the Bible and for the ancient Near East—needed to be viewed as important witnesses involved in reconstructing the history of their civilizations, but also with similar criteria. For example, the Bible should not be studied with more historical skepticism than analogous ancient Near Eastern sources.[33] As he writes in a later work, "Methodologically, it continues to make

---

[31] On Hallo see, e.g., William W. Hallo, *The World's Oldest Literature: Studies in Sumerian Belles-Lettres* (Leiden, NL: Brill, 2010), xvii–xxi; Peter Machinist and Piotr Michalowski, "Introduction: William Hallo and Assyriological, Biblical, and Jewish Studies," in *World's Oldest Literature*, xxiii–xxxii; William W. Hallo, "Suche nach den Ursprüngen," in *Vergegenwärtigungen des zerstörten jüdischen Erbes. Franz-Rosenzweig-Gastvorlesungen, Kassel 1987-1998*, ed. Wolfdietrich Schmied-Kowarzik, (Kassel: Kassel University Press, 1997), 139–46; and David B. Weisberg, "William W. Hallo: An Appreciation," in *The Tablet and the Scroll: Near Eastern Studies in Honor of William W. Hallo*, ed. Mark E. Cohen, Daniel C. Snell, and David B. Weisberg, (Bethesda, MD: CDL, 1993), ix–xvi.

[32] William W. Hallo, "The Limits of Skepticism," *Journal of the American Oriental Society* 110, no. 2 (1990): 187–99.

[33] See also William W. Hallo, "Sumer and the Bible: A Matter of Proportion," in *The Future of Biblical Archaeology: Reassessing Methodologies and Assumptions: The Proceedings of a Symposium, August 12-14, 2001 at Trinity International University*, ed. James K. Hoffmeier and A. R. Millard (Grand Rapids: Eerdmans, 2004), 163–75; William W. Hallo, "Introduction: Ancient Near Eastern Texts and Their Relevance for Biblical Exegesis," in

sense to treat Mesopotamian history and Israelite history alike—to exempt neither from criticism, to expose neither to unreasonable tests of authenticity."[34] Some sort of historical critical work has begun for certain ancient Near Eastern texts and traditions, but by and large such study has shown the hypothetical nature of such work, and how textual criticism and the comparative approach from the archaeological record are on firmer ground.[35]

It should thus not surprise us that scholars from the background of ancient Near Eastern studies were more attuned to these issues than those trained primarily in biblical studies, where the various tenants of the historical critical method so often serve as an unquestioned starting point. The earliest of these scholars—William Martin, Kenneth Kitchen, Edwin Yamauchi, Donald Wiseman, and Alan Millard—were all trained in ancient Near Eastern archaeology and philology. For example, Kitchen was trained as an Egyptologist, Yamauchi's doctorate was in ancient Mediterranean Studies

---

The Context of Scripture Volume One: Canonical Compositions from the Biblical World, ed. William W. Hallo and K. Lawson Younger, Jr. (Leiden, NL: Brill, 2002), xxv–xxviii; William W. Hallo, "Introduction: The Bible and the Monuments," in *The Context of Scripture Volume Two: Monumental Inscriptions from the Biblical World*, ed. William W. Hallo and K. Lawson Younger, Jr. (Leiden, NL: Brill, 2002, xxi–xxvi; William W. Hallo, "New Directions in Historiography (Mesopotamia and Israel)," in *Dubsar anta-men: Studien zur Altorientalistik: Festschrift für Willem H.Ph. Römer zur Vollendung seines 70. Lebensjahres mit Beiträgen von Freunden, Schülern und Kollegen*, ed. Manfried Dietrich and Oswald Loretz (Münster: Ugarit-Verlag, 1998), 109–28; William W. Hallo, "The Concept of Canonicity in Cuneiform and Biblical Literature: A Comparative Appraisal," in *The Biblical Canon in Comparative Perspective*, ed. K. Lawson Younger, Jr., William W. Hallo, and Bernard Frank Batto (Lewiston, NY: Edwin Mellen Press, 1991), 1–20; William W. Hallo, "Compare and Contrast: The Contextual Approach to Biblical Literature," in *The Bible in the Light of Cuneiform Literature*, ed. William W. Hallo, Bruce William Jones, and Gerald L. Mattingly (Lewiston, NY: Edwin Mellen Press, 1990), 1–30; William W. Hallo, "Biblical History in its Near Eastern Setting: The Contextual Approach," in *Scripture in Context: Essays on the Comparative Method*, ed. Carl D. Evans, William W. Hallo, and John B. White (Eugene, OR: Pickwick, 1980), 1–26; and William W. Hallo, "New Viewpoints on Cuneiform Literature," *Israel Exploration Journal* 12, no. 1 (1962): 13–26.

[34] Hallo, "New Directions," 122. On the same page he continues, "Absent an overabundance of documentation such as applies to some much more recent periods, the historian of antiquity has no alternative but to use every scrap of evidence available—making allowances for its biases, for the intentions of its presumed authors and the expectations of its presumed audiences in order to reconstruct a remote past."

[35] See, e.g., Raymond F. Person, Jr. and Robert Rezetko, "Introduction: The Importance of Empirical Models to Assess the Efficacy of Source and Redaction Criticism," in *Empirical Models Challenging Biblical Criticism*, ed. Raymond F. Person, Jr. and Robert Rezetko (Atlanta, GA: SBL Press, 2016), 1–35; Sara J. Milstein, "Outsourcing Gilgamesh," in *Empirical Models*, 37–62; Alan Lenzi, "Scribal Revision and Textual Variation in Akkadian Šuila-Prayers: Two Case Studies in Ritual Adaptation," in *Empirical Models*, 63–108; and Y. S. Chen, *The Primeval Flood Catastrophe: Origins and Early Development in Mesopotamian Traditions* (Oxford, UK: Oxford University Press, 2013).

specializing in Mandaic literature, and Wiseman was an Assyriologist. With training much akin to Hallo's, these scholars studied the biblical texts as they were trained to study other ancient Near Eastern texts. Since the 1970s, even more challenges have come from scholars outside of evangelical traditions. It is to this history from the latter half of the twentieth century into the beginning of the twenty-first century that we now turn.

WILLIAM MARTIN ON STYLISTIC CRITERIA

William Martin, the Rankin Professor of Hebrew and Ancient Semitic Languages (who would be succeeded in that chair by Alan Millard) was an important evangelical ancient Near Eastern specialist who engaged the work of Pentateuchal source critics. Working in the 1950s through 1970s, he made a modest contribution to the critique of Pentateuchal criticism with his slender twenty-three-page booklet *Stylistic Criteria and the Analysis of the Pentateuch*. Though short, this study was utilized and cited by most of the scholars we will discuss later.[36] The likely reasons for the popularity of Martin's text are its brevity, which enabled it to be read widely; its insightful use of parallels from Homeric scholarship, which lay at the very foundation of the history of the Documentary Hypothesis; and the prestige of its author, as Martin was a scholar not easily dismissed. In a very brief review of Martin's work in 1958, Luis Alonso-Schökel concluded with the following: "The article is worth pondering, because all science needs from time to time to reflect on its methods. We could say two things to the author: that many of the investigators of the OT have already renounced similar methods; that his final conclusion about the unity of Genesis appears very exaggerated."[37]

Like Cassuto before him, Martin sees Wellhausen's theory as in some sense indebted to the Homeric scholarship of Wolff.[38] Martin recognizes "the close parallelism between Homeric and Pentateuchal criticism."[39] Much of the volume, in fact, pertains to Homeric criticism, showing how most of the criteria, indebted to Wilamowitz, Wolff, et al., were no longer useful, thus demonstrating how the arguments against the primary unity of Homer were somewhat passé. The same is true, he argues, for the similar analysis of the Pentateuch that the Documentary Hypothesis represents, indebted as it is to the methods of Homeric scholarship. Martin argues that

---

[36] W. J. Martin, *Stylistic Criteria and the Analysis of the Pentateuch* (London: Tyndale House, 1955).

[37] Luis Alonso-Schökel, S.J., review of *Stylistic Criteria and the Analysis of the Pentateuch* by W. J. Martin, *Biblica* 39, no. 1 (1958): 106.

[38] Martin, *Stylistic Criteria*, 5.

[39] Martin, *Stylistic Criteria*, 6n3.

S. R. Driver, more than Wellhausen, was in fact responsible for systematizing a method utilizing the Documentary Hypothesis.[40] Martin writes, with regard to the criterion of stylistic and vocabulary variation:

> The invalidity of such criteria has long been recognized by classical scholars, and no one would now think of attaching any significance to, say, the fact that beans are mentioned in the Iliad but not in the Odyssey; that the Iliad is rich in words for wounds and wounding, whereas such words are rare in, or absent from, the Odyssey.[41]

Turning to a specific criterial instance in Driver, Martin observes that:

> In Genesis the personal pronoun occurs only nine times in passages assigned by Driver to P. Why a particular form of a personal pronoun should be associated with P when in one document of considerable size it is found in only nine passages, whereas J and E use it on numerous occasions, would seem to savour a little of arbitrariness in the enlistment of characteristics.[42]

On the use of different names for God, which he shows as problematic as a criterion (as had others before, and as would others after him), Martin explains:

> The use of the various names for God first gave Astruc the idea of dividing up the Pentateuch on this basis, and until the present day Pentateuchal criticism still uses the occurrence of the different divine names as evidence of different documents. The removal of this verse [Exodus 6:3] would deprive Pentateuchal criticism of its one piece of indisputably objective evidence, for varieties in style can be classed only as subjective.[43]

---

[40] Martin, *Stylistic Criteria*, 10–11. He cites, e.g., the 11th ed. of Driver's *The Book of Genesis*. We cite here the 6th edition of that volume because it was the one we had access to, and it too contains the criteria Martin discusses. S. R. Driver, *The Book of Genesis: With Introduction and Notes*, 6th ed. (London: Methuen, 1907 [1904]).

[41] Martin, *Stylistic Criteria*, 13.

[42] Martin, *Stylistic Criteria*, 14.

[43] Martin, *Stylistic Criteria*, 17. He explains the problem in more detail earlier: "The locus classicus was to be found, not in Genesis, but in Exodus vi. 3: 'I appeared to Abraham, to Isaac, and to Jacob, as God Almighty, but by my name the LORD I did not make myself known to them'. . . . It is on the basis of the accepted translation of this verse, that the theory of the composite character of the Pentateuch has been most confidently defended. On examination, it becomes apparent that the argument depends . . . on a single word and that a mere particle, the negative lo. Probably never in the whole history of exegesis,

Martin concludes his brief treatment by arguing for the literary genius of the author of Genesis, which he takes to be a single author, likely Moses.

KENNETH KITCHEN: EGYPTOLOGIST AND BIBLICAL SCHOLAR EXTRAORDINAIRE: PENTATEUCHAL CRITICISM

Kenneth Kitchen has written voluminously on various aspects of Egyptology and the Old Testament.[44] For present purposes, we focus on his work concerning the historical reliability of the Old Testament, including the Pentateuch.[45] His most neglected work on the topic was also his most sus-

---

whether classical or biblical, has so much been made to depend on a single word. There was something strangely paradoxical about this attitude to a tiny word on the part of men who were ready to believe that otherwise the text had suffered extensive admixture. In the interpretation of the text at the outset a recognized and generally accepted canon of exegesis seemed to have been neglected, namely that a passage should be interpreted in the light, not only of the local context, but also of the remote, for, to be fair to any statement, the, mediate as well as the immediate must be taken into consideration. . . . a simple solution would have been to read it not as the negative but as the emphatic particle. This would have involved merely replacing the vowel o by u, as has been done in at least one other place in the Old Testament (1 Samuel xviii. 12). Why this particle should have been treated as if it were sacrosanct must be one of the most extraordinary examples of inverted scrupulosity" (16–17).

[44] On Kitchen see, e.g., Kenneth A. Kitchen, *In Sunshine and Shadow: An Autobiographical Sketch in a Family Context* (Liverpool, UK: Abercromby Press, 2016); and Mark Collier and Steven Snape, eds., *Ramesside Studies in Honour of K. A. Kitchen*, vii (Bolton, UK: Rutherford Press, 2011), preface.

[45] E.g., Kenneth A. Kitchen, "The Hebrew Bible and its Critics—A Verdict from the Ancient Near East," *Bulletin of the Anglo-Israel Archaeological Society* 26 (2008): 149–50; Kenneth Kitchen, "Ancient Near Eastern Studies: Egypt," in *The Oxford Handbook of Biblical Studies*, ed. Judith M. Lieu and J.W. Rogerson (Oxford, UK: Oxford University Press, 2006), 89–98; K. A. Kitchen, *On the Reliability of the Old Testament* (Grand Rapids: Eerdmans, 2003); Kenneth A. Kitchen, "The Desert Tabernacle: Pure Fiction or Plausible Account?" *Bible Review* 16, no. 6 (2000): 14–21; Kenneth A. Kitchen, "The Patriarchal Age: Myth or History?," *Biblical Archaeology Review* 21, no. 2 (1995): 48–57, 88, 90–92, and 94–95; Kenneth A. Kitchen, "Genesis 12–50 in the Near Eastern World," in *He Swore an Oath: Biblical Themes from Genesis 12–50*, ed. Richard S. Hess, Gordon J. Wenham, and Philip E. Satterthwaite (Grand Rapids: Baker, 1994), 67–92; Kenneth A. Kitchen, "New Directions in Biblical Archaeology: Historical and Biblical Aspects," in *Biblical Archaeology Today, 1990: Proceedings of the Second International Congress on Biblical Archaeology: Jerusalem, June–July 1990* (Jerusalem: Israel Exploration Society, 1993), 34–52; Kenneth A. Kitchen, "The Tabernacle—A Bronze Age Artifact," *Eretz-Israel* 24 (1993): 119–29; Kenneth A. Kitchen, "Ancient Egypt and the Old Testament," *Bulletin of the Anglo-Israel Archaeological Society* 11 (1991–1992): 48–51; Kenneth A. Kitchen, *The Bible in its World: The Bible and Archaeology Today* (Exeter, UK: Paternoster Press, 1977); K. A. Kitchen, "From the Brickfields of Egypt," *Tyndale Bulletin* 27 (1976): 137–47; K. A. Kitchen, "The Old

tained critique of the Documentary Hypothesis, a rather short book (or lengthy booklet) consisting of roughly fifty pages of very thorough notes from three lectures Kitchen delivered in 1965, which were informally type-set and printed by the Theological Students' Fellowship.[46]

In the notes from his first lecture, Kitchen covers the matter of alleged internal evidence for the various documentary theories that developed into the Documentary Hypothesis.[47] He begins by summarizing rather briefly the prehistory of the hypothesis,[48] covering the basic criteria whose cumulative effect is used to justify it.[49] Kitchen challenges the criteria on internal grounds. When it comes to the classical case of Genesis 1–2, almost universally recognized now as two separate creation accounts, Kitchen underscores their complementarity.[50] He views Genesis 1:1–2:3 as a "balanced outline of the whole creation with mankind as the climax."[51] Moreover, he points out that what remains in Genesis 2 is not a complete creation account, as we have in Genesis 1.[52]

Testament in its Context 6," *Theological Students' Fellowship Bulletin* 64 (1972): 2–10; K. A. Kitchen, "The Old Testament in its Context 2: From Egypt to the Jordan," *Theological Students' Fellowship Bulletin* 60 (1971): 3–11; K. A. Kitchen, "The Old Testament in its Context 1: From the Origins to the Eve of the Exodus," *Theological Students' Fellowship Bulletin* 59 (1971): 2–10; Kenneth A. Kitchen, "Moses: A More Realistic View," *Christianity Today* 12 (21 June 1968): 8–10; K. A. Kitchen, *Ancient Orient and Old Testament* (London: InterVarsity Press, 1966); K. A. Kitchen, "Historical Method and Early Hebrew Tradition," *Tyndale Bulletin* 17 (1966): 63–97; K. A. Kitchen, "Some Egyptian Background to the Old Testament," *Tyndale Bulletin* 5–6 (1960): 4–18; and K. A. Kitchen, "A Recently Published Egyptian Papyrus and its Bearing on the Joseph Story," *Tyndale Bulletin* 2 (1956–1957): 1–2. Even some of his book reviews prove helpful in how he brings up relevant archaeological evidence in support of the historicity of the Pentateuch, e.g., K. A. Kitchen, review of *Ancient Israel: A Short History from Abraham to the Roman Destruction of the Temple*, ed. Hershel Shanks, *Themelios* 15, no. 1 (1989): 25–28; K. A. Kitchen, review of *A Study of the Biblical Story of Joseph* by Donald B. Redford, *Oriens antiquus* 12 (1973): 233–42; and K. A. Kitchen, review of *Joseph en Égypte. Genèse chap. 37–50 à la lumière des études égyptologiques récentes*, by Jozef Vergote, *Journal of Egyptian Archaeology* 47 (1961): 158–64.

46 Kenneth A. Kitchen, *Pentateuchal Criticism and Interpretation: Notes of Three Lectures Given at the Annual Conference of the Theological Students' Fellowship, held at The Hayes, Swanwick, Derbyshire from December 27 to 31, 1965* (Leicester: Theological Students' Fellowship, 1965). Below the table of contents, just prior to page 1, there's an NB clarifying that, "This typescript does NOT constitute a formal publication and cannot be cited as such; its contents and views can be referred to as notes of lectures, however."

47 Kitchen, *Pentateuchal Criticism* [lecture notes], 1–24.

48 Kitchen, *Pentateuchal Criticism* [lecture notes], 1–3.

49 Kitchen, *Pentateuchal Criticism* [lecture notes], 5–6.

50 Kitchen, *Pentateuchal Criticism* [lecture notes], 6.

51 Kitchen, *Pentateuchal Criticism* [lecture notes], 6.

52 His notes on Genesis 2:19 are worth quoting at length: "The matter can be made perfectly

As with Cassuto, Kitchen recognizes that Elohim functions in passages like Genesis 1–3 as a general name for God, whereas Yahweh is God's personal name.[53] Historically, source critics have identified the use of Elohim with one source (e.g., E or P), and the use of Yahweh as indicative of another source (e.g., J or D). When it is combined as Yahweh-Elohim, source critics posit editorial activity splicing the names together. And yet, as Kitchen points out in his notes, "Outside of Ex 9.30, the compound YHWH-Elohim occurs only here [Gen 2–3] in the whole Pentateuch, and fittingly serves as a transitional form: it identifies the supreme God of Gen 1, the creator of all, as the same God YHWH who is vitally concerned with His people."[54]

Kitchen addresses variation in style as a common literary technique, which he will discuss further in his next lecture.[55] He then lists the places Yahweh appears where, according to the theory, it should not in E and P and, likewise, the many places Elohim (apart from "fixed phrases") appears in J.[56] After discussing vocabulary differences,[57] Kitchen's notes bring up an important but often neglected point about P in Genesis:

---

clear if one renders 2.19 into English with an English pluperfect as follows: 'Now, out of the ground the Lord God *had* formed every beast of the field (. . . etc.), and he brought them to the man to see what he would call them'. However, conventional literary critics simply cannot bear to hear of a pluperfect translation, as it so simply removes their precious contradiction at one fell swoop. S. R. Driver and his adherents allege that for a Waw-consecutive-Imperfective a Pluperfect rendering 'would be contrary to idiom', trying to explain away the various possible or alleged examples of this construction where a Pluperfect would be an appropriate rendering. While this construction is by form and origin a continuative tense, yet in *function* in contexts it is an equivalent of the Perfective (for which no one objects to a Pluperfect translation where suitable), and so (like the Perfect) it comes to express *complete action in the past*—which covers both the Perfect and the Pluperfect in English. There is no special Pluperfect form in Hebrew, other Ancient Semitic languages, or Egyptian; hence there are only the attested completed-action forms to express it" (Kitchen, *Pentateuchal Criticism* [lecture notes], 7–8, all underlining has been changed to italics here and in the rest of this book for purposes of style).

53   Kitchen, *Pentateuchal Criticism* [lecture notes], 8.

54   Kitchen, *Pentateuchal Criticism* [lecture notes], 8. On the same page and in the same context, Kitchen notes, "in Gen 2–3, YHWH is combined with Elohim as YHWH Elohim (the LORD God of English versions), and does not stand alone as it *should* do (as in Gen 4) if Gen 2–3 is really 'J' and if terms for Deity are really the label-markers that they are alleged to be. Elohim in this compound throughout two J . . . chapters should indicate that 'J' knew and used Elohim when and as he wished; if so, the distinction of authors by divine names is pointless and erroneous. The only expedients open to conventional literary criticism are to emend Elohim out of the text or to attribute it to a later redactor or the like, to explain away somehow or anyhow the physical evidence of the Hebrew text. . . ."

55   Kitchen, *Pentateuchal Criticism* [lecture notes], 10–11.

56   Kitchen, *Pentateuchal Criticism* [lecture notes], 11.

57   Kitchen, *Pentateuchal Criticism* [lecture notes], 11–13.

For a century no-one even recognized P. Hupfeld's division simply siphoned-off most of the lists, statistical, genealogical data, etc. to form his first E (our P). P is only really continuous in Gen 1–2, 6–9, 10–11, 17 and more bits up to about 20. After that—apart from 23—the rest of P in Genesis is the merest little fragments. Curiously, E proper only begins about Gen 20 and thence continues. I.e., P + E looks suspiciously like *one* document cut in half.[58]

Kitchen's lecture notes proceed to cover the matter of alleged doublets, which he divides into various types, such as supposed double narratives.[59] He maintains that in the cases of alleged double stories, they are simply different stories rather than contradictory accounts of the same event. Repetitions, he maintains, need to be read in light of ancient Near Eastern and Hebrew writing styles, rather than anachronistically in light of modern assumptions. The remainder of his notes for his first lecture cover the other areas of the hypothesis, like supposedly divergent theologies, etc., where he cites a number of helpful secondary sources. This is where he also walks through the various alleged developmental stages in Wellhausen's approach and that of his followers, challenging them on internal literary grounds.

Kitchen's second lecture looks at the Documentary Hypothesis in light of the background of the ancient Near East.[60] He begins by noting the problem others before him have recognized, namely that the Documentary Hypothesis developed as a purely internal literary theory without recourse to the broader ancient Near Eastern literature. He recognizes that, for the first hundred or more years of the hypothesis's development in the eighteenth and nineteenth centuries, ancient Near Eastern literature was simply not available. Since the time of Wellhausen, however, such has not been the case.[61] Throughout this lecture, Kitchen uses comparable ancient Near Eastern material in order to situate the biblical texts within their appropriate historical context so as better to understand their compositional methods and assess the validity of the criteria used in the Documentary Hypothesis.

For the substantive portion of this second lecture, Kitchen begins by discussing the question of multiple names for God, something Gordon, Cassuto, and others had already addressed.[62] Kitchen cites and quotes from Egyptian texts known to have only one author, which nonetheless use different names for the same deity to emphasize specific roles or functions the

---

[58] Kitchen, *Pentateuchal Criticism* [lecture notes], 13.
[59] Kitchen, *Pentateuchal Criticism* [lecture notes], 14–15.
[60] Kitchen, *Pentateuchal Criticism* [lecture notes], 25–38.
[61] Kitchen, *Pentateuchal Criticism* [lecture notes], 25.
[62] Kitchen, *Pentateuchal Criticism* [lecture notes], 27–28. He cites Gordon in this context (27–28).

deity played. For the names being varied on stylistic grounds, he includes texts from a broader range of sources: Egyptian, Babylonian, Canaanite (Ugaritic), Hittite, Hurrian, as well as Old South Arabian. Regarding compound divine names comparable to Yahweh-Elohim, Kitchen provides examples from Egyptian and Canaanite texts. In none of these instances from the ancient Near East is there any question of multiple authorship or sources. Kitchen does the same (with fewer examples from primary sources but more citations from secondary sources) for diversity of vocabulary.[63]

Kitchen uses the same method, drawing from several Egyptian examples, for diversity of style.[64] He also provides a number of case studies when it comes to the matter of alleged doublets.[65] For example, he explains:

> The Karnak Poetical Stela of Tuthmosis III, *c* 1460 BC, has the god Amun address the king on the latter's political supremacy over foes (i) in a varied style, lines 1–12 (J/E?), (ii) in a very stately and slightly more detailed poem (p?), far more rigid in pattern than Gen 1, and (iii) in lines 23–25 again in more varied style (J2/E2?).[66]

He provides further illustrations of the same sort of diversity in texts patently and indisputably by the same author. These texts also exhibit other traits that Wellhausen and other source critics have taken as evidence of multiple sources, such as divergent theologies.[67]

Finally, Kitchen's third lecture situates the Pentateuch itself within its ancient Near Eastern context, showing how that ancient comparative lens is a far more appropriate framework for understanding the Pentateuch's composition than the more arbitrary literary theories that evolved into the Documentary Hypothesis.[68] Here he considers potential post-Mosaic aspects, as well as pre-Mosaic material, and attempts to sum up some conclusions. He walks through several of the key passages typically identified as anachronisms. For most of the examples, Kitchen has a plausible explanation showing how the passages do not need to be read as anachronistic. He concedes that Genesis 36:31 might be anachronistic. Here's what he claims:

> "before the reigning of a king in Israel." This phrase is the *sole* possible post-Mosaicum that has any weight in the entire book. Two views are possible: (a) That this clause was added under the

---

[63] Kitchen, *Pentateuchal Criticism* [lecture notes], 28.

[64] Kitchen, *Pentateuchal Criticism* [lecture notes], 28.

[65] Kitchen, *Pentateuchal Criticism* [lecture notes], 28–30.

[66] Kitchen, *Pentateuchal Criticism* [lecture notes], 28.

[67] Kitchen, *Pentateuchal Criticism* [lecture notes], 30–32.

[68] Kitchen, *Pentateuchal Criticism* [lecture notes], 39–50.

Hebrew monarchy to make clear the pre-monarchic date of the
Edomite kings; this could have occurred in a hypothetical recension
of the Pentateuchal writings under (for example) David or Solomon. . . . (b) That this phrase is of the same date (Mosaic period
or earlier) as the rest of the book. One *should* remember that it was
the Hebrews who were the odd people out in *not* having a king
. . . everyone else in their world did! . . . Either (a) or (b) is feasi-
ble. (a) seems simplest, (b) cannot be wholly excluded (curiously,
impressively defended by Astruc. . . .)[69]

He has a lot of material here concerning the authentic historical framework of the texts that he will flesh out more thoroughly in later publications.
For the moment it will suffice to include one excerpt:

The literary scheme of Gen 1–9, with its Mesopotamian background (Flood, and remember, Abraham & co came from Ur!),
is now paralleled not only implicitly by the "final" editing of
the Sumerian King List (*c* 1800 BC), but also more explicitly by
the reconstructed Atrakhasis Epic of the Old Babylonian period
(*c* 1900–1700 BC)—in both cases; the Patriarchal Age. It is not too
bold to suggest that these traditions came from Mesopotamia with
Abraham.[70]

Kitchen likewise points to the important work on Hittite covenants,
showing how well Deuteronomy fits that ancient second millennium BCE
pattern.[71] This is especially significant regarding Wellhausen's formulation

---

[69] Kitchen, *Pentateuchal Criticism* [lecture notes], 40. In the case of Deuteronomy, Kitchen
explains these lecture notes, "Deut 34: the Death of Moses: this is the one absolutely
cast-iron post-Mosaicum in the text. Deut 34.1–9 could easily have been written just after
Moses' death; verses 10–12 might be later. . . . The narrative framework running through
Deuteronomy with Moses in the third person. Two views are theoretically possible here:
(i) That Moses himself wrote of himself in the third person (common, eg, in titles of Near
Eastern texts [Wisdom, monumental, etc.], and in classics) or dictated in the first person
and was written down in the third person. This is possible but not wholly free of difficulty
in certain passages (eg, Deut 31.9). (ii) That Moses gave the addresses that the text attributes to him, and the actions likewise (eg, writing out the full matter in Deut 1.1–30.8
except for the third person connecting-headings and narrative of 4.41ff, etc.), and that at
his death a contemporary (such as Eleazar the priest?) . . . wrote out the whole, supplying
the third-person record of Moses' activities and the headings as needful" (42).

[70] Kitchen, *Pentateuchal Criticism* [lecture notes], 41.

[71] We will see more on this with the work of Joshua Berman below. Here in his lecture notes,
however, Kitchen provides a very helpful condensed history of comparing the relatively newly
discovered Hittite covenants up to 1965, a history which has since been better fleshed out:

of the Documentary Hypothesis, because, as Kitchen here points out, "The very concept of 'covenant' was arbitrarily late-dated by Wellhausen—a position now impossible on the ANE data."[72]

THE RELIABILITY OF THE OLD TESTAMENT

More important than Kitchen's informal critique of the Documentary Hypothesis—as helpful as that has been to review—are his decades of publications highlighting the massive evidence for the authenticity, antiquity, and reliability of the Old Testament, perhaps especially the Pentateuch. In addition to the articles already cited above, his earliest major relevant monograph on the topic is his 1966 *Ancient Orient and Old Testament*.[73] He covers the history of source criticism and especially the development of the Documentary Hypothesis in a more general way than he had in his lectures.[74] Buried in a footnote, Kitchen notes an important omission in Wellhausen:

> Wellhausen's famous *Prolegomena zur Geschichte Israels*, even in its sixth edition of 1905 (repr. 1927), was not marked by any acquisition or use of new, factual data (esp. from the Ancient Orient) so

---

"Over the decades, much information on covenants and treaties in the Near East has come to light. From *no less than* 25 treaties from the archives of the Hittites, Ugarit, etc., it has been possible to establish the clear pattern of such covenants or treaties for the late 2nd millennium BC (14th–13th centuries). . . . This was all worked out for the Hittite treaties by V Korosec . . . 1931. It was first utilized for OT covenants by G E Mendenhall . . . 1954 . . . reprinted . . . 1955. However, he applied the data only to Exodus and Josh 24, curiously overlooking Deuteronomy. In 1955 I dealt with Deuteronomy, but was not able to publish it. In 1963 appeared M G Kline's *Treaty of the Great King*, applying this material to Deuteronomy effectively. . . . From my own and esp Kline's work, it is absolutely clear that Deuteronomy mirrors the 14th–13th century pattern (age of Moses). . . . There can be no doubt that, as Mendenhall established for Exodus and Josh 24 and Kline published for Deuteronomy, that the Sinai covenant and its renewal belong to the 2nd-millennium group" (43–44).

[72] Kitchen, *Pentateuchal Criticism* [lecture notes], 44. Most recently, Kitchen has done the world of ancient Near Eastern and biblical scholarship a major service in publishing more than 1600 pages of transliterations along with English translations of all the major covenants (more than 100 examples written in ten different ancient Near Eastern languages) from the ancient Near East that have been discovered and examined, including their historical contexts and commentary. See Kenneth A. Kitchen and Paul J. N. Lawrence, *Treaty, Law and Covenant in the Ancient Near East Part 1: The Texts* (Wiesbaden: Harrassowitz, 2012); *Treaty, Law and Covenant in the Ancient Near East Part 2: Text, Notes and Chromograms* (Wiesbaden: Harrassowitz, 2012); and *Treaty, Law and Covenant in the Ancient Near East Part 3: Overall Historical Survey* (Wiesbaden: Harrassowitz, 2012).

[73] Kitchen, *Ancient Orient and Old Testament*.

[74] Kitchen, *Ancient Orient and Old Testament*, 17–20.

much as by its remoulding of history to accord with his *a priori* philosophical principles.[75]

Kitchen proceeds to trace the development of ancient Near Eastern studies, showing how it split from biblical studies, and how they subsequently developed separately, cutting off much of biblical studies (in its historical critical mode) from the archaeology and literature of the ancient Near East.[76]

Of most help here, Kitchen walks through the antediluvian and Flood material in light of the ancient Near Eastern context, showing how well the format and ideas fit other texts from that general time period.[77] He then situates the patriarchal narratives within their ancient historical context, underscoring their historical plausibility in light of material from the archaeological sources uniquely situated to the early second millennium.[78] After this, Kitchen delves into the exodus, wilderness, and conquest material, showing its authentic mid-second millennium ancient Egyptian context.[79] He addresses some of the alleged anachronisms in the Pentateuch, showing how in fact they can be reconciled with archaeological findings,[80] especially the covenantal traditions which fit so well with sources from the second millennium.[81]

Kitchen then devotes an entire chapter to the matter of literary criticism,[82] beginning with a focus on the Documentary Hypothesis,[83] which expands some of the material he had presented earlier in his lecture. He cites a number of the figures we have already covered here, including Kaufmann, whom he believes is justified in dating the material attributed to P to the pre-exilic period. In fact, Kitchen considers Kaufmann's work to be one of the most important scholarly sources proving the antiquity of P.[84] Utilizing the same sort of primary sources from the ancient Near East (mainly from Egypt, his own specific area of expertise), Kitchen dissolves the problem of doublets, building on the work of other scholars as well, including Cassuto.[85] He then addresses the issue of double names more thoroughly than he did in his lecture, referencing the work of Gordon and others, as well as many primary sources.[86]

---

[75] Kitchen, *Ancient Orient and Old Testament*, 19n5.
[76] Kitchen, *Ancient Orient and Old Testament*, 20–28.
[77] Kitchen, *Ancient Orient and Old Testament*, 35–41 and 88–90.
[78] Kitchen, *Ancient Orient and Old Testament*, 41–55 and 153–56.
[79] Kitchen, *Ancient Orient and Old Testament*, 57–68 and 156–58.
[80] Kitchen, *Ancient Orient and Old Testament*, 79–81.
[81] Kitchen, *Ancient Orient and Old Testament*, 91–102.
[82] Kitchen, *Ancient Orient and Old Testament*, 112–38.
[83] Kitchen, *Ancient Orient and Old Testament*, 112–29.
[84] Kitchen, *Ancient Orient and Old Testament*, 114.
[85] Kitchen, *Ancient Orient and Old Testament*, 116–20.
[86] Kitchen, *Ancient Orient and Old Testament*, 121–25.

After *Ancient Orient and Old Testament,* one of Kitchen's most significant contributions was in the form of a book chapter concerning the patriarchal narratives in Genesis.[87] One of the most important points he brings up in this essay is the ancient Near Eastern background to Genesis 14, highlighting how well it fits the geopolitics of the time. Pointing out that the four kings in the battle came from Mesopotamia, he isolates the patriarchal age, roughly 2000–1700, as the only time period in history that the actual events covered in Genesis 14 could possibly have taken place:

> In Mesopotamia, the dominance of alliances of kings (often in rival groups) belongs to only two historical periods. The earlier is that of the old Sumerian city-states of the 3rd millennium BC, before the empires of Akkad and Ur III; this is too early to be relevant. The only other such period is broadly 2000–1700 BC, *i.e.* between the fall of the 3rd Dynasty of Ur, and the supremacy of Shamshi-Adad I of Assyria and Hammurabi of Babylon. After their time, Mesopotamia proper was dominated by just these two kingdoms until Persia swallowed all. But within 2000–1700 BC, just such alliances proliferate. . . . It is this political configuration for eastern powers which—alone—fits the situation in Genesis 14. And it is only in this period that the distant realm of Elam was ever involved in international politics anywhere west of Babylonia and Assyria proper.[88]

He also shows, as he had elsewhere, how well the covenants in the patriarchal narratives fit the early second millennium covenant texts and treaties that have been discovered.[89] He explains, "So far as one may determine on the data we have, the treaty-reports of Abraham, Isaac and Jacob belong with the treaties of the first half of the 2nd millennium BC—and not with those of earlier or later epochs."[90] Anticipating the work of his younger contemporary James K. Hoffmeier, Kitchen proceeds to show the abundance of evidence for Semites in Egypt during the period from Joseph through the Israelite subjugation, underscoring how well the Joseph narratives fit with what we know of early second millennium Egypt, including the price for which he was sold into slavery.[91]

Kitchen's real *tour de force* is his nearly seven-hundred-page tome, *On the Reliability of the Old Testament,* which boasts more than one

---

[87] Kitchen, "Genesis 12–50," 67–92.
[88] Kitchen, "Genesis 12–50," 72–73.
[89] Kitchen, "Genesis 12–50," 74–77.
[90] Kitchen, "Genesis 12–50," 77.
[91] Kitchen, "Genesis 12–50," 77–89.

hundred pages of endnotes and copious references (including images) of primary sources.[92] The portions most relevant to our discussion concern his situating Genesis 1–11 within its early second millennium context,[93] his discussion of the historicity of the patriarchal narratives,[94] and his massively documented treatment on the historical reliability of the exodus and wilderness traditions.[95] In some ways this volume updates all of his prior work on the historical reliability of the Old Testament, but with more thorough arguments and more recent evidence that has come to light from the archaeological record, representing more than forty years of his scholarship—indeed, almost fifty by the time that volume was published.[96]

Although he is responding to more recent minimalists who push Wellhausen's skepticism beyond the edge, locating the origin of Israel late in the Hellenistic period, Kitchen's comments on the general historical reliability of the Genesis material, in light of the large quantity and convergence of lines of evidence, applies as well to the late dating of material by Wellhausen:

> *WHY*, then, is the literary profile of Gen. 1–11 basically identical with the profiles of comparable Mesopotamian literature relating to creation, flood-catastrophe, and long "linkup" human successions—and, as a search of the ancient literatures shows, as a topos in vogue creatively *only* in the early second millennium BC (and earlier?), not later? . . . *WHY*, then, do main features in the much-maligned patriarchal narratives fit so well (and often, *exclusively*) into the framework supplied by the independent, objective data of the early second millennium? (E.g., details in Gen. 14; Elamite activity in the west, uniquely then; basic slave price of twenty shekels for Joseph; etc.) . . . *WHY*, then, do the human and other phenomena at the exodus show clearly Egyptian traits (not Palestinian, not Neo-Babylonian . . .), and especially of the thirteenth century? . . . Tabernacle-type worship structures are known in the Semitic world (Mari, Ugarit, Timna) specifically for the nineteenth to twelfth centuries; the Sinai tabernacle is based directly on Egyptian technology of the thirtieth to thirteenth centuries (with the concept extending into the eleventh). The Sinai/plains of Moab covenant (much of Exodus-Leviticus, Deuteronomy, Josh. 24) is squarely tied in format and content *exclusively* to the massive

---

92 Kitchen, *On the Reliability*.
93 Kitchen, *On the Reliability*, 421–48.
94 Kitchen, *On the Reliability*, 313–72.
95 Kitchen, *On the Reliability*, 241–312.
96 The earliest of his publications we were able to find was Kitchen, "Recently Published," 1–2 which dates from 1956–1957.

document format of the fourteenth-thirteenth centuries, before and after which the formats were wholly different; we have ninety original exemplars that settle the matter decisively. . . . *WHY*, then, does Merenptah (in his Year 5, 1209/1208) report a *people* Israel, a foreign tribal grouping by the very accurate determinative signs (in a very accurately written text) who are west of Ascalon and Gezer, and south of Yenoam, and hence in the central Canaanite hill country, if no such named people existed?[97]

In another lengthy excerpt, Kitchen summarizes his conclusions based on the massive amount of evidence for the authentic second millennium Egyptian background to the exodus and wilderness traditions, making the figure of Moses, and Moses as author of the Pentateuch, seem more likely than ever before:

The particular and special form of covenant evidenced by Exodus-Leviticus and in Deuteronomy (and mirrored in Josh. 24) could not possibly have been reinvented even in the fourteenth/thirteenth centuries by a runaway rabble of brick-making slaves under some uncouth leader no more educated than themselves. The formal agreeing, formatting, and issuing of treaty documents belongs to governments and (in antiquity) to royal courts. . . . So, how come documents such as Exodus-Leviticus and Deuteronomy just happen to embody very closely the framework and order and much of the nature of the contents of such treaties and law collections established by kings and their scribal staffs at court . . . in the late second millennium? . . . To exploit such concepts and formats for his people's use at that time, the Hebrew's leader would *necessarily* had to have been in a position to know of such documents at first hand. . . . In short, to explain what exists in our Hebrew documents we need a Hebrew leader who had had experience of life at the Egyptian court, mainly in the East Delta . . . including knowledge of treaty-type documents and their format, as well as of traditional Semitic legal/social usage more familiar to his own folk. In other words, somebody distressingly like that old "hero" of

---

[97] Kitchen, *On the Reliability*, 459–60.

biblical tradition, Moses, is badly needed at this point, to make any sense of the situation as we have it.[98]

THE VIEW OF AN ANCIENT HISTORIAN: EDWIN YAMAUCHI[99]

Kitchen's contemporary Edwin Yamauchi published in broader fields than perhaps any scholar we have covered thus far, apart from Albright and Gordon, Yamauchi's mentor. His wide range of scholarship includes Gnosticism,[100] Church history, classical Greek and Roman studies,[101] ancient Persia,[102] Egyptology,[103] Assyriology,[104]

---

[98] Kitchen, *On the Reliability*, 295.

[99] On Yamauchi see, e.g., Jeffrey L. Morrow, "Yamauchi, Edwin Masao (b. 1937)," in *Encyclopedia of Christian Civilization*, ed. Kurian, 2549–50; Kenneth R. Calvert, "Edwin M. Yamauchi," in *The Light of Discovery: Studies in Honor of Edwin M. Yamauchi*, ed. John D. Wineland (Eugene, OR: Pickwick, 2007), 1–23; Paul L. Maier, "Foreword," in *Light of Discovery*, xi–xiv; John D. Wineland, "Preface," in *Light of Discovery*, xv–xvii; and Edwin M. Yamauchi, "An Ancient Historian's View of Christianity," in *Professors Who Believe: The Spiritual Journeys of Christian Faculty*, ed. Paul M. Anderson (Downers Grove, IL: InterVarsity Press, 1998), 192–99.

[100] E.g., Edwin M. Yamauchi, "Pre-Christian Gnosticism in the Nag Hammadi Texts?" *Church History* 48 (1979): 129–41; Edwin M. Yamauchi, *Pre-Christian Gnosticism? A Survey of the Proposed Evidence* (London: Tyndale, 1973); Edwin M. Yamauchi, *Gnostic Ethics and Mandaean Origins* (Cambridge, MA: Harvard University Press, 1970); Edwin M. Yamauchi, *Mandaic Incantation Texts* (New Haven, CT: American Oriental Society, 1967); Edwin M. Yamauchi, "The Present Status of Mandaean Studies," *Journal of Near Eastern Studies* 25 (1966): 88–96; and Edwin M. Yamauchi, "Aramaic Magic Bowls," *Journal of the American Oriental Society* 85 (1965): 511–23.

[101] E.g., Edwin M. Yamauchi, "Homer and Archaeology: Minimalists and Maximalists in Classical Context," in *Future of Biblical Archaeology*, 69–90; Edwin M. Yamauchi, "Herodotus—Historian or Liar," in *Crossing Boundaries and Linking Horizons: Studies in Honor of Michael C. Astour*, ed. Gordon D. Young, Mark W. Chavalas, and Richard E. Averbeck (Bethesda, MD: CDL Press, 1997), 599–614; and Edwin M. Yamauchi, "Homer, History, and Archaeology," *Near Eastern Archaeological Society Bulletin* 3 (1973): 21–42.

[102] E.g., Edwin M. Yamauchi, "Persians," in *Peoples of the Old Testament*, ed. Alfred J. Hoerth, Gerald L. Mattingly, and Edwin M. Yamauchi (Grand Rapids: Baker Academic, 1994), 107–24; Edwin M. Yamauchi, "Mordecai, the Persepolis Tablets, and the Susa Excavations," *Vetus Testamentum* 42 (1992): 272–75; Edwin M. Yamauchi, *Persia and the Bible* (Grand Rapids: Baker Book House, 1990); and Edwin M. Yamauchi, "The Achaemenid Capitals," *Near Eastern Archaeological Society Bulletin* 8 (1976): 5–81.

[103] E.g., Edwin M. Yamauchi, *Africa and the Bible* (Grand Rapids: Baker Academic, 2004); and Edwin M. Yamauchi, "Obelisks and Pyramids," *Near Eastern Archaeological Society Bulletin* 24 (1985): 111–15.

[104] E.g., Edwin M. Yamauchi, "Babylon," in *Major Cities of the Biblical World*, ed. R. K. Harrison (Nashville, TN: Thomas Nelson, 1985), 32–48; Edwin M. Yamauchi, *Greece and*

the Scythians,[105] early Christianity,[106] Reformation history,[107] and both Old[108] and New Testaments.[109] These are reflected in the doctoral dissertations in ancient history he directed—e.g., in Egyptology, ancient Greek and Roman studies, Gnosticism, Second Temple Judaism, and early Coptic Christianity—as well as the courses he taught: Greek Grammar; Homer (in Greek); Herodotus (in Greek); Plato (in Greek); the Greek New Testament; Minoan Linear B; Coptic; Syriac; Greek History; Near Eastern History; Persian History; Religions in the Roman Empire; Mesopotamian History;

Babylon: Early Contacts between the Aegean and the Near East (Grand Rapids: Baker Book House, 1967); Edwin M. Yamauchi, "Additional Notes on Tammuz," *Journal of Semitic Studies* 11 (1966): 10–15; and Edwin M. Yamauchi, "Tammuz and the Bible," *Journal of Biblical Literature* 81 (1965): 283–90.

[105] E.g., Edwin Yamauchi, "The Scythians—Who Were They? And Why Did Paul Include Them in Colossians 3:11?" *Priscilla Papers* 21, no. 4 (2007): 13–18; Edwin M. Yamauchi, "The Scythians: Invading Hordes from the Russian Steppes," *Biblical Archaeologist* 46, no. 2 (1983): 90–99; and Edwin M. Yamauchi, *Foes from the Northern Frontier: Invading Hordes from the Russian Steppes* (Grand Rapids: Baker Book House, 1982).

[106] Edwin M. Yamauchi, "Elchasaites, Manichaeans, and Mandaeans in Light of the Cologne Mani Codex," in *Beyond the Jordan: Studies in Honor of W. Harold Mare*, ed. Glenn A. Carnagey, Sr., Glenn Carnagey, Jr., and Keith N. Schoville (Eugene, OR: Wipf & Stock, 2005), 49–60; Edwin M. Yamauchi, "Christians and the Jewish Revolts against Rome," *Fides et Historia* 23 (1991): 11–30; and Edwin M. Yamauchi, "The Crucifixion and Docetic Christology," *Concordia Theological Quarterly* 46, no. 1 (1982): 1–20.

[107] Edwin M. Yamauchi, "Erasmus' Contribution to New Testament Scholarship," *Fides et Historia* 19, no. 3 (1987): 6–24.

[108] E.g., Edwin M. Yamauchi, "Was Nehemiah the Cupbearer a Eunuch?" *Zeitschrift für die alttestamentliche Wissenschaft* 92, no. 1 (1980): 132–42; Edwin M. Yamauchi, "The Archaeological Background of Ezra," *Bibliotheca Sacra* 173, no. 3 (1980): 195–211; Edwin M. Yamauchi, "The Archaeological Background of Esther," *Bibliotheca Sacra* 137, no. 2 (1980): 99–117; Edwin M. Yamauchi, "The Archaeological Background of Daniel," *Bibliotheca Sacra* 137, no. 1 (1980): 3–16; Edwin M. Yamauchi, "A Decade and a Half of Archaeology in Israel and Jordan," *Journal of the American Academy of Religion* 42 (1974): 710–26; and Edwin M. Yamauchi, "The Greek Words in Daniel in the Light of Greek Influence in the Near East," in *New Perspectives on the Old Testament*, ed. J. Barton Payne (Waco, TX: Word Books, 1970), 170–200.

[109] E.g., Edwin M. Yamauchi, "Jesus Outside the New Testament: What Is the Evidence?" in *Jesus Under Fire*, ed. Michael J. Wilkins and J. P. Moreland (Grand Rapids: Zondervan, 1995), 207–29; Edwin M. Yamauchi, "Archaeology and the Gospels: Discoveries and Publications of the Past Decade (1977–1987)," in *The Gospels Today: A Guide to Some Recent Discoveries*, ed. John H. Skilton (Philadelphia, PA: Skilton House, 1990), 1–12; Edwin M. Yamauchi, "The Episode of the Magi," in *Chronos, Kairos, and Christos: Nativity and Chronological Studies Presented to Jack Finegan*, ed. Jerry Vardaman and Edwin M. Yamauchi (Winona Lake, IN: Eisenbrauns, 1989), 15–39; Edwin M. Yamauchi, "Magic or Miracle? Demons, Diseases and Exorcisms," in *Gospel Perspectives*, vol. 6, *The Miracles of Jesus*, ed. David Wenham and Craig Blomberg (Sheffield, UK: Journal for the Study of the Old Testament Press, 1986), 89–183; and Edwin M. Yamauchi, *The Archaeology of New Testament Cities in Western Asia Minor* (Grand Rapids: Baker Book House, 1980).

Egyptian History; Roman Republic; and Early Church History. These areas are reflected in his teaching both as an ancient historian at Rutgers University and at Miami University (Ohio) where he spent the overwhelming majority of his teaching career. Quite a few of his publications are like Kitchen's in supporting the historical reliability of the Pentateuch and challenging various aspects of the Documentary Hypothesis.[110]

In reviewing Cassuto's work, *The Documentary Hypothesis*, Yamauchi opines that "Cassuto's cogent criticisms were limited in their influence

---

[110] E.g., Edwin M. Yamauchi, "Abraham and Archaeology: Anachronisms or Adaptations?" in *Perspectives on Our Father Abraham: Essays in Honor of Marvin R. Wilson*, ed. Steven A. Hunt (Grand Rapids: Eerdmans, 2010), 15–32; Edwin M. Yamauchi, "Akhenaten, Moses, and Monotheism," *Near Eastern Archaeological Society Bulletin* 55 (2010): 1–15; Edwin Yamauchi, "The Current Status of Old Testament Historiography," in *Faith, Tradition, and History: Old Testament Historiography in Its Near Eastern Context*, ed. A. R. Millard, James K. Hoffmeier, and David W. Baker (Winona Lake, IN: Eisenbrauns, 1994), 1–36; Edwin M. Yamauchi, "Archaeology and the Bible," in *The Oxford Companion to the Bible*, ed. Bruce M. Metzger and Michael D. Coogan (Oxford, UK: Oxford University Press, 1993), 46–54; Edwin M. Yamauchi, "History and Hermeneutics," *Evangelical Journal* 5, no. 2 (1987): 55–66; Edwin M. Yamauchi, "The Proofs, Problems and Promises of Biblical Archaeology," *Journal of the American Scientific Affiliation* 36, no. 3 (1984): 129–38; Yamauchi, *The Scriptures and Archaeology*; Donald J. Wiseman and Edwin Yamauchi, *Archaeology and the Bible: An Introductory Study* (Grand Rapids: Zondervan, 1979); Edwin M. Yamauchi, "Documents from Old Testament Times," *Westminster Theological Journal* 41, no. 1 (1978): 1–32; Edwin M. Yamauchi, "The Patriarchal Age," in *Wycliffe Bible Encyclopedia*, ed. Charles F. Pfeiffer, Howard F. Vos, and John Rhea (Chicago: Moody Press, 1975), 1287–91; Edwin M. Yamauchi, "Archaeology and the Scriptures," *Seminary Journal* 25 (1974): 163–241; Edwin M. Yamauchi, "The Archaeological Confirmation of Suspect Elements in the Classical and Biblical Traditions," in *The Law and the Prophets: Old Testament Studies Prepared in Honor of Oswald Thompson Allis*, ed. John H. Skilton, Milton C. Fisher, and Leslie W. Sloat (Nutley, NJ: Presbyterian and Reformed, 1974), 54–70; Yamauchi, *The Stones and the Scriptures*; Edwin M. Yamauchi, "Stones, Scripts, and Scholars," *Christianity Today* 13 (February 14, 1969): 432–34 and 436–37; Edwin Yamauchi, Edwin Yamauchi, *Composition and Corroboration in Classical and Biblical Studies* (Philadelphia, PA: Presbyterian and Reformed, 1966); Edwin M. Yamauchi, "Do the Bible's Critics Use a Double Standard?" *Christianity Today* 10 (19 November 1965): 179–82; Edwin M. Yamauchi, "Joseph in Egypt," *The Way* (September 1965): 28–36; and Edwin M. Yamauchi, "Abraham and Mesopotamia," *The Way* (September 1965): 1–5. Yamauchi's important 1984 article was republished the following year in a more accessible venue as Edwin M. Yamauchi, "The Proofs, Problems and Promises of Biblical Archaeology," *Evangelical Review of Theology* 9, no. 1 (1985): 117–38. As with Kitchen, some of Yamauchi's book reviews are themselves little treasures of arguments against aspects of the Documentary Hypothesis and in favor of the historical reliability of the Pentateuch, e.g., Edwin Yamauchi, review of *Before Abraham Was* by Isaac M. Kikawada and Arthur Quinn, *Journal of the American Oriental Society* 108, no. 2 (1988): 310–11; and Edwin M. Yamauchi, review of *The Documentary Hypothesis and the Composition of the Pentateuch* by Umberto Cassuto, *Journal of the American Oriental Society* 85, no. 4 (1965): 582–83.

on biblical scholarship because until recently [1961] this work was available only in Hebrew."[111] He writes further, adding to Cassuto's critique: "If the criteria used to establish the documentary hypothesis of the Pentateuch were transferred to the study of other Near Eastern literatures, one would see that in many cases the criteria would prove to be arbitrary and artificial. For example, were we to apply the criterion of different names (and words) as indications of different documents, we would have to postulate multiple authorships for works that are transparently unitary."[112] Yamauchi recounts further, "Not only were various synonyms used, but various styles were employed in a single document. The biography of the Egyptian Uni (c. 2300 BC) contains the flowing narrative about his various employments, stereotyped refrains, and also a victory hymn."[113] After surveying multiple examples from documents emerging from the archaeological record, Yamauchi concludes, "Composite styles therefore do not necessarily require multiple authors as a single writer may employ several styles."[114]

In an essay surveying the history of Old Testament scholarship, Yamauchi points out that:

> Modern biblical criticism has been characterized by anti-supernaturalism. Literary criticism as influenced by Julius Wellhausen (1844–1918), Herman Gunkel (1862–1932), and Gerhard von Rad (1901–71) has sought the prehistory of the texts and concluded that though one may recover *Heilsgeschichte*, the expression of Israel's faith, her *Historie* can no longer be established.[115]

In the context of early dating for the patriarchal narratives, Yamauchi mentions that "many of the divine names in the patriarchal narratives, El Elyon, El Ro'i, El Olam, and El Bethel, were not current names of the first millennium BC but of the second millennium BC."[116] As others had before

---

[111] Yamauchi, review of *Documentary Hypothesis*, 582.

[112] Yamauchi, review of *Documentary Hypothesis*, 582–83.

[113] Yamauchi, review of *Documentary Hypothesis*, 583. On the same page, Yamauchi provides other examples as well: "But Ramesses II celebrated his so-called 'victory' at Kadesh both in prose and in poetic accounts on various walls throughout the land of Egypt. Hammurabi's Law Code is structured with a prose body between a poetic prologue and epilogue. . . . Khety, a writer under the pharaoh Amenemhet I (c. 1990 B.C.), composed the Satire of the Trades, probably gave literary form to the 'Teaching of Amenemhet I,' and may have written a well-known Hymn to the Nile."

[114] Yamauchi, review of *Documentary Hypothesis*, 583.

[115] Yamauchi, "Current Status," 5.

[116] Yamauchi, "Current Status," 11.

him, Yamauchi also underscores "The similarity of the Mosaic covenant to the Hittite suzerainty treaties, which date from the second millennium BC."[117] In a more recent work, Yamauchi explains many of the apparent anachronisms in the Pentateuch as either not anachronistic at all but entirely in keeping with the cultural and historical context (as in the case of the domestication of camels), or later scribal emendations (as in the case of the mention of the Philistines)—but hardly an airtight case for late dating the Pentateuch.[118]

In the next chapter we continue to see how evangelical ancient Near Eastern scholars in the 1980s through the twenty-first century carried this work further. In more recent times, scholars from Catholic, mainline Protestant, and Jewish backgrounds have joined the discussion. We will cover some of these other scholarly works as well, showing how diverse have been the many challenges to the Documentary Hypothesis for more than a century.

---

[117] Yamauchi, "Current Status," 13.
[118] Yamauchi, "Abraham and Archaeology," 15–32.

CHAPTER 3

MORE RECENT DIRECTIONS IN THE STUDY OF THE PENTATEUCH'S ORIGINS:

CHALLENGES TO THE DOCUMENTARY HYPOTHESIS FROM THE END OF THE TWENTIETH CENTURY TO TODAY

In the last chapter we took a look at the many challenges to the Documentary Hypothesis from roughly the midpoint of the twentieth century, mainly coming from archaeology and ancient Near Eastern studies. In this chapter, we continue along this trajectory and see how challenges mounted, especially as the literature of the ancient Near East, uncovered by decades of archaeological excavations, was increasingly studied by scholars. By and large, many of the proponents of the Documentary Hypothesis were trained in biblical studies or theology as their primary disciplines, with varying levels of competence in the languages and literatures of the ancient Near East. Some of the more prominent challenges to the Documentary Hypothesis since the 1970s, however, were from scholars, Protestant and otherwise, who had been trained in Egyptology, Assyriology, and related ancient Near Eastern and Mediterranean studies.

The Patriarchal Narratives in Evangelical Scholarship from 1980

In 1980, Donald Wiseman joined Alan Millard to edit an important volume challenging Wellhausen-style skepticism on the historical reliability of the patriarchal narratives in Genesis.[1] The volume brought together leading evangelical biblical and ancient Near Eastern scholars highlighting the historical reliability of the patriarchal narratives.[2] It includes a variety of topics. The first essay, by John Goldingay, explores the patriarchs in history.[3] Goldingay situates the narratives within their biblical and historical context, showing how well they fit within the matrix of the ancient Near East of the second millennium.

In the next essay, Alan Millard takes a look at the question of appropriate methodology for studying the patriarchal narratives.[4] Millard has produced numerous works helping demonstrate the historical reliability of aspects of the Pentateuch (indeed, of the entire Bible).[5] In this essay, Millard

---

[1] On Millard see Edwin M. Yamauchi, with contributions from Paul J. N. Lawrence and Daniel I. Block, "In Praise of a Venerable Scribe: A Bibliographic Tribute to Alan R. Millard," in *Write That They May Read: Studies in Literacy and Textualization in the Ancient Near East and in the Hebrew Scriptures: Essays in Honour of Professor Alan R. Millard*, ed. Daniel I. Block, David C. Deuel, C. John Collins, and Paul J. N. Lawrence (Eugene, OR: Pickwick, 2020), 392–415; and Piotr Bienkowski, Christopher Mee, and Elizabeth Slater, preface to *Writing and Ancient Near Eastern Society: Papers in Honour of Alan R. Millard* (New York: T&T Clark, 2005), 7–8.

[2] A. R. Millard and D. J. Wiseman, ed., *Essays on the Patriarchal Narratives* (Leicester, UK: InterVarsity Press, 1980).

[3] John Goldingay, "The Patriarchs in Scripture and History," in *Essays*, 11–42.

[4] Alan R. Millard, "Methods of Studying the Patriarchal Narratives as Ancient Texts," in *Essays*, 43–58.

[5] See, e.g., Alan R. Millard, "Deuteronomy and Ancient Hebrew History Writing in Light of Ancient Chronicles and Treaties," in *For Our Good Always: Studies on the Message and Influence of Deuteronomy in Honor of Daniel I. Block*, ed. Jason S. DeRouchie, Jason Gile, and Kenneth J. Turner (Winona Lake, IN: Eisenbrauns, 2013), 3–15; Alan Millard, "Ramesses Was Here . . . And Others Too!," in *Ramesside Studies in Honour of K. A. Kitchen*, ed. Mark Collier and Steven Snape (Bolton, UK: Rutherford Press, 2011), 305–12; Alan R. Millard, "Were the Israelites Really Canaanites?" in *Israel—Ancient Kingdom or Late Invention?*, ed. Daniel I. Block (Nashville, TN: B&H Academic, 2008), 156–68; Alan R. Millard, "The Tablets in the Ark," in *Reading the Law: Studies in Honour of Gordon J. Wenham*, ed. J. G. McConville and Karl Möller (New York: T&T Clark, 2007), 254–66; Alan R. Millard, "Archaeology," in *Dictionary for Theological Interpretation of the Bible*, ed. Kevin J. Vanhoozer, Craig G. Bartholomew, Daniel J. Treier, and N.T. Wright (Grand Rapids: Baker Academic, 2005), 60–63; Alan R. Millard, "Where Was Abraham's Ur: The Case for the Babylonian City," *Biblical Archaeology Review* 27, no. 3 (2001): 52–53, 57; Alan Millard, "How Reliable is Exodus?" *Biblical Archaeology Review* 26, no. 4 (2000): 50–57; Alan R. Millard, "On Giving the Bible a Fair Go," *Buried History* 35, no. 4 (1999):

challenges prior studies of the patriarchal narratives—both Wellhausen's as well as Gunkel's—on their lack of reliance upon appropriate ancient Near Eastern historical and literary sources. Millard concedes the point made by more recent skeptical scholars that many of the optimistic parallels Cyrus Gordon and others of his generation found in ancient Near Eastern texts were not always fittingly or consistently applied to the biblical accounts. What Millard shows, however, is that the proper methodology for studying them is a more comprehensive approach to ancient Near Eastern literature and archaeological discoveries, as opposed to the haphazard approach of the past or the selective and skeptical approach of the present.

After Millard's essay, John Bimson writes an important contribution on studying the patriarchal narratives in light of the archaeological record.[6] Bimson covers the various arguments for dating the patriarchs, highlighting problems with the various proposals. In the end he argues for a slightly earlier dating of the patriarchal period than is typical. After Bimson's chapter comes Martin Selman's important look at the patriarchal narratives in light of comparative customs evidenced in ancient Near Eastern literature, wherein he reviews and evaluates earlier comparative claims of Gordon, et al.[7]

Selman begins by reviewing the consensus between what we might call the schools of Albright, Gordon, and Ephraim Speiser on the general historical reliability of the patriarchal narratives. Speiser was the most open of the three to the Documentary Hypothesis, assuming its basic literary form,

---

5–12; Alan Millard, "Books in the Late Bronze Age in the Levant," *Israel Oriental Studies* 18 (1998): 171–81; Alan R. Millard, "Die Geschichte Israels auf dem Hintergrund der Religionsgeschichte des alten Vorderen Orients," in *Israel in Geschichte und Gegenwart*, ed. Gerhard Maier (Wuppertal: R. Brockhaus; Giessen & Basel, CH: Brunnen, 1996), 25–42; Alan R. Millard, "Archaeology and the Reliability of the Bible," *Evangel* (Summer 1991): 22–25; Alan R. Millard, "How Can Archaeology Contribute to the Study of the Bible?" *Evangel* (Spring 1991): 9–12; Alan Millard, *Discoveries from Bible Times: Archaeological Treasures Throw Light on the Bible* (Oxford, UK: Lion, 1985); Alan R. Millard, "Archaeology and Ancient Israel," *Faith and Thought* 108 (1981): 53–62; Alan R. Millard, "The Text of the Old Testament," in *A Bible Commentary for Today*, ed. G. C. D. Howley, F. F. Bruce, and H. L. Ellison (London: Pickering & Inglis, 1979), 27–39; A. R. Millard, *The Bible BC: What Can Archaeology Prove?* (Leicester, UK: InterVarsity Press, 1977); and Alan R. Millard, "A New Babylonian 'Genesis' Story," *Tyndale Bulletin* 18 (1967): 3–18.

6 John J. Bimson, "Archaeological Data and the Dating of the Patriarchs," in *Essays*, 59–92.

7 Martin J. Selman, "Comparative Customs and the Patriarchal Age," in *Essays*, 93–138. Selman wrote other works that support the historical reliability of the patriarchal age and thus challenge that aspect of the Documentary Hypothesis. See, e.g., Martin J. Selman, "Social Environment of the Patriarchs," *Tyndale Bulletin* 27 (1976): 114–36; and Martin J. Selman, "Published and Unpublished Fifteenth Century B.C. Cuneiform Documents and Their Bearing on the Patriarchal Narratives of the Old Testament," (Ph.D. diss., University of Wales, 1975).

but all three found apparent parallels in patriarchal customs evidenced from ancient Near Eastern documents, especially the Nuzi tablets. Selman then shows how that near consensus was shattered, reverting to a more skeptical position.

Selman walks through a host of parallels Albright, Gordon, and/or Speiser posited for the patriarchal narratives and concedes that the skeptics are correct to challenge the fit. Notwithstanding the legitimacy of these challenges, Selman shows how many of these parallels do show a general ancient Near Eastern context, even if they are not tied to specific ancient literary motifs. After reviewing proper methodology in evaluating both ancient Near Eastern customs as well as biblical, Selman concludes, "When the biblical and nonbiblical material is subject to proper control, the way is still open for the social customs of the patriarchal narratives to be legitimately illustrated and supported from a variety of historical contexts in the ancient Near East."[8] After surveying more than a dozen legitimate examples of such customs, Selman argues that:

> Since the majority of these examples show that the patriarchal customs can be compared without difficulty with a wide range of material from the ancient Near East, it may be concluded that the patriarchal narratives accurately reflect a social and historical setting which belongs to the second and first millennia BC. . . . From the independent viewpoint of the historian, therefore, the social parallels make the historical existence of the patriarchs more likely.[9]

After Selman comes Donald Wiseman's essay on Abraham in his historical context.[10] Wiseman, as we have mentioned above, was a prolific Assyriologist who helped demonstrate the Old Testament's historicity, especially various aspects of the historical reliability of the Pentateuch in the light of ancient Mesopotamian evidence.[11] In this essay, he shows decisively,

---

[8] Selman, "Comparative Customs," 125–26.

[9] Selman, "Comparative Customs," 128.

[10] Donald J. Wiseman, "Abraham Reassessed," in *Essays*, 139–56.

[11] See, e.g., Donald J. Wiseman, "They Lived in Tents," in *Biblical and Near Eastern Studies: Essays in Honor of William Sanford LaSor*, ed. Gary A. Tuttle (Grand Rapids: Eerdmans, 1978), 195–200; Donald J. Wiseman, "Abraham in History and Tradition Part II: Abraham the Prince," *Bibliotheca Sacra* 135 (1977): 228–37; Donald J. Wiseman, "Abraham in History and Tradition Part I: Abraham the Hebrew," *Bibliotheca Sacra* 134 (1977): 123–30; D. J. Wiseman, "Law and Order in Old Testament Times," *Vox Evangelica* 8 (1973): 5–21; Donald J. Wiseman, "Archaeology and Scripture," *Westminster Theological Journal* 33, no. 2 (1971): 133–52; Donald J. Wiseman, "Archaeological Confirmation of the Old Testament," in *Revelation and the Bible: Contemporary Evangelical Thought*, ed. Carl F. H. Henry (Grand Rapids: Baker, 1958), 301–16; D. J. Wiseman, "Annual Address:

contrary to more recent skeptical scholars, how well the narratives about Abraham fit a second millennium historical context.

After Wiseman's chapter, Gordon Wenham treats the religious context of the patriarchs, focusing especially on the various names for God used in Genesis.[12] Among Wenham's conclusions is that "certain aspects of patriarchal religion are so different from later practice, that to suppose the traditions were invented in the first millennium seems unlikely . . . [and] the complete absence of Baal from the patriarchal tradition points to its antiquity."[13] The fact that Jerusalem is nowhere mentioned, something Munro brought up more than half a century earlier, is a point Wenham drives home.

The final chapter is by David W. Baker and pertains to the literary structure of the patriarchal narratives, arguing for a unified reading focusing on the various ancient rhetorical devices present in the text. Baker explains indications of literary diversity as evidence of literary unity.[14] He concludes:

> The Hebrew text of Genesis fits well into its contemporary literary milieu as far as structure is concerned. . . . There is nothing out of the ordinary in the structure of the book which might indicate that

---

The Place and Progress of Biblical Archaeology," Journal of the Transactions of the Victoria Institute 88 (1956): 117–28; D. J. Wiseman, "Secular Records in Confirmation of the Scriptures," Journal of the Transactions of the Victoria Institute 87 (1955): 25–36; D. J. Wiseman, "Genesis 10: Some Archaeological Considerations," *Journal of the Transactions of the Victoria Institute* 87 (1955): 13–24; and D. J. Wiseman, "Some Recent Trends in Biblical Archaeology," *Journal of the Transactions of the Victoria Institute* 82 (1950): 1–18.

[12] Gordon J. Wenham, "The Religion of the Patriarchs," in *Essays*, 157–88. Wenham wrote a number of other works that challenge various aspects of the Documentary Hypothesis. See, e.g., Gordon J. Wenham, "Sanctuary Symbolism in the Garden of Eden Story," in *Proceedings of the Ninth World Congress of Jewish Studies, Jerusalem, August 4–12, 1985* (Jerusalem: World Union of Jewish Studies, 1986), 19–25; Gordon Wenham, "The Date of Deuteronomy: Linch-Pin of Old Testament Criticism: Part Two," *Themelios* 11, no. 1 (1985): 15–18; Gordon Wenham, "The Date of Deuteronomy: Linch-Pin of Old Testament Criticism: Part One," *Themelios* 10, no. 3 (1985): 15–20; and Gordon J. Wenham, "The Coherence of the Flood Narrative," *Vetus Testamentum* 28, no. 3 (1978): 336–48.

[13] Wenham, "Religion of the Patriarchs," 184.

[14] David W. Baker, "Diversity and Unity in the Literary Structure of Genesis," in *Essays*, 189–205. Baker has written a number of other works which challenge (implicitly or explicitly) aspects of the Documentary Hypothesis, especially showing the historical antiquity of parts of the Pentateuch. See, e.g., David W. Baker, "Approaches to Genesis: A Review Article," *Ashland Theological Journal* 31 (1999): 103–7; David W. Baker, "The Mosaic Covenant Against Its Environment," *Ashland Theological Journal* 20 (1989): 9–18; David W. Baker, "The Old Testament and Criticism," *Journal of Theology for Southern Africa* 48 (1984): 13–20; and David W. Baker, "Division Markers and the Structure of Leviticus 1–7," in *Studia Biblica 1978 I: Papers on Old Testament and Related Themes: Sixth International Congress on Biblical Studies: Oxford 3–7 April 1978*, ed. Elizabeth A. Livingstone (Sheffield, UK: Journal for the Study of the Old Testament Press, 1979), 9–15.

it is a heterogenous amalgam of originally separate sources which have been melded. . . . Genesis appears to be a well-structured literary document.[15]

Numerous other evangelical biblical and ancient Near Eastern scholars could be added to this list of those who have contributed to challenging the Documentary Hypothesis.[16]

---

[15] Baker, "Diversity and Unity," 201.

[16] Richard E. Averbeck, "Reading the Torah in a Better Way: Unity and Diversity in Text, Genre, and Compositional History," in *Paradigm Change in Pentateuchal Research, ed.* Matthias Armgardt, Benjamin Kilchör, and Markus Zehnder (Wiesbaden: Harrassowitz, 2019), 21–44; Richard E. Averbeck, "The Cult in Deuteronomy and Its Relationship to the Book of the Covenant and the Holiness Code," in *Sepher Torath Mosheh: Studies in the Interpretation of Deuteronomy,* ed. Daniel I. Block and Richard L. Schultz (Peabody, MA: Hendrickson, 2017), 232–60; Richard S. Hess, "Onomastics of the Exodus Generation in the Book of Exodus," in *"Did I Not Bring Israel Out of Egypt?" Biblical, Archaeological, and Egyptological Perspectives on the Exodus Narratives,* ed. James K. Hoffmeier, Alan R. Millard, and Gary A. Rendsburg (Winona Lake, IN: Eisenbrauns, 2016), 37–48; Benjamin J. Noonan, "Egyptian Loanwords as Evidence for the Authenticity of the Exodus and Wilderness Traditions," in *Did I Not Bring Israel,* 49–68; Richard E. Averbeck, "The Egyptian Sojourn and Deliverance from Slavery in the Framing and Shaping of the Mosaic Law," in *Did I Not Bring Israel,* 143–76; Peter T. Vogt, "'These Are the Words Moses Spoke': Implied Audience and a Case for a Pre-Monarchic Dating of Deuteronomy," in *For Our Good,* 61–80; Richard E. Averbeck, "Pentateuchal Criticism and the Priestly Torah," in *Do Historical Matters Matter to Faith? A Critical Appraisal of Modern and Postmodern Approaches to Scripture,* ed. James K. Hoffmeier and Dennis R. Magary (Wheaton, IL: Crossway, 2012), 151–80; Harry A. Hoffner, Jr., "Ancient Israel's Literary Heritage Compared with Hittite Textual Data," in *Future of Biblical Archaeology: Reassessing Methodologies and Assumptions: The Proceedings of a Symposium, August 12–14, 2001 at Trinity International University,* ed. James K. Hoffmeier and A. R. Millard (Grand Rapids: Eerdmans, 2004), 176–92; Richard E. Averbeck, "Factors in Reading the Patriarchal Narratives: Literary, Historical, and Theological Dimensions," in *Giving the Sense: Understanding and Using Old Testament Historical Texts,* ed. David M. Howard, Jr. and Michael A. Grisanti (Grand Rapids: Kregel, 2003), 115–37; Harry A. Hoffner, Jr., "Hittite-Israelite Cultural Parallels," in *The Context of Scripture,* vol. 3, *Archival Documents from the Biblical World,* ed. William W. Hallo and K. Lawson Younger, Jr. (Leiden, NL: Brill, 2002), xxix–xxxiv; K. Lawson Younger, Jr., "The 'Contextual Method': Some West Semitic Reflections," in *Archival Documents,* xxxv–xlii; Walter C. Kaiser, Jr., *The Old Testament Documents: Are They Reliable and Relevant?* (Downers Grove, IL: InterVarsity Press, 2001); Mark W. Chavalas and Murray R. Adamthwaite, "Archaeological Light on the Old Testament," in *The Face of Old Testament Studies,* ed. David W. Baker and Bill T. Arnold (Grand Rapids: Baker Academic, 1999), 59–96; John D. Currid, *Ancient Egypt and the Old Testament* (Grand Rapids: Baker, 1997); Richard S. Hess, "One Hundred and Fifty Years of Comparative Studies on Genesis 1–11: An Overview," in *"I Studied Inscriptions from Before the Flood": Ancient Near Eastern, Literary, and Linguistic Approaches to Genesis 1–11,* ed. Richard S. Hess and David Toshio Tsumura (Winona Lake, IN: Eisenbrauns, 1994), 3–26; David Toshio Tsumura, "Genesis and Ancient Stories of Creation

OTHER STUDIES FROM THE 1980S AND 1990S
ISAAC KIKAWADA (AND ARTHUR QUINN) ON THE
PENTATEUCH'S LITERARY ARTISTRY

The year 1985 saw the publication of Isaac Kikawada and Arthur Quinn's slender but significant volume *Before Abraham Was*.[17] Kikawada wrote a few other important and related studies beyond this book, but it was this work that has posed the most serious challenges to the Documentary Hypothesis.[18] Unlike many of the prior studies mentioned here, Kikawada and Quinn take

and Flood: An Introduction," in *I Studied Inscriptions*, 27–57; Richard E. Averbeck, "The Sumerian Historiographic Tradition and Its Implications for Genesis 1–11," in *Faith, Tradition, and History: Old Testament Historiography in Its Near Eastern Context*, ed. A. R. Millard, James K. Hoffmeier, and David W. Baker (Winona Lake, IN: Eisenbrauns, 1994), 79–102; John D. Currid, "An Examination of the Egyptian Background of the Genesis Cosmogony," *Biblische Zeitschrift* 35 (1991): 18–40; Richard S. Hess, "Genesis 1–2 in its Literary Context," *Tyndale Bulletin* 14, no. 1 (1990): 143–53; K. Lawson Younger, Jr., *Ancient Conquest Accounts: A Study in Ancient Near Eastern and Biblical History Writing* (Sheffield, UK: Journal for the Study of the Old Testament Press, 1990); Richard S. Hess, "The Genealogies of Genesis 1–11 and Comparative Literature," *Biblica* 70, no. 2 (1989): 241–54; T. C. Mitchell, *Biblical Archaeology: Documents from the British Museum* (Cambridge, UK: Cambridge University Press, 1988); Barry J. Beitzel, "From Harran to Imar Along the Old Babylonian Itinerary: The Evidence from the Archives Royales de Mari," in *Biblical and Near Eastern Studies*, 209–19; Walter C. Kaiser, Jr., "The Literary Form of Genesis 1–11," in *New Perspectives on the Old Testament*, ed. Barton Payne (Waco, TX: Word Books, 1970), 48–65; Harry A. Hoffner, Jr., "Some Contributions of Hittitology to Old Testament Study," *Tyndale Bulletin* 20 (1969): 27–55; Harry A. Hoffner, Jr., "Hittite Tarpiš and Hebrew Terāphîm," *Journal of Near Eastern Studies* 27, no. 1 (1968): 61–68; and T. C. Mitchell, "Archaeology and Genesis i–xi," *Faith and Thought* 91 (1959): 28–49.

17 Isaac M. Kikawada and Arthur Quinn, *Before Abraham Was: The Unity of Genesis 1–11* (Nashville, TN: Abingdon Press, 1985).

18 E.g., Isaac M. Kikawada, "A Quantitative Analysis of the 'Adam and Eve,' 'Cain and Abel,' and 'Noah' Stories," in *Perspectives on Language and Text: Essays and Poems in Honor of Francis I. Andersen's Sixtieth Birthday July 28, 1985*, ed. Edgar W. Conrad and Edward G. Newing (Winona Lake, IN: Eisenbrauns, 1987), 195–203; Isaac M. Kikawada, "The Double Creation of Mankind in Enki and Ninmah, Atrahasis I 1–351, and Genesis 1–2," *Iraq* 45, no. 1 (1983): 43–45; Isaac M. Kikawada, "Genesis on Three Levels," *Annual of the Japanese Biblical Institute* 7 (1981): 3–15; Isaac Mitzuru Kikawada, "Literary Conventions Connected with Antediluvian Historiography in the Ancient Near East," (Ph.D. diss., University of California, Berkeley, 1979); Isaac M. Kikawada, "The Unity of Genesis 12:1–9," in *Proceedings of the Sixth World Congress of Jewish Studies, held at the Hebrew University of Jerusalem 13–19 August 1973, under the auspices of the Israel Academy of Sciences and Humanities*, vol. 1, ed. Avigdor Shinan (Jerusalem: World Union of Jewish Studies, 1977), 229–35; Isaac M. Kikawada, "Literary Convention of the Primaeval History," *Annual of the Japanese Biblical Institute* 1 (1975): 3–21; and Isaac M. Kikawada, "The Shape of Genesis 11:1–9," in *Rhetorical Criticism: Essays in Honor of James Muilenburg*, ed. Jared J. Jackson and Martin Kessler (Pittsburgh, PA: Pickwick Press, 1974), 18–32.

a far more respectful tone toward Wellhausen. In demonstrating the literary unity of Genesis 1–11, however, they have isolated where the hypothesis is strongest, and have a more compelling alternative to supply: namely, unitary authorship.

Kikawada and Quinn begin by underscoring the apparent literary diversity contained within Genesis 1–11, which shows the reason why this section of the Pentateuch provides the strongest examples for the Documentary Hypothesis, such as the different names for God, which historically has functioned as the most significant criterion in the development of the paradigm.[19] They explain different options for such diversity, including multiple authorship or a single author, as in the case of St. Thomas Aquinas alternating between using "God" and "the Holy Trinity."[20] They point out, however, that "the change in divine names is paralleled by other changes in vocabulary."[21] Following classical Documentarian arguments, Kikawada and Quinn point out the strength of the Documentary Hypothesis:

> Vocabulary changes are themselves but local manifestations of broader stylistic contrasts. The Elohim sections are organized formulaically. . . . The Yahwist section could scarcely read more differently. Here, rather than formulas, we have colorful human dramas, dramas in which Yahweh himself is a member of the cast. . . . In short, the contrasting styles of narrative seem to express contrasting conceptions of God. Apparently, the divergent traditions had incompatible theologies . . . what we find in Genesis 1–5 are not only changes in vocabulary, narrative styles, and theologies, but also unnecessary, even contradictory repetitions—and all these obey the general sectioning of Genesis 1–5 suggested by the divine names.[22]

Kikawada and Quinn, however, are not satisfied with this answer because it does not fit what they have encountered in the broader context of ancient Near Eastern literature, nor what they find elsewhere in Genesis. They will argue for a unitary authorship. Here is what they explain in light of this apparent stark contrast between the various texts in Genesis 1–5:

> If Genesis 1–5 is the product of a single author, then that author is capable of two quite different narrative styles and has no

---

19 Kikawada and Quinn, *Before Abraham Was*, 17–35.
20 Kikawada and Quinn, *Before Abraham Was*, 19.
21 Kikawada and Quinn, *Before Abraham Was*, 19.
22 Kikawada and Quinn, *Before Abraham Was*, 19–20.

compunction about using them to express two quite different conceptions of God. He would be a very sophisticated author, indeed. Presumably he would think that his two apparently divergent theologies were ultimately reconcilable. . . . we would expect him to attempt a synthesis . . . that would exhibit to an even greater degree his theological profundity and literary virtuosity. If we could find a story in which such a synthesis was achieved, then we would have the strongest possible argument in favor of a unitary reading and against the Documentary Hypothesis. . . . The story that at first seems to meet our requirements could not in fact be any closer to Genesis 1–5, for it is the story of Noah that occupies Genesis 6–10 and dominates the latter half of the primeval history.[23]

In the end, they conclude this chapter by underscoring the strength of the Documentary Hypothesis for reading the Noah narratives, showing how it can appear to be read as two separate stories about Noah.[24]

In their second chapter, Kikawada and Quinn take a look at other ancient Near Eastern primeval histories and flood accounts.[25] They point out, for example, that the so-called double creation of humanity in Genesis 1 and 2 has parallels in comparable ancient Near Eastern literature, e.g., the Sumerian Epic of Enki and Ninmah and the Akkadian Atrahasis Epic, indicating that such "doublets" were a common literary style.[26] They go through other ancient texts as well, including an ancient Iranian flood story, showing how Genesis 1–11 fits the basic pattern of creation and flood motif, including expected repetitions, as found in unitary ancient Near Eastern stories.

Next they turn to the documentary accounts of the genealogies. Based on their study of comparable ancient Near Eastern material, they explain:

We suggested in the last chapter that Genesis 1–11 shares structural features with the old Babylonian history of Atrahasis. A distinctive feature of this structure is that the middle three episodes are repetitive. Episode 1 is a creation; episode 5 is a resolution; but episodes 2–4 are three threats to mankind. Their repetitive character is fairly obvious in Atrahasis, but not so obvious in Genesis. If the author of Genesis 1–11 was thinking in terms of this older primeval historiographic structure, then we would expect a closer examination of

---

[23] Kikawada and Quinn, *Before Abraham Was*, 21.

[24] Kikawada and Quinn, *Before Abraham Was*, 22–34.

[25] Kikawada does this elsewhere as well, in his "Double Creation," 43–45; "Literary Conventions"; and "Literary Convention," 3–21.

[26] Kikawada and Quinn, *Before Abraham Was*, 39–49; as well as Kikawada, "Double Creation," 43–45.

the Adam and Eve, Cain and Abel, and Noah and the flood stories to reveal significant similarities. Moreover, if he was as skillful in putting together these episodes as he was in exploiting the relatively unpromising form of genealogy, then we would expect more than repetition. We would expect him to find a way to repeat with sufficient variations to give a real sense of movement and progression. To expect both repetition and progression is no small order, but we believe this is exactly what we find.[27]

They then show how this in fact fits the basic form and pattern found in Atrahasis. In summing up what they find in the early Genesis material, they explain:

When the stories of Adam and Eve, Cain and Abel, and Noah's flood are viewed quantitatively we notice that the greatest portion of the narrative is spent for the stage setting part of the story in the Adam and Eve story; the greatest portion of the narrative of Cain and Abel is reserved for the middle of the story; then, in the Noah narrative, we find the conclusion of the story becoming the story in itself and all of the other parts being reduced to a brief prelude. So the interrelationship among these three stories reflects a progressive dramatic development in three stages that can be observed even quantitatively.[28]

In their fourth chapter, Kikawada and Quinn show how the flood narrative appears to be a carefully constructed whole with a chiastic structure.[29] We reproduce here the structure they outline in their volume (originally laid out by Gordon Wenham), underscoring how the narrative appears not as a conglomerate of disparate sources, but rather as a carefully constructed unified whole:

A Noah (vi. 10*a*)
B Shem, Ham, and Japheth (10*b*)
C Ark to be built (14–16)
D Flood announced (17)
E Covenant with Noah (18–20)
F Food in the ark (21)
G   Command to enter the ark (vii. 1–3)

---

[27] Kikawada and Quinn, *Before Abraham Was*, 62–63.
[28] Kikawada and Quinn, *Before Abraham Was*, 67–68.
[29] Kikawada and Quinn, *Before Abraham Was*, 83–104.

H	7 days waiting for flood (4–5)
I	7 days waiting for flood (7–10)
J	Entry to ark (11–15)
K	Yahweh shuts Noah in (16)
L	40 days flood (17*a*)
M	Waters increase (17*b*–18)
N	Mountains covered (19–20)
O	150 days waters prevail (21–24)
P	GOD REMEMBERS NOAH (viii. 1)
O'	150 days waters abate (3)
N'	Mountain tops visible (4–5)
M'	Waters abate (5)
L'	40 days (end of) (6*a*)
K'	Noah opens window of ark (6*b*)
J'	Raven and dove leave ark (7–9)
I'	7 days waiting for waters to subside (10–11)
H'	7 days waiting for waters to subside (12–13)
G'	Command to leave ark (15–17 [22])
F'	Food outside ark (ix. 1–4)
E'	Covenant with all flesh (8–10)
D'	No flood in future (11–17)
C'	Ark (18*a*)
B'	Shem, Ham, and Japheth (18*b*)
A'	Noah (19)[30]

They conclude their volume looking at the unity of the rest of Genesis in light of what they identify as a similar pattern to what they found in Genesis 1–11.

A DISCIPLE OF CYRUS GORDON: GARY RENDSBURG

Gary Rendsburg is another scholar whose publications have challenged aspects of the Documentary Hypothesis.[31] His most important work in this regard is his monograph *The Redaction of Genesis*. Rendsburg builds on the work of a number of other scholars to show how Genesis can be seen as a carefully constructed work of brilliant literary artistry. Michael Fishbane

---

[30] Wenham, "Coherence," cited in Kikawada and Quinn, *Before Abraham Was*, 104.

[31] Gary A. Rendsburg, "The Literary Unity of the Exodus Narrative," in *Did I Not Bring Israel*, 113–32; Gary A. Rendsburg, *The Redaction of Genesis* (Winona Lake, IN: Eisenbrauns, 1986).

had already shown how Genesis 25–35, concerning Jacob, formed a chiastic pattern—much as Kikawada and Quinn had argued for Noah.[32] Jack Sasson claimed something similar in Genesis 1–11 based on the narrative concerning the Tower of Babel.[33] Rendsburg's first chapter focuses on the unity of Genesis 1–11.[34] He concludes, "There can be little doubt that the structure of the Primeval History set forth in the above pages was deliberately produced by the redactor of Genesis. Too many overall themes, general story links, key vocabulary items, and other details are shared . . . for the structure of 1:1–11:26 to be coincidental."[35]

Rendsburg's second chapter explores the narratives concerning the patriarch Abraham.[36] Following especially the work of Cassuto, Rendsburg underscores the chiastic structure evident in the Abraham cycle, but also other literary devices—linking phrases, etc.—that show it to be a unified text.[37] He notes, "The presence of these devices in the narrative betokens a well-conceived blueprint expertly executed by the individual responsible for bringing together the various traditions surrounding Israel's first patriarch."[38] After this chapter, Rendsburg examines the narratives concerning Jacob.[39] Again, following Fishbane, whose arguments he acknowledges he merely modifies and puts in his own words, Rendsburg explains how "the stories of the Jacob Cycle are aligned in perfectly symmetrical fashion."[40]

One of the key insights turns on the apparent interruption in the narrative with Rebekah and Dinah, which, on its face, just does not seem to fit; their appearance makes it seem more likely that diverse sources spliced together accounts for the composition. Fishbane and Rendsburg demonstrate, however, how well these stories fit with one another: "the Jacob Cycle is symmetrical even within its symmetry."[41] After surveying the lit-

---

[32] Michael Fishbane, "Composition and Structure in the Jacob Cycle (Gen. 25:19–35:22)," *Journal of Jewish Studies* 26 (1975): 15–38.

[33] Jack M. Sasson, "The 'Tower of Babel' as a Clue to the Redactional Structuring of the Primeval History (Gen. 1–11:9)," in *The Bible World: Essays in Honor of Cyrus H. Gordon*, ed. Gary A. Rendsburg, Ruth Adler, Milton Arfa, and Nathan H. Winter (New York: Ktav, 1980), 211–19.

[34] Rendsburg, *Redaction of Genesis*, 7–25.

[35] Rendsburg, *Redaction of Genesis*, 22.

[36] Rendsburg, *Redaction of Genesis*, 27–52.

[37] U. Cassuto, *A Commentary on the Book of Genesis Part II: From Noah to Abraham, Genesis VI 9–XI 32, with an Appendix: A Fragment of Part III* (Jerusalem: Magnes Press, 1964 [1949]).

[38] Rendsburg, *Redaction of Genesis*, 52.

[39] Rendsburg, *Redaction of Genesis*, 53–69.

[40] Rendsburg, *Redaction of Genesis*, 53. See Fishbane, "Composition and Structure," 15–38.

[41] Rendsburg, *Redaction of Genesis*, 61–62. Rendsburg continues, "Not only are the stories of Jacob's leaving and homecoming matched, but there are two reasons for parting from Canaan and thus two routes for returning to Canaan" (62).

erary evidence, Rendsburg summarizes what he found: "The Jacob Cycle reflects deliberate structure in which the compiler has organized twelve individual units into reverse sequences. . . . The Jacob Cycle is unquestionably a masterpiece, well-conceived, brilliantly constructed, and expertly executed."[42] Rendsburg explains further that "As in the Primeval History and in the Abraham Cycle, incorporated into the Jacob Cycle are a series of nexuses linking successive units."[43]

Rendsburg's fourth chapter takes a look at material in the patriarchal narratives that at first may appear not to fit very well. Rendsburg shows how such apparently misplaced passages function as linking material helping structure the whole, and thus, they are not misplaced at all but very carefully woven narratives.[44] As he remarks, "nothing is accidental in the redaction of Genesis."[45] The fifth chapter takes a look at the Joseph narrative.[46] It is more commonplace to see an overall unity in the Joseph story than in the prior narratives examined, but what Rendsburg's study contributes on this score is quite significant, especially regarding the apparent interruption of the story concerning Judah and Tamar. He points out that the story concerning Judah and Tamar, as well as the story concerning Jacob's final testament, "have been skillfully worked into the redactional plan of

---

[42] Rendsburg, *Redaction of Genesis*, 66–67. He elaborates, "We are introduced to the Jacob narratives in A, then comes an interlude in B, and next follows Jacob's fear of Esau and his departure from Canaan in C, his encounter with messengers in D, his arrival at Haran in E, and his success through the fertility of his wives in F. At this juncture comes the focal point . . . 30:22–25 which bridges F and F'. The favored wife, Rachel, at long last gives birth, to the son who will eventually be the patriarch's favorite, Joseph. . . . Jacob has been successful throughout F, but the ultimate success is not realized until Rachel herself produces a son in 30:22–24. The very next verse, 30:25 . . . connects this fact with Jacob's desire to return home. . . . After this point all the themes and episodes of A through F are repeated in reverse order. In F' we read about Jacob's success through the fertility of his flocks, then comes his flight from Haran in E', his encounter with messengers in D', and the resolution of his fear of Esau and his return to Canaan in C', next occurs an interlude in B', and finally we have the development of the whole narrative in A'" (66–67).

[43] Rendsburg, *Redaction of Genesis*, 67. Rendsburg is referring to the following: "The root šb', 'swear,' is used in A at 25:33 and in B at 26:32–34. Esau's marriages and the concern they caused his parents are the subject of a brief notice at the end of B at 26:34–35; this issue is echoed in C at 27:46–28:9. In C Jacob receives a blessing from his father at 27:27–29; and in D he gains God's blessing at 28:13–15. D and E share the word 'eben, 'stone,' in 28:18 and 29:10, with Jacob utilizing it in each instance. In E Jacob gains his two wives and their maid servants in 29:23–30, and these four produce his children in F in 29:31–30:24. F and F' have a number of nexuses because they are not only successive but also paired in the redactional structure. Moreover, we may point to the focal point where 30:22–24 and 30:25 both mention Rachel's giving birth to Joseph in F and F' respectively" (67).

[44] Rendsburg, *Redaction of Genesis*, 71–77.

[45] Rendsburg, *Redaction of Genesis*, 72.

[46] Rendsburg, *Redaction of Genesis*, 79–97.

the cycle."[47] Rendsburg isolates seventeen theme words between these two apparent interruptive narratives.[48]

After concluding his examination of the Genesis material, Rendsburg turns in his sixth chapter to an examination of source criticism in light of his study of redactional activity.[49] Rendsburg is aware of the limits of his study, and mentions how it could go hand-in-hand with a documentary approach, wherein the skilled redactor made use of J, E, and P sources.[50] He emphasizes, however, that "it must be admitted that wherever the basic unity of a section can be established the Documentary Hypothesis can be called into question."[51] Rendsburg's deft critique, based on the literary evidence he has amassed throughout his volume, is well worth quoting at length:

> The corresponding units in each of the cycles were seen as parallel not just because of their similar themes and motifs, but just as importantly because of the numerous theme-words which link them. Now, when traditional source criticism assigns corresponding units to different sources, we must wonder how it is that source X uses theme-words a, b, c, d, e, f, g, etc., and that source Y uses the exact same theme-words. This is no better seen than in a comparison of 12:1–9 and 22:1–19. . . . The first of these is usually divided between J . . . and P . . . and the second of these is viewed as E. We should ask: how is it that J uses *lek lekā* in 12:1 and that E does so in 22:1; that J uses the second person masculine singular pronoun suffix three times in 12:1 and that E does so in 22:2; that J has Abram go to Moreh in 12:6 and that E takes Abraham to Moriah in 22:2; that J reads *wayyiben šām mizbēaḥ laYHWH* in 12:7 and that E uses *wayyiben šām 'abrāhām 'et hammizbēaḥ* in 22:9; that J's blessing in 12:2–3 is remarkably similar to E's blessing in 22:17–18; that J reads *wayyēlek 'ittô lôṭ* in 12:4 and that E states *wayyēlekû šenêhem yaḥdāw* in 22:6, 22:8; that J uses *meqôm* in 12:6 and that E uses *hammāqôm* in 22:3–4, both times meaning 'hallowed site'; that the root *škm* occurs in J in 12:6 and in E in 22:3; that J uses *wayyērā' YHWH* in 12:7 and that E includes the toponym *YHWH yir'eh* in 22:14; that J's story ends in the Negev and that E's story ends in Beersheba; and that both stories have God speaking to the patriarch in two parts, in J at 12:1–3, 12:7, and in E

---

[47] Rendsburg, *Redaction of Genesis*, 80.
[48] Rendsburg, *Redaction of Genesis*, 84–86.
[49] Rendsburg, *Redaction of Genesis*, 99–106.
[50] Rendsburg, *Redaction of Genesis*, 100–102.
[51] Rendsburg, *Redaction of Genesis*, 102. He adds, "This is even more the case when specific evidence can be forwarded to show the failing of this school of source criticism" (102).

at 22:12, 22:16–18? All of this becomes extremely coincidental and much too difficult to explain if one retains the JEP source analysis of Genesis. The evidence points to one author for these two units.[52]

He follows this up by pointing out how the same goes for the rest of the Book of Genesis, e.g., with the creation and flood as well as Abrahamic narratives.[53] Rendsburg dates the material much later than the time of Moses (his final chapter is about dating)—most likely, he thinks, from the early first millennium, perhaps during the united monarchy, and he concedes that it might contain earlier source material.[54]

ROGER WHYBRAY'S CASE FOR A SINGLE AUTHOR OF THE PENTATEUCH

Roger Whybray is one of the more unique and unusual figures in the history of Pentateuchal studies. An ordained Anglican priest with D.Phil. in Old Testament studies from Oxford, he spent his teaching career (1965–1982) at the University of Hull—scarcely a bastion of religious conservatism. Retiring from active teaching in 1982 to devote himself to research and publication, the first fruits of his retirement appeared in 1987 as the provocative *The Making of the Pentateuch*, which, although dating the Pentateuch late, made a strong case for unitary authorship, thus posing a major challenge to the Documentary Hypothesis.[55] The first part of his volume, "Literary Hypotheses," details the documentary approach and highlights the weaknesses of such interrelated hypotheses.[56] He raises an important but often neglected point at the outset of his study: "The Documentary Hypothesis has to prove, up to the hilt, that its hypothetical documents—and *only* they—possess a sufficient degree of *unity* to compel belief in their existence. Its proponents must justify their thesis at every point if they are to show that it is an *indispensable* theory and that the other, simpler solutions to the problem are inadequate."[57]

---

[52] Rendsburg, *Redaction of Genesis*, 102–3.

[53] Rendsburg, *Redaction of Genesis*, 103–4. On such careful narrative structure and literary artistry in the Book of Genesis, see also Jon D. Levenson, "Response," in *The State of Jewish Studies*, ed. Shaye J. D. Cohen and Edward L. Greenstein (Detroit, MI: Wayne State University Press, 1990), 47–54.

[54] Rendsburg, *Redaction of Genesis*, 107–20.

[55] R. N. Whybray, *The Making of the Pentateuch: A Methodological Study* (Sheffield, UK: Journal for the Study of the Old Testament Press, 1987).

[56] Whybray, *Making of the Pentateuch*, 17–131.

[57] Whybray, *Making of the Pentateuch*, 19.

Whybray unmasks Wellhausen's developmental approach as philosoph-ical, more than merely historical.[58] He remarks further that, "It is to a large extent inevitable that the study of the biblical narrative should reflect the literary standards of the literary world of the critics themselves rather than those of the period in which the narratives were composed, since very little is known about the latter."[59] The point he emphasizes is that this is not simply scientific or merely historical work, deriving directly from the texts, but rather a very specific literary hermeneutic is imposed on the texts by the critics. This includes the long-standing and extensive modern discussion about apparent doublets, which lie at the root of the hypothesis; such "evi-dence" of multiple authorship, standard since the eighteenth century, are modern constructs imposed on the text as criteria rather than evidence of composition based on ancient canons of literary style.[60] He also reveals the inconsistencies of assumptions source critics employ, such as that "authors" of sources are always internally consistent and unrepetitious, but "redac-tors" are completely unbothered by inconsistencies and repetition.

In the final portion of his volume, Whybray makes the case for a single author of the Pentateuch.[61] In criticizing more recent scholars who allow for the bulk of the Pentateuch to be compiled by a single redactor, but who balk at the suggestion of the Pentateuch being a unified original whole, Whybray points out: "There appears to be no reason why (allowing for the possibility of a few additions) the *first* edition of the Pentateuch as a comprehensive work should not also have been the *final* edition, a work composed by a single historian. . . . insufficient allowance has been made for deliberate vari-ations of style and compositional method on the part of a single author."[62] This is in fact what Whybray concludes.

MORE RECENT SCHOLARSHIP:
FROM THE END OF THE TWENTIETH CENTURY AND THE
BEGINNING OF THE TWENTY FIRST CENTURY

Two of the most important recent figures from the end of the twentieth century and the beginning of the twenty first century are James Hoffmeier and Joshua Berman. Hoffmeier is an evangelical Protestant scholar who

---

[58] Whybray, *Making of the Pentateuch*, 43.

[59] Whybray, *Making of the Pentateuch*, 55.

[60] Whybray, *Making of the Pentateuch*, 72–91. On the importance of such so-called "double narratives" or "doublets" in the history of the development of source criticism, and particu-larly within Pentateuchal Criticism, see Nahkola, *Double Narratives in the Old Testament*.

[61] Whybray, *Making of the Pentateuch*, 221–42.

[62] Whybray, *Making of the Pentateuch*, 232–33.

specializes in Egyptology, the field in which he earned his doctorate at the University of Toronto.[63] Two of Hoffmeier's most important contributions to this debate have been his Oxford University Press monographs, *Israel in Egypt: The Evidence for the Authenticity of the Exodus Tradition* (1996);[64] and *Ancient Israel in Sinai: The Evidence for the Authenticity of the Wilderness Tradition* (2005).[65] Also important, although not dealing directly with the Pentateuch, is his 1994 essay, "The Structure of Joshua 1–11 and the Annals of Thutmose III," because it demonstrates the intimate knowledge of New Kingdom Egypt and of Egyptian military scribal traditions in particular from that time, which makes sense if the author of Joshua emerged out of Egypt from that era.[66]

Israel in Egypt mainly tackles matters related to the Documentary Hypothesis indirectly, as Hoffmeier's intention in this volume is primarily to demonstrate the extensive evidence for Semites in Egypt, as well as evidence for the exodus event itself. He addresses the Documentary Hypothesis directly near the beginning of his volume when he surveys studies of Israel's origins, showing the increasing challenges scholars have mounted against the Documentary Hypothesis.[67] Hoffmeier's third chapter is the most significant for surveying the evidence for the presence of Semites in Egypt prior to and during the New Kingdom period.[68] It is in his fourth chapter that he hones in on the Egyptian evidence for the authenticity of the Joseph narrative in Genesis.[69] Most scholars of the Hebrew Bible have little to no firsthand knowledge of the discipline of Egyptology. Hoffmeier points out that "Scholars with Egyptological training have long recognized the Egyptian elements in the Joseph story."[70] After reviewing the more recent

---

[63] James K. Hoffmeier, "Egyptian Religious Influences on the Early Hebrews," in *Did I Not Bring Israel*, 3–36; James K. Hoffmeier, "The Exodus and Wilderness Narratives," in *Ancient Israel's History: An Introduction to Issues and Sources*, ed. Bill T. Arnold and Richard S. Hess (Grand Rapids: Baker Academic, 2014), 46–90; James K. Hoffmeier, *Ancient Israel in Sinai: The Evidence for the Authenticity of the Wilderness Tradition* (Oxford, UK: Oxford University Press, 2005); James K. Hoffmeier, *Israel in Egypt: The Evidence for the Authenticity of the Exodus Tradition* (Oxford, UK: Oxford University Press, 1996); James K. Hoffmeier, "The Structure of Joshua 1–11 and the Annals of Thutmose III," in *Faith, Tradition, and History*, 165–79; and James K. Hoffmeier, "Some Thoughts on Genesis 1 & 2 and Egyptian Cosmology," *Journal of the Ancient Near Eastern Society* 15 (1983): 39–49.

[64] Hoffmeier, *Israel in Egypt*.

[65] Hoffmeier, *Ancient Israel in Sinai*.

[66] Hoffmeier, "Structure of Joshua 1–11," 165–79.

[67] Hoffmeier, *Israel in Egypt*, 7–10.

[68] Hoffmeier, *Israel in Egypt*, 52–76.

[69] Hoffmeier, *Israel in Egypt*, 77–106.

[70] Hoffmeier, *Israel in Egypt*, 83. He quotes and cites, as an example, Alan R. Schulman, "On the Egyptian Name of Joseph: A New Approach," *Studien zur Altägyptischen Kultur* 2 (1975): 235–43. The more recent work of Susanne Binder could be added to this, e.g.,

evidence for the authentic second millennium Egyptian background to the Joseph narrative, Hoffmeier concludes that, "the indirect evidence . . . tends to demonstrate the authenticity of the story."[71]

The remainder of Hoffmeier's book deals with the historical background to the exodus account, looking in turn at the evidence for the Israelites in Egypt,[72] the figure and story of Moses,[73] potential routes,[74] geography and toponymy,[75] and the location of the body of water ("Red Sea" or "sea of reeds") that was parted.[76] Relying upon the literary analysis of Charles Isbell,[77] Hoffmeier explains how "the linguistic and literary criteria used in the past to identify different sources can no longer be sustained," since key thematic words systematically link the portions variously identified with distinct sources (J, E, or P).[78]

Hoffmeier's sequel, *Ancient Israel in Sinai*, tackles more aspects related to the Documentary Hypothesis head on, as it walks through the second millennium Egyptian evidence for the Pentateuchal wilderness tradition. He recounts the history of Pentateuchal scholarship prior to Wellhausen[79] and then explains Wellhausen's significance within this history: "With his *Die Composition des Hexateuch* (1877), Wellhausen left an enduring mark on critical Old Testament scholarship, for he brought order out of the dating chaos that had prevailed in the field of Old Testament studies."[80] Hoffmeier proceeds to show how Wellhausen's formulation dominated Pentateuchal studies, and Old Testament studies more broadly, and how it began to be challenged.[81]

As he patiently works through the biblical material, such as the Book of Numbers, in light of the Egyptian evidence, Hoffmeier clarifies how

---

Susanne Binder, "Joseph's Rewarding and Investiture (Genesis 41:41–43) and the Gold of Honour in New Kingdom Egypt," in *Egypt, Canaan and Israel: History, Imperialism, Ideology and Literature*, ed. S. Bar, D. Kahn, and J. J. Shirley, 44–64 (Leiden, NL: Brill, 2011).

[71] Hoffmeier, *Israel in Egypt*, 97.

[72] Hoffmeier, *Israel in Egypt*, 107–34.

[73] Hoffmeier, *Israel in Egypt*, 135–63.

[74] Hoffmeier, *Israel in Egypt*, 164–75.

[75] Hoffmeier, *Israel in Egypt*, 176–98.

[76] Hoffmeier, *Israel in Egypt*, 199–222.

[77] Charles Isbell, "The Structure of Exodus 1:1–14," in *Art and Meaning: Rhetoric in Biblical Literature*, ed. David J. A. Clines, David M. Gunn, and Alan J. Hauser (Sheffield, UK: JSOT Press, 1982), 37–61.

[78] Hoffmeier, *Israel in Egypt*, 107–8.

[79] Hoffmeier, *Ancient Israel in Sinai*, 9–11. Hahn and Morrow covered some of this history in *Modern Biblical Criticism*, and we will cover it in more detail in the chapters that follow in this present volume.

[80] Hoffmeier, *Ancient Israel in Sinai*, 11.

[81] Hoffmeier, *Ancient Israel in Sinai*, 12–17.

poorly some of these literary theories fit the biblical texts and yet, at the same time, how well these texts fit their ancient Egyptian context. Numbers 33, for example, is almost always attributed to P, the Priestly Source, but, as Hoffmeier underscores, "The toponym list or itinerary as presented in Numbers 33 shares a number of features with Egyptian toponym lists, or itineraries, found on New Kingdom monuments."[82] After surveying all of the geographic evidence—the region and potential route for the parting of the sea—Hoffmeier concludes:

> The toponyms of Exodus 14:2 have a specificity that was certainly not necessary for a writer inventing the story or drawing on his creative imagination. The names themselves seem to serve no theological or aetiological agenda, and they are not contrived and garbled. If P were historicizing an original mythic version of the sea-crossing episode, he did a remarkable job of identifying toponyms known in New Kingdom Egypt, and they fit into a geographical zone that accords well into the generally wet paleoenvironmental situation of the late second millennium BC.[83]

The authentic Egyptian background, which Hoffmeier demonstrates for names (including toponyms), geography, and even diet, make it increasingly likely that the author had firsthand knowledge of New Kingdom Egypt, which makes the stories' origins in multiples sources from later dates without a direct connection to New Kingdom Egypt increasingly less likely.[84]

After looking through the covenantal legislation at Sinai, Hoffmeier shows how well it fits its second millennium context, but he also shows how carefully crafted the text is. Specifically, Exodus 19:1–24:2 utilizes "a

---

[82] Hoffmeier, *Ancient Israel in Sinai*, 51.

[83] Hoffmeier, *Ancient Israel in Sinai*, 108.

[84] Consider Hoffmeier's observations about diet: "this list [Numbers 11:5] of vegetables and fruit [cucumbers, melons, leeks, onions, and garlic] looks authentically Egyptian.... The foods mentioned here are typically associated with the common folk in Egypt, both in Pharaonic and modern times.... they are often depicted on [Egyptian] funerary stelae and on false doors of tombs, and on vignettes from the Book of the Dead papyri. Such scenes are found from the Old Kingdom through the Greco-Roman periods. . . . people at all levels of [Egyptian] society . . . ate cucumbers, melons, leeks, onions, and garlic.... These five food items, interestingly, occur only in this passage [Numbers 11:5].... they do not occur [again] in the Bible among the many references to food. The people's complaint about the lack of vegetables and fruits in the wilderness appears to be an authentic one of a people accustomed to such food in Egypt, which obviously were not available in Sinai. These five food items seem out of place in Canaan or Israel and hardly seem to reflect the dietary passions of an exilic or postexilic community" (*Ancient Israel in Sinai*, 175).

common narrative framework."[85] He goes on to point out the implications of this:

> Even if one were to argue that the redactor was responsible for the chiastic structure and the blending of the various sources or traditions, it seems that they become so blurred by the structuring process that they are no longer distinguishable. . . . The use of a common literary framework and chiastic pattern demonstrate that a brilliant author or editor stands behind this material. If the latter used earlier and divergent sources, then his skill at weaving the material together is so effective that sources have become blurred, preventing critics from successfully delineating the sources behind the pericope.[86]

One further frontal assault Hoffmeier makes against Wellhausen's theories concerns Wellhausen's baseless assertions that the tabernacle was a fictional and anachronistic invention of Israel based on their later temple. Hoffmeier devotes an entire chapter showing the long history of tabernacle structures, primarily in Egypt during the New Kingdom period (but not later) and much earlier, abundantly attested in the archaeological record to which Wellhausen had no recourse.[87] Hoffmeier closes his volume with a detailed examination of the authentic second millennium Egyptian background to personal names, Egyptian laws, and related material in the Pentateuch.[88]

Joshua Berman of Bar-Ilan University has more recently joined these scholars in challenging the very foundations of the Documentary Hypothesis.[89] His significant 2011 *Journal of Biblical Literature* article on Deuteronomy 13 in light of an important Hittite parallel firmly grounded

---

[85] Hoffmeier, *Ancient Israel in Sinai*, 183. Hoffmeier is relying here in part on the work of D. Patrick, "The Covenant Code Structure," *Vetus Testamentum* 27 (1977): 145–57; Gregory C. Chirichigno, "The Narrative Structure of Exod. 19–24," *Biblica* 68 (1987): 457–79; and T. D. Alexander, "The Composition of the Sinai Narrative in Exodus XIX I–XXIV II," *Vetus Testamentum* 49, no. 1 (1999): 2–20.

[86] Hoffmeier, *Ancient Israel in Sinai*, 183.

[87] Hoffmeier, *Ancient Israel in Sinai*, 193–222.

[88] Hoffmeier, *Ancient Israel in Sinai*, 223–49.

[89] Joshua Berman, "The Biblical Criticism of Ibn Hazm the Andalusian: A Medieval Control for Modern Diachronic Method," *Journal of Biblical Literature* 138, no. 2 (2019): 377–90; Joshua A. Berman, Inconsistency in the Torah: Ancient Literary Convention and the Limits of Source Criticism (Oxford, UK: Oxford University Press, 2017); and Joshua Berman, "CTH 133 and the Hittite Provenance of Deuteronomy 13," *Journal of Biblical Literature* 130, no. 1 (2011): 25–44.

the structure of Deuteronomy in the second millennium.[90] His most important work in this context, however, is his 2017 Oxford University Press volume, *Inconsistency in the Torah*.[91] He opens his book urging for Pentateuchal criticism to forge a new path, unshackled from the documentary source critical theories of the nineteenth century that have for too long limited the vision of biblical scholars by overly restricting the very sort of questions they can ask concerning the Pentateuch's composition.[92]

In his first major chapter, Berman turns to ancient Egypt and looks at Ramesses II's famous Kadesh inscriptions, which we saw Kitchen address earlier in this chapter.[93] When we find in the Bible similarly divergent material to what we have in the various Kadesh inscriptions, scholars typically posit different authors or sources; and yet, the Kadesh inscriptions, with their vast differences (in both style and content) were all commissioned by the same Pharaoh.[94] This very type of literature the Kadesh inscription represents, "triumphal literature," is found in ancient Egypt and the Old Testament but is absent from literature produced in the other places ancient Israel dwelt, like the Ugaritic texts from Canaan.[95]

Berman revisits the Kadesh inscriptions in his next chapter, comparing them with Exodus 13–15, the account of the parting of the sea.[96] After reviewing the shared themes and styles of these two traditions, Berman explains:

> The poetics of the Kadesh Poem alone call into question the validity of the source-critical methodology of establishing a text's compositional history on the basis of doublets and inconsistencies with the text. . . . the Kadesh Poem is universally recognized to be a unitary, synchronically composed composition. . . . the poetics of the Kadesh Poem demonstrate that source critics read ancient texts employing anachronistic notions of consistency, which were not shared by ancient writers.[97]

---

90 Berman, "CTH 133," 25–44.
91 Berman, *Inconsistency in the Torah*.
92 Berman, *Inconsistency in the Torah*, 1–11.
93 Berman, *Inconsistency in the Torah*, 17–34.
94 See Berman, *Inconsistency in the Torah*, 20, where he comments, "the pharaoh commissioned two differing, and even conflicting, accounts of the Battle of Kadesh and had them carved side by side at several monumental sites across Egypt."
95 Berman, *Inconsistency in the Torah*, 34. Berman here suggests that perhaps this evidence for a common "triumphal literature" tradition may be explained by Israel's scribes adopting an ancient "Egyptian literary tradition."
96 Berman, *Inconsistency in the Torah*, 35–60.
97 Berman, *Inconsistency in the Torah*, 53–54.

In his third and fourth chapters, Berman turns to an area in which he has already made a significant impact: using Hittite literature to illuminate the historical and chronological setting for the Bible.[98] Examining Hittite treaties leads Berman to the conclusion that similarities between Deuteronomy and the Hittite treaty tradition might account for the differences between Deuteronomy and the early Sinai tradition, in that Deuteronomy might be retelling the history while having both traditions retained, much as Hittite treaties did.

Berman then moves to explain biblical Pentateuchal law traditions in light of their ancient Near Eastern counterparts, showing how modern biblical critics tend to misread such traditions because of their anachronistic recourse to modern legal analogues.[99] He points out how the shift in legal analogues really took place between the eighteenth and nineteenth centuries as European legal traditions were transforming from a common law culture—more similar to the ancient Near East—to a modern statutory law culture, which, Berman explains, was a reason eighteenth-century biblical critics failed to find fault with the variations in biblical law. It was only later, after the legal culture changed, that biblical critics began to find a problem with the Pentateuchal legal material on this score.[100]

In his sixth and seventh chapters, Berman looks to Mesopotamian texts, such as Hammurabi's Code, to shed further light on these legal traditions.[101] Chapters nine and ten continue Berman's examination of biblical law codes, wherein he argues, based on ancient Near Eastern parallels, for the inclusion of disparate legal traditions. These do not require multiple authorship or sources but rather different notions of law, much as his earlier chapters argued divergent histories evidenced different notions of historiography.[102]

The remainder of his volume takes a broad look over the history of Pentateuchal source criticism, which we will cover in our present volume, and the real methodological problems inherent in modern source criticism, especially of the documentary mode, wherein he uses the example of the Flood narrative in Genesis to demonstrate his point.[103] He closes his volume with a plea for a "new path forward," where he joins other contemporary scholars in calling for a rethinking of Pentateuchal criticism.[104]

A number of other contemporary scholars have joined Berman in a quest for forging a new path for the analysis of the Pentateuch. One of

---

[98] Berman, *Inconsistency in the Torah*, 63–103.
[99] Berman, *Inconsistency in the Torah*, 107–17.
[100] Berman, *Inconsistency in the Torah*, 117.
[101] Berman, *Inconsistency in the Torah*, 118–47.
[102] Berman, *Inconsistency in the Torah*, 171–98.
[103] Berman, *Inconsistency in the Torah*, 201–68.
[104] Berman, *Inconsistency in the Torah*, 269–80.

the most promising is Benjamin Kilchör, who has written several studies challenging the traditional construal of the relationship of the sources identified as "D," "P," and "H."[105] In our own ways, we have contributed to this trend already—John Bergsma directly with his studies on various aspects of the Pentateuch,[106] and Jeffrey Morrow with his studies on the history of scholarship.[107]

---

[105] Benjamin Kilchör, "Wellhausen's Five Pillars for the Priestly Priority of D over P/H: Can They Still Be Maintained," in *Paradigm Change*, 101–14; Benjamin Kilchör, "Sacred and Profane Space: The Priestly Character of Exodus 20:24–26 and Its Reception in Deuteronomy 12," *Bulletin for Biblical Research* 29, no. 4 (2019): 455–67; Benjamin Kilchör, "Did H Influence D on an Early or a Late Stage of the Redaction of D?" *Old Testament Essays* 29, no. 3 (2016): 502–12; Benjamin Kilchör, "Levirate Marriage in Deuteronomy 25:5–10 and Its Precursors in Leviticus and Numbers: A Test Case for the Relationship between P/H and D," *Catholic Biblical Quarterly* 77 (2015): 429–40; Benjamin Kilchör, "The Direction of Dependence between the Laws of the Pentateuch: The Priority of a Literary Approach," *Ephemerides Theologicae Lovanienses* 89, no. 1 (2013): 1–14; Benjamin Kilchör, "Frei aber arm? Soziale Sicherheit als Schüssel zum Verhältnis der Sklavenfreilassungsgesetze im Pentateuch," *Vetus Testamentum* 62, no. 3 (2012): 381–97.

[106] E.g., John S. Bergsma, "A 'Samaritan' Pentateuch? The Implications of the Pro-Northern Tendency of the Common Pentateuch," in *Paradigm Change*, 287–300; John Bergsma and Brant Pitre, *A Catholic Introduction to the Bible*, vol. 1, *The Old Testament* (San Francisco: Ignatius Press, 2018); John S. Bergsma, "The Year of Jubilee and the Ancient Israelite Economy," *Southwestern Journal of Theology* 59, no. 2 (2017): 155–64; John S. Bergsma, "The Biblical Manumission Laws: Has the Literary Dependence of H on D been Demonstrated?" in *A Teacher for All Generations: Essays in Honor of James C. VanderKam*, vol. 1, ed. Eric F. Mason, Samuel I. Thomas, Alison Schofield, and Eugene Ulrich (Leiden, NL: Brill, 2012), 65–89; John Sietze Bergsma, *The Jubilee from Leviticus to Qumran: A History of Interpretation* (Leiden, NL: Brill, 2007); Scott Walker Hahn and John Sietze Bergsma, "What Laws Were 'Not Good'?: A Canonical Approach to the Theological Problem of Ezekiel 20:25–26," *Journal of Biblical Literature* 123, no. 2 (2004): 201–18; and John S. Bergsma, "The Jubilee: A Post-Exilic Priestly Attempt to Reclaim Lands?" *Biblica* 84 (2003): 225–46.

[107] E.g., Jeffrey L. Morrow, "Methods of Interpreting Scripture and Nature: The Influence of the Baconian Method on Spinoza's Bible Criticism," in *Studies in the History of Exegesis, ed. Mark W. Elliott, Raleigh C. Heth, and Angela Zautcke (Tübingen: Mohr Siebeck, 2022), 157–73;* Jeffrey L. Morrow, *Pretensions of Objectivity: Toward a Criticism of Biblical Criticism* (Eugene, OR: Pickwick, 2019); Jeffrey L. Morrow, "Spinoza and the Theo-Political Implications of his Freedom to Philosophize," *New Blackfriars* 99 (2018): 374–87; Jeffrey L. Morrow, *Theology, Politics, and Exegesis: Essays on the History of Modern Biblical Criticism* (Eugene, OR: Pickwick, 2017); Jeffrey L. Morrow, *Three Skeptics and the Bible: La Peyrère, Hobbes, Spinoza, and the Reception of Modern Biblical Criticism* (Eugene, OR: Pickwick, 2016); Jeffrey L. Morrow, "Faith, Reason and History in Early Modern Catholic Biblical Interpretation: Fr. Richard Simon and St. Thomas More," *New Blackfriars* 96 (2015): 658–73; and Jeffrey L. Morrow, "French Apocalyptic Messianism: Isaac La Peyrère and Political Biblical Criticism in the Seventeenth Century," *Toronto Journal of Theology* 27, no. 2 (2011): 203–13.

As should be clear from the survey in these past two chapters on the history of challenges to the Documentary Hypothesis, the figures brought together are really only united in their recognition of the limits of that hypothesis. They disagree on most other specifics, from theological and religious issues; to whether or not anything is salvageable or useful in the Documentary Hypothesis; to whether the Pentateuch is from the second or first millennium. We intend our present volume to be a further contribution to this discussion, as kindred spirits to the work of scholars like Berman and Kilchör, representing between the four of us Jewish, Protestant, and Catholic traditions. In the next part of the book, we will look at new lines of evidence supporting the antiquity of the Pentateuch.

PART 2

NEW EVIDENCE FOR THE ANTIQUITY OF THE PENTATEUCH

CHAPTER 4

THE LAW BEFORE THE PROPHETS OR THE PROPHETS BEFORE THE LAW?

One of the most characteristic and revolutionary features of Wellhausen's paradigm for the history of the composition of the Old Testament was his reversal of the traditional order of the Law (the Pentateuch) and the Prophets (Isaiah through Malachi). Whereas the canonical literature invariably places the revelation of the Law to Moses at the beginning of Israel's history as a nation, and the literary (writing) prophets as beginning their careers in the much later monarchic epoch, Wellhausen argued that the bulk of the laws of Moses, which became classified as the "Priestly Source," were, for the most part, composed only after the Babylonian Exile—that is, largely in the fifth century BCE.[1] Wellhausen wrote about his "conversion" to this position in a very telling passage in the introduction to his great *Prolegomena*:

> In the summer of 1867, I learned that Karl Heinrich Graf placed the law after the prophets and almost without knowing the reason for his hypothesis, I was won over: I allowed myself to confess that Hebraic antiquity could be understood without the book of the Torah.[2]

---

[1] For discussion, see Konrad Schmid, "The Prophets after the Law or the Law after the Prophets?—Terminological, Biblical, and Historical Perspectives," in *The Formation of the Pentateuch: Bridging the Academic Cultures of Europe, Israel, and North America*, ed. Jan C. Gertz, Bernard M. Levinson, Dalit Rom-Shiloni, and Konrad Schmid (Tübingen: Mohr Siebeck, 2016), 841–50.

[2] J. Wellhausen, *Prolegomena zur Geschichte Israels*, 5th ed. (Berlin: Reimer, 1899), 4, my

In hindsight, we can probably all agree that this is a classic example of the so-called "Freudian slip" and admit that Wellhausen, only twenty-three years old at the time, actually accepted Graf's hypothesis *without knowing the reason,* simply because it fit his biases and worldview. It was a forgivable mistake for a young scholar, but Wellhausen should have followed up with a careful study of those passages of the Pentateuch and the Prophets that exhibit striking verbal parallels—of which there are many—demonstrating that, in at least most instances, the direction of literary dependence was clearly from the Prophets to the Pentateuch. This he never did.[3] The task would be left to later generations, and the results would not support Wellhausen's paradigm.

The purpose of this chapter is to demonstrate, using key examples, that the close examination of passages exhibiting significant verbal parallels between the legal material of the Pentateuch (both "Priestly" and "Deuteronomic") and the oracles of the Latter Prophets consistently betrays a direction of literary dependency that flows *from* the Law *to* the Prophets. In other words, close readings of the Prophets show they knew the Torah, and not vice-versa.

The primary objects of study in our demonstration will be the books of Ezekiel and Jeremiah, which are especially useful for our purposes because they abound in close verbal parallels with Pentateuchal texts, and their linguistic profile as well as other factors enable them both to be dated with confidence to the sixth century BCE. Therefore, if these books exhibit dependence on the Pentateuchal legislation, that legislation must predate the sixth century, and Wellhausen's paradigm, particularly as it relates to the Priestly Source, cannot be correct. However, it is not just Ezekiel and Jeremiah that exhibit dependence on the Pentateuch, and we will conclude the chapter with a brief look at dependence on the Pentateuch in Isaiah, Hosea, and other prophetic books.

EZEKIEL AND THE PENTATEUCH

Background. Scholars have long recognized the close relationship between Ezekiel and the Pentateuch, particularly that part of the Priestly Source known as the Holiness Code ("H"; approx. Lev 17–27).[4] The number of

---

translation.

3 See Michael A. Lyons, *From Law to Prophecy: Ezekiel's Use of the Holiness Code* (LHBOTS 507; New York: T&T Clark, 2009), 37–39: "Wellhausen's literary analysis is so superficial that it cannot yield significant results" (39).

4 The so-called "Holiness Code" (roughly Lev 17–27) is very closely related to the so-called "Priestly" materials that extend from Exodus 25–Numbers 36 and is usually thought to

shared locutions between Ezekiel and the Holiness Code, if not the entire Priestly legislation, is so great—and the similarities often so precise—that most scholars publishing on the subject over the past century have been convinced that there is a relationship of literary dependence between the documents *as written texts* and not merely a shared oral tradition or some other, less definite relationship.[5]

Wellhausen became aware, sometime before completing the *Prolegomena*, that the literary relationship between Ezekiel and the Pentateuch was very strong, but he incorporated this fact into his overarching paradigm by declaring Ezekiel to represent an early form of the Priestly tradition, and thus the Priestly authors—particularly those of the Holiness Code—were drawing on Ezekiel, rather than the prophet reusing the Law. In fact, Ezekiel became the central document in Wellhausen's revisionist re-writing of the religious history of Israel, a kind of keystone on which the whole arch of his reconstruction depended:

> Ezekiel is the forerunner of the priestly legislator in the Pentateuch; his prince and people . . . are the antecedents of the congregation of the tabernacle and the second temple. Against this supposition there is nothing to be alleged.[6]

> Jehovist, Deuteronomy, Ezekiel, are a historical series; Ezekiel, Law of Holiness, Priestly Code, must also be taken as historical steps, and this in such a way as to explain at the same time the dependence of the Law of Holiness on the Jehovist and on Deuteronomy.[7]

---

come from the same priestly circles, only at a later or earlier time in the history of the priest-hood. Some scholars, like Richard Elliot Friedman and his students (e.g., Levitt Kohn), do not recognize "H" as a separate or distinct source and simply consider it a part of the Priestly materials generally. In the chapters that follow, we are not endorsing the source divisions "P," "H," and "D" but simply employing them as they are used in academic writing to refer to recognized sections of the Pentateuch.

[5] For discussion of the literature on Ezekiel and H through 2007, see John Sietze Bergsma, *The Jubilee from Leviticus to Qumran: A History of Interpretation* (Leiden, NL: Brill, 2007), 177–80. Menahem Haran argues that P (including H) and Ezekiel do not know each other but stem from the same tradition (Menahem Haran, "Ezekiel, P, and the Priestly School," *Vetus Testamentum* 58 [2008]: 211–18).

[6] Julius Wellhausen, *Prolegomena to the History of Israel*, trans. J. Sutherland Black and Allan Menzies (Edinburgh: Adam & Charles Black, 1885), 107.

[7] Wellhausen, *Prolegomena*, 379.

> Ezekiel . . . is the connecting link between the prophets and the law. . . . The chapters xl.-xlviii. [40–48] are the most important in his book, and have been called . . . the key of the Old Testament.[8]

Whether or not Ezekiel 40–48 really are the "key of the Old Testament," they certainly are the key to Wellhausen's *interpretation* of the Old Testament. So, if it can be shown that Wellhausen's understanding of Ezekiel is fundamentally incorrect, his reconstruction collapses, like an arch with its keystone removed.

Wellhausen's view of Ezekiel was regarded as standard at least through the end of the twentieth century. By the early twenty-first century, however, Wellhausen's approach had been abandoned by most international scholars publishing on the prophet,[9] and Ezekiel scholarship since has fallen basically into two camps. The first continues to maintain Wellhausen's fifth-century dating of the Priestly Source and thus pushes the composition and/or redaction of Ezekiel into the late fifth or fourth century or even later.[10] The second recognizes Ezekiel as a sixth-century document and thus affirms the Priestly legislation as extant already in pre-exilic Judah.[11] Very few if any Ezekiel scholars, however, still accept a direction of dependence *from* Ezekiel *to* the Holiness Code ("H") or Priestly Source ("P") for reasons that will become evident below.[12]

Two landmark monographs on the relationship of Ezekiel to the Pentateuch appeared in the first decade of the twenty-first century and contributed to a paradigm change in the study of this prophetic book. Facilitated by the availability of electronic resources for the study of the biblical text, the authors of these monographs were able to systematically identify and analyze shared diction between the different Pentateuchal books and Ezekiel at a level of precision beyond anything possible in earlier scholarship.

Risa Levitt Kohn published a study in 2002 examining ninety-seven terms found only in the Priestly texts of the Pentateuch (including H) and

---

[8] Wellhausen, *Prolegomena*, 421.

[9] As Michael Konkel admits: "Es ist nicht mehr möglich, Ez 40–48 [. . .] als Bindeglied zwischen dem Deuteronomium und der Priesterschrift zu verstehen," ["It is no longer possible to understand Ez 40–48 as the intermediary between Deuteronomy and the Priestly Source"] (*Architektonik des Heiligen: Studien zur zweiten Tempelvision Ezekchiels (Ez. 40–48)*, Bonner Biblische Beiträge 129 [Berlin: Philo, 2001], 350).

[10] E.g. Konkel, *Architektonik des Heiligen*.

[11] E.g. Michael A. Lyons, *An Introduction to the Study of Ezekiel* (London: Bloomsbury T& T Clark, 2015).

[12] See Benjamin Kilchör, *Wieder-Hergestellter Gottesdienst: Eine Deutung der zweiten Tempelvision Ezechiels (Ez 40–48) am Beispiel der Aufgaben der Priester und Leviten* (Herders Biblische Studien 95: Freiburg: Herder, 2020), 38.

Ezekiel, and an additional twenty-one uncommon words present in Ezekiel, Deuteronomy, and other Deuteronomistic literature (e.g., Deuteronomistic Historian [DtrH],[13] Jeremiah).[14] Wherever a direction of dependence could be determined by context or other factors, Levitt Kohn showed it was always *from* P and D *to* Ezekiel (P/D → Ezekiel). Levitt Kohn argued based on a principle some scholars have called *interpretability*.[15] A proposed direction of dependence between two texts that share a significant degree of vocabulary is *interpretable* when *the way* the proposed dependent text re-uses the language of the proposed source text *makes sense* in light of the interests, concerns, and historical circumstances of the (proposed) later author. In the case of Ezekiel, Levitt Kohn showed that when the prophet shares language with a Pentateuchal source and the respective contexts are compared, it is seldom difficult to interpret how Ezekiel is reusing the older, authoritative texts; but, typically, there is no plausible scenario that would explain why the Pentateuchal authors would be reusing language from Ezekiel in the way they (presumably) have.[16]

Moreover, in many passages of Ezekiel (e.g., Ezekiel 20), a very strong

---

[13] "DtrH" is an abbreviation for the "Deuteronomistic History," a reference to the books Judges through 2 Kings, understood as a single composition edited together in the Babylonian Exile to show the unfolding and fulfillment of theological themes articulated in Deuteronomy. This view was first advanced and popularized by Martin Noth in his work, *Überlieferungsgeschichtliche Studien: Die sammelnden und bearbeitenden Geschichtswerke im Alten Testament* (Tübingen: M. Niemeyer, 1957), translated in English as *The Deuteronomistic History, Journal for the Study of the Old Testament* Supplement 15 (Sheffield, UK: University of Sheffield, 1981).

[14] Risa Levitt Kohn, *A New Heart and a New Soul: Ezekiel, the Exile, and the Torah* (Sheffield, UK: Sheffield Academic Press, 2002). See also Risa Levitt Kohn, "A Prophet Like Moses? Rethinking Ezekiel's Relationship to the Torah," *Zeitschrift für die alttestamentliche Wissenschaft* 114 (2002): 236–54; Jacob Milgrom, "Leviticus 26 and Ezekiel," in *The Quest for Context and Meaning: Studies in Biblical Intertextuality in Honor of James A. Sanders*, ed. Craig A. Evans and Shemaryahu Talmon, 57–62 (Leiden, NL: Brill, 1997); and Jacob Milgrom, *Leviticus 17–22: A New Translation with Introduction and Commentary* (New York: Doubleday, 2000), 1362.

[15] B. J. Oropeza and Steve Moyise, eds., *Exploring Intertextuality: Diverse Strategies for New Testament Interpretation of Texts* (Eugene, OR: Wipf & Stock, 2016), 96, 102.

[16] Particularly persuasive are Levitt Kohn's examples of "reversals" in Ezekiel's use of Priestly/Holiness terminology, in which positive terminology from P/H is re-used in a strikingly negative sense in Ezekiel: "Ezekiel parodies P language by using terms antithetically. It is virtually impossible to image that the Priestly Writer would have composed Israelite history by transforming images of Israel's apostasy and subsequent downfall from Ezekiel into images conveying the exceptional covenant and unique relationship between Israel and Yahweh. Indeed, it is difficult to imagine that the Priestly Writer could have turned Ezekiel's land of exile (אֶרֶץ מְגֻרֵיהֶם) into Israel's land of promise, Israel's enemies (קְהַל עַמִּים) into a sign of fecundity, or Israel's abundant sin (בִּמְאֹד מְאֹד) into a sign of Yahweh's covenant. It is, however, plausible that Ezekiel, writing in exile, re-evaluated P's portrayal of

indicator of literary dependency can be observed: *conflation*. Conflation, simply defined, is the recognizable mixing (juxtaposition, interweaving, mingling) of distinct literary sources in the process of creating a new text. In the Pentateuch there are two large bodies of legislation, each of which exhibit a consistent and unique style throughout: the so-called Priestly Source that extends, albeit discontinuously, from Exodus 25 though Numbers 36; and the Book of Deuteronomy, with its law code proper extending from Deuteronomy 12–26. As Bergsma has shown elsewhere, these two literary divisions have their own unique literary style and vocabulary preferences—they use different language even when dealing with the same or similar legal circumstances, and the lexical overlap between the two bodies of legislation is very small (i.e., they do not borrow each other's unique diction).[17] However, in Ezekiel, distinctive language from both "P" and "D" is readily combined throughout the book. And, as one of the foremost international authorities on biblical intertextuality, David Carr of Union Theological Seminary (NY) has pointed out, when faced with a text that conflates the diction characteristic of two or more distinct literary sources, one should conclude that the conflating text is later than, and dependent on, those literary sources.[18] In a detailed empirical study of four Second Temple texts in the biblical tradition universally recognized as dependent on the Pentateuch,[19] Carr evaluated the usefulness of various criteria proposed by scholars since Wellhausen for the determination of the direction of literary dependence, and found that two of the most consistently accurate criteria for determining the later or dependent text were forms of literary conflation:

> One prominent mark of relative lateness across all four of the texts studied here was the tendency to conflate materials found in disparate parts of the Pentateuch into one location. More specifically, each of our exemplars tended to follow a given base text closely, enriching it with fragments or blocks of material from disparate locations [in the Pentateuch].[20]

Israel's uniqueness, cynically inverting these images so that what was once a "pleasing odor to Yahweh" now symbolizes impiety and irreverence" (Levitt Kohn, *New Heart*, 77–78).

[17] See Levitt Kohn, *New Heart*, 96–104.

[18] David Carr, "Method in Determination of Direction of Dependence: An Empirical Test of Criteria Applied to Exodus 34, 11–26 and its Parallels," in *Gottes Volk am Sinai: Untersuchungen zu Ex 32–34 and Dtn 9–10*, ed. Matthias Köckert and Erhard Blum (Gütersloh: Gütersloh Verlaghaus, 2001), 107–40, here 124–26.

[19] These texts are 4QPaleoExodusᵐ, 4QReworkedPentateuch, the Samaritan Pentateuch, and the Temple Scroll.

[20] Carr, "Method," 124.

The only linguistic phenomenon that did seem to make sense as the basis for a criterion is a variant of [the criterion of conflation]: a text tends to be later than its parallels when it combines linguistic phenomena from disparate strata of the Pentateuch.[21]

Just such conflation of P and D terms lay at the heart of Levitt Kohn's argument that Ezekiel was the recipient and not precursor of the Priestly literature. At the conclusion of her work, Levitt Kohn described Ezekiel not as the forerunner of P, as Wellhausen had supposed, but as the forerunner of "R" (the Pentateuchal "Redactor" or editor) inasmuch as the prophet, like the (presumed) later redactor, combined in one work the legal traditions of both P (including H) and D.

Four years after the publication of Levitt Kohn's monograph, Michael A. Lyons released a milestone in the history of biblical scholarship: the first exhaustive study of shared locutions between Ezekiel and the Holiness Code.[22] It seems remarkable that it took more than a century for any scholar to put Wellhausen's paradigm for the relationship of Ezekiel and H to a systematic test. Lyons did so, and reached the conclusion that in all instances where a direction of dependence could be demonstrated, it was in the direction from H to Ezekiel.

Three years later, Jason Gile, a student of noted Ezekiel commentator Daniel I. Block, successfully defended a dissertation demonstrating that the same literary relationship Lyons had discovered between Ezekiel and the Holiness Code also held true for Deuteronomy and Ezekiel.[23] Using strategically selected passages from Ezekiel 8, 16, 20, and elsewhere, Gile produced convincing evidence of Ezekiel's strategy of literary reworking of Deuteronomy to advance the theological message of his work.[24] Israeli scholar Tova Ganzel had already made a similar argument on a smaller scale, showing the interesting phenomenon that Ezekiel, in his critique of the idolatrous practices of his contemporaries, very clearly combined the distinctive terminology for idolatry used in both Deuteronomy and the Priestly literature.[25]

---

[21] Carr, "Method," 125.

[22] Lyons, *From Law to Prophecy*.

[23] Jason Gile, "Deuteronomic Influence on the Book of Ezekiel" (Ph.D. diss, Wheaton College, 2013).

[24] Gile's dissertation would later appear as *Ezekiel and the World of Deuteronomy*, The Library of Hebrew Bible/Old Testament Studies 703 (London: Bloomsbury/T & T Clark, 2021).

[25] Tova Ganzel argues that Ezekiel combines D and P, and in fact knew nearly all of Deuteronomy in a written form in her "Transformation of Pentateuchal Descriptions of Idolatry," in *Transforming Visions: Transformations of Text, Tradition, and Theology in*

Although not all Pentateuchal scholars are aware of the sea change, within Ezekiel scholarship it is no longer controversial to characterize the prophetic book as a post-priestly fusion of Priestly and Deuteronomic language and theology.[26] But Ezekiel does not just conflate language and concepts from P and D; he also integrates both of them with *Zion theology*. "Zion theology" is the name given by Bible scholars to a theological system attested in most Old Testament books (outside of the Pentateuch) that stresses the importance of the infallible commitment the LORD has made by granting a royal covenant to David and his heirs, establishing David's capital Zion (i.e. Jerusalem) as the permanent dwelling place of God's presence in the Temple. We could use the letter "Z" to refer to this Zion theology, the concepts and language of the Zion tradition so characteristic of the Deuteronomistic History, the Psalms, and the other prophets.[27] In the examples that follow, we will examine four texts from Ezekiel that illustrate this fusion of P, D, and Z. Our point is to show that, already in the sixth century BCE, practically the entire corpus of Pentateuchal law was known to Ezekiel and, under the inspiration of the Holy Spirit, the prophet was already moving beyond the theology of the Pentateuch to a new theological synthesis that included the Zion theology based on the Davidic covenant, as reflected in 2 Samuel 7, Psalms 2, 72, 89, and 132, and other key texts.

Examples. On the following pages, we provide three examples from Ezekiel of the fusion of language or concepts from the parts of the Pentateuch classified as "Priestly" (i.e., Leviticus and Numbers), the Book of Deuteronomy, and the Zion tradition.

Ezekiel, ed. William A. Tooman and Michael A. Lyons, Princeton Theological Monograph Series 127 (Eugene, OR: Pickwick, 2010), 33–49.

[26] For example, speaking of Ezekiel's dependence on Priestly literature, German biblical scholar Michael Konkel of Tübingen writes that the "consensus is palpable" among Ezekiel scholars concerning the relative dating of P/H prior to Ezekiel, if not on the absolute date of either composition ("Ezekiel 40–48 and P: Questions and Perspectives," paper given at the Society of Biblical Literature Annual Meeting, San Diego, Nov. 22, 2014, p. 12).

[27] On Zion theology generally, see Jon D. Levenson, *Sinai & Zion: An Entry into the Jewish Bible* (San Francisco: Harper One, 1985), 89–217. On Zion theology in Ezekiel, see Thomas Renz, "The Use of the Zion Tradition in the Book of Ezekiel," in *Zion, City of Our God*, ed. Richard S. Hess and Gordon J. Wenham (Grand Rapids: Eerdmans, 1999), 77–103; Daniel I. Block, "Transformation of Royal Ideology in Ezekiel," in *Transforming Visions*, 208–46; Daniel I. Block, "Zion Theology in the Book of Ezekiel," in *Beyond the River Chebar: Studies in the Kingship and Eschatology in the Book of Ezekiel* (Eugene, OR: Cascade Books, 2013); Jon D. Levenson, *Theology of the Program of Restoration of Ezekiel 40–48* (Missoula, MT: Scholars Press, 1976), 57–69.

EXAMPLE I: ZION AS DEUTERONOMIC CENTRAL SANCTUARY
EZEK 20:39–41 [28]

Pentateuchal Sources	Ezek 20:39–40
	[39] "As for you, O house of Israel . . . Go serve every one of you his idols . . . if you will not listen to me; but <u>my holy name you shall no more profane</u>[1] with your gifts and your idols.
Lev 22:32, cf. 20:3 "<u>You shall not profane my holy name</u>"	
Deut 12:5-6 But <u>you shall seek the place which the LORD your God will choose out of all your tribes to put his name and make his habitation</u> **there; there** you shall go, and **there** you shall bring your burnt offerings and your sacrifices, your tithes and the <u>contributions of your hand</u>, your votive offerings, your freewill offerings, and the firstlings . . .	[40] "<u>For on my holy mountain, the mountain height of Israel</u>,[2] says the Lord GOD, **there** all the house of Israel, all of them, shall serve me in the land; **there** I will accept them, and **there** <u>I will seek your contributions</u> and the choicest of your gifts, with all your sacred offerings.[3]

[1] This expression forbidding the profanation of the holy name is common and significant in H (Lev 20:3; 21:6; 22:2, 32).

[2] Ezekiel replaces Deuteronomy's "place which the LORD your God will choose" with "my holy mountain," a reference to Zion. For Zion as "my holy mountain," see Ps 2:6; 3:5; 15:1; 24:3; 43:3; 48:1; 99:9; Isa 11:9; 56:7; 57:13; 65:11, 25; 66:20; Joel 2:1; 3:17; Obad 16; Zeph 3:11; Dan 9:16, 20; for the "mountain height of Israel" as Zion, see Ezek 17:23; cf. Ps 48:1–2; 68:16–17, 19; 78:68–69.

[3] Ezek 20:40 reflects the concepts and diction of the cult centralization commands of Deuteronomy, esp. Deut 12:5–6: note shared distinctive *triple repetition* of "there" (Heb. *šām/šommâ*), the verb "to seek" (Heb. *dāraš*), and the noun "(your) contributions" (Heb. *těrûmōtêkem*). The other terms for offerings in Ezek 20:40 can be paralleled in other cult-centralization passages of Deuteronomy (Deut 12:26; 26:2, 10).

---

[28] Gile discusses Ezekiel's reuse of Deuteronomic terminology for Israel's scattering and regathering (*Ezekiel and Deuteronomy*, 140–204.)

EXAMPLE I: ZION AS DEUTERONOMIC CENTRAL SANCTUARY
(CONT.) EZEK 20:39–41

Pentateuchal Sources	Ezek 20:41
Lev 26:31 I will not smell your <u>pleasing odor</u> . . . Deut 30:3 <u>He will gather you from all the peoples where the LORD your God scattered you there</u> . . .	[41] As a <u>pleasing odor</u> I will accept you,[4] when <u>I bring you out from the peoples, and gather you out of the countries where you have been scattered;</u>[5]
Num 20:12 To <u>sanctify me in the eyes of</u> the people of Israel . . . Lev 26:45 I brought them forth from the land of Egypt <u>in the eyes of the nations</u> . . .	and <u>I will sanctify myself</u>[6] among you <u>in the eyes of the nations.</u>[7]

[4] "Pleasing odor" (*rêaḥ nîḥōaḥ*) occurs frequently in P/H and Ezekiel, but never elsewhere in MT. The Hebrew phrasing of Ezek 20:41 and Lev 26:31 are unusually similar, suggesting a specific literary connection.

[5] The three Hebrew words "people"(*'am*), "gather" (*qābaṣ*), and "scatter" (*pûṣ*) only occur together in Deut 30:3 and several verses of Ezekiel (11:17; 20:34, 41; 28:25; 29:13). Verbs *qābaṣ* and *pûṣ* are not priestly vocabulary, but appear in Deut 4:27; 28:64; 30:4. Observe that Ezekiel has taken a single clause from Deuteronomy 30:3 ("He will gather you from all the peoples") and constructed from it a classic Hebrew synonymous bicola ("I bring you out from the peoples//and gather you out of the countries").

[6] The phrase "sanctify in the eyes of" occurs only in Numbers (20:12; 27:14) and Ezekiel (20:41; 28:25; 36:23; 38:16; 39:27).

[7] The phrase "in the eyes of the nations" occurs only in Lev 26:45; Ps 98:2, and Ezekiel (5:8; 20:9, 14, 22, 41; 28:25; 39:27).

EXAMPLE II: JERUSALEM AS FOCUS OF COVENANT CURSES ON ISRAEL EZEK 4:13–17

Pentateuchal Sources	Ezek 4:13–15
Deut 30:1 And when all these things come . . . and you call them to mind among all the nations whither the LORD your God has driven you, Lev 22:8 That which dies of itself or is torn by beasts he shall not eat, defiling himself by it . . . Lev 19:7 If it is eaten at all on the third day, it is foul; it will not be accepted . . .	*113* And the LORD said, "Thus shall the people of Israel eat their bread unclean, among the nations whither I will drive them."[1] *14* Then I said, "Ah Lord GOD! behold, I have never defiled myself . . . I have never eaten what died of itself or was torn by beasts,[2] nor has foul flesh come into my mouth."[3] *15* Then he said to me, "See, I will let you have cow's dung instead of human dung, on which you may prepare your bread."

[1] The Hebrew phrase "among the nations whither I will scatter them there" is a Deuteronomism from Deut 30:1 imitated in Jer 29:14, 18; 43:5; 46:28; 49:36 and here in Ezek 4:13. The verbal root for "scatter" (Heb. *n-d-ḥ*) ever occurs in Priestly texts of the Pentateuch, so Ezekiel is likely drawing on the vocabulary of Deuteronomy.

[2] Ezek 4:14 incorporates a near quote of Lev 22:8. The similarity—easy enough to see in English—is even more striking in Hebrew, with five contiguous, identical Hebrew lemmas with just minor syntactical reformulation. The inversion of quoted clauses is known as "Seidel's Law." See Bernard M. Levinson, *Deuteronomy and the Hermeneutics of Legal Innovation* (New York: Oxford University Press, 1997), 18 n. 51.

[3] "Foul" (Heb. *pigûl*) is a rare word occuring only in Lev 7:18; 19:7; Isa 65:4; and Ezek 4:14. Ezekiel is clearly affirming his compliance with the regulations in Leviticus 7:18 and 19:7, just as earlier he affirmed compliance with Lev 22:8.

EXAMPLE II: JERUSALEM AS FOCUS OF COVENANT CURSES
ON ISRAEL (CONT.) EZEK 4:13–17

Pentateuchal Sources	Ezek 4:16–17
Lev 26:26 When <u>I break your staff of bread</u>, ten women shall bake your bread in one oven, and shall deliver <u>your bread again by weight, and you shall eat,</u> and not be satisfied.	[16] Moreover he said to me, "Son of man, behold, <u>I will break the staff of bread</u> **in Jerusalem;** <u>they shall eat bread by weight[4]</u> and with fearfulness; and they shall drink water by measure and in dismay.
Deut 8:9 A land in which without scarcity <u>you will eat bread, you will not lack anything in it</u> . . . Lev 26:39 The remnant among you shall <u>rot away in their iniquity.</u>	[17] I will do this that <u>they may lack bread and water,</u>[5] and look at one another in dismay, and <u>rot away in their iniquities.</u>[6]

[4] In Hebrew, there are six nearly contiguous and identical words between Ezekiel 4:16 and Leviticus 26:26 ("bread," *leḥem* [2x]; "break," *š-b-r*; "staff," *maṭṭēh*; "eat," *'-k-l*; "by weight," *bammišqāl*). Ezekiel's unique contribution is to specify the location as "in Jerusalem," in keeping with his consistent pattern of re-applying geographically nonspecific statements of Leviticus to Jerusalem/Zion in particular.

[5] Here Ezekiel alludes to, and inverts, the promised blessings of Deut 8:7-10 . The expression "lack bread" (Heb. *ḥāsar leḥem*) never occurs in priestly texts of the Pentateuch, so Ezekiel is likely drawing on the vocabulary of Deuteronomy.

[6] The expression "to rot away in iniquities" is extremely rare, occuring only in Lev 26:39, Ezek 4:17, and 24:23.

EXAMPLE III: JERUSALEM AS THE CENTER OF THE NATIONS
EZEK 5:5–17

Pentateuchal Sources	Ezek 5:5–7
Deut 17:14 When you come to the land which the LORD your God gives you, . . . and then say, 'I will set a king over me, like all the nations that are round about me'	[5] Thus says the Lord GOD: **"This is Jerusalem**; I have set her in the center of the nations, with countries round about her.[1] [6] And she has rebelled against my ordinances more than the nations . . .
Lev 26:43 But the land shall be left by them . . . because they spurned my ordinances, and their soul abhorred my statutes.	for they spurned my ordinances and did not walk in my statutes."
Deut. 6:14 You shall not go after other gods, of the gods of the peoples who are round about you . . .	[7] Therefore thus says the Lord GOD: "Because you are more turbulent than the nations that are round about you,[2] and
Lev 18:4 You shall do my ordinances and keep my statutes and walk in them . . .	have not walked in my statutes or done my ordinances[3]
Lev 20:23 And you shall not walk in the customs of the nation which I am casting out before you . . .	but have acted according to the ordinances of the nations that are round about you . . . ."[4]

[1] Interestingly, the Hebrew roots for "surrounding," "say," "land," "set," and "nation" (Heb. *sabîb, 'āmar, 'āreṣ, śîm, gôy*) occur together in the same clause in the MT only in Ezek 5:5 and Deut 17:14. Ezekiel may have formulated his declaration about Jerusalem in light of the famous Deuteronomic king law, implying that Jerusalem is the monarch-city among the nations.

[2] Polemic against the "the nations round about" is absent from P/H, but characteristic of D and DtrH: Deut 6:14, 12:10, 13:7, 17:14; Judg 2:12; 2 Kgs 17:15. The Holiness Code polemicizes against the "nation(s) the LORD casts out": Lev. 18:24; 20:23.

[3] The inversion of quoted clauses (cf. Ezek 4:14 above) is another example of "Seidel's Law," cf. Lev 26:25//Ezek 5:17.

[4] D lacks the idea "laws of the nations," which occurs only in H (Lev 20:23). Ezekiel draws the idea from Lev 20:23 and modifies the linguistic formulation to fit his context, changing "customs" (*ḥuqqôt*) to "ordinances" (*mišpaṭîm*) to contrast the divine "ordinances" in the previous clause, and "nation I am casting out" to the Deuteronomism "nations round about" to match v. 5 above (cf. 2 Kgs 17:8).

EXAMPLE III: JERUSALEM AS THE CENTER OF THE NATIONS
(CONT.) EZEK 5:5–17

Pentateuchal Sources	Ezek 5:16–17
Deut 32:23–24 "'And I will heap evils upon them; I will spend my **arrows** upon them, emptiness of **famine** . . . Deut 32:42 I will make my **arrows** drunk with **blood** . . . Lev 26:26 When I break your staff of bread . . . Lev 26:22 And I will send the wild beasts among you, which will bereave you . . . Lev 26:25 I will bring a sword upon you, vengeance for the covenant; and if you gather within your cities I will send pestilence among you . . .	16 When I loose against you my deadly **arrows** of **famine, arrows**⁵ for destruction, which I will loose to destroy you, and when I bring more and more **famine** upon you, and break your staff of bread. 17 I will send **famine** and wild beasts against you, and they will bereave you; pestilence and **blood** shall pass through you; and I will bring the sword upon you. I the Lord have spoken.⁵

5   Greenberg, Block, Gile, and others recognize Ezek 5:16–17 as a mosaic assembled from the covenant curses of Lev 26 and Deut 32 (Gile, Ezekiel and Deuteronomy, 96). The terms in Ezek 5:16–17 bolded above—famine, arrows, and blood—are absent from Lev 26, and appear borrowed from Deut 32. In all the Hebrew Bible, these three nouns appear together exclusively in Deut 32 and Ezek 5, so the connection seems secure.

Admittedly, it takes time and patience to digest all the textual information on these tables and gradually recognize Ezekiel's characteristic way of
blending together material primarily from the priestly texts of the Pentateuch
(Leviticus-Numbers) with allusions or quotes from Deuteronomy and affir-
mations of Zion theology. Readers with facility in Hebrew who may wish to
see a more technical presentation of the texts are referred to Bergsma's study
of them in a different publication.[29] But here we will present a brief discussion for a more general readership. Example I (Ezek 20:39–41) is taken
from a famous review of the history of Israel found in Ezekiel 20:1–44 that
has long been recognized as interweaving language and concepts from both
priestly texts and Deuteronomy. Its final oracle, Ezek 20:33–44, promises
a future restoration of Israel. Our example lies in the middle of this oracle.
Verses 39 and 41 borrow generously from terms and expressions found in
Leviticus and Numbers, but the central verse, Ezek 20:40, constitutes a bold
rewriting of the cult centralization command(s) of Deuteronomy 12:5–6,
only now as an eschatological prophecy of a restored liturgy on "my holy
mountain, the mountain heights of Israel," an obvious poetic reference to
Jerusalem.[30] The triple repetition of "there" in Ezek 20:40 is an unmistak-
able evocation of Deut 12:5–6, in which "there" or "thither" are repeated
four times for emphasis. Deuteronomy's "the place which the Lord your
God shall choose" becomes in Ezekiel "my holy mountain, the mountain
heights of Israel," because the prophet has no doubt that Jerusalem is the
place the Lord has chosen—this is a central tenet of Zion theology and the
Davidic covenant (see Ps 132:13–14). Deuteronomy speaks of the people of
Israel "seeking" out this place of worship, but Ezekiel cleverly reverses the
image to *the Lord* "seeking" the offerings of Israel at the holy place. Finally,
Ezekiel does not repeat the lengthy list of sacrifices and offerings found in
Deut 12:6, but summarizes them more succinctly with "your contributions
and the choicest of your gifts, with all your sacred offerings" (Ezek 20:40).

In Examples II (Ezek 4:13–17) and III (Ezek 5:5–17), the prophet cre-
ates new oracles of judgment by splicing together terms and phrases from
legal material and the covenant curses of both Leviticus and Deuteronomy.
Moreover, he respecifies the object of divine judgment as *Jerusalem* in particular, and not the people or land of Israel generally, as is the case in his
Pentateuchal source texts. This is because in the Zion tradition the holy city
Jerusalem constitutes the mystical center not only of the nation of Israel but

---

[29] John Bergsma, "The Relevance of Ezekiel and the Samaritans for Pentateuchal Compo-
sition: Converging Lines of Evidence," in *Exploring the Composition of the Pentateuch:
Conference Papers 2016, Bulletin for Biblical Research* Supplement 27 (Winona Lake, IN:
Eisenbrauns, 2020), 230–48.

[30] Cf. Ps 2:6; 48:1; 87:1; 99:9; Joel 2:1; 4:17; Zeph 3:11; Isa 66:20; Dan 9:16, 20.

of all nations generally (Ezek 5:5; cf. Ps 2:6–10; 48:2 *et passim*; 87:1–6, etc.). In Example II (Ezek 4:13–17), the prophet mixes a few Deuteronomic allusions with the central famine expression of Leviticus 26—"breaking of the staff of bread"—and applies this curse specifically to *Jerusalem* (Ezek 4:16). In Example III (Ezek 5:5–17), Ezekiel composes an oracle of judgment that mixes distinctive words and phrases from Leviticus and Deuteronomy (esp. Lev 26 & Deut 32) and states at the beginning of the entire oracle the identity of one to be judged: "This is Jerusalem!" (Ezek 5:5).[31]

We only present here three examples, but they are by no means isolated or idiosyncratic: the fusion of priestly, Deuteronomic, and Zion theology, images, language, and phrases is characteristic of Ezekiel both at the close textual level and also on a more macroscopic scale, involving elements like the structure and themes of the book and its major sections.[32] What is the implication for Ezekiel's relationship to the Pentateuch? First of all, it becomes obvious why contemporary scholars have abandoned Wellhausen's paradigm that Ezekiel was a source first for the Holiness Code, and then the Priestly Source as a whole. Simply put, if we imagine Jerusalem priest-scribes composing and editing the Priestly materials of the Pentateuch in the 400s BCE while using Ezekiel as a source—as Wellhausen envisioned—then we cannot explain why the Deuteronomisms and Zionisms embedded in several of Ezekiel's oracles *never* find their way into the text of the priestly laws or Holiness Code. Why would fifth-century Jerusalem priests use the work of the prophet Ezekiel but *edit out* any mention of Jerusalem and all his Deuteronomic language?[33] If they objected so strongly

---

[31] For brevity, Example III analyzes only the beginning (Ezek 5:5–7) and end (Ezek 5:16–17) of this oracle, to capture the strongest references to Zion (Ezek 5:5) and examples of dependence on D (Ezek 5:16–17) present in this unit. The missing verses, Ezekiel 5:8–15, are also rich in literary reuse of P, H, and D texts: see Moshe Greenberg, *Ezekiel 1–20* (Garden City, NJ: Doubleday, 1983), 113–16.

[32] John S. Bergsma, "A 'Samaritan' Pentateuch? The Implications of the Pro-Northern Tendency of the Common Pentateuch," in *Paradigm Change in Pentateuchal Research*, ed. Matthias Armgardt, Benjamin Kilchör, and Markus Zehnder (Wiesbaden: Harrassowitz, 2019), 287–300.

[33] It is common in critical scholarship to attribute the Priestly and Deuteronomic texts to the work of Jerusalem priests: "[The Priestly Document] is closely linked to the rebuilding of the Temple [and] the legitimation of the Second Temple community in Jerusalem. [. . .] The writing down of P also betrays the claims of the priestly class in Jerusalem" (Christophe Nihan, *From Priestly Torah to Pentateuch: A Study in the Composition of the Book of Leviticus* [Tübingen: Mohr Siebeck, 2007], 614). Similarly, Ziony Zevit describes Deuteronomy as the work of a "Jerusalem Temple loyalist" (Ziony Zevit, "Deuteronomy and the Temple: An Exercise in Historical Imagining," in *Mishneh Todah: Studies in Deuteronomy and Its Cultural Environment in Honor of Jeffrey H. Tigay*, ed. Nili Sacher Fox, David A. Glatt-Gilad, and Michael J. Williams [Winona Lake, IN: Eisenbrauns, 2009], 217).

to these elements of Ezekiel's thought and diction, why did they nonetheless venerate him so much to use him as a source? The whole scenario is, from an historical perspective, completely implausible. On the other hand, for the prophet, writing in the sixth century BCE, to be using older sacred texts already familiar to the people of Israel and creatively combining them to make application to their current historical and theological crisis poses no implausibilities whatsoever.

EZEKIEL, THE "MAN WHO KNEW TOO MUCH"

For Wellhausen, the whole Pentateuch is not fused together until around 444 BC when it's priestly redactors publish it. Ezekiel, however, makes himself inconvenient to this theory by the fact that he "knows too much" of the Pentateuchal narrative already in the sixth century BC. A parade example of Ezekiel's inconvenient knowledge is Ezek 20:1–31, a text in which the prophet rehearses the sacred history of Israel from the sojourn in Egypt (Ezek 20:5–9) to the entrance into the promised land (Ezek 20:28). Many scholars have recognized that, as he retells this story, he both alludes to and reuses the diction of both priestly texts and passages of Deuteronomy.[34]

Daniel I. Block analyzes the literary structure of Ezek 20:5–26 as consisting of three "panels" (vv. 5–9, 10–17, and 18–26) that correspond to the three stages of Israel's exodus and wilderness wanderings:

1. The first panel (Ezek 20:5–9) concerns the LORD's dealings with Israel in Egypt.
2. The second panel (Ezek 20:10–17) concerns the first generation in the wilderness and the Sinai event.
3. The third panel (Ezek 20:18–26) with the second generation in the wilderness and the second giving of the law (i.e. Deuteronomy) on the plains of Moab.[35]

---

[34] In what follows, I am summarizing arguments presented in greater detail in my article with Scott W. Hahn, "What Laws Were Not Good? A Canonical Approach to the Theological Problem of Ezekiel 20:25–26," *Journal of Biblical Literature* 123 (2004): 201–18.

[35] Cf. Block's layout of the divisions of the text (The Book of *Ezekiel: Chapters 1–24*, New International Commentary on the Old Testament [Grand Rapids: Eerdmans, 1997], 622–24). Corrine Patton also recognizes the correspondence between the narrative of Ezekiel 20 and the narrative sequence of the Pentateuchal accounts of the exodus: "The clearest references to the exodus in the book of Ezekiel occur in ch. 20. The text shows clear familiarity with the exodus tradition: sojourn in Egypt (5–8), deliverance by the LORD (9–10), two generations in the wilderness (10–25), the giving of the law in the wilderness (11–13 and 25–26) and entry into the land (28). . . . The scheme certainly matches historical

In the course of his retelling of the sacred history of Israel, the prophet refers or alludes to several pivotal events recorded in the canonical text of the Pentateuch. Ezekiel 20:10–12 state that the LORD "brought them out of Egypt," "led them into the wilderness," and then "gave them My laws," which summarizes the exodus event (Exod 12–18) and the giving of the law at Sinai (Exod 19–31). In Ezekiel 20:13 the prophet insists, "the House of Israel rebelled against Me in the wilderness," probably an allusion to the incident of the Golden Calf (Exod 32). In response, the LORD's threatens to destroy Israel in the desert, but decides to refrain for the sake of his name (v.13b–14), a recognizable synopsis of Exod 32:7–14, where Moses averts the wrath of God by interceding on behalf of the people. Next, Ezekiel describes a divine oath *not* to bring Israel into the land, which we discover in the Pentateuch in the account of Israel's rebellion after the twelve spies scouted the land (Num 13–14), when the LORD did indeed swear concerning the first wilderness generation that "none of the men . . . shall see the land I promised on oath to their fathers" (Num 14:20–23, cf. Deut 2:14).

In Ezek 20:18–26 we find reference to the second generation of Israel in the wilderness, corresponding to the Pentateuchal narrative from Num 25 through the end of Deuteronomy. But the second generation *also* rebels against the LORD in the desert (Ezek 20:21; "The children rebelled against Me,"), an event recorded in the Pentateuchal text in Num 25:1–18, the account of the great sin of the people at Beth-Peor, which some commentators recognize as *the* catastrophic event for the second generation, as the golden calf was for the first.[36]

Thus, we are clearly in the context of the second generation when we come to Ezek 20:23, where clear allusions to Deuteronomic material first occur. The prophet states on behalf of the LORD, "I swore to them in the wilderness that I would scatter them among the nations," which can be understood as a synthetic interpretation of the covenant curses in Deut 27–31, which threaten Israel to be scattered among the nations (28:64), followed by the climactic divine oath at the end of the Song of Moses, "For I lift up my hand to heaven, and swear . . . I will take vengeance. . ." (32:40–41

---

reviews present and presumed in Deuteronomic texts, including the historical review in Deuteronomy 1–11, the speech of Solomon in 1 Kings 8, and the speech of Joshua in Joshua 24. ("'I Myself Gave Them Laws That Were Not Good': Ezekiel 20 and the Exodus Traditions," *Journal for the Study of the Old Testament* 69 [1996]: 74–75).

[36] Cf. Jacob Milgrom, *Numbers*, JPS Torah Commentary (Philadelphia: Jewish Publication Society, 1990), xv, 211, 214.

RSV).[37] The allusion to Deuteronomy is confirmed by the use of the Deuteronomic term for scattering (*hāpîṣ*, the *hip'îl* of *pûṣ*).[38]

Thus, when we reach v. 25 in Ezekiel's recital of Israel's history, we are in the period of Detuteronomy, the second major law-giving event recorded in the Pentateuch, delivered to the second generation. This helps explain Ezekiel's much-debated statement, "Moreover, I gave them laws that were not good and rules by which they could not live" (Ezek 20:25). Why would Ezekiel describe the laws of Deuteronomy as "not good" and "by which they could not live"? Several reasons are suggested by the canonical narrative of the Pentateuch. The law code of Deuteronomy, given forty years after the so-called "Priestly" and "Holiness" legislation associated with Sinai, selectively revises cultically important aspects of the P/H ritual system: No longer must the very firstborn animal itself be brought to slaughter (Ex 13:12; Num 18:17; Lev 27:10, 26, 28, 33), but another can be purchased and offered in its stead (Deut 14:22–26). No longer must every animal be sacrificed as an act of worship at the Tabernacle (Lev 17:1–8), but now clean animals may be slaughtered just for meat and their blood be poured out like game animals (Deut. 12:15, 16, 20–24). No longer is it sufficient to drive out the inhabitants of the land (Num 33:52), but now they must be put to death (Deut 20:16–18). And perhaps most significantly, although in the P/H corpus, covenant-breaking and exile are envisaged as a real possibility (Lev 26:14–46), in Deuteronomy they are explicitly predicted and prophesied as *inevitable* (see Deut 27:15–26; 28:15–68; 29:1–4, 22–28; 30:1–3; 31:16–22).[39] Thus, according to the text of Deuteronomy itself, the law

---

[37] David Rolph Seely, "The Raised Hand of God as an Oath Gesture," in *Fortunate the Eyes that See: Essays in Honor of David Noel Freedman*, ed. Astrid B. Beck et al. (Grand Rapids: Eerdmans, 1995), 411–21, esp. 413.

[38] See Deut 4:27, 28:64, and 30:3. When the Holiness Code speaks of "scattering" it uses a different term, *zārāh* (cf. Lev 26:33, Ezek 20:23b).

[39] Consider the following: (1) Deut 4:25–31, if the introductory *kî* is taken as "when" rather than "if" (see previous note) it reads as Moses's sworn prediction that Israel will break the Deuteronomic covenant and experience judgement (i.e. dispersion and exile); (2) although there ought to be corresponding blessings for the Levites to pronounce in ch. 27, only the curses are given (Deut 27:11–26); (3) the curses for disobedience (28:15–68) are two to three times longer than the promises for obedience (28:1–14), as well as being far more detailed and programmatic; (4) the threats for disobedience in 29:16–30:10 are, again, oddly long and programmatic, as if the author is not really in doubt about which of the two options (obedience or disobedience) the Israelites will choose; (5) Deut 31:16–22 consists of a divine prophesy of Israel's inevitable disobedience and actualization of the covenant curses; (6) 31:26–29 consists of Moses's solemn prediction to the Israelites of their future complete violation of the covenant; (7) the Song of Moses (32:2–43) castigates the Israelites so thoroughly for their rebelliousness against the LORD that when in v. 41 the LORD swears to "take vengeance on my adversaries and requite those who hate me," the reader is tempted to take this as a reference to the Israelites themselves, who from v.

code being given to them would not be obeyed and would not lead to "life," i.e. the flourishing of the community. Thus Ezekiel's perspective: "I gave them laws that were not good and rules by which they could not live" (Ezek 20:25).

The canonical narrative of the Pentateuch, in which the "Priestly" legislation is followed and revised by Deuteronomy, can also explain the notoriously puzzling comment of Ezekiel in the following verse: "I rendered them defiled by their gifts, when they offered every opener of the womb, in order that I might render them desolate . . ." (Ezek 20:26, my translation). This refers to the change in cultic law in Deuteronomy. Whereas under the priestly legislation, as noted above, animals sacred or dedicated to the LORD could not be sold or exchanged (Num 18:17; Lev 27:10, 26, 28, 33), Deuteronomy permitted firstling animals and others dedicated for sacrifice to be sold and the money used to buy substitutes at the place of the central sanctuary (Deut 14:22–26). Judged by the higher standards of the earlier priestly legislation, the manner of offering the first-born in Deuteronomy was cultically inferior and even profane.[40]

To summarize, the narrative sequence of Ezekiel 20 strongly suggests familiarity with the general narrative of the canonical Pentateuch, and even certain of its subtleties. Ezekiel is cognizant of two major dispensations of the Law during the Exodus and wilderness wanderings, one to the first generation (Exod 20–Num 10) and one to the second (Num 27–Deut 34, note Num 27:64–65). Ezekiel 20:23–26 describes a second law-giving to Israel as sandwiched between the rebellion of the second generation in the wilderness (Ezek 20:21–22; cf. the apostasy of Baal-Peor, Num 25:1–16), and the entrance into the land (Ezek 20:27–29; Josh 3–4). In the Pentateuchal narrative, Moses delivers the Deuteronomic code at this very point. Ezekiel's reference to the *inevitability* of scattering, which is unique to Deuteronomy, along with the use of Deuteronomic diction, serve to corroborate that vv. 23–26 refer to this body of law. This is a striking example, of which many others could be provided, of Ezekiel "knowing too much" of the Pentateuchal narrative for an Israelite of the sixth century BC—at least according to Wellhausen's ideologically-driven reconstruction of the history

---

5 through v. 38 have never responded to the LORD with anything but rebellion. Corinne Patton astutely comments that according to Ezek 20:25, "Israel has been set up for failure" ("I Myself," 79). One can only agree; that would seem to be the same conclusion one would draw from a canonical reading of Deuteronomy. The end of the book "takes for granted that the people will indeed fail to be the true people of the covenant and that this will result in the full force of the curses of ch. 28 falling on them" (J. Gordon McConville, *Grace in the End: A Study in Deuteronomic Theology* [Grand Rapids: Zondervan, 1993], 135).

40 For a more detailed argument, see Bergsma and Hahn, "What Laws Were Not Good?," 211–18.

of Israelite religion. But if we jettison the Wellhausenian paradigm, Ezekiel and his book can be allowed to sit in peace in their historical and canonical position, without appeal to hypothetical, interventionist redactors in order to save an old paradigm at the expense of the empirical textual data.

JEREMIAH AND THE PENTATEUCH

The same phenomenon of conflation of Pentateuchal literary corpora that we have witnessed in Ezekiel is also evident in Jeremiah. In the following, we will present examples of such conflation from different literary genres of Jeremiah: from poetic passages typically attributed to the prophet himself; from historical narration some believe to be the work of Baruch; and from "additions" to the book found in the Masoretic Text (MT)[41] but not the Septuagint (LXX), thought by some to be the work of exilic redactors.

---

[41] The Masoretic Text is the traditional Jewish text of the Hebrew Bible, standardized between 700–1000 CE by a scribal movement that flourished around the Sea of Galilee in the land of Israel.

Example I: Conflation in the Poetry of Jeremiah
Jeremiah 2:20–25

Pentateuchal Sources	Jer 2:20–21
Lev 26:13 I am the LORD your God, who brought you out of the land of Egypt, that <u>you should not be their servants</u>. And <u>I have broken the bars of your yoke</u> and <u>made you walk erect.</u> Deut 12:2 You shall surely destroy all the places where the nations . . . served their gods, <u>upon the high mountains and upon the hills and under every green tree</u> . . . Deut. 22:9 "<u>You shall not sow your vineyard with mixed seed</u> . . .	20"For long ago, <u>I broke your yoke</u> <u>and burst your bonds;</u>[1] <u>but you said, 'I will not serve.'</u>[2] <u>Yes, upon every high hill</u> <u>and under every green tree</u>[3] <u>you bowed down as a harlot.</u>[4] 21 Yet <u>I planted you a choice vine, wholly of pure seed.</u>[5] How then have you turned degenerate and become a wild vine?

[1] Outside of Jeremiah, "break" (*šābar*) and "yoke" (*'ōl*) only occur in Lev 26:13 and a nearly verbatim quote in Ezek 34:27. Arguably, Jeremiah borrows the expression from Leviticus (cf. also Jer 5:5; 28:2-14; 30:8). Notice that Jeremiah makes a poetic bicola of a single statement of the Law, a phenomenon also seen in Ezekiel (e.g. Lev 26:4//Ezek 34:26).

[2] We have used "servants" (*'ăbadîm*) in Lev 26:13 and "serve" (*'ābad*) in Jer 2:20 to highlight the common root *'-b-d*, "work, serve, worship."

[3] This famous phrase from the cult centralization law (Dt. 12:2) is reused in DtrH (1 Kgs 14:23; 16:4; 17:10), Jeremiah (2:20; 3:6,13; 17:2), and Ezekiel (6:13). It is absent in P/H.

[4] Jeremiah makes an intentional contrast, in that the LORD intended them to "walk erect" (Heb. *qômĕmîyût*) yet Israel "bowed down," "bent over," or "reclined" (Heb. *ṣō'āh*) like a harlot.

[5] Lit. "all of it seed of truth," that is, unmixed, according to the prohibition of mixed seed in the Law, which only occurs in Deuteronomy 22:9.

EXAMPLE I: CONFLATION IN THE POETRY OF JEREMIAH (CONT.)
JEREMIAH 2:20–25

Pentateuchal Sources	Jer 2:22–23
Lev. 17:16 "But if he does not wash them or bathe his flesh, he shall bear his iniquity." Num. 5:12 "If any man's wife goes astray and acts unfaithfully against him¹³... and she is undetected though she has **defiled** herself, and there is no witness against her¹⁴... and he is jealous of his wife who has **defiled** herself; or if the spirit of jealousy comes upon him ... though she has not **defiled** herself;¹⁵ then the man shall bring his wife to the priest....¹⁹ Then the priest shall make her take an oath, saying...²⁰ "If you have **defiled** yourself...²¹ then...²² may this water that brings the curse pass into your bowels....' And the woman shall say, 'Amen, Amen.' ²⁷ If she has **defiled** herself ... the water that brings the curse shall enter into her ...²⁸ But if the woman has not **defiled** herself and is clean, then she shall be free....²⁹ "This is the law ... when a wife ... **defiles** herself....³¹ The man shall be free from iniquity, but the woman shall bear her iniquity."	²² Though you wash⁶ yourself with lye and use much soap, the stain of your iniquity is still before me, says the Lord GOD. ²³ How can you say, '**I am not defiled**,⁷ I have not gone after the Baals?' Look at your way in the valley; know what you have done—a restive young camel interlacing her tracks, ²⁴ a wild ass used to the wilderness, in her heat sniffing the wind! Who can restrain her lust? None who seek her need weary themselves; in her month they will find her. ²⁵ Keep your feet from going unshod and your throat from thirst. But you said, 'It is hopeless, for I have loved strangers, and after them I will go.'

---

6. "Wash" (Heb. *kābās*): 42 of 48 occurences of this verb in the MT are in P, but never in D. The idea of "washing" because of "iniquity" (Heb. *'āwôn*) is Priestly, attested only in Lev. 16:21-18; Lev 17:16, and echoed in Ps. 51:2,7 ET.

7. Heb. *ṭāmē'* in the *niphal* (passive stem), only 18x in MT: 2x re: food uncleanliness (Lev. 11:43;18:24); 7x re: literal female adultery, all in Numbers 5 (vv. 13,14 [2x],20,27,28,29); 9x figuratively of idolatry (Jer. 2:23; Ezek. 20:30,31,43; 23:7,13,30 Hos. 5:3; 6:10). Never in D or DtrH.

EXAMPLE II: CONFLATION IN HISTORICAL NARRATIVE IN
JEREMIAH 34:8–13

Pentateuchal Sources	Jer 34:8–9
Lev. 25:10 And you shall hallow the fiftieth year, and <u>proclaim liberty</u> throughout the land to all its inhabitants; it shall be a jubilee for you, when each of you shall turn back to his property and each of you shall turn back to his family. Deut. 15:12 "<u>If your brother, a Hebrew or a Hebrewess, is sold to you, he shall serve you six years, and in the seventh year you shall let him go free from you.</u> Lev. 25:39 "<u>And if your brother . . . sells himself to you, you shall not make him serve as a slave:</u> 40 he shall be with you as a hired servant. . . . 42 For they are my servants . . . <u>they shall not be sold as slaves</u> . . .	8The word which came to Jeremiah from the LORD, after King Zedekiah had made a covenant with all the people **in Jerusalem**[1] <u>to make a proclamation of liberty to them,</u>[2] 9that <u>every one should set his manservant and maidservant, a Hebrew or Hebrewess, free,</u>[3] <u>so that no one should enslave a Jew, his brother.</u>[4]

[1] References to Jerusalem or the Temple are **bolded** as part of the Zion tradition absent from Deuteronomy and Priestly sources.

[2] "To proclaim liberty," Heb. *qārā' děrôr*, is absent from D or DtrH but comes from the Holiness Code's jubilee legislation (Lev. 25:10).

[3] "Free" (Heb. *ḥopšî*) occurs in slave laws of Exodus 21:2,5,26,27 and Deuteronomy 15:12,13,18; but not the Holiness Code (Leviticus), which uses "liberty" (*děrôr*), "to go out" (*yāṣā'*), or "redeem" (*gā'al*) to describe freedom. Emphasis on *both male and female slaves* comes from Deut 15:12-18, not Exod 21:1-11, which limits release to males.

[4] The only blanket prohibition of enslaving a fellow Israelite in the Pentateuch is found in the Holiness Code, Lev 25:39-42. Notice Jeremiah's use of "Jew" (Heb. *yěhûdî*)— a late Biblical Hebrew term absent in the MT from Genesis 1 through 2 Kings 15— for the Holiness Code's "brother."

EXAMPLE II: CONFLATION IN HISTORICAL NARRATIVE IN JEREMIAH 34:8–13 (CONT.)

Pentateuchal Sources	Jer 34:10–13
Deut. 15:12 "If your brother, a Hebrew or a Hebrewess, is sold to you, he shall serve you six years, and in the seventh year you shall let him go free from you. Lev. 25:10 And you shall . . . proclaim liberty throughout the land to all its inhabitants; it shall be a jubilee for you, when each of you shall _turn back_ to his property and each of you shall _turn back_ to his family. Deut. 29:25 They forsook the covenant of the LORD, the God of their fathers, which he made with them when he brought them out of the land of Egypt . . . Deut. 5:6 "'I am the LORD your God, who brought you out of the land of Egypt, out of the house of bondage.	[10]And they obeyed, all the princes and all the people . . . that each one would set his slave, whether man or maidservant, free; so that they would not be enslaved again; they obeyed and set them free. [11]But afterward they _turned back_[5] around and _turned back_ the male and female slaves they had set free, and brought them into subjection as slaves. . . . [13]"Thus says the LORD, the God of Israel: I made a covenant with your fathers when I brought them out of the land of Egypt, out of the house of bondage,[6] saying . . .

[5] We translate Heb. *šûb* as "turned back" to approximate its range of senses: "turn," "return," "repent," "go back," etc. The two elements of the Jubilee (Lev 25:10) are "proclamation of liberty" (*qārā' děrôr*) and "return" (*šûb*). Jeremiah engages in creative and ironic wordplay on the Jubilee idea of "return," *šûb*, throughout Jeremiah 34: First the Judeans "turned" (repented; 34:15) and proclaimed liberty to their slaves; then they "turned" (backslid; 34:11,16) and took them back as slaves, so God will make the Babylonians "turn" (return; 34:22) and destroy the city.

[6] The concatenation of "LORD," "God," "covenant," "fathers," "brought," and "Egypt" occurs in the MT only in Deut 29:25 and Jer 34:13.

EXAMPLE II: CONFLATION IN HISTORICAL NARRATIVE IN
JEREMIAH 34:8–13 (CONT.)

Pentateuchal Sources	Jer 34:14–16
Deut. 15:12 "If your brother, a Hebrew or a Hebrewess, is sold to you, he shall serve you six years, and in the seventh year you shall send him forth from you, free.	[14] 'At the end of six years each of you must send forth his Hebrew brother who has been sold to you and has served you six years; you must send him forth free from being with you'[7] . . .
1 Kings 8:43 "That all the peoples of the earth may know your name and fear you ... and that they may know that **this house that I have built is called by your name.**	[15]You recently *turned back* and did what was right in my eyes by proclaiming liberty, each to his neighbor, and you made a covenant before me **in the house which is called by my name;**[8] [16]but then you *turned back* around and profaned my name[9] when each of you took back his male and female slaves, whom you had set free according to their desire, and you brought them into subjection to be your slaves.
Lev. 22:32 And you shall not profane my holy name, but I will be hallowed among the people of Israel; I am the LORD . . .	

[7] Jeremiah 34:14 is virtually a quote of Deut 15:12.

[8] The phrase "house *called* by my name" is part of the Zion tradition and occurs elsewhere only in1 Kgs 8:43 and the parallel 1 Chr 6:33. Similar expression abound in the DtrH and Chronicler: 2 Sam 7:13; 1 Kgs 3:2; 5:3,5; 8:16-20, 29, 44, 48; 9:3,7; 2 Kgs 21:4,7; 23:27; 1 Chr 22:7-8; 22:10,19; 28:3; 29:16; 2 Chr 2:4; 6:5,7-10,20,34,38; 7:16,20; 20:9; 33:4,7.

[9] The expression "profane the name" (Heb. *hillēl et-šēm*) is absent from D and DtrH, but is very common in the Holiness Code (Lev 18:21; 19:12; 20:3; 21:6; 22:2,32) and Ezekiel (20:9,14,22,39; 36:20-23; 39:7).

EXAMPLE II: CONFLATION IN HISTORICAL NARRATIVE IN JEREMIAH 34:8–13 (CONT.)

Pentateuchal Sources	Jer 34:17
Lev. 25:10 And you shall . . . <u>proclaim liberty</u> throughout the land to all its inhabitants . . . Deut. 15:2 Every creditor shall release what he has lent to his neighbor; <u>he shall not exact it of his neighbor, his brother</u>, because the LORD's release has been proclaimed. Lev. 26:25 <u>And I will bring a *sword* upon you, that shall execute vengeance for the covenant; and if you gather within your cities I will send *pestilence* among you, and you shall be delivered into the hand of the enemy.</u> ²⁶ <u>When I *break your staff of bread*, ten women shall bake your bread in one oven.</u> . . . Deut. 28:25d <u>"You shall be a horror to all the kingdoms of the earth."</u>	¹⁷ Therefore, thus says the LORD: You have not obeyed me by <u>proclaiming liberty</u>, <u>every one to his brother and to his neighbor;</u>¹⁰ behold, <u>I proclaim to you liberty</u> to the *sword*, to *pestilence*, and to *famine*,¹¹ says the LORD. <u>I will make you a horror to all the kingdoms of the earth.</u>¹²

---

¹⁰ Jeremiah's "each to his brother and each to his neighbor" appears influenced by the debt release (Heb. *šĕmiṭṭâ*) law of Deut 15:1-6 (esp. v. 2) which is conceptually similar to both Lev 25:10-55 and Deut 15:12-18, and also the only Pentateuchal law that juxtaposes "brother" and "neighbor" in the same clause.

¹¹ The phrase "sword, pestilence, and famine" is a stock list of curses in Jeremiah (Jer 14:12; 15:2; 18:21; 21:7, 9; 24:10; 27:8,13; 29:17-18; 32:24,36; 34:17; 38:2; 42:17,22,13) absent from Deuteronomy, but may ultimately derive from the sequence of "sword" (Heb. *ḥereb*), "pestilence" (Heb. *deber*), and description of famine in the covenant curses of Lev 26:25-26. It also occurs in Ezek 5:17; 6:11; 7:15; 12:16; 14:21. Cf. esp. Lev 26:22-26//Ezek 14:21, where Ezekiel's dependence is clear.

¹² Essentially a quote of Deut 28:25d, also in Jer 15:4; 24:9; 29:18.

EXAMPLE II: CONFLATION IN HISTORICAL NARRATIVE IN
JEREMIAH 34:8–13 (CONT.)

Pentateuchal Sources	Jer 34:18-22
Gen. 15:7 "Bring me a heifer, . . . a she-goat, . . . a ram, . . . a turtle-dove, and a young pigeon." [13] And [Abram] brought him all these, cut them in two, and laid each half over against the other. . . . [17] When the sun had gone down and it was dark, behold, a smoking fire pot and a flaming torch passed between these pieces. [18] On that day the LORD made a covenant with Abram . . . Lev. 25:10 And you shall . . . proclaim liberty throughout the land to all its inhabitants; it shall be a jubilee for you, when each of you shall *turn back* to his property and each of you shall *turn back* to his family.	[18] And the men who transgressed my covenant and did not keep the terms of the covenant which they made before me, I will make like the calf which they cut in two and passed between its halves— [19] the princes of Judah, the princes of Jerusalem, the eunuchs, the priests, and all the people of the land who passed between the halves of the calf . . . [22] Behold, I will command, says the LORD, and will make them *turn back*[14] to **this city** and they will fight against it, and take it, and burn it with fire.

[13] The covenant ritual of passing between the parts of slain sacrificial animals in Jeremiah 34 bears some relationship to the covenant ritual of Gen 15:7-18, the only other place in the HB/OT where such a covenant-making rite occurs. "Half part" (Heb. *beter*) occurs in the MT only in Gen 15:10 and Jer 24:18-19.

[14] Jeremiah's final, ironic use of "turn back" or "return" (Heb. *šûb*) concludes his inversion of the Jubilee motif: rather than the Israelites "returning" to their lands, the Babylonians will "return" to destroy "this city," Jerusalem/Zion.

EXAMPLE III: CONFLATION IN A MT "PLUS" OF JEREMIAH
JER 33:20–22

Pentateuchal Sources	Jer 33:20-21b
Gen. 8:21 And when the LORD smelled the pleasing odor, the LORD said in his heart . . . 22 "While the earth remains, seedtime and harvest, cold and heat, summer and winter, **day and night**, shall not cease." 9:8 Then God said to Noah and to his sons with him, 9 "Behold, I establish my covenant with you and your descendants after you, 10 and with every living creature that is with you. . . 11 I establish my covenant with you, that never again shall all flesh be cut off by the waters of a flood . . . Ps 89:20 I have found David, my servant . . . 28 My steadfast love I will keep for him for ever, and my covenant will stand firm for him. 29 I will establish his line forever and his throne as the days of the heavens . . . 36 His line shall endure for ever, his throne as long as the **sun** before me. 37 Like the **moon** it shall be established for ever; it shall stand firm while the skies endure."	20 "Thus says the LORD: If you can break my covenant with the **day and** my covenant with the **night**, so that **day and night** will not come at their appointed time,[1] 21 then also my covenant with David my servant may be broken, so that he shall not have a son to reign on his throne . . .[2]

[1] Jeremiah's "covenant with the day and with the night" has to be a reference to the creation covenant renewed with Noah, drawing on the language of Gen 8:20–9:17, most of which is traditionally attributed to the Priestly source. Jeremiah's association of the Davidic covenant with Noah's "covenant with the day and night" may have been catalyzed by texts like Ps 89:36-37, which may already have been traditional by Jeremiah's day, where the Davidic covenant is as firm as the *sun* and the *moon* and the cycles of the *skies* and the *heavens*.

[2] Jeremiah's language about the Davidic covenant is traditional and reflected in several biblical texts. Psalm 89, which we have excerpted in the left column, closely represents the same concepts.

EXAMPLE III: CONFLATION IN A MT "PLUS" OF JEREMIAH (CONT.) JER 33:20–22

Pentateuchal Sources	Jer 33:21-22
Deut. 18:1 "The *Levitical priests*, all the tribe of Levi, shall have no portion or inheritance with Israel . . . Deut. 21:5 Then *the priests, the sons of Levi*, shall come forward, for the LORD your God has chosen them *to minister to him* . . . Gen. 22:16 "By myself I have sworn . . .¹⁷ I will multiply your seed as the stars of heaven and as the sand which is on the seashore. Gen. 15:5 And [God] said, "Look toward heaven, and number the stars, if you are able to number them." Then he said to him, "So shall your seed be." Gen. 32:12 I will do you good, and make your seed as the sand of the sea, which cannot be numbered for multitude.	²¹ Then also my covenant with David my servant may be broken, so that he shall not have a son to reign on his throne, and my covenant with the *Levitical priests my ministers*.[3] ²² As the host of heaven cannot be numbered and the sands of the sea cannot be measured, so I will multiply the seed[4] of David my servant, and the *Levitical priests who minister to me*."

---

[3] "Levitical priests," *hakkōhǎnîm halwîyim*, is a Deuteronomism (Deut 17:9,18; 18:1; 24:8; 27:9; Josh 3:3; 8:33) absent from priestly texts but borrowed in Jer 33:18,21,22 and Ezek 43:19; 44:15. In P, Levites minister (*š-r-t*) to Aaron and sons (Num 3:6; 8:26; 18:2); but in Jeremiah as in Deuteronomy the Levites minister to the LORD (Deut 10:8; 18:7; 21:5).

[4] Jeremiah 33:22 seems to point directly to Gen 22:16-17, the solemnization of the Abrahamic covenant by divine oath, the only two places "sand" (*ḥôl*), "heavens" (*šāmayim*), and "I will multiply seed" (*'arbbeh zera'*) concur in the MT. Jeremiah respecifies the Abrahamic covenant promises to the House of David. We also see the influence of other statements of the Abrahamic promises (Gen 15:5; 32:12) that emphasize the infinite number of both the stars and the sand, respectively.

Discussion. *Example I.* The pericope Jer 2:20–25, begins with an evocation of Lev 26:13, a locution that may have been well known, since it was the last statement of the covenantal blessings section of the Holiness Code (Lev 26:13). The verb "break," *šābar*, with "yoke," *'ōl*, as its object occurs outside of Jeremiah only in Lev 26:13 and the quotation of Lev 26:13 in Ezek 34:27. Jeremiah both employs and develops this image of the broken yoke more than any other biblical author, especially in Jer 28 (see verses 2, 4, and 11). Jeremiah uses the expression ironically in Jer 5:5 to describe Israel's rebellion rather than God's liberation, but in Jer 30:8 his re-deployment of the motif is very similar to its original sense in Lev 26:13, essentially promising a future realization of God's liberation, which was actualized in the past in a singular way through the Exodus from Egypt.

In Jer 2:20, the prophet splits his Pentateuchal source stich, "I have broken the bars of your yoke," into a classic Hebrew bicola: "I broke your yoke//I burst your bonds."[42] But then there is a contrast. Whereas Lev 26:13 speaks of God freeing Israel so that they should not serve the Egyptians ("that you should not be their servants"), Jeremiah continues by insisting Israel refused to serve the LORD ("but you said, 'I will not serve'"). Jeremiah now inserts a Deuteronomism describing the promiscuity of Israel's idolatry ("upon every high hill and under every green tree," Jer 2:20//Deut 12:2), and concludes with an inversion of the Holiness Codes' description of the Exodus: whereas God freed Israel from Egypt so that they could walk "erect" (*qômemîyût*), Israel of her own free will has decided to "bend over" (*ṣō'āh*) like a harlot.

God insists that, in keeping with divine purity laws governing planting and forbidding mixed seed in vineyards (Deut 22:9), he had planted Israel as a "choice vine, wholly of pure seed." Nonetheless, she changed into a wild vine. Jeremiah switches metaphors to that of washing, using "*kābas*," a characteristic term of the priestly texts for washing for ritual cleanliness, to describe Israel's inability to wash herself clean: her iniquity will always remain.[43] The only texts outside of Jer 2:22 that correlate washing with iniquity are Lev 17:16 and Ps 51:2. Leviticus 17:16 insists that if a man *does not* wash or bathe, his iniquity remains; Jeremiah insists that *even if* Israel washes *with lye and soap*, her iniquity remains, so Jeremiah may be intending a heightened contrast over against Lev 17:16 or the priestly principles reflected in that text.

---

42 This practice of constructing a bicola of a single source line can also be observed in Ezekiel: for example, Lev 26:4a "Then I will give you your rains in their season," becomes in Ezek 34:26: "I will send down the rains in their season//they shall be rains of blessing."

43 Of 48 total occurrences in the Hebrew Bible, 41 (approx. 85%) are in priestly texts from Exod 19:10 to Num 31:24. *Kābas* never occurs in Deuteronomy and only once in DtrH (2 Sam 19:24).

Finally, in Jer 2:23–25, the prophet presents Israel as a wife who denies that she is sexually defiled from chasing other men. The use of "defiled," *ṭāmē᾽*, in the passive/reflexive *niphal* stem evokes the one passage of the Hebrew Bible with the highest concentration of this specific form of the verb (7x), the ritual ordeal for the wife suspected of adultery but without clear evidence (Num 5:11–31). This legislation describes a sacred ordeal administered by the priest for a woman who denies adultery but is suspected of it by her husband. Israeli Bible scholar Dalit Rom-Shiloni of Tel Aviv University argues persuasively that Jer 2:23–25 evokes this priestly pericope, based on (1) the use of the uncommon *nip῾al* of "defiled" (*ṭāmē᾽*); (2) the shared theme of the wife "going astray," stated in Num 5:12 and described very graphically in Jer 2:23–25; and (3) the shared image of "iniquity," (*῾āwōn)* that remains (Num 5:31; Jer 2:22).[44]

Example II. Our second example comes from the historical narrative of Jeremiah. Our passage Jeremiah 34:8–22 is a very well-known example of a literary reworking of texts of the Torah, and the passage has been analyzed by many scholars including Martin David, Nahum Sarna, Bernard Levinson, Mark Leuchter, Simeon Chavel, Moshé Anbar, Kenneth Bergland, John Bergsma, and others.[45] No one disputes the obvious fact that Jeremiah reworks the manumission law of the Deuteronomic Code, Deut 15:12–18. More recent work has recognized the presence of terms and concepts in common with the Holiness Code as well, leading some (Leuchter, Chavel, Anbar) to try to make Jeremiah 34 a middle term between Deut 15:12–18

---

[44] Dalit Rom-Shiloni, "'How can you say, "I am not defiled . . ."?' (Jeremiah 2:20–25): Allusions to Priestly Legal Traditions in the Poetry of Jeremiah," *Journal of Biblical Literature* 133 (2014): 757–75.

[45] Some significant contributions include Martin David, "The Manumission of Slaves under Zedekiah," *Oudtestamentische studiën* 5 (1948): 63–79; Johannes B. Baur, "The Law of Manumission in Jer 34," *Biblische Zeitschrift* 15 (1971): 105–8; Nahum Sarna, "Zedekiah's Emancipation of Slaves and the Sabbatical Year," in *Occident and Orient: Essays Presented to C. H. Gordon on the Occasion of his Sixty-Fifth Birthday*, ed. Harry A. Hoffner, Jr. (Neukirchen-Vluyn: Neukirchener Verlag, 1973), 143–49; Niels P. Lemche, "The Manumission of Slaves—The Fallow Year—The Sabbatical Year—The Jobel Year," *Vetus Testamentum* 26 (1976): 38–59, esp. 51–53; Innocenzo Cardellini, *Die biblischen "Sklaven"-Gesetze im Lichte des keilschriftlichen Sklavenrechts: ein Beitrag zur Tradition, Überlieferung und Redaktion der alttestamentlichen Rechtstexte* (Königstein: Hanstein, 1981), 312–21; Patrick D. Miller, "Sin and Judgment in Jeremiah 34:17–19," *Journal of Biblical Literature* 103 (1984): 611–23; Simeon Chavel, "'Let My People Go!': Emancipation, Revelation, and Scribal Activity in Jeremiah 34:8–14," *Journal for the Study of the Old Testament* 76 (1997): 71–95; Moshé Anbar, "La liberation des esclaves en temps de guerre: Jer 34 et ARM XXVI.363," *Zeitschrift für die alttestamentliche Wissenschaft* 111 (1999): 253–55; Bergsma, *Jubilee*, 160–70; Kenneth Bergland, "Jeremiah 34 Originally Composed as a Legal Blend of Leviticus 25 and Deuteronomy 15," in *Paradigm Change*, 189–205.

and Lev 25:10–55 in the development of biblical manumission law. This is special pleading, however, because Jeremiah is the conflationary text that includes diction and concepts from both the others, whereas Deut 15:12–18 and Lev 25:10–55 do not betray any literary dependence on one another or on Jeremiah 34.[46] According to standard principles of literary analysis (as articulated by Carr, for example), conflation is a key sign of dependence. Therefore, Jeremiah, as the only conflated text of the three, must be considered diachronically as the last rather than the intermediate text.[47]

In Jer 34:8–22, we first recognize the centrality of Jerusalem to the historical setting and even the theology of this pericope, a centrality lacking in the Pentateuch, which never mentions Jerusalem or Zion at all. Like Ezekiel, Jeremiah incorporates Jerusalem and Zion theology into texts interwoven from different Pentateuchal literary corpora.

At the start of the pericope, Jeremiah describes a recent edict of Zedekiah in language from the Jubilee legislation of Lev 25:10: *qārā᾽ dĕrôr*, "proclaim liberty," a rare phrase found only in Lev 25:10 and a handful of prophetic texts dependent on it (Jer 34:8, 15, 17; Isa 61:1; cf. Ezek 46:17 [*šĕnat dĕrôr*, "year of liberty"]).[48] But the rest of the decree description is filled in with language from Deuteronomy 15:12–18 (e.g. *šālaḥ ḥopšî*, "to send forth free," Deut 15:12, 13, 18). What is particularly distinctive is Jeremiah's reuse of the rare phrase "Hebrew or Hebrewess," which is unique to these two passages, Deuteronomy 15 and Jeremiah 34. In fact, the term "Hebrewess" in the singular is only used in Jer 34:9 and Deut 15:12 in the entire Hebrew Bible.

Throughout the passage, Jeremiah engages in wordplay with the two central actions of the Jubilee year as stated in Lev 25:10—to proclaim liberty (*qārā᾽ dĕrôr*) and to "return" (*šûb*) everyone to his family and property. But the Hebrew "*šûb*" has a wide range of meanings. We rendered it "turn back" in our example table, an expression that can communicate most of the nuances of this word, which include "turn," "turn around," "turn back," "backslide," "return," and "repent." Jeremiah exploits all these senses in Jer 34:8–22 in order to convey an impression of the fittingness or poetic

---

[46] On the independence of Deut 15:12–18 and Lev 25:10–55 from each other, see Bergsma, "The Biblical Manumission Laws," in *A Teacher for All Generations: Essays in Honor of James C. VanderKam*, vol. 1, ed. Eric F. Mason, Samuel I. Thomas, Alison Schofield, and Eugene Ulrich (Leiden, NL: Brill, 2012), 65–89.

[47] Thus Bernard M. Levinson: "This text is a response to the legal sources of the Pentateuch, not a transition point between them" ("Zedekiah's Release of Slaves as the Babylonians Besiege Jerusalem: Jeremiah 34 and the Formation of the Pentateuch," in *The Fall of Jerusalem and the Rise of the Torah*, ed. Dominik Markl, Jean-Pierre Sonnet, and Peter Dubovský [Tübingen: Mohr Siebeck, 2016], 319).

[48] See Bergsma, *Jubilee*, 164.

justice in God's eventual judgment on the people: God's punishment fits their crime. The basic plot is this: At first, the people "repent" (*šûb*) and "proclaim liberty" to their slaves. Then, they "backslide" (*šûb*) and take back all their slaves. Therefore, God "proclaims liberty" to them—a liberty to "sword, pestilence, and famine"! (This is a traditional sequence of covenant curses articulated in that order in Lev 26:25–26, but Jeremiah adds a nearly verbatim covenant curse from Deut 28:25: "I will make you a horror to all the kingdoms of the earth" Jer 34:17d.) Then the Babylonians will "return" (*šûb*) and destroy the city! So we see that the author of Jer 34:8–22 has built up the entire passage in dialogue with two key phrases and concepts from the Jubilee legislation of the Holiness Code. Meanwhile, he intersperses phrases from the Zion tradition like "the house which is called by name" (Jer 34:15//1 Kgs 8:43) and other motifs from the Holiness Code, like "profane my name" (Jer 34:16; cf. Lev 18:21; 19:12; 20:3; 21:6; 22:2, 32). Near the end of the pericope, we have a curious connection with Gen 15:7–21, the "Covenant Between the Pieces," as Jeremiah's contemporaries are portrayed as engaging in a very similar covenant-making ritual.

In the end, we come to recognize that Jer 34:8–22 is a literary mosaic consisting of "tiles" from Pentateuchal texts and the Zion tradition arranged artistically to form a composition.

Example III. Our third text is an excerpt from an oracle, Jer 33:14–26, that belongs to that set of oracles omitted from the LXX of Jeremiah, which could therefore be suspected of being added by later redactors.[49] However, the precipitating *Sitz-im-Leben* of the oracle is the people's abandonment of any confidence in the priesthood or royal house (Jer 33:24), a very natural reaction in the immediate aftermath of the decimation of the royal house and exile of the king (Jer 52:8–11), the destruction of the Temple (Jer 52:12–23), and the execution of the chief priests and royal officers (Jer 52:24–27). In other words, the existential situation that provoked the composition of this oracle would have taken place in the lifetime of the prophet, so there is no pressing need to date it decades later. Furthermore, all the themes of this oracle are attested in parts of Jeremiah that *are* found in the LXX. For the perdurance of the Levitical priesthood, see Jer 38:14 LXX (=31:14 MT): "μεγαλυνῶ καὶ μεθύσω τὴν ψυχὴν τῶν ἱερέων υἱῶν Λευι." For the perdurance of the Davidic dynasty, see Jer 37:8–9 LXX (=30:8–9 MT) and Jer 23:5–6 (LXX/MT). If it is the work of later redactors, they have maintained the style and thought of the rest of Jeremiah. For this and other reasons, no less an authority than Emanuel Tov argues Jer 33:14–26 is

---

[49] See the discussion in Gerald L. Keown, Pamela J. Scalise, and Thomas G. Smothers, *Jeremiah 26–52* (WBC 27; Grand Rapids: Zondervan, 1995), 172–73.

genuine Jeremianic material that was accidently omitted from the Hebrew *Vorlage* of LXX Jeremiah.[50]

Our chosen excerpt is an affirmation of God's covenant fidelity to the priestly house of Levi and the royal house of David. It begins with a reference to the creation covenant that was renewed with Noah in Genesis 8:20–9:17 (sometimes called the "Noahic" covenant), which is usually classified as a predominantly priestly text because of certain distinctive priestly diction (e.g. *rēaḥ nîḥōaḥ*, "a pleasing aroma," 8:21) and the extensive references to the so-called Priestly account of creation, Gen 1:1–2:3. The text of Jeremiah speaks of God's "covenant with the day and the night" such that they will always "come at their appointed time," a clear reference to the divine promise of Gen 8:22 that "while earth remains … day and night shall not cease." It then draws an analogy between God's faithfulness to this creational covenant and his fidelity to the Davidic covenant, described in terms characteristic of the Zion tradition as reflected in the Psalms (e.g. Ps. 89:34–37) and various passages of the historical books (i.e. DtrH). It is not just David's covenant but also the Levitical covenant that is unbreakable, as the text incorporates key phrases and concepts from Deuteronomy: "and my covenant with the *Levitical priests my ministers*." This odd phrase "Levitical priests," *hakkōhănîm halwîyim*, is a clear Deuteronomism[51] absent from any priestly texts but borrowed by both Jeremiah (33:18, 21, 22) and Ezekiel (43:19; 44:15). Then, the "Levitical priests" are defined as "my ministers," which is a concept from Deuteronomy, which describes the Levites as "ministers to the LORD"[52] whereas texts of the Pentateuch attributed to the Priestly Source describe the Levites as ministers to Aaron and his sons.[53]

Thus, in vv. 20–21 we observe references to three covenants: the Noahic, the Davidic, and the Levitical. In verse 22, there is a clear evocation of the Abrahamic covenant, in which God promised, "I will multiply your seed as the stars of the heaven and as the sand which is on the seashore" (Gen 22:16). Jeremiah 33:22 reworks this promise under the influence of similar Abrahamic covenant texts (Gen 15:5; 32:12) and respecifies the recipients to be not just any "seed" or descendants of Abraham, but specifically the seed of David and Levi: "As the host of heaven cannot be numbered and the sands of the sea cannot be measured, so I will multiply the seed of David my servant and the Levitical priests who minister to me."

Thus, in the space of three verses, we observe the phenomenon seen so

---

50 Emanuel Tov, "The Literary History of the Book of Jeremiah in the Light of its Textual History," in *Empirical Models for Biblical Criticism*, ed. Jeffrey H. Tigay (Philadelphia, PA: University of Pennsylvania Press, 1985), 216.

51 Deut 17:9, 18; 18:1; 24:8; 27:9; Josh 3:3; 8:33.

52 Cf. Deut 10:8; 18:5, 7; 21:5.

53 Cf. Num 3:6; 8:26; 18:2.

often elsewhere in Jeremiah and Ezekiel: the interweaving of Priestly and Deuteronomic texts and theology with those of the Zion tradition (i.e. the Davidic covenant). The text is almost completely composed of words and phrases lifted from earlier sacred texts, but that is not to say Jeremiah makes no innovations. The concept of God's relationship with the "Levitical priests" as a *covenant* may be implied (cf. Num 25:13)—but is never stated—in the Pentateuch. Only a few late biblical texts make explicit mention of a "covenant with Levi" (Neh 13:29; Mal 2:4, 8); Jer 33:21 may in fact be the first (i.e. oldest) biblical text to do so. So, while reusing older sacred texts, Jeremiah is also developing their thought and making explicit that which was previously only implicit: that the relationship between the LORD and the tribe of Levi constituted a formal covenant.

Finally, it should be clear from all the examples we have examined from both Ezekiel and Jeremiah that it will not do to try to eliminate either the Priestly or the Deuteronomic elements from these texts by recourse to an imaginary "Priestly" or "Deuteronomistic" redactor. Elements from both these Pentateuchal corpora are embedded and interwoven deeply into both the thought and the diction of several of these examples, such that to remove them would eviscerate the pericope of its force and purpose. Removing the allusions to Deuteronomy 12 from Ezekiel 20, for example, would rip the heart out of the prophet's message; and with respect to Jeremiah 34, Bergland has demonstrated in detail how neither source can be eliminated without reducing the pericope to a husk.[54]

OTHER PROPHETS AND THE PENTATEUCH

There is not space here to provide closely analyzed examples from every prophetic book, nor is such necessary. It will suffice to make some reference to the literature on the dependence of some of the other prophetic books on the Torah/Pentateuch.

In the case of Isaiah, we are in need of more scholarship on the relationship of the first part of the book, Isa 1–39, to the Pentateuch, although there is good reason to expect such work to bear fruit. Key passages of the first part of Isaiah, such as Isaiah 11, clearly draw on Zion theology (Isa 11:1–5//2 Sam 7:12–16), Edenic/Creation imagery (Isa 11:6–9//Gen 1:29–30 & 2:8–14), and Exodus traditions (Isa 11:10–15//Exod 14:21–22). However, work remains to be done to determine if such allusions are to specific

---

[54] See Bergland, "Jeremiah 34," esp. 199–202, where he graphically demonstrates what would result to the text from the removal of references to either of its primary Pentateuchal sources.

texts or simply to commonly known traditions. In the case of the second half of the book (Isaiah 40–66), more has been written on possible literary dependency on Pentateuchal sources. Michael Fishbane has argued that several passage of Isaiah[55] draw from the so-called "Priestly" creation story of Gen 1:1–2:4a.[56] He also argues Isaiah 58 betrays awareness and reuse of ideas and language from the Jubilee legislation of Lev 25:10–55 and the Day of Atonement regulations Lev 16:1–34.[57] Klaus Baltzer argues that the Isaianic "Servant" is modeled on the figure of Moses, and that there are specific catch-words and allusions to Pentateuchal texts scattered among the Servant Songs.[58] Benjamin Sommer has dedicated a monograph, *A Prophet Reads Scripture*, to analyzing the way that the prophetic author reads, interprets, and redeploys older Israelite sacred texts.[59] Sommer identifies the following Pentateuchal texts reflected in specific passages of Isaiah: Isa 40:18//Gen 1:26; Isa 40:28//Gen 2:2; Isa 45:6–7//Gen 1:1–3; Isa 45:14–19//Deut 33:26–29; Isa 45:18–19//Gen 1:2; Isa 50:1//Deut 24:1–3; Isa 51:2//Gen 22:15–17; Isa 56:1–8//Exod 31:12–16; Isa 58:11–14//Deut 32:9–13; Isa 59:8–10//Deut 28:28–29; Isa 61:1//Lev 25:10; Isa 61:5–6 & 56:4–7//Num 18:1–10, 22; Isa 63:8–9//Exod 23:20, 23 & 33:14–15.

Moving to the minor prophets, many have proposed a literary relationship of some kind between Hosea and earlier Israelite Scriptures.[60] In fact, the obvious and pervasive dependence of the preaching of Hosea on references to the sacred history of Israel was immediately seized upon by opponents of Wellhausen in order to argue against his theory.[61] Hosea seems to presume

---

[55] Isa 40:18, 13–14, 25, 28; 42:5; 44:24; 45:7, 18; 46:5.

[56] Michael Fishbane, *Biblical Interpretation in Ancient Israel* (Oxford, UK: Clarendon Press, 1985), 322–26.

[57] Fishbane, *Biblical Interpretation*, 304–7.

[58] Klaus Baltzer, *Deutero-Isaiah: A Commentary on Isaiah 40–55* (Minneapolis, MN: Fortress Press, 2001), 18–22 and throughout.

[59] Benjamin Sommer, *A Prophet Reads Scripture: Allusion in Isaiah 40–66* (Stanford, CA: Stanford University Press, 1997).

[60] See, for example, Dwight R. Daniels, *Hosea and Salvation History: The Early Traditions of Israel in the Prophecy of Hosea* (Berlin: de Gruyter, 1990); Else K. Holt, *Prophesying the Past: The Use of Israel's History in the Book of Hosea* (Sheffield, UK: Sheffield Academic Press, 1995); Jerry Hwang, "'I Am Yahweh Your God from the Land of Egypt': Hosea's Use of the Exodus Traditions," in *Did I Not Bring Israel*, 243–53; Heinz-Dieter Neef, *Die Heilstraditionen Israels in der Verkündigung des Propheten Hosea* (Berlin: de Gruyter, 1987).

[61] See Stanely Leathes, *The Law in the Prophets* (London: Eyre and Spottiswoode, 1891); Umberto Cassuto, "The Prophet Hosea and the Books of the Pentateuch," in *Biblical and Oriental Studies*, trans. Israel Abrahams (Jerusalem: Magnes Press, 1973), 79–100. A partial list of parallel passages would include: Hos 1:2//Lev 19:29; Hos 1:2–9//Exod 34:15–16; Hos 1:9//Exod 3:14; 6:7; 2:17; 12:9,13; 13:4; Hos 2:1//Gen 15:5; 22:17; Deut 32:8; Hos 2:2//Deut 30:3; Hos 2:4–15//Deut 24:1–4; Hos 2:9//Deut 28:45; Hos 2:20//

that his readership has a strong familiarity with the sacred history of Israel in a way not discernibly different from how it is presented in the Pentateuch; in fact, the author of Hosea is arguably engaged in an interpretive actualization of Israel's traditional Scriptures for his contemporaries.[62] This phenomenon has sparked studies of Hosea's hermeneutical techniques by Cassuto, Fishbane, Rooker, and Bass.[63] The evidence of Hosea's dependence on Pentateuchal sources is particularly significant, since the prophet ministered not in Judah but Northern Israel, and in a time period prior to the reign of Josiah, with which the publication of Deuteronomy is often tied. According to Wellhausen's paradigm, Deuteronomy should not be in existence during the career of Hosea. Yet Hosea appears to depend on Deuteronomy as well as other parts of the Pentateuch, including texts Wellhausen attributed to P and H.

Some scholars have tried to maintain Wellhausen's paradigm in the face of this evidence by making Hosea the forerunner of the Deuteronomic movement, a kind of proto-Deuteronomist. However, the evidence doesn't lend itself to a direction of dependence from Hosea to Deuteronomy, in part because Hosea frequently exhibits ironic or negative reversals or inversions of his Deuteronomic source, which makes sense in the context of his proclamation of judgment.[64] It is difficult to imagine, however, a Deuteronomic author undoing Hosea's irony in order to produce positive oracles. This same phenomenon appears in Jeremiah and Ezekiel, where it also seems to indicate the prophetic dependence on the Law, and not vice-versa.[65] In a recent review of the arguments for different directions of dependence, Carsten Vang concludes that Hosea's dependence on a written

---

     Gen 1:30; Hos 3:1//Deut 31:18, 20; Hos 4:2//Decalogue; Hos 4:5, 5:5b//Lev 26:37; Hos 4:10, 13:6//Lev 26:26; Hos 4:13//Deut 12:2; Hos 5:2b//Lev 26: 18, 28; Hos 5:10// Deut 27:17; Hos 5:14, 13:7–8 // 26:22; Hos 5:15–6:1//Deut 4:29–30; Hos 6:11//Deut 30:3; Hos 8:1//Deut 28:49; Hos 8:3//Lev 26:36; Deut 28:25,31,48, 53, 55, 57, 68; Deut 30:7; Hos 9:3–4//Deut 26:14; Hos 9:10//Num 25:1–5; Hos 9:11,16//Deut 28:18; Hos 9:17//Deut 28:40, 64; Hos 9:15–17//Deut 28:62–64 (ibid., 52–65) Hos 11:1//Exodus from Egypt; Deut 7:7–8; Deut 14:11; Hos 11:6,13:16//Lev 26:25; Hos 12:3–5, 13//Gen 25:11–35:22; Hos 12:14//Deut 18:15,18; Hos 13:2//Deut 4:16–18; Hos 13:6//Deut 8:12–14; Hos 14:2–5//Deut 30:1–10; Hos 14:4//Deut 4:28; Hos 14:9//Deut 29:16–28.

[62] See David Drummond Bass, "Hosea's Use of Scripture: An Analysis of His Hermeneutics," (Ph.D. diss., Southern Baptist Theological Seminary, 2009), 2–4.

[63] See Cassuto, *Biblical and Oriental Studies*, 79–140; Fishbane, *Biblical Interpretation*, 298–300; 360–62, 376–79; Michael Lee Catlett, "Reversals in Hosea: A Literary Analysis" (Ph.D. diss., Emory University, 1988); Mark F. Rooker, "The Use of the Old Testament in the Book of Hosea," *Criswell Theological Review* 7 (1993) 51–66; Bass, "Hosea's Use of Scripture."

[64] See Catlett, "Reversals in Hosea."

[65] See discussion above in n. 338.

text of Deuteronomy is the best explanation of the literary evidence for a number of reasons, including the presence in Hosea of the "splitting" phenomenon also seen in Jeremiah and Ezekiel, in which a single stich from a source text—in this case, Deuteronomy—is split and augmented to create a classic Hebrew bicola.[66] Vang's case could be bolstered by the observation that Hosea is a *conflate text* with respect to Deuteronomy, since Hosea also reflects concepts and even specific language from priestly-holiness texts (e.g. Hos 1:2//Lev 19:29; Hos 4:5, 5:5//Lev 26:37) that are completely absent from Deuteronomy.

The other minor prophets may be dealt with more quickly. Several are quite brief and occasional in nature, and thus one cannot expect much in the way of intertextual allusions and references. Nonetheless, evidence of dependence on different Pentateuchal corpora is not absent.

Micah includes many possible echoes or allusions to various Pentateuchal laws (e.g. Mic 1:7; 2:2; 3:11; 5:12–14; 6:11–12; 7:3, 6), and a very specific reference to the narrative of Balak, Balaam, and the Beth-Peor incident in Num 22–25 (Mic 6:5).

Habakkuk likewise displays a number of allusions to both Priestly and Deuteronomic texts: Hab 1:3//Num 23:21; Hab 1:8//Deut 28:49–50; Hab 2:15–16//Gen 9:20–27.

Zephaniah opens with what seems to be an intentional evocation of the Flood narrative (Zeph 1:2–3//Gen 6:7, 7:4) followed by a rebuke of Israel for violation of various Pentateuchal prohibitions (e.g. Zeph 1:5//Deut 4:19, Lev 18:21, 20:2–5).

Haggai appears to allude to the covenant curses of Deuteronomy (Hag 1:6, 10–11//Deut 28:48, 51) and his questions to the priests (Hag 2:10–14) presuppose the principles of cleanliness and holiness of the priestly legislation (Num 19:13; Num 18:8, 18; Exod 29:27–34, 37; Lev 6:27).

Malachi interacts substantially with Mosaic legislation: Fishbane studies the reuse and reinterpretation of Num 6:23–27 in Mal 1:6–2:9,[67] and Hugenberger argues Mal 2:15–16 draws on Gen 2:20–24 for its view of marriage.[68] We see references to many moral and social justice laws of the Pentateuch in Mal 3:5, and the subsequent verses (Mal 3:6–12) are dependent on the tithing laws of the Torah (Lev 27:30; Num 18:21–28; Deut 12:6–17; Deut 14:22–28; 26:12–14). Malachi 3:17–18 evokes both Exod

---

[66] Carsten Vang, "When a Prophet Quotes Moses: On the Relationship Between the Book of Hosea and Deuteronomy," in *Sepher Torath Mosheh: Studies in the Interpretation of Deuteronomy*, ed. Daniel I. Block and Richard L. Schultz (Peabody, MA: Hendrickson, 2017), 295.

[67] Fishbane, *Biblical Interpretation*, 332–34.

[68] Gordon P. Hugenberger, *Marriage as Covenant: Biblical Law and Ethics as Developed from Malachi* (Leiden, NL: Brill, 1994), 124–67.

19:5–6 and Exod 4:22–23. Finally, Mal 4:4, in what is probably the touch of the redactor of the minor prophets, shows that those who treasured and curated the Book of the Twelve[69] understood these prophets as heralds who called for fidelity to the covenant of Moses and all its commandments.

Thus, our brief survey of the books of Isaiah and the Twelve reveal that, although the density of references to the Pentateuch is less in some cases, the same phenomena observed in Ezekiel and Jeremiah holds with these prophetic works as well: a conflation of several Pentateuchal *corpora*, including Deuteronomy and the Priestly/Holiness tradition, as well as Pentateuchal texts Wellhausen ascribed to other sources.

MOVE THE PROPHETS LATER STILL?

Many scholars over the past century have come to recognize, upon studying the prophetic literature, that Wellhausen's "Prophets before the Law" paradigm is just untenable as an explanation for the literary relationships. But their response has been to continue to accept Wellhausen's dating of the priestly legislation to the sixth through fifth centuries BCE and move the prophetic books—or at least the extensive redaction of them—*even later still*.[70] This is ironic, since Wellhausen appealed to the supposed absence of references to the Law in the prophetic literature as evidence of the Law's late date. Now the *reason* for the dating is rejected, but the dating continues to be accepted and used to place the prophets into a time period of Israel's history in which they are very much out of place.

We will cite examples of this procedure from Ezekiel. Ezekiel scholar Michael Konkel of the University of Tübingen is a good example of the tendency, especially in Continental scholarship, to retain Wellhausen's dates even after rejecting Wellhausen's reasoning. Konkel engages in extensive redaction-critical work on Ezekiel, dividing the book into many editorial layers over a long time period.[71] He makes no pretense of using literary-critical markers to distinguish the late layers of Ezekiel's work, but baldly admits it is merely the presence of dependence on the Priestly Source that leads

---

[69] It is generally understood that the twelve minor prophets circulated together as a single composite book written on one scroll in antiquity.

[70] Benjamin Kilchör discusses this phenomenon in his article "Überlegungen zum Verhältnis zwischen Levitikus 26 und Ezechiel und die tempeltheologische Relevanz der Abhängigkeitsrichtung" ("Reflections on the Relationship between Leviticus 26 and Ezekiel and the Relevance of the Direction of Dependence for the Temple-Theology"), *Zeitschrift für altorientalisch und biblische Rechtsgeschichte* 24 (2018): 295–306, esp. 295–306.

[71] See Konkel, *Architektonik des Heiligen*.

him to distinguish those parts of Ezekiel as "late" and "redactional."[72] To our mind, this is a completely unacceptable case of re-arranging data to fit a paradigm, rather than revising the paradigm to accommodate the data. Furthermore, Konkel and others appear to lose sight of the forest for the trees—that is, lost in imaginative redactional-critical scenarios concerning individual pericopes, they fail to ask the question whether a document like Ezekiel, in either its LXX or MT form, really *fits* anywhere in Jewish society of the fifth or fourth centuries? Let us simply *read* the MT Ezekiel, for example: it is a document *unrelentingly* concerned with the issues of Judah and the Judean exiles in the *sixth century*, and it concludes with *wildly inaccurate* predictions about the character of the imminent restoration of the nation of Israel, and an extensive body of legislation (Ezek 40–48) largely *at odds with the legislation of Moses*. Why would any priestly author of fifth- or fourth-century Jerusalem waste the time, ink, and parchment to compose a document which purports to be the *unfulfilled* predictions and *potentially heretical law code* of a sixth-century Israelite prophet?[73] The answer is: he wouldn't! Moreover, almost exactly the same question may be asked of those who place the redaction of Jeremiah in the post-exilic or Second Temple time period, with the difference that Jeremiah, at least, does not include a code of law at odds with Moses. Both Jeremiah and Ezekiel make *perfect* sense as compositions of the early- to mid-sixth-century Judean society, and the further their date of composition and redaction is moved from the sixth century, the *less* sense they make as literary and theological compositions.[74]

There is also the linguistic evidence. With respect to the Book of Ezekiel, Avi Hurvitz made the basic case for recognizing the language of the book as

---

[72] See Michael Konkel, review of *The Book of Ezekiel: Chapters 25–48*, by Daniel I. Block, *Biblische Zeitschrift* 44 (2000): 296–98. For a revealing discussion of Konkel's views, see Benjamin Kilchör, "Wellhausen's Five Pillars for the Priority of D of P/H: Can They Still Be Maintained?," in *Paradigm Change*, 101–11, esp. 108.

[73] Indeed, Konkel admits that he cannot propose a realistic setting or author for Ezekiel according to his reconstruction, nor for the Priestly literature either: "This leads to the question of supporters behind the texts [of Ezekiel and P]. Today, it is more difficult than ever to answer it. . . . Who were these priestly groups, who wrote these late Fortschreibungen of Lev and Num [sic]? It's hard to believe that Zadokite priests should not have been involved in forming these texts. The intriguing question I want to ask Pentateuch researchers as a researcher in Ezekiel: Who the heck wrote P?" ("Ezekiel 40–48 and P," 14).

[74] For a coherent reading of Ezekiel as a sixth-century document, see Michael A. Lyons, *An Introduction to the Study of Ezekiel* (London: Bloomsbury T&T Clark, 2015). For Jeremiah, see Aaron Hornkohl, *Ancient Hebrew Periodization and the Language of the Book of Jeremiah: The Case for a Sixth-Century Date of Composition* (Leiden, NL: Brill, 2014). For both, see Dalit Rom-Shiloni, *Exclusive Inclusivity: Identity Conflicts between the Exiles and the People Who Remained (6th–5th Centuries BCE)*, Library of Hebrew Bible/Old Testament Studies 543 (New York: T&T Clark, 2013); and Rom-Shiloni, *Voices from the Ruins: Theodicy and the Fall of Jerusalem in the Hebrew Bible* (Grand Rapids: Eerdmans, 2021).

a form of transitional Hebrew between Standard Biblical Hebrew ("SBH," Genesis–Kings) and Late Biblical Hebrew ("LBH," Ezra-Nehemiah, Chronicles, Esther, Daniel, etc.) in a monograph published in 1982.[75] A decade later, Mark Rooker built on Hurvitz's work, including not just lexical but also grammatical and syntactical considerations in order to place the Hebrew of Ezekiel firmly in the sixth century in terms of linguistic development.[76] For Jeremiah, Aaron Hornkohl has performed a similar service, analyzing the linguistic data to place the book, as would be expected from its contents, in the late-pre-exilic and exilic period of Judah's history.[77] One of the best observations on the date and composition of the books of Ezekiel and Jeremiah comes from renowned American Catholic Old Testament scholar Lawrence Boadt, who devoted much of his long and illustrious career to the study of these prophets and was certainly aware of all the proposals for many stages of post-exilic redaction for their respective books. Nonetheless, a few years before the end of his life, Boadt addressed the Ezekiel section of the Society of Biblical Literature and declared his view:

> So much work has been done on this question that it need not be in doubt that the editorial process involved written materials both from and about the two prophets, and that both books were put together within a relatively short period of time. Ezekiel perhaps not much after 571, since there is no evidence of any awareness of the world of Second Isaiah after 547; and Jeremiah perhaps in the 550's after Jehoiachin's release.[78]

Thus, considerations of both linguistics and content lead to the conclusion that Jeremiah and Ezekiel are literary products of the first half of the sixth century BCE. Responsible historical reasoning would accept that as given data, and if these books show signs of extensive reuse and conflation of the material of Deuteronomy and the Priestly literature, then we should accept that both these literary corpora were in written form and considered authoritative *at least* by the late pre-exilic period.

---

[75] Avi Hurvitz, *A Linguistic Study of the Relationship between the Priestly Source and the Book of Ezekiel* (Paris: Gabalda, 1982).

[76] Mark F. Rooker, *Biblical Hebrew in Transition: The Language of the Book of Ezekiel* (Sheffield: JSOT Press, 1990).

[77] Hornkohl, *Ancient Hebrew Periodization*.

[78] Lawrence Boadt, "Do Jeremiah and Ezekiel Share a Common View of the Exile?" (paper presented at the annual meeting of the Society of Biblical Literature, Atlanta, 22 November 2003), 40.

CONCLUSION: THE PROPHETS BEFORE THE LAW OR THE LAW BEFORE THE PROPHETS?

Intellectual honesty requires us to recognize that Wellhausen's embrace of Graf's priority of the prophets over the law was never the result of careful studies of the literary parallels between these two bodies of literature and an objective adjudication of the question of direction of dependence. Rather, it was the product of the pleasing fit of the Graf-Kuenen hypothesis with Wellhausen's philosophical and theological commitments and biases. The hypothesis is counterintuitive and has proved to be an impediment and burden to biblical scholarship for more than a century. It was not until the twenty-first century, for example, that Ezekiel scholarship finally broke free of the shackles that forced Ezekiel to serve as a precursor of the Holiness Code, which continually rendered nonsensical the actual literary and theological relationship of the two works.

Using the two books of the sixth-century priest-prophets Ezekiel and Jeremiah, we have shown that both works exhibit many instances of the *conflation* of the distinctive diction and concepts of the Pentateuchal texts ascribed to the priestly and holiness schools on the one hand, and of Deuteronomy on the other. This phenomenon can also be seen in Isaiah 40–66, Hosea, and several others of the Twelve. *Yet, for the most part, we do not find conflation of "P" and "D" in the Pentateuch itself,*[79] in which a certain consistent set of terms and theological preferences prevails roughly from Exodus 25 through Numbers 36 (i.e. "P" and "H"), and then Deuteronomy represents a new and distinct literary and theological style.[80] This is strong

---

[79] On the distinction between the diction of the so-called "Priestly" materials of the Pentateuch and Deuteronomy, see Moshe Weinfeld, *Deuteronomy and the Deuteronomic School* (Oxford: Clarendon Press, 1972), esp. 179–89. On the *lack* of conflation of these styles in the Pentateuch itself, see Bergsma, "The Biblical Manumission Laws," in Mason, Thomas, Schofield, and Ulrich, ed., *A Teacher for All Generations,* 1:65–89; and Markus Zehnder, "Leviticus 26 and Deuteronomy 28," in *Paradigm Change,* 115–78.

[80] Notice that our analysis is not the same as Wellhausen's source-criticism, which was largely based on *narrative* texts in Genesis and then forced to fit the other Pentateuchal books. Our division of (roughly) Exodus 25–Numbers vs. Deuteronomy is largely based on *legal* texts. The content of Exodus 25–Numbers 36 and Deuteronomy consists mostly of cultic and civil laws and instructions. The canonical explanation of the difference in style and specifics between Exodus 25–Numbers 36 and Deuteronomy is (1) an elapse of time, (2) a change in context, and (3) a different rhetorical situation. The laws of Exodus 25 through Leviticus 27 are dictated by God to Moses on Sinai. Then various legal addenda are added through the wilderness wanderings in Numbers. According to the Pentateuch, Deuteronomy comprises legal material delivered orally by Moses to Israel *forty years after* Exod 25–Lev 27 was written down, in the context of the *imminent entrance to the land*, as part of Moses's pre-death *valedictory*. These are the canonical explanations for the difference in literary style and specific content.

evidence that, at least from the sixth century and probably from much earlier (based on the evidence of Hosea), both so-called "P" and so-called "D" were extant and considered authoritative for the people of Israel. Could they, at that time, have still been merely oral and not written sources? We think not, for at least two reasons.

First, the archaeological evidence shows that the seventh century BCE was a period of prosperity of the Kingdom of Judah, and by its end if not already much earlier, the level of literacy was very high.[81] There is no reason, then, that culturally authoritative texts would not have been written down during this century, and possibly much earlier, as it is often only an accident of history and archaeological preservation that provides us with the proof of literacy.[82] Secondly, the evidence of Ezekiel and Jeremiah shows that, already in the sixth century, authors *who were themselves priests or Levites* were freely mixing and interweaving the texts and concepts of both P and D. How then would we expect that other priestly authors writing centuries later would have either the *motivation* or the *capability* to strain a "pure" P/H strand out of the conflated traditions they had inherited in order to compose a "pure" P/H document free of all the language and concepts of "D" and the Zion tradition? The fact is that the parts of the Pentateuch typically attributed to the Priestly Source are *archaic* and *anachronistic* already in fifth- and fourth-century Judah. The primary concerns of the texts identified with P and D are not those of post-exilic Judaism and vice-versa, especially the fact that both P and D are absolutely unconcerned with Zion/Jerusalem, David, and the Temple, as we will demonstrate in subsequent chapters.

---

[81] See Israel Finklestein, "Jerusalem and Judah 600–200 BCE: Implications for Understanding Pentateuchal Texts," in *The Fall of Jerusalem and the Rise of Torah*, ed. Peter Dubovsky, et al., Forschungen zum Alten Testament 107 (Tübingen: Mohr Siebeck, 2016), 3–18, esp. 6–7; Abigail R. Zammit, "To Read, or Not to Read: The Question of Literacy in Lachish 3," in *To Gaul, to Greece and into Noah's Ark: Essays in Honour of Kevin J. Cathcart on the Occasion of His Eightieth Birthday*, ed. Laura Quick, Ekaterina E. Kozlova, Sona Noll, and Philip Y. Yoo (Oxford, UK: University of Manchester/Oxford University Press, 2019), 111–22.

[82] See Matthieu Richelle, "Elusive Scrolls: Could Any Hebrew Literature Have Been Written Prior to the Eighth Century BCE?," *Vetus Testamentum* 66 (2016): 556–94; and Richelle, "When Did Literacy Emerge in Judah?," *Biblical Archeology Review* 46, no. 2 (Spring, 2020): 58, 60–61.

CHAPTER 5

THE ELEPHANT NOT IN THE ROOM:

THE IMPLICATIONS OF THE ABSENCE OF ZION AND THE NORTHERN ISRAELITE CHARACTER OF THE PENTATEUCH

There is a hypothetical scenario that lies behind the cliché, "the elephant in the room." Detectives are called to the scene of a crime. The interior of the house is severely damaged. Tables and furniture are squashed flat. Large gashes are torn out of the dry wall. Elephant scat lies on the floor. The detectives mill about, scratching their heads and asking one another, "Who could have done this?" In the middle of the room, an elephant dozes, but none seem to notice him.

The situation in Pentateuchal scholarship is almost the inverse of this cliché scenario. It is more like the following: The local zoo declares the opening of a new elephant exhibit. Along with thousands of others, you crowd the zoo to see the rare beast. The curtain drops on the elephant habitat, but there is no elephant. You notice a donkey wandering inside, but no pachyderm. "Behold, the elephant!" cry a panel of dozens of zookeepers, zoologists, biologists, and naturalists. At first the crowd is uncertain, but soon all the students of zoology, biology, ecology, and related sciences, eager to please their professors, take up the cry as well, "Behold, the elephant!" And soon the crowd is convinced they see it.

The elephant that is "not in the room" of the Pentateuch is Zion theology. Specifically, we see in the Pentateuch not a single occurrence of the toponyms "Zion" or "Jerusalem," the name "David," or even the word "temple" (Heb. *hêkhāl*). Nowhere does Moses ever command, urge, insist, or request the people of Israel to build a permanent structure for the worship of the LORD, much less specify where such a structure should be built. Later biblical texts openly admit this. The one chapter that constitutes *the* quintessential statement of Zion theology in the Hebrew Bible/Old Testament acknowledges that the Temple was never anticipated or requested in the Mosaic or post-Mosaic era of Israel's history:

> But that same night the word of the LORD came to Nathan, "Go and tell my servant David, 'Thus says the LORD: Would you build me a house to dwell in? I have not dwelt in a house since the day I brought up the people of Israel from Egypt to this day, but I have been moving about in a tent for my dwelling. In all places where I have moved with all the people of Israel, did I speak a word with any of the judges of Israel, whom I commanded to shepherd my people Israel, saying, 'Why have you not built me a house of cedar?'" (2 Sam 7:4–7)

This is an absolutely remarkable statement at the heart of the so-called Deuteronomistic History (Deuteronomy–2 Kings), a sprawling document that becomes ever more fixated on Jerusalem, the Temple, and the Davidic dynasty as it progresses. Nonetheless, when recording David's first inklings of building a temple for the LORD, the Deuteronomistic historian acknowledges that the Temple was never required by earlier divine revelation.

Despite the absence of the Temple, Zion, Jerusalem, or any connection with the Davidic dynasty, Wellhausen and most Pentateuchal scholars after him have held that the Pentateuch received its final redaction, and then was promulgated, by the *priesthood of Jerusalem* in the fifth century, with the figure of Ezra playing a pivotal role in popularizing the document.[1] Why would a priesthood whose theology, faith commitments, fate, and livelihood had been inextricably bound up with the sacred site of Zion/Jerusalem and the holy house that stood there promulgate a sacred document that portrays the founder of their religion not only *not* authorizing their sacred site, *nor* commanding a temple to be built, but actually giving *extensive* instructions for a small, portable tent shrine whose dimensions did not correspond to any structure ever built in Jerusalem, and whose location could be shifted

---

1   "[The Priestly Document] is closely linked to the rebuilding of the Temple [and] the legitimation of the Second Temple community in Jerusalem. [. . .] The writing down of P also betrays the claims of the priestly class in Jerusalem" (Christophe Nihan, *From Priestly Torah to Pentateuch: A Study in the Composition of the Book of Leviticus* [Tübingen: Mohr Siebeck, 2007], 614). Cf. Julius Wellhausen, *Prolegomena to the History of Israel*, trans. J. Sutherland Black and Allan Menzies (Edinburgh: Adam & Charles Black, 1885), 408.

arbitrarily? Let's recall the sentiments of the priests and Levites who were forcibly exiled from Jerusalem and the Temple:

> How shall we sing the LORD's song
> > in a foreign land?
> If I forget you, O Jerusalem,
> > let my right hand wither!
> Let my tongue cleave to the roof of my mouth,
> > if I do not remember you,
> if I do not set Jerusalem
> > above my highest joy! (Ps 137:4–6)

Actually, the difficulty is much worse than this because not only does the Pentateuch fail to mention, much less authorize, the central elements of the Zion theology (city, temple, dynasty) that, by the time of the Babylonian Exile, had constituted the heart of Judah's faith for centuries, it actually *valorizes* the rival sacred sites and the ancestors of the northern Israelites, the Samaritans—who, in the post-exilic period, operated a competing Yahwistic sanctuary on Mt. Gerizim to the north of Jerusalem. Again, why would the Jerusalem priesthood compose, redact, and publish a sacred document that strongly favored the religious claims of their Samaritan rivals to the north?

The Pentateuch, however, is so commonly read in the academy through the distorting lens of the Documentary Hypothesis or its later revisions that many may not be conscious of the way the books of Moses favor the claims and fortunes of what would become the northern tribes and the Kingdom of Israel over those of the tribe of Judah, with its Davidic dynasty and sacred site of Jerusalem. Therefore, the burden of this chapter is to re-read the Common Pentateuch[2] from a Samarian[3] (i.e. northern Israelite) perspective, especially by surveying key macroscopic narrative elements from Genesis through Deuteronomy such as (1) the locations dignified by patriarchal cultic activity, and (2) the valorization of Judah and Joseph and

---

[2] By "Common Pentateuch" we mean the presumed *Urtext* from which the Samaritans developed their unique Samaritan Pentateuch, and the Judean tradition eventually developed the Masoretic Text. It could also be defined as that content which is held in common between the MT and Samaritan forms of the Pentateuch.

[3] "Samarian" is a term coined by scholars to describe the people and culture in the territory of Samaria prior to the schism between Judaism and Samaritanism, which Gary Knoppers dates to the destruction of the Samaritan temple by John Hyrcanus c. 111–110 BCE. Others would date the schism earlier, to the building of the Yahwistic sanctuary on Mt. Gerizim in the 5th century BCE. See Magnar Kartveit, "The Samaritan Temple and Rewritten Bible," in *Holy Places and Cult*, ed. Erkki Koskenniemi and J. Cornelis de Vos, Studies in the Reception History of the Bible 5 (Winona Lake, IN: Eisenbrauns, 2014), 85–99, esp. 95–99.

their descendant tribes in the narrative. We will then contrast the Pentateuchal portrayal of these issues with the approach of the *Book of Jubilees*,
a second-century BCE pro-Judean, pro-Zion rewriting of the Pentateuch
narrative from creation to the Sinai event. The contrast between the Pentateuch and *Jubilees* brings into sharp relief the fact that the Pentateuch—even
in its Masoretic form, lacking the peculiar pluses of the Samaritan text—
lends itself better to the legitimation of the claims of Northern Israel and
the Samaritans than those of Judah and the Jerusalem priesthood.

Sacred Sites in the Pentateuch

At least nine different locations are recorded in Genesis as sites of worship
or theophany for the patriarchs. These are, in order of their introduction
into the narrative,

- Shechem (12:6; 33:18; 35:4);
- an unnamed halfway point between Bethel and Ai (12:8;
  13:3–4);
- Hebron in the hill country of Judah (13:18; 18:1; [as the burial
  site of Abraham, Sarah, Isaac, Rebecca, Jacob and Leah: 23:19;
  25:9; 35:29; 49:30–31; 50:13]);
- Beersheba in the Negev (21:33; 26:23–25; 46:1–4);
- an unidentified mountain in "the land of Moriah" (Gen
  22:2–18);
- Gerar (26:1–6);
- Bethel (Gen 28:17–21; 31:13; 35:1–15);
- Mahanaim (32:12); and
- Peniel (32:22–31).

The four most significant locations among these are Shechem and Bethel in
the territory of Northern Israel (later Samaria), and Hebron and Beersheba
in the territory of southern Judah.

The text of Genesis never mentions Jerusalem or Zion. The sensitive
reader might notice some subtle connections:[4] Genesis 2:13 mentions
the Gihon as one of the rivers flowing from Eden, and this name is shared

---

[4] For a detailed consideration of the possible allusions to Jerusalem in the books of Moses,
see Umberto Cassuto, "Jerusalem in the Pentateuch," in *Biblical & Oriental Studies*, vol,
1, *Bible* (Jerusalem: Magnes Press/The Hebrew University, 1973), 71–78. See also Gary
Rendsburg, *"The Genesis of the Bible,"* The Blanche and Irving Laurie Chair in Jewish
History Investiture Address, October 14, 2004, and Inaugural Lecture, October 28, 2004;
New Brunswick, NJ: Rutgers University, 2004.

with the spring that constituted Jerusalem's only continuous source of fresh water (cf. 1 Kgs 1:33); Genesis 14:18 mentions that the mysterious Melchizedek is king of "Salem," arguably an archaic name of Jeru-salem (cf. Ps 76:2), although a text-critical issue makes this uncertain;[5] and Genesis 22:2 informs us that the binding of Isaac (the *Aqedah*) occurs on a mountain in the land of Moriah which the Chronicler later identifies with the site of Solomon's Temple (2 Chron 3:1 and *Jubilees* 18:13). Remarkably, however, the supposed priestly redactors, working in Jerusalem in the early post-exilic/Persian Period, never introduced into the text even a small gloss like הִיא יְרוּשָׁלָם, "this [is] Jerusalem,"[6] to make explicit the connection of the sacred city with Melchizedek and the *Aqedah*, even though these are both attested interpretative traditions in late biblical and post-biblical Jewish literature.[7] The result is that even these subtle connections are not completely certain. For example, "Salem" (Gen 14:18) could actually be understood as another name for the site of Shechem based on Gen 33:18, and the name "Moriah" (Gen 22:2), a *hapax* in the Pentateuch, could be a variant form of the more familiar "Moreh," which was also near Shechem (Gen 12:6).[8] It is a bit disconcerting, then, that the Hebrew text of Genesis leaves open the possibility that even the two strongest candidates for an allusion to Jerusalem are actually references to Shechem, the sacred city of the Samaritans. Therefore, as there is no completely unambiguous reference to Jerusalem in the text of Genesis, we cannot agree with Cassuto and others that the sacred author intended to anticipate the future role of Zion in Israel's history, or that the text betrays signs of redaction after Jerusalem had become the central site of the cult.[9]

We readily grant that there is no mention of Mt. Gerizim in Genesis either, but Gerizim does benefit indirectly from the valorization of Shechem, the sacred city lying between Mounts Ebal and Gerizim, either or both of which offered a suitable site for a shrine associated with the city. Genesis grants an honored place to Shechem: it is the first site in the land

---

[5] See Antti Laato, "The Cult Site on Mount Ebal: A Biblical Tradition Rewritten and Reinterpreted," in *Holy Places and Cult*, 63–64. Genesis 33:18 can be translated, "Jacob came to Salem, the city of Shechem," as the LXX does. Pseudo-Eupolemos, following this translation, connects Melchizedek with "holy Argarizin" (=Mt. Gerizim; see Kartveit, "The Samaritan Temple and Rewritten Bible," in *Holy Places and Cult*, 89).

[6] As is done with Jebus in Joshua and Judges: Josh 15:8; 18:28; Judg 19:10.

[7] Josephus (*War* 6:438) associates Melchizedek with Jerusalem. Likewise, 2 Chron 3:1 and *Jubilees* 18:13 identify the mount of the *Aqedah* as Jerusalem.

[8] Since "Moriah" is a *hapax*, but "Moreh" has an important role (Gen 12:6; Deut 11:30; cf. Judg. 7:1), some suggest taking "Moriah" as a variant of the better-known "Moreh" near Shechem. See Laato, "Cult Site on Mt. Ebal," 63–64.

[9] Pace Cassuto, "Jerusalem," 78; Rendsburg, *Genesis of the Bible*, 16–25.

of Canaan at which Abraham offers worship to the LORD (Gen 12:7), and both Abraham and Jacob build altars there (Gen 12:7; 33:20). The sons of Israel conquer Shechem already in the patriarchal period (Gen 34), exterminating all males and assimilating the rest of its pagan citizens.[10] In fact, Jacob considers it a territory he himself conquered, and therefore he feels free to bequeath it to Joseph (Gen 48:22). It is a curious fact that, in the canonical biblical narrative, Shechem appears to remain uninhabited for the intervening centuries until the arrival of the Israelites under Joshua, at which point it becomes their base of operation in the land—there is no record of a siege or conquest of Shechem in the entire text of the Book of Joshua. Shechem also becomes identified as a place of conquest over the pernicious habit of idolatry, inasmuch as Jacob buries the idols of his household under the oak associated with the site (Gen 35:4),[11] which may anticipate Joshua's triumph over idolatry at the same location years later (Josh 24:1–28, esp. 26).[12]

There are no references to sacred sites in the land of Israel in Exodus through Numbers. It is not until Deuteronomy that the attention of the sacred author turns once more to places of worship within the land, and there we read that Moses chooses the area of Shechem as the future site for the solemnization ritual of the covenant between Israel and the LORD (Deut 11:30). Moses does not anticipate that Shechem will need to be conquered—in keeping with the narratives of Genesis (Gen 34:25–29; 48:22), it is assumed to be Israelite territory. Shechem was bracketed by two mountains—Gerizim and Ebal—which offered ideal platforms for the declaration of the curses and blessings that characteristically concluded ancient Near Eastern covenant-making rituals:

> And when the LORD your God brings you into the land . . . you shall set the blessing on Mount Gerizim and the curse on Mount Ebal. Are they not beyond the Jordan, west of the road . . . over against Gilgal, beside the oak of Moreh? (Deut 11:29–30)

---

[10] Amit reads Genesis 34 as anti-Shechemite polemic (so Yairah Amit, "Shechem in Deuteronomy: A Seemingly Hidden Polemic," in *History, Memory, Hebrew Scriptures: A Festschrift for Ehud Ben Zvi*, ed. Ian Douglas Wilson and Diana V. Edelman [Winona Lake, IN: Eisenbrauns, 2015], 6), but it could as easily be understood as identifying the first city in Canaan conquered by Israel, just as it was the first sacred site when Abraham entered the land. The Pentateuchal as a whole seems to have a consistently favorable view of Shechem, so this reading would be preferable.

[11] That is, the "oak of Moreh" mentioned in Gen 12:6, Deut 11:30, and Judg 9:6.

[12] Contra Amit ("Shechem," 6), the burial of the idols under the oak of Shechem does not defile the site but associates the site with a radical commitment to true worship, and a sanctuary to the LORD is later constructed there (Josh 24:26), a cultural practice similar to the construction of Christian churches over ancient pagan sites of worship.

We can observe here the significance of the "Oak of Moreh" to the entire Pentateuchal narrative: it serves as the marker of the sacred precinct employed by Abraham as the first place of worship in Canaan (Gen 12:7), and at the end of the Pentateuch it serves to designate the place of covenant solemnization as Abraham's descendants enter to possess the land God promised by covenant to their ancestor (Deut 11:30; cf. Josh 24:25–26).

Joshua 8:30–35 informs us that Moses's instructions were executed by the Israelites under Joshua's leadership faithfully once they had taken possession of the land. There is some manuscript evidence to suggest that the Masoretic Text has actually been redacted in order to relocate the site of the altar in Deut 24:7 and Josh 8:30 from *Gerizim* to *Ebal*, in order to subvert the legitimacy of Gerizim as a claimant for site of cult centralization for Israel. If such an emendation took place, it would be strong evidence that later Judaism felt the force of Deuteronomy's valorization of Gerizim as providing legitimation to the Samaritan's cultic site.[13]

In sum, the Pentateuch mentions Jerusalem not at all, and Gerizim only twice, so one would have to conclude that neither Judean nor Samaritan interests were heavily at work in the redaction of the text of the "Common Pentateuch"; otherwise, one would expect more decisive interventions in the text resolving the controversy of the location of the central sanctuary—such interventions as we do, indeed, find in the Samaritan Pentateuch. Certainly Genesis, with its emphasis on the sacrality of several locations within the land—especially Bethel, but also Shechem, Hebron, and Beersheba—has the potential to subvert or destabilize Deuteronomy's insistence on a single place of worship for the whole nation.

Having said that, if one were constrained to justify a choice of location of a central sanctuary based only on the data that the Pentateuch itself supplies, surely the Samaritans made the better choice since a much stronger case can be made for Gerizim or at least the Shechem vicinity than for the invisible Jerusalem. At least the text mentions Gerizim and designates

---

[13] James H. Charlesworth makes this argument; see "The Discovery of an Unknown Dead Sea Scroll: The Original Text of Deuteronomy 27?", http://blogs.owu.edu/magazine/the-discovery-of-an-unknown-dead-sea-scroll-the-original-text-of-deuteronomy-27/"; Charlesworth, "What is a Variant?: Announcing a Dead Sea Scrolls Fragment of Deuteronomy," *Maarav* 16 (2009): 201–12 and 273–74, citing Old Latin Manuscript Codex 100, Greek manuscript Papyrus Giessen 19, and a recently recovered Dead Sea Scroll. See also Eugene Ulrich, "4QJosha," in *Qumran Cave 4: IX: Deuteronomy, Joshua, Judges, Kings*, ed. Eugene Ulrich et al. (Oxford, UK: Clarendon Press, 1995), 145–46; Ingrid Hjelm, "Northern Perspectives in Deuteronomy and its relation to the Samaritan Pentateuch," *Hebrew Bible and Ancient Israel* 4 (2015): 203; Kartveit, "Samaritan Temple," 90–95; and Martin Abegg, Peter Flint, and Eugene Ulrich, *The Dead Sea Scrolls Bible* (San Francisco: Harper, 1999), 201–2.

it as the mountain of the blessing of the twelve tribes during the covenant solemnization ritual (Deut 11:29; 27:12). Gerizim is a mountain adjacent to Shechem, the first site of patriarchal worship in the promised land (Gen 12:7), the first site Israel possesses of her inheritance (Gen 34:25–29), the site that symbolizes rejection of idolatry and commitment to the covenant (Gen 35:4; cf. Josh 24:19–24), the site Moses himself designated for the ratification of the covenant upon entry to the land (Deut 11:30; some manuscripts of Deut 27:4). Etienne Nodet summarizes the situation succinctly: "The Pentateuch, considered as a whole, goes better with Shechem than Jerusalem."[14]

The case for Shechem as the holy site becomes only stronger when we include the entire Hexateuch in our analysis. As mentioned, Joshua never besieges or conquers Shechem (cf. Gen 34:25–29), and mysteriously encounters no opposition when he gathers the tribes there to ratify the covenant (Josh 8:30–33). At the end of his life he regathers the tribes at the same site (Josh 24:1) and, in an action that evokes memories of Genesis 35:4, he persuades the Israelites to abandon their idols and foreign gods, reaffirm the covenant (24:25), and establish a sacred stone in the *miqdash* or "sanctuary" of the LORD (apparently an early shrine) adjacent to the ancient oak known already by the patriarchs (Josh 24:26; cf. Gen 12:6; 11:30). Shechem is even dignified by hosting the mortal remains of Joseph (Josh 24:32), whom Genesis clearly designates as the primary heir of the patriarchal promises (Gen 48:1–20). Thus, when we take in the narrative arc of the Hexateuch as a whole, we observe a "from Shechem to Shechem" *inclusio* (Genesis 12–Joshua 24) concluding with an emphatic endorsement of this city as the unifying cultic site for all Israel, the only place to host a permanent sanctuary already in the days of Moses's immediate successor. It is difficult to dismiss these narrative facts as unintended by the author(s) and redactor(s). As Hjelm remarks:

> Is it sheer accident that the Masoretic Hexateuch forms a continuum in its compositional form of "promise (Genesis 12) and fulfillment" (Joshua 24), which may also be defined as "from Shechem to Shechem" (Genesis 12–Joshua 24), in which yet another continuum is included (Genesis 35–Joshua 24)?[15]

---

[14] Etienne Nodet, *A Search for the Origins of Judaism: From Joshua to the Mishnah*, trans. Ed Crowley (Sheffield, UK: Sheffield Academic Press, 1997), 152. Also see discussion in Laato, "Cult Site on Mt. Ebal," 59–66.

[15] Hjelm, "Northern Perspectives," 188.

THE CHARACTERIZATIONS OF JUDAH AND JOSEPH IN THE PENTATEUCH

A. THE PATRIARCHS JUDAH AND JOSEPH

Joseph was considered by the Samaritans to be their forefather, and Knoppers and others are willing to concede that the Samarian population of the Persian and Second Temple period was composed of the descendants of Israelites who had inhabited the territories traditionally associated with Joseph's sons, Ephraim and Manasseh.[16] On the other hand, it is abundantly clear that the Judeans claimed the ancestor Judah, from whom they took their name, as their forefather.[17] Thus, in reading the Pentateuch, especially when looking for clues to the time of its composition or redaction(s), one needs to be attentive to the valorization or pejorativization of these two characters, since their status in the sacred history would be understood as legitimation or de-legitimation of the social, political, and cultic claims of their descendants.

This is the profile of Joseph in Pentateuch: Jacob favors Joseph above all his brothers (Gen 37:3) since he is the first born of Rachel, Jacob's most beloved wife (30:24). God blesses Joseph with prophetic insight, and grants him multiple dreams that transparently represent the rest of his family venerating him (Gen 37:5–11). His brothers reject him and Judah in particular betrays him (37:26–28), but despite this serious opposition divine providence contrives that he rise to become, for all practical purposes, the governor of the ancient Near East by virtue of his role as prime minister of Egypt (41:40). Pharaoh gives him a very honorable wife, Asenath, a highborn daughter of an Egyptian priest of the chief deity Amon-Re (41:50–52),[18] and his father Jacob/Israel directly adopts his two sons Ephraim and Manasseh (48:5), making them the direct heirs of the patriarchal blessings originating with Abraham (Gen 48:15–16). Jacob/Israel *reaffirms* this blessing yet a second time in Gen 49:22–26, in which Joseph's blessing is distinguished

---

[16] Ingrid Hjelm, "Lost and Found? A Non-Jewish Israel from the Merneptah Stele to the Byzantine Period," in *History, Archeology, and the Bible Forty Years after "Historicity,"* ed. Ingrid Hjelm and Thomas Thompson (London: Routledge, Taylor & Francis Group, 2016), 112–29; Hjelm, "Northern Perspectives," 188–90; and Gary Knoppers, *Jews and Samaritans: The Origins and History of Their Early Relations* (New York: Oxford University Press, 2013), 18–44.

[17] Cf. Josephus, *Antiquities* 11:340. Also Knoppers: "Samaritans claimed to be descendants of the northern tribes of Joseph . . . while Judeans claimed to be descendants of the southern tribes, most notably Jacob's progeny of Judah" (*Jews and Samaritans*, 2)

[18] We can determine this because her father served in On (Gen 41:45), i.e. Heliopolis, the center for the worship of the sun god.

from those of his other brothers by its length and effusiveness. His father even designates Joseph as the "prince" (*nāzîr*) over his other brothers (Gen 49:26b). Very significantly, Moses repeats the core elements of this blessing and expands upon them considerably in Deut 33:13–17, just prior to his death and the end of the Pentateuch as a literary document. It can hardly be overemphasized that the Pentateuch concludes with every expectation that the Joseph tribes will be at the center of the covenantal blessings as sacred history progresses.

Let us contrast this profile with that of Judah: He is the fourth son of Leah, she of "weak eyes," Jacob's less-favored wife whom he was forced to marry (Gen 29:23–28). His gradual increase in status within the family appears largely to be the result of the missteps and foolhardiness of his three older brothers (Reuben, Simeon, and Levi), each of whom provokes upon himself a paternal curse (49:3–7). God does not bless Judah with prophetic insight, nor grant him omens of future greatness. He distinguishes himself early in his career as the betrayer of his brother Joseph (37:26–27). His marital life leaves much to be desired and gives bad example to his descendants: his wife was a Canaanitess (38:2) who bore him three half-Canaanite sons (38:3–5). Far from redeeming themselves by acts of faith, as some "righteous Gentiles" do in the pages of the Pentateuch, Judah's first two sons act so wickedly they provoke God to slay them by direct divine agency (38:7–10). Judah's youngest and only surviving son by his legitimate wife, however, is *not* the progenitor of the majority of his descendants (1 Chron 4:21–23). Rather, the tribe of Judah is primarily built up through Perez and Zerah (1 Chron 2:1–4:20), the sons of the Canaanitess Tamar (38:27–30), who was given in marriage to Judah's two wicked sons, but afterward conceived by her father-in-law by seducing him under the guise of a cult prostitute (38:12–19).

Granted, there is a gradual rehabilitation of Judah's character after Genesis 38. By stages Judah rises to be the leader of his brothers (43:1–10) and shows himself increasingly to have the welfare of his father at heart (44:18–34). Indeed, it falls upon Judah to deliver the climactic soliloquy in Genesis 44:18–34 that demonstrates his moral maturity, sways the hardened heart of the embittered Joseph (45:1–3), and breaks open the impasse of fear, resentment, and unforgiveness between Joseph and his brothers. Perhaps in view of this service, Jacob bestows on Judah in Genesis 49:8–12 the promise of leadership of his kinfolk (49:8) and even the status of royalty (49:10), but both of these promises seem temporally limited.[19] Strikingly, at

---

[19] Genesis 49:10 appears to limit Judah's possession of the "scepter" by the phrase "until Shiloh comes" or "until he comes to whom it belongs," taking "Shiloh" as a compound noun meaning "him to whom it is [i.e. 'belongs']." See discussion of Gen 49:10 in Nahum

the end of the Pentateuch, Moses himself chooses *not* to reiterate the royal blessing to Judah, but instead grants him a simple prayer for general divine assistance one verse in length (33:7) in stark contrast to the lengthy benedictions on his brothers Levi (33:8–11) and Joseph (33:13–17).

But it is necessary to return to the scandalous text of Genesis 38 and consider the force of this narrative in the post-exilic context, in which so many scholars presume to place the formative redaction of the Pentateuch. The implications of Genesis 38 are that the majority of Jews are of half-Canaanite ancestry through an immoral union (*zĕnût*) of Judah and his own daughter-in-law (*kallāh*). The Mosaic law explicitly condemns such unions (Lev 18:15) and punishes them with death (20:12). Not that Judah's own marriage was admirable: he marries a Canaanitess, which Moses explicitly forbids (Deut 7:1–3) under pain of divine annihilation (Deut 7:4). Thus even his legitimate children through Shelah are half-Canaanite.

How could such a text have failed to be a grave embarrassment to the Judean exiles returned from Babylon in the early Persian Period, and how could it not have threatened to subvert the pretensions of racial purity reflected in the agenda of Ezra and Nehemiah to prohibit intermarriage with the surrounding peoples (cf. Ezra 10:2–44; Neh 13:26–27)? One could almost suspect the pericope was composed by Samaritan partisans to humble their cousins to the south. If the Jerusalem priesthood had felt comfortable redacting the text of the Pentateuch in the late sixth or fifth centuries BCE, Genesis 38 would have been removed. The fact that it was not indicates the text was considered canonical—and therefore unalterable—already in the early post-exilic period. Further below we will examine the evidence from the *Book of Jubilees* that shows the discomfort this text caused within Second Temple Judaism.

There is no doubt, then, that Joseph is the dominant and valorized son of Jacob/Israel in the Pentateuch. Although Judah does grow in moral maturity and leadership qualities, his own father places a limit on his period of leadership over the tribes ("until he comes to whom it belongs," Gen 49:11), and it is hard for Judah to outlive or escape the stigma of having betrayed his brother Joseph and begotten all his sons by Canaanite women, some in the most illicit and immoral fashion. On the other hand, the text of the Pentateuch has almost nothing negative to communicate about Joseph. God marks him with prophetic insight and knowledge of the future, engineers his rise to universal power, and moves on both his father and Moses to confirm his leadership role among his kinfolk and his special status as primary recipient of the patriarchal blessings. The Pentateuch ends with every

---

M. Sarna, *Genesis*, JPS Torah Commentary (Philadelphia: JPS, 1989), 336–37: "Judah's hegemony over Israel will last until the secession of the north" (337).

expectation that the future of Israel rests largely on the shoulders of Joseph's sons Ephraim and Manasseh (Deut 33:17), especially since Moses's successor, Joshua, comes from the tribe of Ephraim (Num 13:8,16).

B. The Descendants of Judah and Joseph

The Pentateuchal narrative from Exodus through Deuteronomy casts the descendants of both Judah and Joseph—that is, their tribes—favorably. The representatives of Judah and Joseph, namely Joshua of Ephraim and Caleb of Judah, are the faithful spies who trust in the power of the LORD God of Israel and counsel courage in the face of the inhabitants of the land (Num 14:6–10). Yet Joshua and Caleb are not equals: Joshua becomes Moses's successor as leader over all the tribes—perhaps a temporary fulfillment of the prophecy given to Joseph in Gen 49:26/Deut 33:16–17. In the Book of Numbers, we observe Joseph overcoming Judah. Although in the first census the tribe of Judah outnumbers the combined Joseph tribes, by the end of the book Judah has only barely increased, whereas Joseph's total now exceeds Judah by almost nine thousand persons.[20] The patriarchal blessing had consisted primarily in fruitfulness and multiplication (Gen 28:3; 35:11) and the author of Numbers is affirming that his promise was experienced by Ephraim and Manasseh in a particular way, as prophesied by Jacob/Israel himself (Gen 48:1–20 and 49:22–26; cf. 41:52).

Even the structure of the Book of Numbers places emphasis on the Joseph tribes. A possible way of understanding the structure of Numbers is to perceive two major units, each enclosed with an *inclusio*: Num 1–26, begun and concluded with censuses (found in Num 1 and 26); and Num 27–36, begun and concluded with discussion about the inheritance of the descendants of Zelophehad of Manasseh, who had only daughters (Num 27:1–11 and 36:1–13).[21] The two narratives about the daughters of Zelophehad seem to belong together, and appear to have been split by the redactor in order to encompass the second half of the book (Num 27–36).[22] As a result, the book still ends with a focus on, and even assurance of, the inheritance of the twelve tribes, despite the ten rebellions against God narrated during the wilderness wanderings (Num 11–25). The theological message is: Despite Israel's sins, they will still inherit the promises by the grace of God, not their own merit. But the family, clan, and tribe chosen by the sacred author as an

---

[20] In the first chapter of Numbers we see the tribe of Judah has 74,600 people (1:27) while the combined tribes of Joseph have 72,700 (1:32–35). By the end of Numbers Judah has only 76,500 tribal members (26:22), and Joseph has 85,200 (26:34–37).

[21] See Dean R. Ulrich, "The Framing Function of the Narratives about Zelophehad's Daughters," *JETS* 41 (1998): 529–38.

[22] Ulrich, "Framing," 530–31.

icon of God's faithfulness in fulfilling his promises is that of Zelophehad of Machir of Manasseh, son of Joseph.[23]

In Wellhausen's paradigm, Numbers is classified predominantly as a "P" book, perhaps forming the end of a priestly Tetrateuch before "R," the final redactor, appended Deuteronomy to the collection.[24] If that is the case, it is even more striking that the two chapters that conclude the two major sections of the book (chs. 26 and 36) are pro-Josephite: Joseph takes over the role of largest tribe(s) in Numbers 26; and in Numbers 36, the inheritance rights of Joseph's descendants, even if they should only be women, is affirmed. One can and should raise the question: Why would such solicitude for the Joseph tribes be in the interests of the post-exilic Jerusalem priesthood?[25] The obvious answer is that it wouldn't. The tendencies of the Book of Numbers only serve to bolster the political and theological claims of the Samarians/Samaritans, who claimed descent from Joseph and continued to inhabit the tribal territory of Ephraim and Manasseh, and whose temple lay on Mt. Gerizim adjacent Shechem in the heart of the traditional inheritance of Manasseh. Thus, any objective reading of the Pentateuchal narrative must acknowledge that it valorizes Joseph and his descendants over Judah.

This situation is only exacerbated if we include Joshua in our purview and make an assessment of the entire Hexateuch. We have already noted how Moses's successor Joshua is an Ephraimite. It is this Ephraimite judge who distributes the land among the twelve tribes and assigns Joseph's tribes to the well-watered and more easily defensible central heartland (Josh 16–17), with the other ten tribes gathered around to form a buffer between the Joseph tribes and foreign incursions (Josh 14–15; 18–19). Then, Joshua ratifies the covenant of Moses at Shechem early in his career (Josh 8) and renews it at the same location at the end of his life (Josh 24) within the precincts of the sanctuary (*miqdāš*) that already existed there at that time (Josh 24:26). Finally, Joshua buries there at Shechem the bones of Joseph, whom Jacob and Moses blessed as primary heir of the covenant.

All of this could only serve to strengthen the claim of Persian-Period Samarians and Second Temple Samaritans that they descended from the

---

[23] Machir is mentioned several times in the Pentateuch: see Gen 50:23; Num 26:29; Deut 3:15.

[24] See discussion in Baruch Levine, *Numbers 1–20: A New Translation with Introduction and Commentary* (New York: Doubleday, 1993), 64–72, 101–3.

[25] By the time of the Second Temple, the tribe of Manasseh had either been completely obliterated and/or exiled, if one follows 2 Kings 17; or else had become a component of the Samaritan people, if the claims of the Samaritans themselves were accepted. In either case, redacting the end of the Tetrateuch to emphasize the endurance of land inheritance to the clans of Manasseh (Num 27:1–11; Num 36:1–13) did nothing to serve the interests of the Judean Jerusalem priesthood.

great Joseph and therefore were the primary heirs of the covenant with Abraham. It was only fitting, then, that the natural capital of their territory, Shechem—the "navel of the land" according to Judges 9:37—should also host the central sanctuary, especially since Moses designated the adjacent mountains for cultic acts, and Joshua constructed a sanctuary there.

THE REWRITING OF THE PENTATEUCH IN *JUBILEES*

One might object that, in the Persian or Second Temple Period, the biblical text was already so sacrosanct that the Jewish readers of it did not feel the force of the pro-Josephite, pro-northern tendency of the Pentateuch as we have it. Or one could argue that by this time the Judeans considered themselves heirs of all the patriarchs, such that the elevation of Joseph and the disgraces of Judah meant little to them. However, any such proposal that the narrative bias of the Pentateuch went unnoticed is undermined by the character of the *Book of Jubilees*, a Second Temple (early Hasmonean) rewriting of Genesis through Exodus from the perspective of a zealous Jew of the time period, probably one with close connections to the priesthood.[26]

When one compares the Pentateuch with the rewritten narrative of Jubilees, several illuminating contrasts emerge. Whereas the Pentateuch never mentions Jerusalem/Zion, the city appears in *Jubilees* eight times.[27] One has only to read its first chapter to discover that Zion is holy and destined to serve in the eschaton as the source and origin of the new creation. Indeed, Zion/Jerusalem is one of the four sacred places of the earth (*Jub* 4:26), characterized as the "center of the navel of the earth" (*Jub* 8:19), the site where Abraham attempted to sacrifice Isaac (*Jub* 18:13). And what of Gerizim? It is never mentioned in *Jubilees*.

The author of *Jubilees* is clearly uncomfortable with the narrative of Judah's fathering of his sons through Tamar in Genesis 38, but apparently feels unable to omit it. Nonetheless, he makes the following changes to the story to pull its message into line with his purposes in writing:

1. While the biblical text implies that Tamar is simply a local woman, i.e. a Canaanite (Gen 38:6), *Jubilees* transforms her into an Aramaen (Jub 41:1), the same ethnic group as the

---

[26] James C. VanderKam, *The Book of Jubilees* (Sheffield, UK: Sheffield Academic Press, 2001) 17–21; and O. S. Wintermute, "Jubilees," in *The Old Testament Pseudepigrapha*, Anchor Bible Reference Library, 2 vols., ed. James H. Charlesworth (New York: Doubleday, 1985), 2:35–142, here 43–45.

[27] Jub 1:28 [3x]; 1:29 [2x]; 4:26; 8:19; 18:13.

matriarchs Rebekah, Leah, and Rachel, and therefore an eligible bride.

2. *Jubilees* portrays Er, Jacob's son, as detesting Tamar because he wants a Canaanite wife like his Canaanite mother, but, paradoxically, Judah forbids Er to marry a Canaanitess (*Jub* 41:2).

3. In *Jubilees*, Tamar's marriages with Er and Onan were conveniently unconsummated (*Jub* 41:27), with the result that she is still a virgin when she conceives by her father-in-law Jacob, which may exculpate him from the prohibitions of Lev 18:15 & 20:12.

4. Judah makes a great show of repentance after his illicit union with Tamar, complete with lamentation, confession, and supplication for forgiveness, thus transforming Judah's greatest moral failure into the occasion for him to become the model of repentance and reconciliation (*Jub* 41:23–25).

5. According to *Jubilees*, it is to Judah's credit that he showed great zeal for the Law by his intention to execute Tamar by burning her (*Jub* 41:28), a punishment apparently reserved for very serious cases of fornication (Lev 21:9).

6. Finally, *Jubilees* makes it abundantly clear to its readership that Judah's example in these marital/sexual matters is not normative and should not be followed (*Jub* 41:25–26).

In contrast to the Pentateuch, which gives excessive attention to Joseph's sons and marks them as the primary heirs of the covenant (Gen 48:1–22), *Jubilees* suppresses information about Ephraim and Manasseh, mentioning them just once, briefly, in a genealogical notice (*Jub* 44:24). The account of Jacob blessing Ephraim and Manasseh (Gen 48:1–22) is omitted entirely in *Jubilees*, which instead includes an account of *Isaac* blessing Jacob's sons *Levi* and *Judah* with a priestly and royal blessing respectively (*Jub* 31:1–32). According to *Jubilees*, Levi already served as a priest at the altar of the Bethel shrine in his own lifetime (*Jub* 32:9), long before his descendants gained the priesthood for their zeal during the calf debacle (Exod 32:29). For all that, *Jubilees* refuses to authorize Bethel as place of worship: Jacob is solemnly warned to build no temple there because it is "not the place" for an "eternal sanctuary" (*Jub* 32:22), which of course will be reserved for Zion/Jerusalem.

What is abundantly clear from *Jubilees'* rewriting of the biblical narrative is the intense discomfort zealous Judeans felt with many of the features of the canonical Pentateuch during the Second Temple period, such as the cultic activity of the patriarchs at a wide variety of shrines and locations, the valorization of Joseph and the Josephite tribes, the embarrassing sexual unions of Judah, and the absence of any explicit reference to Zion.

Although *Jubilees* is the best evidence of this discomfort, signs of it may also be found in other Second Temple texts. For example, in what is almost certainly an effort by Judean redactors to remove legitimation of the Samaritan's central sanctuary near Shechem, LXX Joshua adjusts the account of Joshua 24 to place the sanctuary in *Shiloh* instead of *Shechem*.[28] Somewhat less certain is the possibility that the MT reading of "Ebal" instead of "Gerizim" in Deut 27:4 and Josh 8:30 is also motivated by anti-Samaritanism.[29] Finally, the famous Temple Scroll of Qumran, which purports to be a set of instructions for the building and management of the Temple addressed from God to Moses in the second person,[30] is ample witness to the "felt need" of Second Temple Judeans to ground the legitimacy of the Jerusalem Temple in God's revelation to Moses rather than merely in the oracles to David and Solomon, as the canonical text does (2 Sam 7:13–16; 1 Kings 5:1–6).

CONCLUSION: THE FACT OF THE NORTHERN ISRAELITE PERSPECTIVE OF THE PENTATEUCH

What conclusions may be drawn from our observations that the Common Pentateuch tends to exult Joseph and his descendants over Judah and his tribe, and to valorize Shechem while omitting mention of Zion/Jerusalem? We propose the following three points:

First, the Pentateuch is not the product of the post-exilic Jerusalem priesthood. Especially in light of the work of the late Gary Knoppers, who called the attention of Pentateuchal scholars to the fact that there is strong archaeological evidence for a Yahwistic shrine on Mt. Gerizim from the mid-fifth century BCE (c. 450 BCE) on, it has become increasingly difficult to explain the development of the Pentateuch solely in terms of Judean history.[31] Already during the careers of Ezra and Nehemiah, there was a rival claimant for the "place the LORD your God will choose" either under

---

[28] Laato, "Cult Site," 66; see also Hjelm, "Northern Perspectives," 188.

[29] Kartveit, "Samaritan Temple," 91–93: "The change to 'Ebal' must have been made at the hands of Jews and could be a polemical alteration: an altar in the North was to be built on the mountain of curse. The conclusion is that the reading 'Gerizim' in Deut 27:4 is older than the reading 'Ebal' of the Masoretic Text (cf. BHQ)." See also Ulrich, "4QJosha," 145; Abegg, Flint, and Ulrich, *Dead Sea Scrolls Bible*, 201–2; Charlesworth, "Discovery of an Unknown Dead Sea Scroll"; and Charlesworth, "What Is a Variant?"

[30] See Johann Maier, *The Temple Scrolls: An Introduction, Translation & Commentary, Journal for the Study of the Old Testament* Supplement 34 (Sheffield: JSOT Press, 1985), 1–7.

[31] Knoppers, *Jews and Samaritans*, 11: "The Jerusalem Temple had a Yahwistic rival to the north significantly earlier than most scholars had assumed," i.e. from "the mid-fifth century onward."

construction or already functioning in the center of Samaria to the north. As we have seen, the Pentateuch gives far too much support to the ideological claims of the Samarians/Samaritans to be the editorial product of their rivals to the south. The Pentateuch cannot have been the product of the post-exilic Jerusalem priesthood for the strongest possible reason: *it did not and does not support their interests*, but rather those of their rivals. Ingrid Hjelm comments:

> There is nothing Jerusalemite about the Pentateuch as such and were it not for tradition's assumption of a biblical Israel with a common past in which Jerusalem always had priority over against other Yahwistic cult centers in Palestine, no one would suggest that the Pentateuch had an origin in Jerusalem. . . . Although Deuteronomy has an all Israel perspective, it nevertheless focuses on Shechem and Gerizim/Ebal . . . which does not correspond well with an assumed origin in a Jerusalemite court at any time when looking at the book from a Pentateuchal perspective.[32]

Second, there is no evidence for the common opinion that the Pentateuch is a Judean document that incorporates some northern Israelite elements.[33] Rather, the converse is true. All the evidence points to the Pentateuch as a northern Israelite document that incorporates a few Judean traditions. For example: it would only take the excision of a single passage (Gen 49:8–10) to remove any basis in divine revelation for Judah's claim to hegemony over the heirs of Israel. For this reason, too, we can rule out the proposal of Knoppers, Nihan, and others that the Pentateuch is a "compromise" project between Samarian and Judean interest groups—there simply is no "compromise" between Shechem and Jerusalem in the Pentateuch. Shechem is glorified and Jerusalem suppressed.[34] If indeed Persian-Period Judean and Samarian scribes collaborated on the Pentateuch, which we think is hopelessly anachronistic given the evidence in the previous chapter that Ezekiel and Jeremiah already knew the Pentateuch as a document in the early sixth century, then it would be better to characterize the Pentateuch

---

[32] Hjelm, "Northern Perspectives," 202, 204.

[33] E.g., Reinhard Pummer, "The Samaritans and Their Pentateuch," in *The Pentateuch as Torah: New Models for Understanding Its Promulgation and Acceptance*, ed. Gary N. Knoppers and Bernard M. Levinson (Winona Lake, IN: Eisenbrauns, 2007), 265: "The Pentateuch is accommodating toward the Samaritans . . . besides Jerusalem traditions (Genesis 14, 22), traditions about Ebal and Gerizim are included." But the Pentateuch is not just "accommodating"; it looks at salvation history from a primarily northern perspective and anticipation.

[34] Knoppers, *Jews and Samaritans*, 194–216.

as a "concessionary" or "capitulatory" document because it seems our poor Judean scribes conceded and capitulated to the interests of their northern kinfolk. Actually, at no time in the history of Judah from the establishment of Jerusalem as David's capital (2 Samuel 5) to the destruction of the Second Temple in AD 70 would it have been in the interests of the Jerusalem priesthood to promulgate a document like the Common Pentateuch, which (1) says nothing of their sacred site, (2) presents Moses as authorizing a portable tent shrine rather than a permanent stone temple (Exod 25–40), (3) appears to authorize the vicinity of Shechem as the *de facto* national capital and site for covenant renewal rituals (Deut 11:26–30; Deut 27:1–14), and (4) concludes with a grant of pre-eminence to the Josephite tribes (Deut 33:13–17).

Finally, even though what we have called the "Common Pentateuch" better supports the claims of the Samarians/Samaritans than those of the Judeans, in point of fact there is no clear evidence of an awareness of the rivalry between these groups at all. Joseph, Judah, and all the brothers reconcile by the end of Genesis, and the Pentateuch ends with an expectation of a united twelve tribes of Israel under the Josephite leadership of Joshua. If either the Samaritans or the Judeans had redacted the Common Pentateuch from the mid-fifth century BCE on, we would expect to find redactional elements that would clarify God's intended place for his sanctuary—the kind of elements we *do* find, for example, in the Samaritan Pentateuch.[35] The absence of these redactional elements, as well as the curious absence of any redactions to make explicit the presence of Zion/Jerusalem even in those passages (e.g. Gen 14:18; 22:2) where Second Temple Jews clearly saw it, make it necessary to postulate that the text of the Pentateuch was already considered unalterable (i.e. canonical) in a much earlier, necessarily *pre-exilic* period of the history of Israel and Judah.[36] This agrees with our

---

[35] On the question of the origin of the schism between Samaritans and Judeans, we follow Magnar Kartveit in seeing the *construction* of the Gerizim sanctuary (c. 450 BCE) rather than its *destruction* (c. 129 BCE) as marking the beginning of the Judean-Samaritan schism (Kartveit, "Samaritan Temple," 99). At least by the second half of the third century BCE, distinct *Samaritan* synagogues were being built around the Mediterranean rim (Pummer, "Samaritans," 239), which indicates a definitive schism had already taken that prevented common prayer in shared synagogues. Indeed, the hatred of Samaritanism that motivated the destruction of their temple by John Hyrcanus *presupposes* the prior existence of a considerable animosity between the two groups.

[36] Cf., Pummer, "Samaritans," 263: "Given the shared culture and longstanding substantial contacts, then, there is no reason that the interactions between the two communities should not have included participation in the development of some of the narrative and legal traditions that came to constitute the Pentateuch," and "the fall of the Northern Kingdom in the eighth century B.C.E. would have brought about a more concentrated effort to preserve the common patrimony . . . in writing," quoting Joseph Blenkinsopp,

evidence from the Prophets in the previous chapter. After the rise of Zion theology in Judah, it would have been impossible to convince the Jerusalem priesthood to embrace as foundational to their faith a document devoid of Zion and all it stood for, so we must look for a time of canonization prior to the rise of Zion theology. If J. J. M. Roberts is correct that Zion theology arose during the Davidic-Solomonic empire, then we should look for a pre-Davidic origin of the Pentateuch.[37] Although such a proposal is radically at odds with "consensus" views of the composition of the Pentateuch in the academy, we have arrived at this position not on the basis of faith commitments but via a properly historical critical argument, engaging the claims of the Pentateuchal text directly—without the mediation of the Wellhausenian interpretive tradition—and asking the question: at what point in the history of Israel could such a text have been promulgated and accepted as authoritative by the entire nation, both North and South?

The Pentateuch: An Introduction to the First Five Books of the Bible (New Haven, CT: Yale University Press, 2000), 234.

[37] J. J. M. Roberts, "The Davidic Origin of the Zion Tradition," *Journal of Biblical Literature* 92 (1973): 329–44; and J. J. M. Roberts, "The Historicity of David's Imperial Conquests," *Theology Today* 70 (2013): 109–18.

CHAPTER 6

DID POST-EXILIC JUDAISM REALLY ABANDON ZION THEOLOGY?

THE PROBLEM OF THE ABSENCE OF ZION THEOLOGY FROM THE PENTATEUCH

As we have discussed, the starting points for the analysis of the composition of the Pentateuch for the past century and a half were popularized by Julius Wellhausen and summarized in his rendition of the Documentary Hypothesis, in which the final form of the Pentateuch was shaped and edited by the post-exilic Jerusalem priesthood in the fifth century BCE, around the time of the ministry of Ezra.[1] A major problem for Wellhausen's theory of such a late final form of the Pentateuch was (and is) the absence of any Zion theology in the books of Moses. "Zion theology" describes the theological system or economy that arose concurrent with the rise of the Davidic monarchy and revolved around a triad of binding choices or elections made by the Lord: of David and his line as kings; of Jerusalem as God's holy city; and of the Temple as God's holy dwelling.[2] Zion theology tends to be a

---

[1] "The Priestly Code, worked into the Pentateuch as the standard legislative element in it, became the definite 'Mosaic law.' As such it was published and introduced in the year 444 BC, a century after the exile. . . . The man who made the Pentateuch the constitution of Judaism was the Babylonian priest and scribe, Ezra. He had come from Babylon to Jerusalem as early as the year 458 BC" (Julius Wellhausen, *Prolegomena to the History of Israel*, trans. J. Sutherland Black and Allan Menzies [Edinburgh: Adam & Charles Black, 1885], 405).

[2] On Zion theology, see the works of J. J. M. Roberts, helpfully collected in: *The Bible and the Ancient Near East: Collected Essays* (Winona Lake, IN: Eisenbrauns, 2000); and the festschrift *David and Zion: Biblical Studies in Honor of J. J. M. Roberts*, ed. Bernard F. Batto and Kathryn L. Roberts (Winona Lake, IN: Eisenbrauns, 2004). See also Tomoo Ishida, *The Royal Dynasties in Ancient Israel: A Study on the Formation and Development of Royal-Dynastic Ideology* (New York: de Gruyter, 1977); and Jon D. Levenson, *Sinai &*

dominant theme in most of the books of the Old Testament: certainly in the Deuteronomistic History (Deuteronomy through 2 Kings), the Chronicler, the Psalms, and the major and minor Prophets. There are even important connections to it in the wisdom literature. However, Zion theology is absent from the Pentateuch. Neither David, nor Jerusalem, nor the Temple are ever mentioned in Genesis through Deuteronomy. Canonically, Jerusalem is mentioned for the first time in Joshua 10:1; Zion in 2 Samuel 5:7; the word "temple" *(hêkāl)* in 1 Samuel 1:9; David in 1 Samuel 16:13.[3] Actually, Zion theology is not only absent from the Pentateuch, it is also absent from Joshua, Judges, and 1 Samuel. In the primary history of the canonical narrative, the reader does not get an inkling of the role of the Davidic dynasty, the Temple, or the holy city of Jerusalem in salvation history until 2 Samuel 7, even though this triple reality of sacred king, house, and city will dominate the faith and hope of the people of Israel for the rest of their history.

How can this be explained? In particular, how could Zion theology be absent from the Pentateuch if these five books were composed and redacted so late in Israel's history—after the Babylonian Exile—when the desire to restore and rebuild Jerusalem was the motivating religious factor for most of the Judeans who returned to their homeland under Persian rule? Until recently, most scholars have been satisfied with the explanation that Jerusalem and the Temple, at least, went unmentioned as part of the guise of Mosaic authorship, but were transparently identified by the oft-used term, "the place which the LORD your God will choose," employed throughout Deuteronomy as a reference to the central sanctuary (Deut 12:5 *et passim*). This was never a satisfactory explanation: since Moses was a prophet, there was absolutely no reason the imagined exilic or post-exilic priestly redactors of the Pentateuch could not have inserted prophecies of Jerusalem and the Temple into his mouth. However, with only a few exceptions, no one pressed this issue against Wellhausen's theory.[4]

In recent decades, though, several scholars have begun to abandon the notion that Deuteronomy's "place that the LORD your God will choose" is or was ever intended to be a thinly-guised cipher for Jerusalem.[5] One of

---

Zion: An Entry into the Jewish Bible (New York: HarperCollins, 1985). On the triad of Davidic King, Temple, and Mt. Zion, see Levenson, *Sinai & Zion*, 97–98.

[3] In Christian canonical order, David is first mentioned in Ruth 4:17; in Jewish canonical order, 1 Sam 1:13.

[4] An important exception was Terrence Fretheim, who raised this painful issue in his essay, "The Priestly Document: Anti-Temple?" *Vetus Testamentum* 18 (1968): 313–29, but received no response at all from the guild.

[5] See, for example, the arguments in Gary Knoppers, *Jews and Samaritans: The Origins and History of Their Early Relations* (New York: Oxford University Press, 2013), 212; and Etienne Nodet, "Israelites, Samaritans, Temples, Jews," in *Samaria, Samarians, Samaritans:*

the major factors motivating this rethinking has been the discovery of a Yahwistic sanctuary on Mt. Gerizim dating from the mid-fifth century BCE at least, or around 450 BCE, coinciding approximately with the mission of Ezra to Jerusalem.[6] Thus, Pentateuchal scholars have begun to realize that in the fifth century BCE, there was at least one viable rival candidate to be the "place that the LORD your God would choose" besides Jerusalem, and the Jerusalem priesthood would have needed to be much more explicit about the divinely chosen city and sanctuary if they wished the Pentateuch to provide religious legitimation for Jerusalem and its Temple. As Knoppers points out, "It would not have been difficult for the framers of Deuteronomy (or the editors of the Pentateuch) to clarify Yhwh's choice if they wanted to do so."[7] In retrospect, this new perspective undermines the arguments of Wellhausen and others for attaching Deuteronomy to the Josianic reform: the text of Deuteronomy as we have it is *not* specific enough to have served Josiah's agenda in destroying all sanctuaries except the Jerusalem Temple (2 Kings 23:4–20). If Deuteronomy were a Josianic composition, we would expect explicit mention of Jerusalem and the Temple. As we have seen, Shechem and other sacred locations have a stronger claim to legitimacy based on Deuteronomy and the rest of the Pentateuch than does Zion/Jerusalem. Thus, the failure to mention Jerusalem and the Temple in the Pentateuch—even though other sacred sites of rival sanctuaries like Bethel, Shechem, Hebron, and Beersheba *are* mentioned and even valorized in the Pentateuch—has come back on the table for discussion within Pentateuchal scholarship, and various explanations are being proposed.

One theory—currently put forward by Knoppers, Christophe Nihan, and others—is that the Pentateuch is a collaborative document between the Jerusalem and Gerizim priesthoods designed to provide a common foundational religious text that allowed latitude in the interpretation of the exact location of the one central sanctuary.[8] Judeans took it to be Jerusalem, Samaritans Gerizim, but otherwise both could accept the Torah. We have critiqued this theory in the previous chapter.[9]

Studies on Bible, History and Linguistics, ed. József Zsengellér, Studia Judaica 66, Studia Samaritana 6 (Berlin: De Gruyter, 2011), 121–71, esp. 146–47.

[6] Gary Knoppers, "Mt. Gerizim and Mt. Zion: A Study in the Early History of the Samaritans and Jews," *Studies in Religion* 34 (2005): 309–38.

[7] Knoppers, *Jews and Samaritans*, 212.

[8] Knoppers, *Jews and Samaritans*, 194–219; Christophe Nihan, "Cult Centralization and the Torah Traditions in Chronicles," in *The Fall of Jerusalem and the Rise of Torah*, ed. Peter Dubovský, Dominik Markl, and Jean-Pierre Sonnet, Forschungen zum Alten Testament 107 (Tübingen: Mohr Siebeck, 2016) 253–88.

[9] John S. Bergsma, "A 'Samaritan' Pentateuch? The Implications of the Pro-Northern Tendency of the Common Pentateuch," in *Paradigm Change in Pentateuchal Research*, ed.

Another proposal for the absence of Jerusalem and the Temple from the Pentateuch has been advanced by Jean-Louis Ska.[10] Ska argues that cities destroyed by foreigners in the ancient Near East were considered accursed, and this in part explains why post-exilic Judeans omitted Jerusalem from their sacred history as recorded in the Pentateuch. Further, Ska proposes, the contemporary state of Jerusalem was so pathetic during the post-exilic period that the Judeans relegated the city to their glorious past and their eschatological future, but in their present omitted it from their thought and "took refuge in a Temple of words, not of stone"; in other words, neglected the Temple in order to focus on the Torah.

We may immediately recognize that Ska's position on the redaction of the Pentateuch represents a tremendous pendulum shift within Pentateuchal studies. Since the time of Wellhausen to the present, it has been taken for granted that the final form of the Pentateuch was the product of the Jerusalem priesthood who redacted it to support their socio-religious position and ideology. Ska, however, is to be commended for recognizing a problem that is only slowly dawning on the rest of the field of Pentateuchal studies: the failure to mention Jerusalem/Zion or the Temple poses a problem for the assumed Persian Period priestly context of the final redaction of Pentateuch, one that cannot be ignored or overlooked by responsible scholarship. Serious scholars must propose an explanation for the ostentatious absence of any mention of the sacred place and sacred sanctuary that was so dear to the interests of the (presumed) editors of this text.

Ska is quite correct directly to address this problem—the "elephant not in the room" as we have called it—with a creative explanation: post-exilic Judaism gave up on Jerusalem. However, Ska's explanation immediately encounters weighty counterevidence. None of the ostensibly post-exilic books of the Bible nor the non-canonical Second Temple Literature reflect the attitude toward the Temple and the Law that Ska associates with his hypothetical redactors of the Pentateuch. There is, in fact, *no literary evidence whatsoever* that any group or sect within Palestinian post-exilic Judaism responded to the trauma of Jerusalem's destruction and delayed recovery by abandoning the centrality of Jerusalem to their faith, seeking refuge instead in a purely legal religion focused on the Mosaic Torah.[11] In

---

Matthias Armgardt, Benjamin Kilchör, and Markus Zehnder (Wiesbaden: Harrassowitz, 2019), 287–300.

[10] Jean Louis Ska, "Why Does the Pentateuch Speak so Much of Torah and so Little of Jerusalem?," in *Fall of Jerusalem*, 113–28.

[11] To be sure, there are references in the Prophets to those who lost their faith in the LORD God of Israel due to the destruction of Jerusalem and the Babylonian Exile (e.g. Jer 33:24), but one can hardly attribute the composition and redaction of the Pentateuch to these disillusioned and scandalized persons.

what follows, we intend briefly to survey the literature of post-exilic Judaism by genre: the Prophets, the historical books, the Psalms, the wisdom literature, the (non-canonical) Second Temple Literature, and the Dead Sea Scrolls to see if any of the texts which we know to have been, or are supposed to have been, composed or redacted during the Persian Period or shortly thereafter give evidence of the "Torah-instead-of-Jerusalem" worldview that Ska attributes to the redactors of the Pentateuch.

The [Latter] Prophets

Zion theology is prominent in the prophetic books of Isaiah, Jeremiah, Ezekiel, and Daniel, and in many of the Twelve as well. Beginning with Isaiah, Zion theology is dominant through all three of the customary scholarly divisions of the book (chs. 1–39, 40–55, 56–66), with Zion or Jerusalem being mentioned explicitly ninety-five times, in a fairly even distribution throughout the work. In fact, the centrality of Zion to Isaianic theology is scarcely debatable; as von Rad put it so succinctly, "The Zion tradition . . . was determinative for the whole of Isaiah's prophecy."[12] By contrast, the law (*torah*) is only mentioned twelve times, and of these only six or less are possible references to the Mosaic Torah.[13] Moses is only mentioned twice, near the end of the work (Isa 63:11–12). David is mentioned ten times, twice in the context of a divine promise to restore the Davidic dynasty (9:7; 16:5). In addition, there are other such promises that refer to David poetically rather than explicitly (e.g., Isa 11:1–5).

Of course, it is commonly supposed that Second Isaiah (40–55) and Third Isaiah (56–66) were composed during the Exile and the immediate post-exilic period, respectively, and so these are especially important texts for the evaluation of Ska's proposal. Do we see in Second and Third Isaiah a response to the 587 BCE calamity that involves a rejection of Jerusalem in the present and a retreat into the Mosaic Torah? Far from it! From the famous opening line of the second half of this prophetic book: "Comfort, comfort my people . . . speak tenderly to Jerusalem" (40:1–2) until the triumphant final vision when the LORD describes all the "brethren" of the prophet coming on "horses, and in chariots, and in litters, and upon mules, and upon dromedaries, to my *holy mountain Jerusalem*," where "From new moon to new moon, and from sabbath to sabbath, all flesh shall come to

---

[12] Gerhard von Rad, *Old Testament Theology*, vol. 2, *The Theology of Israel's Prophetic Traditions*, trans. D. M. G. Stalker (San Francisco: Harper and Row, 1965), 192.

[13] E.g. Isa 5:24; 24:5; 30:9; 42:21, 24. See JiSeong James Kwon, "Re-Examining the Torah in the Book of Isaiah," *Revue biblique* 126 (2019): 547–64.

worship before me" (66:20–23), the city of Jerusalem remains completely central to the theological focus of the author(s).[14] To be sure, there are allusions and references of various kinds to different texts or narratives of the Pentateuch, but in the one place Moses is mentioned (Isa 63:11–12), he is not in the posture of a law-giver, and there is no hint that Judah's response to the trauma of the Exile and return should be to retreat into the world of Moses and Sinai.

Jeremiah and Ezekiel, as we have seen, are late-monarchic and exilic prophets, and although there is nothing in the text of either of these prophetic books that requires a dating more than a few years after the death of the prophets to which they are attributed; nonetheless, there are many scholars who imagine these works as undergoing a long period of continuous redaction nearly to the end of the Persian period.[15] In any event, even if not redacted, they had to be copied and recopied throughout those centuries, and certainly they were read and treasured by at least some within post-exilic Judaism during that time. So what response to the destruction and exile of Jerusalem do these prophets (and their tradents or adherents) advocate?

First, the lexical facts about Jeremiah: Jerusalem (106x) or Zion (17x) are mentioned 123 times in the MT, David fourteen times, half of those in contexts of divine promise that the Davidic dynasty will be restored. Sinai/Horeb is never mentioned, and Moses only once, incidentally (Jer 15:1). The law (*torah*) is mentioned twelve times, all but once (31:33) being probable references to the Mosaic Torah.[16]

Obviously, the major burden of the Book of Jeremiah is to stress that Jerusalem and its inhabitants have fallen under judgment and a curse from the LORD for violation of his laws and statues; however, this does not result

---

[14] On Zion theology in First Isaiah, see recently Jaap Dekker, *Zion's Rock-Solid Foundations: An Exegetical Study of the Zion Text in Isaiah 28:16* (Leiden, NL: Brill, 2007), esp. 265–338. On Zion theology in Second Isaiah, see Maggie Low, *Mother Zion in Deutero-Isaiah* (New York: Peter Lang, 2013); and Lena-Sofia Tiemeyer, *For the Comfort of Zion: The Geographical and Theological Location of Isaiah 40–55* (Leiden, NL: Brill, 2011). On Zion in Third Isaiah, see Paul V. Niskanen, *Isaiah 56–66* (Collegeville, MN: Liturgical Press, 2014): "The book of Isaiah as a whole is very Zion-centric, and chapters 56–66 are no exception" (xx).

[15] As pointed out by Lawrence Boadt, "Do Jeremiah and Ezekiel Share a Common View of the Exile?" (paper presented at the annual meeting of the Society of Biblical Literature, Atlanta, 22 November 2003), 40: "So much work has been done on this question that it need not be in doubt that the editorial process involved written materials both from and about the two prophets, and that both books were put together within a relatively short period of time. Ezekiel perhaps not much after 571, since there is no evidence of any awareness of the world of Second Isaiah after 547."

[16] Jer 18:18; 26:4; 31:33; 32:23; 44:10; 44:23.

in an abandonment of Jerusalem or all that for which it stands. Rather, there are multiple assurances in the book that God will ultimately and permanently restore his covenant relationship with Jerusalem and all Israel.[17] Indeed, the final oracle of the book in the Masoretic Text is a vision of God saying to Jerusalem, "Behold, I will plead your cause and take vengeance for you" (Jer 51:36) against Babylon, and a plea from the prophet to the exiles, reminiscent of Psalm 137, *not* to forget Jerusalem: "You that have escaped from the sword, go, stand not still! Remember the LORD from afar, and let Jerusalem come into your mind" (51:50).[18] Marvin Sweeney points out that the pro-Zion perspective of Jeremiah is even *stronger* in the presumably later MT edition of the book vis-à-vis the presumably earlier LXX redaction.[19]

Ezekiel has a different character. Jerusalem remains central, mentioned twenty-six times explicitly and also through poetic expressions like "my hill" (34:26) or "the mountain height(s) of Israel" (17:23; 20:40; 34:14). David is mentioned four times explicitly in divine oracles promising the restoration of his dynasty (34:23–24; 37:24–25), and in the Temple vision of Ezekiel 40–48 the Davidide is called the "prince" (*nāśî'*, 19x). Moses and Sinai/Horeb are never mentioned, and strangely the term *torah* is not common (9x), and only twice with reference (arguably) to the Mosaic law (7:26; 22:26); otherwise, *torah* refers to the new laws given in Ezekiel 40–48. "Temple" (*hêkāl*, 10x) or "sanctuary" (*miqdāš*, 31x) occur forty-one times total, but "tabernacle" (*miškān*) is seen only once with reference to the divine dwelling (Ezek 37:27).

Ezekiel's relationship with Jerusalem is complex;[20] nonetheless, he affirms the city as the bride of the LORD (Ezek 16, 23), unfaithful though she may be, and he is in no way uncertain about the eventual forgiveness and restoration of the city and the Davidic dynasty.[21] Although the temple-city

---

[17] Jer 3:17; 30:17; 31:6, 12; 32:44; 33:10–16; 50:5, 28; 51:10.

[18] On Zion theology in Jeremiah, see W. Wessels, "Zion, Beautiful City of God – Zion Theology in the Book of Jeremiah," *Verbum et Ecclesia* 27 (2006): 729–48.

[19] Marvin Sweeney, *The Twelve Prophets*, vol. 1, *Hosea, Joel, Amos, Obadiah, Jonah* (Collegeville, MN: Liturgical Press, 2000), xxxvii.

[20] On Zion theology in Ezekiel, see Thomas Renz, "The Use of the Zion Tradition in the Book of Ezekiel," in *Zion, City of Our God*, ed. Richard S. Hess and Gordon J. Wenham (Grand Rapids: Eerdmans, 1999), 77–103; Daniel I. Block, "Transformation of Royal Ideology in Ezekiel," in *Transforming Visions: Transformations of Text, Tradition, and Theology in Ezekiel*, ed. William A. Tooman and Michael A. Lyons, Princeton Theological Monograph Series 127 (Eugene, OR: Pickwick, 2010), 208–46; Daniel I. Block, "Zion Theology in the Book of Ezekiel," pp.1–9 in *Beyond the River Chebar: Studies in the Kingship and Eschatology in the Book of Ezekiel* (Eugene, OR: Cascade Books, 2013); Jon D. Levenson, *Theology of the Program of Restoration of Ezekiel 40–48*, Harvard Semitic Monographs 10 (Missoula: Scholars Press, 1976), 57–69.

[21] Ezek 16:59–63; 17:22–24; 20:40–44; 34:13–14, 26; 34:24–25; 37:23–24.

described in the final vision (Ezek 40–48) is never explicitly identified, the believing reader, both ancient and modern, is compelled to conclude that it is, in some sense, a new Jerusalem. It must be if the divine promises of Jerusalem's restoration earlier in the book are to be fulfilled.[22]

The specifics of the dating and composition history of the Book of Daniel are disputed.[23] It suffices for our purposes simply to note that in both the Masoretic and the Septuagint forms of this book, the city and temple of Jerusalem and the liturgy celebrated there are *central* to the theological concerns of the document. The book opens with Nebuchadnezzar's abduction of some of the temple vessels of Jerusalem to Babylon (Dan 1:2),[24] and a subtle correlation is implied between these temple vessels and Daniel and his three companions, who struggle to maintain ritual cleanliness while in the service of the pagan king.[25] Nebuchadnezzar's subsequent vision of the human image culminates in an altar stone "not cut out by human hand" (2:34) destroying the kingdoms of men and itself growing into a temple-kingdom "mountain" that fills the earth (2:35). The abduction of the Temple vessels returns in Daniel 5, where the profanation of these vessels becomes the provoking cause for Belshazzar's downfall at the hands of the Medes and Persians (5:2–4). In the following chapter, it is Daniel's loyalty to Jerusalem and his habit of praying toward the city at the times of the morning and evening sacrifice (*tamîd*) that results in his being thrown into the lion's den (6:5, 10). While Jerusalem and temple themes are not explicit in Daniel 7, they return in Daniel 8 where the vision of the ram and the goat culminates in the cessation of the (Jerusalem) *tamid* and the profanation of the (Jerusalem) sanctuary (8:11). Then, in chapter 9—the most theological self-conscious chapter of the book—Daniel prays one of the greatest recorded prayers of intercession in the Bible, which the prophet describes as "confessing my sin and the sin of my people Israel, and presenting my supplication before the Lord my God *for the holy hill of my God*" (9:20). In this theologically central chapter, the concern of the prophet is all for the holy city and its sanctuary, which are mentioned under various terms ("Jerusalem," "holy city," "your city," "holy hill," "your sanctuary") at least

---

22 The prophesies of Jerusalem's restoration are Ezek 16:59–63; 17:22–24; 20:40–44; 34:13–14, 26.

23 See our fuller discussion in John Bergsma and Brant Pitre, *A Catholic Introduction to the Bible*, vol. 1, *The Old Testament* (San Francisco: Ignatius Press, 2018), 892–97.

24 "And the Lord gave Jehoi'akim king of Judah into his hand, with some of the vessels of the house of God; and he brought them to the land of Shinar, to the house of his god, and placed the vessels in the treasury of his god."

25 On cultic and Temple motifs in Daniel, see John S. Bergsma, "Cultic Kingdoms in Conflict: Liturgy and Empire in the Book of Daniel," *Letter & Spirit* 5 (2009): 51–76.

fourteen times.[26] The remaining chapters of the book, Daniel 10–12, are wholly consumed with charting out the sequence of events leading up to the cessation of the *tamid* and the profanation of the Temple, and afterward, the resolution of this crisis.

Moving to the Book of the Twelve, we note that not all of the minor prophets make mention of Jerusalem and the Temple (e.g., Jonah, Nahum, Habakkuk), but most do. Sweeney, in fact, argues vigorously that the MT ordering and redaction of the Book of the Twelve places an increased emphasis on Zion and its Temple vis-à-vis the presumably older LXX edition:

> The Masoretic version of the Book of the Twelve, which focuses especially on the role of Jerusalem at the center of creation and the nations, appears to reflect the concerns of the *later Persian period*, particularly in the time of Ezra and Nehemiah, when concern shifted away from the north to focus *almost entirely on Jerusalem* as the holy center of Persian-Period Yehud.[27]

Here we observe the radical contrast between Sweeney, who takes it for granted that Zion theology *became more intense* in the Persian Period, and Ska's proposal that post-exilic Judaism (or important elements thereof) abandoned Jerusalem. In any event, Sweeney's charcterization of the Twelve as so Jerusalem-focused is obviously contrary to the Pentateuch, as we have seen, which is relentlessly pro-Northern in its valorization of Joseph and his descendants and sacred locations in the north, like Shechem.

Taking the Twelve one by one, we observe that Hosea sees a future in which all Israel will seek out "David their king" in the "latter days" (Hos 3:5), which is inseparable from the restoration of Jerusalem. Joel's theology of Zion is summarized in his prophecy, "I am the LORD your God, who dwell in Zion, my holy mountain. And Jerusalem shall be holy and strangers shall never again pass through it" (Joel 3:17). Amos concludes with a vision of the restoration of the Davidic dynasty as an international empire: "In that day I will raise up the booth of David that is fallen and repair its breaches, . . . that they may possess the remnant of Edom and all the nations who are called by my name" (Amos 9:11–12). Obadiah concludes in a remarkably similar way: "Saviors shall go up to Mount Zion to rule Mount Esau; and the kingdom shall be the LORD's" (Obad v. 21). Micah, for his

---

[26] For a discussion of the structure and interpretation of Daniel 9, see John S. Bergsma, "The Persian Period as Penitential Era: The 'Exegetical Logic' of Daniel 9.1–27," in *Exile and Restoration Revisited: Essays in Memory of Peter R. Ackroyd*, ed. Gary N. Knoppers and Lester L. Grabbe (New York: Continuum/T & T Clark, 2009), 50–64.

[27] Sweeney, *The Twelve*, xxxvii.

part, famously envisions Mt. Zion in the latter days as the highest of mountains, the place of religious pilgrimage and instruction for all the nations of the earth (Mic 4:1–6, parallel to Isa 2:1–4).

Strikingly, the last four of the minor prophets all show great concern for Jerusalem and/or its Temple. Zephaniah concludes with an oracle of consolation for Zion, in which the city becomes virtually synonymous with the nation of Israel itself: "Sing aloud, O daughter of Zion; shout, O Israel! Rejoice and exult with all your heart, O daughter of Jerusalem! The Lord has taken away the judgments against you. . . . The King of Israel, the Lord, is in your midst; you shall fear evil no more" (3:14–15). Haggai, of course, is nothing if not focused on the rebuilding of the Jerusalem Temple under the heirs of the Davidic and Levitical covenants, Zerubbabel the governor and Jehozadak the high priest. In the theology of Haggai, the prosperity of the whole people is tied to their piety toward the Temple and its cult (Hag 2:10–19). Zechariah is the longest and also the most Jerusalem-centric of all the minor prophets. This hardly needs demonstration, but his attitude can be encapsulated in the words he records as the voice of the LORD: "I am jealous for Zion with great jealousy, and I am jealous for her with great wrath. . . . I will return to Zion, and will dwell in the midst of Jerusalem, and Jerusalem shall be called the faithful city, and the mountain of the LORD of hosts, the holy mountain" (Zech 8:2–3). His prophetic book concludes with Zion portrayed as the place of pilgrimage for all nations for the Feast of Tabernacles, which they observe under the threat of divine curse (Zech 14:16–19). The sanctity of the Temple will pervade the entire city such that "every pot in Jerusalem and Judah shall be sacred to the Lord of hosts" (Zech 14:20–21). Finally, Malachi is dominated by the concern to reform the liturgical abuses at the Jerusalem Temple. He criticizes (1) the offering of blemished animals (Mal 1:6–14), (2) the priests who allow this practice (2:1–9), (3) other unspecified profanations of the sanctuary (2:10–12), and (4) the withholding of the tithes from the Temple (3:6:1–12). As a remedy, he foresees the coming of a "messenger" who will purify the priesthood at the Jerusalem Temple, resulting in a proper sacrificial liturgy once more (3:1–4). It is true that Malachi ends with an exhortation to observe the law of Moses given at Horeb (Mal 4:4)—one of only two times Moses is mentioned in the Twelve, and the only time Horeb/Sinai is. Nonetheless, it is completely untenable to put this exhortation in opposition to the concern for the Jerusalem Temple and its cult which dominates Malachi and indeed, all the post-exilic minor prophets.

THE HISTORICAL BOOKS / FORMER PROPHETS

No less than the Prophets, the historical books that were completed or edited in the post-exilic period betray an overarching concern for Jerusalem. The Deuteronomistic History, for example—if we take its narrative arc from Deuteronomy to 2 Kings—begins with Moses prophesying God's choice of "a place to make his name dwell there" (Deut 12:5) and concludes with that place—now clearly identified as Jerusalem—being destroyed (2 Kgs 25:9); yet there is a glimmer of hope for the future in that the Davidide, the traditional temple builder and protector, is shown mercy in exile that his dynasty may continue (2 Kgs 25:27–30).[28] Chronicles is much *more* emphatically liturgical and Jerusalem-centric than its source text DtrH, as it omits discussion of the aberrant, heretical northern kingdom as theologically irrelevant, and tells the story of the southern kingdom by focusing largely on the Davidic kings as liturgical reformers and temple builders.[29] It concludes much more optimistically, with an exhortation from Cyrus for all Jews to go up to Jerusalem. The books of Ezra and Nehemiah, of course, are entirely concerned with the rebuilding of Jerusalem, its Temple, and its walls, and with the restoration of healthy civil, social, and liturgical life in that city. While both Ezra and Nehemiah are concerned with the observance of the Mosaic law, it is always in *support* of the re-establishment of Jerusalem, never as an *alternative to* loyalty to the city.

Even in the late Second Temple works considered histories by Hellenistic Jews in the diaspora and included in the Septuagint (e.g., Tobit, Judith, Maccabees), Jerusalem still remains theologically central. Tobit, for example, prides himself in being the sole member of the tribe of Naphtali that remained faithful to the Jerusalem sanctuary and its liturgy (Tob 3:1–8). Likewise, Judith portrays the high priest in Jerusalem as the religious and civil leader of the nation, and suggests that it is the fasting, prayer, and temple sacrifices of the populace of Jerusalem that merits the eventual deliverance of the people of Israel from the hands of the foreign tyrant Holofernes (Jud

---

[28] Against those who deny that this ending indicates hope for the Davidic dynasty, Rolf Rendtorff's comments are definitive: "It is in fact improbable that Israelite readers would not have thought here of a possible future for the Davidic monarchy" (*The Old Testament: An Introduction*, trans. John Bowden [Philadelphia, PA: Fortress Press, 1986], 187).

[29] Sweeney comments: "The shift from concern with the north to concern with Jerusalem is especially evident in Chronicles, which reworks 1–2 Kings by eliminating most material pertaining to northern Israel in order to present a history that focuses on Judah, Jerusalem, and the Temple" (*The Twelve*, xxxvii). For an exposition of the Davidic and Temple-centered theology of Chronicles, see Scott W. Hahn, *The Kingdom of God as Liturgical Empire: A Theological Commentary on 1–2 Chronicles* (Grand Rapids: Baker Academic, 2012).

4:1–15). Finally, the accounts of the Maccabean insurgency in 1–2 Maccabees are nothing if not obsessed with the control of Jerusalem, the Temple,
and the proper celebration of its liturgy. The Maccabean literature is anti-
thetical to any kind of Judaism that neglects the centrality of Jerusalem.

The Psalms

We hardly need emphasize how central Zion is to the Psalms![30] We think
particularly of the work of Gerald Wilson, who showed that the strategic
placement of royal Davidic psalms—e.g. Psalm 2 at the beginning of Book
1; Psalm 72 at the end of Book 2; Psalm 89 at the end of Book 3—was one of
the keys for determining the intention of the redactors of the Psalter.[31] Even
in the last and certainly latest of the divisions of the Psalter (Book V; Pss
107–150), Zion and the Davidic monarchy continue to play an important
theological role. Psalm 110 assures us that the son of David is a priest forever
after the order of Melchizedek, the ancient king of (Jeru-)Salem according
to Genesis 14. Still later in the Psalter, Psalm 132 reemphasizes the dual elec-
tion of the house of David as the royal dynasty and Jerusalem as the site of
the divine sanctuary. The Psalms of Ascent (Psalm 120–134) are a set of
pilgrimage psalms to the rebuilt Second Temple, which begin far from the
sanctuary (120:5) but conclude inside the Temple courts during the watches
of the night (134:1), representing the geographical but also spiritual progress of the pilgrim.[32] The concluding quintet of the Psalter, the Halleluiah
Psalms 146–150, still leave no doubt that the place from which the LORD
is to be praised is the sanctuary in Zion (146:10; 147:2, 12; 149:2). What
is the official response of the Psalter to the trauma of the destruction of
Jerusalem and the Exile? It is Psalm 137:5–6: "If I forget you, O Jerusalem,
let my right hand wither! Let my tongue cleave to the roof of my mouth, if I
do not remember you, if I do not set Jerusalem above my highest joy!" After
an analysis of the role of Zion theology in the editing of the Psalter, Laura
Gillingham concludes that the editors of the Psalter and Chronicles were
probably the same, since they "shared the same vision . . . to reinforce the

---

[30]   For example, Hans-Joachim Kraus, *The Theology of the Psalms*, trans. Keith Crim (Minne-
       apolis, MN: Fortress, 1992), 73–106. See also Levenson, *Sinai & Zion*, 137–56, 169–78.

[31]   Gerald H. Wilson, *The Editing of the Hebrew Psalter* (Chico, CA: Scholars Press, 1985).

[32]   See the discussion in David G. Barker, "Voices for the Pilgrimage: A Study in the Psalms of
       Ascent," *The Expository Times* 116 (2005): 109–16; Philip E. Satterthwaite, "Zion in the
       Songs of Ascent," in *Zion, City of Our God*, ed. Richard S. Hess and Gordon J. Wenham
       (Grand Rapids: Eerdmans, 1999), 105–28.

belief that Zion was the central locus for Judaism, both for the individual and the community as a whole."[33]

David, Zion, and Jerusalem are all frequently mentioned explicitly in the Psalter, and alluded to in other ways or under other terms on many more occasions.[34] By contrast, how does the Mosaic law compare in the Psalter? The *torah* is mentioned only ten times outside of Psalm 119. Moses is mentioned only eight times, seven of them in Book IV, mostly in the reviews of salvation history found at the end of this book (Pss 105–106). He is never mentioned in Book V. The *torah* is not mentioned again after Psalm 119. Sinai is only mentioned twice as the place the LORD left to come to Zion (68:8, 17), and Horeb only once as the site of the Golden Calf apostasy (106:19). There is truly a stark contrast in what is theologically central and what is theologically peripheral between the Psalter and the Pentateuch. It is remarkable that this contrast between the theology of the Psalter and that of the Pentateuch has never been part of the discussion on the composition of the Pentateuch, even though it has been supposed that essentially the same circles (those of the Jerusalem priesthood) were responsible for the final redaction of both.

The Wisdom Literature

Much of the wisdom literature of Israel is believed to have been composed or redacted during the post-exilic period (Proverbs, Ecclesiastes, Song of Songs, Job). Although the concerns of the wisdom literature are practical ethics and the virtues necessary for daily living—and thus there is much less attention paid to the covenantal history of Israel that dominates the rest of the canon—it is significant that all the Hebrew wisdom books but Job tie themselves to the figure of Solomon, son of David, heir of the Davidic covenant, and king of Jerusalem.[35] Even the wisdom books of the Septuagint canon either project Solomonic authorship (Wis 7:1–14) or model themselves on the proverbs of Solomon.[36] The wisdom books of the MT never mention Moses, and with only a few late exceptions near the end of Proverbs,[37] the *torah* is usually the *torah* of Solomon or the sages rather than that of Sinai.[38] Remarkably, there are references specifically to the Temple in the

---

[33] Susan Gillingham, "The Zion Tradition and the Editing of the Hebrew Psalter," in *Temple and Worship in Biblical Israel*, ed. John Day (London: T&T Clark, 2007), 308–41.

[34] In the Psalter, we see David 85x, Zion 39x, and Jerusalem 17x.

[35] Prov 1:1; 10:1; 25:1; Eccl 1:1, 16; 2:7, 9; Song 1:1, 5; 3:7–11; 8:11–12.

[36] Cf. Sir 2:1; 3:17; 4:1; 6:18 with Prov 1:10; 2:1; 3:1; 5:1; 6:1; 7:1, etc.

[37] Possibly Prov 28:4, 7, 9; 29:18.

[38] E.g., Prov 1:8; 3:1; 4:2; 6:20, 23; 7:2; 13:14.

wisdom literature: a passing reference in Ecclesiastes (5:1) and a description of the body of the bridegroom in the Song of Songs that employs temple imagery, suggesting a correlation between the royal bridegroom's person and the Temple itself (Song 5:10–16). This association with the Davidic covenant economy, personified in Solomon the Son of David and the Jerusalem Temple, only increases in the additional wisdom books found in the canon of the Septuagint. The second-century Wisdom of Solomon presents itself as the instruction of Solomon the temple builder (Wis 9:7–8) to the other kings of the world and embeds itself in the DtrH narrative of the young Solomon who prayed for wisdom[39] and so became the greatest and wisest of kings.[40] Furthermore, it is only in the Book of Sirach, which sees itself as a culmination or synthesis of Israel's wisdom tradition (the "last on watch" who "gleans after the grape-gatherers," Sir 33:16), that we find the Mosaic *torah* integrated into the wisdom worldview. There are many examples, but the most striking is Sirach 24:23, 25, which identifies Lady Wisdom as the Mosaic *torah*:

> All this is the book of the covenant of the Most High God, the law which Moses commanded us as an inheritance for the congregations of Jacob. It fills men with wisdom . . .

At the same time, there is a perfect integration with Jerusalem, the Temple, and Zion theology because the author, Jesus son of Sirach, identifies himself as a Jerusalemite (Sir 50:27) who received wisdom by praying at the Temple (Sir 51:14). Furthermore, although divine wisdom began with Moses and Sinai, she has now taken up permanent residence in the Jerusalem Temple:

> In the holy tabernacle I ministered before him,
>> and so I was established in Zion.
> In the beloved city likewise He gave me a resting place,
>> and in Jerusalem was my dominion.
> So I took root in an honored people,
>> in the portion of the Lord, who is their inheritance,
> and my abode was in the full assembly of the saints. (Sir 24:10–12)

Likewise, when Jesus ben Sirah recounts the salvation history of Israel in the "Praise of the Fathers" (Sir 44–50), he presents it in such a way as to suggest that the sacred history of Israel has a liturgical culmination in great feasts of the Jerusalem Temple celebrated under the legitimate high priest: in his

---

[39] 1 Kings 3:3–15; cf. Wis. 7:1–14.
[40] 1 Kings 4:1–34; cf. Wis 7:17–22.

own day, Simon II, son of Onias II (Sir 50:1–24). So what we see in Sirach is a seamless integration of the Mosaic *torah* tradition into the larger wisdom tradition associated with Jerusalem, with the Jerusalem Temple becoming the earthly locus of divine wisdom for the world.

Non-Canonical Second Temple Literature

We only have space for a brief survey of some of the older and more important non-canonical Second Temple works such as the *Book of Jubilees*, the *Testament of the Twelve Patriarchs,* and the Enochic works later collected as *1 Enoch*. These works demonstrate the continued importance and centrality of Jerusalem and its Temple in the late centuries BCE.[41]

The Enochic literature is concerned with esoteric topics like angelology, astronomy, and calendrical studies that bring it far afield from the worldview more typical of Israelite sacred literature. But we should recall that the astro-calendrical investigations of Enoch were ultimately tied to establishing the liturgical calendar for the Jerusalem Temple feasts. Furthermore, Jerusalem and its Temple continue to play an important role in the theological geography of Enoch, even in the older works of the Enochic tradition.[42]

Jubilees, on the other hand, of all the works of Second Temple Judaism perhaps best demonstrates why we can be certain that the Pentateuch is not a Second Temple document. As we have seen, *Jubilees* represents a rewriting of Genesis and Exodus in such a way as to correct those aspects of the Pentateuch that were theologically awkward for Second Temple Jewish sensibilities, thus bringing the Pentateuch as a whole in line with the Zion theology of the period.[43] The Pentateuch never mentions Jerusalem/Zion; yet *Jubilees* mentions it eight times.[44] Already in its first chapter, *Jubilees* affirms the holiness of Zion and its eschatological role as a source of the new creation (1:28–29), elsewhere describing it as one of the four sacred places of the earth (4:26), the "center of the navel of the earth" (8:19), and the location of the *Aqedah* (18:13). *Jubilees* records a stern warning from the LORD to Jacob not to establish a permanent shrine at Bethel (32:22), and also does extensive "damage control" on the scandalous account of Judah's procreation through fornication with his Canaanite daughter-in-law in Genesis 38, which, in its unedited form, destroys Judean pretensions to

---

[41] See Michael A. Knibb, "Temple and Cult in Apocryphal and Pseudepigraphal Writings from Before the Common Era," in *Temple and Worship*, 401–6.

[42] See Kelley Coblentz Bautch, *"No One Has Seen What I Have Seen": A Study of the Geography of 1 Enoch 17–19* (Leiden, NL: Brill, 2003).

[43] See Bergsma, "'Samaritan' Pentateuch?," 287–300.

[44] *Jubilees* 1:28 [3x]; 1:29 [2x]; 4:26; 8:19; 18:13.

ethnic purity (*Jubilees* 41). *Jubilees* also completely omits Jacob's blessing of Ephraim and Manasseh, the ancestors of the despised Samaritans that posed the threat of a rival cult to Judean Yahwists. Instead, *it* substitutes a narrative in which Jacob presents his two sons Levi and Judah to his father Isaac, who (in a scene clearly modeled on Genesis 48) bestows on these two an extensive priestly and royal blessing, respectively (*Jub* 31:1–32). This fits the theology of the Second Temple period much better: compare the twin blessing of the Davidic and Levitical houses in Jeremiah 33:14–26 and, similarly, the two olive trees of the Davidide and the high priest in Zechariah 4:1–14. Therefore, *Jubilees* reflects the discomfort Second Temple Judaism felt with many prominent features of the Pentateuch: the failure to mention Zion, Judah's scandalous sexual behavior, patriarchal worship at diverse shrines, and the emphasis on Joseph and the Josephite tribes. If the Pentateuch had been composed or redacted by Judean priests in the post-exilic period, it would look like *Jubilees*, not like its form in the MT.

Likewise, the eschatology of the *Testament of the Twelve Patriarchs* contains several references to Jerusalem[45] and its Temple[46] and other reflections of the pre-eminence of the tribes of Judah and Levi[47] and anti-Shechemite (=anti-Samaritan) impulses (Levi 7:2) that are characteristic of Second Temple Literature but absent from the Pentateuch.

THE DEAD SEA SCROLLS

When we approach the Qumran literature, the interest in Moses increases vis-à-vis the late biblical literature, but the centrality of Jerusalem/Zion remains constant. The large number of copies of the *Book of Jubilees* found among the Scrolls indicates the reverence with which the community held that document, and it is a safe assumption that the Qumranites shared the pro-Zion perspective of its author(s) and appreciated its revision of the Pentateuchal narrative in such a way as to mitigate those elements that conflicted with the core commitments of Second Temple Judaism.

Moses is mentioned more in the Scrolls than in all of the non-Hexateuchal books of the Hebrew Bible combined.[48] Thus, we see in the Scrolls a return to a concern for Moses as a person, and not just his laws—a concern that is

---

[45] *T. Levi* 10:3, 5; 14:6; *T. Zeb* 9:8; *T. Dan* 5:12–13; *T. Naph.* 5:1.

[46] *T. Levi* 15:1; 17:10.

[47] *T. Jud.* 1:6; *T. Naph.* 5:3; *T. Levi* 2:11; 8:14; 9:2.

[48] Moses's name occurs 64 times in the non-Hexateuchal books of the Hebrew Bible, but is extant or can be convincingly reconstructed in 175 passages of the non-canonical (sectarian) scrolls. This is based on the electronic text, *Qumran Non-biblical Manuscripts*, version 3.2, ©1999–2009 Martin G. Abegg, Jr., available for the Accordance© software platform

largely absent outside the Hexateuch. However, *this renewal of attention to Moses is not at the expense of the centrality of Zion.* Zion/Jerusalem is mentioned one hundred twenty-three times in the Scrolls, while Sinai/Horeb only sixteen times. Zion remains the focus of the Qumran community's present concern as well as its eschatological future, as one can see from the War Scroll[49] as well as non-canonical Zion hymns like 4Q88, 4Q380 and 11Q5 col. 22. Their future is also tied up with David (mentioned thirty-four times), from whose line the expected Messiah of Israel was to come.[50] We can say that the Scrolls represent a kind of "Zionization" of Moses, since we find among the Scrolls something that never occurs in the Pentateuch or any other canonical literature: a claim that Moses himself received revelation about a permanent stone temple and the liturgy to be performed there. We are referring, of course, to the Temple Scroll (11QTemple), which purports to record a revelation to Moses at Sinai concerning the Temple and liturgy to be established in the promised land when the Israelites have settled it.[51] Contrast this with DtrH's acknowledgement that there had never been such a revelation (2 Sam 7:5–7). Thus, the Temple Scroll responds to a felt need of Second Temple Judaism: the need for Mosaic authorization for the construction of a Temple.[52] Although the extant passages of the Temple Scroll do not specify the location on which the Temple was to be built, there is no doubt that the Qumranites knew it was Jerusalem, "for Jerusalem is the holy camp. It is the place that He chose from all the tribes of Israel, for Jerusalem is the foremost of the camps of Israel."[53] The Qumran covenanters clearly embraced the Zion theology evident in the Prophets, the Psalms, the Chronicler, and elsewhere, which is summed up most succinctly in 4Q504:

> Jerusa[lem, the city that You ch]ose out of all the earth, that Your
> [name] should dwell there forever. Surely You love Israel more than
> all the other peoples; more narrowly, You chose the tribe of Judah.
> You have established Your covenant with David, making him a

---

from Oak Tree Software, Inc. Subsequent frequency statistics above also represent both extant and convincingly reconstructed instances in this electronic text.

[49] 1QM 1:3; 3:11; 7:4; 12:13,17; 19:5.

[50] 4Q161, f. 8, 10:17; 4Q174 f. 1–2, col. I, 10–13; 4Q252 5:1–5; 4Q285 f. 7, 2–4.

[51] See Johann Maier, *The Temple Scrolls: An Introduction, Translation & Commentary, Journal for the Study of the Old Testament* Supplement 34 (Sheffield: JSOT Press, 1985), 1–7.

[52] See Molly M. Zahn, "New Voices, Ancient Words: The Temple Scroll's Reuse of the Bible," in *Temple and Worship*, 435–58.

[53] 4Q394 8 IV, 9–12.

princely shepherd over Your people, that he sit before You upon the throne of Israel eternally.[54]

This is precisely the Zion tradition that we do not find in the Pentateuch, save perhaps in Genesis 49:8–10.[55] The evidence from Qumran is all the more interesting and relevant because it has often been surmised that the nucleus of the Qumran community had close ties to the Jerusalem priesthood that was in power prior to the usurpation of the high priesthood by the Maccabees.[56] Thus, the leadership of Qumran may have been descendants of the priesthood that served in Jerusalem during the Persian Period, the very circles often associated with the final redaction of the Pentateuch. Yet, they seemed to be rather fond of the pro-Temple, pro-Zion revisionism of *Jubilees*, the Temple Scroll, and similar documents.

CONCLUSION

We have sought to demonstrate that the majority of religious texts that are commonly thought to be composed or redacted in Judah during the Persian Period represent a *heightened* focus on the great triad of Zion theology (Davidide, Jerusalem, Temple) over against older texts. We even extended our view into the Hellenistic period (e.g. *Jubilees*, 1–2 Maccabees, Sirach, etc.) to demonstrate that this legacy continues uninterrupted into the following stage of Judean history. Ska states that "the law became the most important pillar of Israel's life in postexilic times, more important than . . . the temple. . . . The postexilic community of Israel preferred to house its renewed identity in a city of words, the Torah, rather than in an uncompleted city of stones, Jerusalem."[57] This statement, however, is not supported by the evidence of the texts produced and curated during this time period. There is no literary evidence of Ska's imagined post-exilic Judean community that gave up on Jerusalem and contented itself with the Mosaic law. To the contrary, the literature produced by post-exilic Judaism was, if anything,

---

[54] 4Q504 1-2 IV, 3–8.

[55] Genesis 49:8–10 is the only passage of the Pentateuch which can be presented convincingly as a reference to the Davidic monarchy, but it appears to limit Judah's possession of the "scepter" by the phrase "until Shiloh comes" (v. 10b). Nahum M. Sarna sees this as a reference to the split after Solomon in 1 Kings 12; see *Genesis*, JPS Torah Commentary (Philadelphia: JPS, 1989), 336–37: "Judah's hegemony over Israel will last until the secession of the north" (337).

[56] See Jerome Murphy-O'Connor, "The Teacher of Righteousness," in *The Anchor Bible Dictionary*, vol. 6, ed. David Noel Freedman (New York: Doubleday, 1992), 340–41.

[57] Ska, "Why Does the Pentateuch Speak So Much of Torah?," 126.

more committed to the sacrality of Jerusalem and its Temple than older Isra-elite literature: compare, for example, Chronicles with Samuel-Kings, or Zechariah with Hosea.

This poses a major challenge not just to Ska's hypothesis but to every theory of Pentateuchal development, including Wellhausen's, that places its composition and/or redaction in the post-exilic period. It will not do to ignore the fact that, unlike all the other literature coming from this time period, the Pentateuch never mentions and cares nothing for the elements of Zion theology—Davidic king, Jerusalem, and the Temple—and could even be interpreted as being opposed to these three institutions.[58]

Let us make the point even sharper. Even though in the Persian Period the region of Judah in general, and Jerusalem in particular, were at the nadir of their socio-economic fortunes, with perhaps less than a thousand per-manent inhabitants in the holy city itself,[59] and despite the fact that there is no direct evidence of Hebrew literacy from Persian-Period Yehud,[60] most scholars are (to our mind erroneously) convinced that this was the time and location of an enormous amount of literary activity: the composition and/or redaction of almost the entire Hebrew Bible.[61] During this time period

---

[58] Opposed to the Davidic king because it has a very limited, and non-sacral, view of the king-ship (Deut 17:14–20); opposed to Jerusalem because it never mentions it while valorizing other sacred sites like Shechem; opposed to the Temple because it authorizes a portable tent shrine instead.

[59] So Oded Lipschits, "Ramat Rachel between Jerusalem and Mizpah," paper presented at the Society of Biblical Literature Annual Meeting, Boston, MA, Nov. 11, 2017; cf. Israel Finklestein, "Jerusalem and Judah 600–200 BCE: Implications for Understanding Pentateuchal Texts," in *The Fall of Jerusalem and the Rise of Torah*, ed. Peter Dubovsky, et al., Forschungen zum Alten Testament 107 (Tübingen: Mohr Siebeck, 2016), 8–10. Finkelstein describes "a dramatic settlement and demographic decline" and "disappear-ance of Hebrew writing" that "contradicts scholars who tend to belittle the scope of the catastrophe" of 586 BCE (9). Further, the return from Babylon "was more a trickle than a flood" (9). "Not a single securely-dated Hebrew inscription has been found for the period between 586–c. 350 BCE . . . scribal activity declined—and significantly so" (10).

[60] Finkelstein comments: "There is almost no evidence for Hebrew writing in Yehud in c. 586–350 BCE, and very little evidence until c. 200 BCE. This should come as no surprise: the destruction of Judah brought about the collapse of the kingdom's bureaucracy and deportation of many of the educated intelligentsia . . . the 'vinedressers and ploughmen' who remained were hardly capable of producing written documents" ("Jerusalem and Judah 600–200 BCE," 14).

[61] Finkelstein is a lonely voice warning against the currently popular pan-Persianization of the Hebrew Bible. Based on the archaeological evidence for the profound impoverishment of Persian Jerusalem, his advice to Bible scholars is to date as much biblical literature as possible to the late iron age (late monarchic period) or the Hellenistic period, or place the provenance in Babylon, but to avoid Persian-Period Yehud as the location for production of sacred texts ("Jerusalem and Judah 600–200 BCE," 14–15). He apologizes for threaten-ing "to shatter slick, fad-driven theories" (15).

and in this city, the following works are thought to have been composed:[62] Third Isaiah, Obadiah, Joel, Haggai, Zechariah, Malachi, Ezra-Nehemiah, 1–2 Chronicles, Ecclesiastes, Song of Solomon, and many individual Psalms. Furthermore, the following compositions, large parts of which were already extant, are thought to have undergone redaction to varying degrees: the Deuteronomistic History and the Books of Isaiah, Jeremiah, Ezekiel, the Twelve, Proverbs, and Psalms. It has even been typical in scholarship to imagine that these different compositions represent "schools" that were in existence in Persian Jerusalem, such as an "Isaianic school"[63] or an "Ezekielan school"[64] or a "Jeremianic School,"[65] each representing a religio-theological movement committed to the views contained in their preferred document.

It begins to strain credibility to the breaking point to postulate that, in the relatively small community of Persian-Period Yehud, in which Isaiah, Jeremiah, Ezekiel, the Twelve, parts of Daniel, the Deuteronomistic History, Chronicles, Ezra-Nehemiah, the Wisdom books, the Psalms, and other documents were being composed, redacted, copied and recopied, there existed a counter-community of influential Judeans who rejected a central tenet that all this literature had in common: adherence and loyalty to the Zion tradition.[66] Nonetheless, this Zion-rejecting or Zion-suppressing Judean minority composed a Zion-less account of the formative period of the nation's history, legal tradition, and religion—namely, the Pentateuch—and persuaded all the other streams and traditions of Second Temple Judaism (and the Samaritans as well!) to accept the resulting Zion-less document as the *foundational* document of their religion *par excellence*.[67] Is this scenario really plausible? Or does it rather seem likely that there was no significant form of

---

[62] We exclude the Pentateuch and its sources here since the date of their composition and redaction is the point in question.

[63] H. G. M. Williamson discusses the plausibility of an Isaianic school in *The Book Called Isaiah: Deutero-Isaiah's Role in Composition and Redaction* (Oxford, UK: Oxford University Press, 1994).

[64] Walther Zimmerli speaks frequently of the "Ezekiel school": *Ezekiel 1* (Philadelphia, PA: Fortress, 1969), 65, 71, 422, et passim.

[65] For a "Jeremianic school," see Rosalie Kuyvenhoven, "Jeremiah 23:1–8: Shepherds in Diachronic Perspective," in *Paratext and Megatext as Channels of Jewish and Christian Traditions: The Textual Markers of Contextualization*, ed. A. A. den Hollander, U. B. Schmid, and W. F. Smelik (Leiden, NL: Brill, 2003), 1–36, esp. 12.

[66] To be sure, the Zion tradition is not homogeneous, and each biblical author has his own unique nuancing of this tradition. But the point here is the significant majority of the texts thought to be composed or redacted in the Persian Period embrace the Zion tradition *in some form*, whereas it is *completely absent* from the Pentateuch.

[67] For as soon as Judean history progresses into the second century BCE, from which we possess greater documentation shedding light on Jewish thought and practice, we discover that the Pentateuch is the one document accepted by every sect and branch of Judaism and Samaritanism.

Judaism in Persian-Period Yehud that rejected or suppressed Jerusalem and all it stood for theologically?

We should remember that the Jews largely responsible for populating Jerusalem and its environs were Babylonian exiles, or descendants thereof, who had made the costly decision to uproot from Babylon and return to a devastated Jerusalem almost solely for the religious significance that location held for them. This demographic and its leadership would be the *least likely* segment of the descendants of historic Israel to agree to the redaction of their sacred history that omitted references to their sacred city for which they had suffered so much. This population had sacrificed a great deal in terms of wealth and social standing to re-establish themselves in Jerusalem and Judah, and this commitment to Zion is reflected in the documents they produced: Ezra-Nehemiah, 1–2 Chronicles, and their redactions of the prophetic works and other traditional literature.

Particularly acute is the problem of the role of the Jerusalem priesthood in the redaction of the Pentateuch. Since so much of the Pentateuch is concerned with cultic purity, the sanctuary, the priesthood, the cultic calendar, and the sacrificial liturgy, it is very difficult to imagine that the document could have been promulgated within Judaism without the consent of the Jerusalem priesthood, which had authority over these matters in the Persian Period. At the same time, it is very difficult to believe that this priesthood, which presumably chanted the psalms of Zion within the Temple courts and embraced the theology of these Psalms, would have consented to the promulgation of a sacred history which expunged or overlooked references to the sacred site they considered the *axis mundi*.[68] Wellhausen never confronted the conflict between the Zion-less theology of his imagined "Priestly Source" and the theology of the Psalms, even though both documents must be attributed to the same priestly community. In a moment of clarity he does observe that, in the Priestly texts, "Jerusalem and the temple, which, properly speaking, occasioned the whole arrangement, are buried in silence with a diligence which is in the highest degree surprising."[69] In the rest of his work, Wellhausen proceeds himself to "bury in silence" this glaring omission of Zion from the Pentateuch. But ignoring a problem does not make it go away.

---

[68] Terence Fretheim's observation from over half a century ago has lost none of its force: "It is incredible that a document promulgated by a priesthood that had been entrenched in Jerusalem for over three hundred years, and so closely bound up with the monarchy and 'Zion theology', would be completely devoid of so much as an allusion to the David-Zion traditions" ("The Priestly Document: Anti-Temple?" *Vetus Testamentum* 18 [1968]: 313–29, at 319). On Jerusalem as the *axis mundi* in biblical literature, see Levenson, *Sinai & Zion*, 115–26.

[69] Wellhausen, *Prolegomena*, 164.

Furthermore, it has often been believed that much of the biblical literature composed or redacted during the Persian Period was done by circles close to the priesthood if not by the priests themselves. Yet we have a fairly continuous sequence of such priestly-associated authors reflected in the documents of the Hebrew Bible: from the early to mid-sixth century, we have Ezekiel and Jeremiah at least; from the late sixth century, Haggai, Zechariah, Malachi; from the fifth century, Ezra-Nehemiah; from the fourth, Chronicles and perhaps the Psalter; from the second, *Jubilees*. All these documents emanate from authors or circles that had strong ties to the priesthood and the Temple. All of them also are committed to Zion theology. It is indeed very surprising that the theological disparity between the Psalms and the Pentateuch, for example, has never elicited much discussion within biblical scholarship, even though both documents have been presumed to emanate from the same Jerusalem hierocracy of the Persian Period. The Books of Chronicles, too, are a particularly important witness since they are widely held to have been written by a priest or Levite serving in Jerusalem in the fourth century BCE and therefore could be presumed to reflect the worldview of the Jerusalem clergy at the heart of the Persian Period.[70] Yet the Chronicler is one of the greatest advocates of Zion theology to be found in the Hebrew Bible. Who, then, are the mysterious figures who abandoned Zion and produced the Pentateuch, and how did they persuade the Jerusalem priesthood to accept their work?

In sum, Ska is quite correct to recognize the absence of Zion theology from the Pentateuch as a problem that demands an explanation, but an explanation is not possible as long as we insist on imagining the Pentateuch as the result of creative redactional activity in the post-exilic/Second Temple Period.[71] We have not even begun to bring the linguistic evidence into play, but William Schniedewind of UCLA, one of the top semiticists in international Biblical studies, assures us that the Pentateuch is *not* a document of post-exilic/Second Temple Judaism linguistically, showing none of the grammatical, syntactical, and lexical features of Hebrew written in

---

[70] Steven L. McKenzie, *1–2 Chronicles* (Nashville, TN: Abingdon, 2004), 27–28, 32; cf. Jacob M. Myers, *1 Chronicles* (New York: Doubleday, 1965), lxxxvi–lxxxix.

[71] By contrast with Ska's prescience, note that not a single contribution to the immense tome edited by Jan C. Gertz, Bernard M. Levinson, Dalit Rom-Shiloni, and Konrad Schmid, *The Formation of the Pentateuch: Bridging the Academic Cultures of Europe, Israel, and North America* (Tübingen: Mohr Siebeck, 2016), addresses the issue of the absence of Zion from the Pentateuch, the role of the Samarians/Samaritans in Pentateuchal composition, or the presence of the rival Gerizim sanctuary during the Persian Period that drives Knoppers and Nihan to propose a "compromise" theory of Pentateuchal redaction. There seems to be a certain studied avoidance of this issue in contemporary Pentateuchal studies.

this time period.[72] Yet some are willing to argue that the archaic Hebrew of the Pentateuch could have been imitated by a Persian Period author. Thus, even more significant than the linguistic evidence is the fact that the Pentateuch as we have it *does not reflect the interests of the Judaism after the Exile,* which—while loyal to the laws of Moses—had moved on to place Zion theology in the center of its religious aspirations. We need to recognize that, as we have said before, and contrary to Ska's proposal, Zion theology does not abate but rather *intensifies* in the Persian Period, as can be seen (as Marvin Sweeney points out)[73] by comparing DtrH with the Chronicler, LXX Jeremiah with MT Jeremiah, LXX Twelve with MT Twelve, Hosea/Amos with Zechariah/Malachi, even Book IV of the Psalms with Book V.[74] This poses a serious challenge not only to Ska's hypothesis, but also to the "Judean-Samarian compromise" view of Nihan and others, which imagines that the Pentateuch arose from a sanguine ecumenism between the priestly leadership of Jerusalem and Gerizim in the Persian Period[75]—an ecumenism unattested and indeed opposed by almost all the religious literature associated with this time period.

We need to acknowledge that the "Common Pentateuch," with its (1) absence of Zion, (2) valorization of northern religious sites (esp. Shechem and Gerizim), and (3) subjugation of (southern) Judah to (northern) Joseph (Deut 33:7 vs. Deut 33:13–17)[76] looks like an outlier when placed among all

---

[72] See William Schniedewind, "Linguistic Dating, Writing Systems, and the Pentateuchal Sources," in *Formation of the Pentateuch*, 345–55; also Lina Peterson, "The Linguistic Profile of the Priestly Narrative of the Pentateuch," in *Paradigm Change*, 243–64.

[73] Sweeney, *The Twelve*, xxxvii.

[74] There is some Zion theology in Book VI, but it is much more vigorous in Book V. Book IV mentions David twice (superscriptions of Pss 101 and 103), but contains seven of the eight mentions of Moses in the Psalter. Jerusalem is mentioned but once, Zion only five times, three of which are part of a plea for God's mercy on the city (102:13, 16, 21). In Book V, by contrast, Moses is not mentioned; David is referred to twenty-six times, Zion fourteen times, and Jerusalem twelve times.

[75] Christoph Nihan, "The Torah between Samaria and Judah: Shechem and Gerizim in Deuteronomy and Joshua," in *The Pentateuch as Torah: New Models for Understanding Its Promulgation and Acceptance*, ed. Gary N. Knoppers and Bernard M. Levinson (Winona Lake, IN: Eisenbrauns, 2007), 187–223, esp. 223.

[76] On the pro-northern character of the Pentateuch, see Bergsma, "A 'Samaritan' Pentateuch?," 287–300; Ingrid Hjelm, "Northern Perspectives in Deuteronomy and its relation to the Samaritan Pentateuch," *Hebrew Bible and Ancient Israel* 4 (2015): 184–204; Hjelm, "Lost and Found? A Non-Jewish Israel from the Merneptah Stele to the Byzantine Period," in *History, Archeology, and the Bible Forty Years after "Historicity,"* ed. Ingrid Hjelm and Thomas Thompson (London: Routledge, Taylor & Francis Group, 2016), 112–29; Kartveit, "The Samaritan Temple and Rewritten Bible," in *Holy Places and Cult*, ed. Erkki Koskenniemi and J. Cornelis de Vos, Studies in the Reception History of the Bible 5 (Winona Lake, IN: Eisenbrauns, 2014), 85–99.

the post-exilic sacred documents of Judaism. Therefore, it must either be a product of the northern Samarians that was then adopted by the Judeans, or else the common patrimony of the Judeans and Samaritans reaching back into the pre-exilic period to a time when the Pentateuchal vision of Israelite unity under Josephite leadership (Gen 37:5–11; 49:26; Deut 33:16) could have been acceptable even to the Judeans. The only possible time periods where this vision of the Pentateuch would have been acceptable to all the tribes including Judah would be either the early settlement period under the Ephraimite leadership of Joshua as Sandra Richter and others have argued,[77] or perhaps during those periods when Northern Israel dominated southern Judah, as during the Omride dynasty. Marvin Sweeney remarks:

> Judah was a vassal of Israel throughout the reigns of the house of Omri and the house of Jehu in the ninth and eighth centuries BCE. . . . The house of Omri was closely allied to the house of David by the marriage of Athaliah . . . to King Jehoram of Judah . . . given Judah's smaller size, it was a suzerain-vassal alliance in which Israel was the suzerain and Judah the vassal. Judah's vassal-age to Israel would explain Judah's place as the fourth son born to Leah.[78]

But many other aspects of the Pentateuch do not fit the ninth and eighth centuries BCE, such as the centralization of the cult at a single location (Deut 12:1–14), the limited subsistence economy presupposed by the

---

[77] See Sandra Richter, "The Archaeology of Mt. Ebal and Mt. Gerizim and Why It Matters to Deuteronomy," in *Sepher Torath Mosheh: Studies in the Composition and Interpretation of Deuteronomy*, ed. Daniel I. Block and Richard L. Schultz (Peabody, MA: Hendrickson, 2017), 304–37. Also see the views summarized by Michael A. Grisanti, "Josiah and the Composition of Deuteronomy," in *Sepher Torath Mosheh*, 110–38, esp. 130–38.

[78] Marvin Sweeney, "Hosea's Reading of Pentateuchal Narratives: A Window for a Foundational E Stratum," in *Formation of the Pentateuch*, 851–71, esp. 864–65. He goes on to propose that "the reign of Jeroboam ben Joash, 786–742 BCE, would provide a suitable setting" for the composition of the E (for Ephraimite) stratum of what later became the Pentateuch (865). However, Sweeney does not recognize the reality that the Pentateuch in its MT form remains, to the very end, committed to the Josephite tribes over Judah (e.g. Deut 33:13–17 vs. 33:7). The cult centralization commands of Deuteronomy, and the Golden Calf incident in Exodus 32, are thought to be anti-northern and thus rule out the possibility of a northern provenance for the Pentateuch. However, it should be remembered that southern Judah, too, had multiple sanctuaries (Deut 12:1–14 notwithstanding, see Jer 2:20), and that the Golden Calf incident can be read equally well as an anti-Aaronide polemic targeting the ancestor of the Jerusalem priesthood (Exod 32:4,24,35; 1 Chr 24:1–19), as an anti-Jeroboam polemic targeting the founder of the northern kingdom (cf. 1 Kings 12:32; 2 Kings 10:29; 2 Kings 17:16).

Holiness and Deuteronomic codes,[79] the limited role of the monarchy envisioned by Deut 17:14–20, the importance of Shechem,[80] and many, many others.[81] Thus, the more one considers the evidence of the entire literary tradition of the people of Israel, the more it seems that the only suitable setting for the promulgation of the Pentateuch within Israel is a setting close to what it suggests for itself.

---

[79] See Sandra Richter, "What's Money Got to Do with It? Economics and the Question of the Provenance of Deuteronomy in the Neo-Babylonian and Persian Periods," in *Paradigm Change*, 301–21.

[80] Deut 11:29–30; 27:2–12; Josh 8:30–35; 24:25–26. Shechem subsided in importance during the monarchic period. Jeroboam made it his first capital, but seems quickly to have moved to Penuel (1 Kings 12:25). Later Tirzah (1 Kings 15:21) and finally Samaria (1 Kings 16:24) served as the northern capital.

[81] For additional considerations, see Pekka Pitkänen, "Reconstructing the Social Contexts of the Priestly and Deuteronomic Materials in a Non-Wellhausian Setting," in *Paradigm Change*, 323–28.

PART 3

The History of Pentateuchal Source Criticism

CHAPTER 7

CHALLENGING MOSES

The Earliest Theo-Political History of the Documentary Hypothesis

The Tradition of Mosaic Authorship

In his marvelous volume on the history of biblical interpretation, *How to Read the Bible*, James Kugel explains how early Jews and Christians approached Scripture:

> [1] They assumed that the Bible was a fundamentally cryptic text: that is, when it said A, often it might really mean B. . . . [2] Interpreters also assumed that the Bible was a book of lessons directed to readers in their own day. It might seem to talk about the past, but it is not fundamentally history. It is instruction, telling us what to do. . . . Ancient interpreters assumed this not only about narratives like the Abraham story but about every part of the Bible. . . . [3] Interpreters also assumed that the Bible contained no contradictions or mistakes. It is perfectly harmonious, despite its being an anthology. . . . In short, the Bible, they felt, is an utterly consistent, seamless, perfect book. . . . [4] Lastly, they believed that the entire Bible is essentially a divinely given text, a book in which God speaks directly or through His prophets.[1]

When it came to the Pentateuch, Jewish and Christian exegetes understood it to have been divinely inspired, and they identified Moses as the

---

[1] James L. Kugel, *How to Read the Bible: A Guide to Scripture, Then and Now* (New York: Free Press, 2007), 14–16.

sacred inspired author.[2] The biblical texts themselves, already in the Old Testament, contain passages that seem to imply Moses is responsible for the Pentateuch.

Deuteronomy 31:9 reads, "Then Moses wrote this law [*Torah*] and gave it to the priests, the sons of Levi . . . and to all the elders of Israel." Regardless of whether or not this "law" referred to the entire Torah, just to Deuteronomy, or to a portion of Deuteronomy, it was one passage that helped associate the figure of Moses with the writing of the entire Pentateuch. Moses's authorship makes sense if he actually existed and if the events recorded about him are true. Who better to take the traditions of Israel (oral and/or perhaps written) and weave them together into Genesis than someone in Moses's position as head of the people liberating them from Egypt? It would explain why so much of Genesis clearly prepares for the exodus event. It would also explain the reason for so much material being shaped by priestly concerns—not only Genesis 1, which source critics identify as coming from P, but also Genesis 2–3 depicting the Garden of Eden as a sort of Holy of Holies and Adam as a priest;[3] Moses was a Levite and the younger brother to the first high priest of Israel, as Richard Averbeck points out.[4] As someone raised both in the Pharaonic court in Egypt as well as coming from the Israelites themselves, called by God to lead the people, Moses would be the most likely candidate from that time to be responsible for such a divine project as the Torah.

Thus, in several passages in the Old Testament, we find reference to "the Book of the Law [*Torah*] of Moses," or simply the "Law" of Moses. Consider the following examples:

- "as it is written in the Book of the Law [*Torah*] of Moses" (Josh 8:31);
- "he wrote on the stones a copy of the law [*Torah*] of Moses" (Josh 8:32);

---

[2] Michael M. Homan, "How Moses Gained and Lost the reputation of Being the Torah's Author: Higher Criticism prior to Julius Wellhausen," in *Sacred History, Sacred Literature: Essays on Ancient Israel, the Bible, and Religion in Honor of R. E. Friedman on His Sixtieth Birthday*, ed. Shawna Dolansky, 111–31 (Winona Lake, IN: Eisenbrauns, 2008), is helpful but limited. In these next three chapters we flesh out the history more thoroughly than he was able to do in his brief essay.

[3] See, e.g., Jeffrey L. Morrow, *Liturgy and Sacrament, Mystagogy and Martyrdom: Essays in Theological Exegesis* (Eugene, OR: Pickwick, 2020), 33–58 and the many references in the footnotes therein.

[4] Richard E. Averbeck, "Factors in Reading the Patriarchal Narratives: Literary, Historical, and Theological Dimensions," in *Giving the Sense: Understanding and Using Old Testament Historical Texts*, ed. David M. Howard, Jr. and Michael A. Grisanti (Grand Rapids: Kregel, 2003), 115–37.

- "do all that is written in the Book of the Law [*Torah*] of Moses" (Josh 23:6);
- "as it is written in the Law [*Torah*] of Moses" (1 Kgs 2:3);
- "according to what is written in the Book of the Law [*Torah*] of Moses" (2 Kgs 14:6);
- "according to all the Law [*Torah*] of Moses" (2 Kigs 23:25);
- "as it is written in the Law [*Torah*] of Moses" (2 Chr 23:18);
- "according to the Law [*Torah*] of Moses" (2 Chr 30:16);
- "as it is written in the Law [*Torah*] of Moses" (Ezra 3:2);
- "He was a scribe skilled in the Law [*Torah*] of Moses" (Ezra 7:6);
- "to bring the Book of the Law [*Torah*] of Moses" (Neh 8:1);
- "are written in the Law [*Torah*] of Moses" (Dan 9:11);
- "As it is written in the Law [*Torah*] of Moses" (Dan 9:13).

Sometimes, instead of "Law" [*Torah*] of Moses, the Old Testament texts simply refer to the "Book of Moses" (sometimes identified with the "Law" [*Torah*], as a synonym) as the following passages exemplify:

- "according to what is written in the Law [*Torah*], in the Book of Moses" (2 Chr 25:4);
- "as it is written in the Book of Moses" (2 Chr 35:12);
- "as it is written in the Book of Moses" (Ezra 6:18);
- "On that day they read from the Book of Moses in the hearing of the people" (Neh 13:1).

It is not clear if these are referring to the entire Pentateuch, the whole Torah, just Deuteronomy, or just the legal corpora to which these refer. It is not difficult to see, however, just how Moses became associated with the Pentateuch. He is, after all, the main figure from Exodus through Deuteronomy, and he is the one God called to Mount Sinai, where God gave him the Ten Commandments and related revelations. Moses is the prime recipient of divine revelation in the very Torah associated with his name. This is likewise the testimony of Philo of Alexandria, before the advent of Christianity.[5] In fact, one scholar has argued that "While the first book [of Philo's *On the Life of Moses*] is primarily occupied with who Moses was, the second book is concerned with affirming the Mosaic authority of the Pentateuch and providing an interpretive key to Moses's corpus and recalling the

---

5   On Philo's treatment of Moses in general, see the excellent work of Louis H. Feldman, *Philo's Portrayal of Moses in the Context of Ancient Judaism* (Notre Dame, IN: University of Notre Dame Press, 2007).

way the corpus was written and translated."[6] Speaking of Moses's "sacred writings" (ἱερῶν γραμμάτων), he identifies them as the "whole law" (ὅλης νομοθεσίας).[7]

If we look to the New Testament, to the time of Jesus and the apostles, we find something similar about Moses's association with the Pentateuch. Consider the following from the New Testament:

- "Teacher, Moses *wrote* for us that if a man's brother dies . . ." (Mark 12:19, emphasis added);
- "And as for the dead being raised, have you not read in the book of Moses, in the passage about the bush" (Mark 12:26);
- "according to the Law of Moses" (Luke 2:22);
- "They have Moses and the Prophets" (Luke 16:29);
- "If they do not hear Moses and the Prophets" (Luke 16:31);
- "Teacher, Moses *wrote* for us that if a man's brother dies" (Luke 20:28);
- "even Moses showed, in the passage about the bush" (Luke 20:37);
- "And beginning with Moses and all the Prophets, he interpreted to them in all the Scriptures the things concerning himself" (Luke 24:27);
- "everything written about me in the Law of Moses and the Prophets and the Psalms must be fulfilled" (Luke 24:44).

Let us note a few points about these New Testament examples from the Gospels: In the parallel passages in Mark 12:19 and Luke 20:28 there is an emphasis on Moses *writing*. Moreover, unlike the Old Testament examples, in which it is unclear whether the reference is to Deuteronomy or the entire Torah, the examples Jesus provides here in Mark 12:26 and its parallel in Luke 20:37 make it clear that the Book of Exodus is also in mind, with the burning bush episode explicitly mentioned. Finally, in Luke 16:29, 31; 24:27, 44, "Moses" is treated like the prophetic books (and Book of Psalms) in the Old Testament. It seems implied here that Genesis through

---

[6] Finn Damgaard, *Recasting Moses: The Memory of Moses in Biographical and Autobiographical Narratives in Ancient Judaism and 4th-Century Christianity* (Frankfurt am Main: Peter Lang, 2013), 66.

[7] Philo, *De Vita Moses* 2.290. For the Greek text of Philo's *On the Life of Moses* see Leopoldus Cohn and Paulus Wendland, ed., *Philonis Alexandrini: Opera Quae Supersunt*, vol. 4 (Berlin: Reimer, 1902). For an English translation see Philo, *The Works of Philo: Complete and Unabridged*, trans. Charles Duke Yonge (Peabody, MA: Hendrickson, 1993). Here, English translations are our own while the numbering follows Cohn and Wendland's critical edition of the Greek text.

Deuteronomy appear to come from Moses. This is also affirmed after the time of the New Testament by the first century Jewish historian Josephus. In his work *Against Apion*, Josephus writes of the authors of Scripture as prophets who learned what they wrote by "inspiration" (ἐπίπνοιαν) from God.[8] In this context, Josephus mentions, "And of these five are of Moses" (ἐστι Μωυσέως).[9] The remaining scriptural works recounting the history of Israel Josephus considered to have been authored by "prophets after Moses" (μετὰ Μωυσῆν).[10]

GNOSTICS AND ROMANS

One further but usually neglected source of testimony to the presumption of Mosaic authorship is the early challenges to it by critics of Judaism and of Christianity. Sometimes questions of Ezra's role in restoring the Torah are used to make it seem that texts like the *Apocalypse of Ezra* challenged Mosaic authorship. In this apocryphal account, God inspires Ezra to transcribe the Torah. The text itself never denies that the original Torah was Mosaic in origin, nor that what Ezra, under divine influence, records was anything other than the Mosaic Torah. Other scholars point to the question in the Talmud of how Moses could have mentioned his own death, as well as the various responses to it. Such critics underscore that such comments were evidence of the existence of doubt about the Mosaic authorship or origin of every portion of the Pentateuch. This is a bit of a straw man argument, since it is difficult to find any adherents to the Pentateuch's Mosaic authorship, even modern ones, who require every single portion (e.g., Moses's death) to have been penned by Moses.

Sometimes the Pseudo-Clementine Homilies, from within the world of early Christianity in the third and fourth centuries, are brought up as early challenges to the Mosaic origin and authorship of the Pentateuch.[11] This is

---

[8] Josephus, *Against Apion* 1.37. For a critical edition of the Greek text see Dagmar Labow, *Flavius Josephus, Contra Apionem, Buch I: Einleitung, Text, Textkritischer Apparat, Übersetzung und Kommentar* (Stuttgart: Kohlhammer, 2005). A useful English edition with helpful notes is available as John M. G. Barclay, *Flavius Josephus: Against Apion* (Leiden, NL: Brill, 2007). The English we use here for Josephus is our own.

[9] Josephus, *Against Apion* 1.39.

[10] Josephus, *Against Apion* 1.40.

[11] On the background of these homilies, see, e.g., Karin Hedner Zetterholm, "Jewish Teachings for Gentiles in the Pseudo-Clementine Homilies: A Reception of Ideas in Paul and Acts Shaped by a Jewish Milieu?" *Journal of the Jesus Movement in its Jewish Setting* 6 (2019): 68–87; Donald H. Carlson, *Jewish-Christian Interpretation of the Pentateuch in the Pseudo-Clementine Homilies* (Minneapolis, MN: Fortress Press, 2013); Annette Yoshiko Reed, "Heresiology and the (Jewish-) Christian Novel: Narrativized Polemics in

because St. Peter, as depicted in these homilies, denies that certain passages from the Pentateuch originated with Moses. Although many scholars now see these as simply Christian homilies, traditionally, they were associated with the Ebionite heresy. Countering this traditional view, which she sees as an oversimplification, Annette Yoshiko Reed instead reads "them as part of the late antique discourse of heresiology."[12] At the same time, like the Ebionites, these homilies present a very laudatory view of Judaism.[13]

When in the Pseudo-Clementines the figure of the apostle Peter challenges Mosaic authorship, he actually affirms the Mosaic origin of the Torah; he simply places the emphasis on what was passed down from Moses verbally, attributing problematic passages that contain difficulties for interpretation to later scribal interpolations.[14] This is connected with the homilies' rejection of allegorical exegesis.[15] As Donald Carlson remarks:

> An integral component of the Homilist's exegesis is the theory that, as it exists in its written form, the Pentateuch is contaminated with "false pericopes." These falsehoods, enmeshed as they are throughout the Pentateuch, are not always easy to detect. But it is essential for any who would interpret the Scriptures "correctly" to be able to recognize them and then deal with them appropriately.[16]

On the one hand, this is an early example of a challenge to the Mosaic origin of some portions of the Pentateuch; on the other hand, it remains an affirmation of its overall Mosaic origin.

Among the earliest to challenge the Pentateuch's Mosaic origins were the Gnostics and non-Christian Roman intellectuals. A group sometimes identified as Nazarenes, Nasarenes, or as Nazarites was one of the earliest to reject wholesale the Mosaic origin of the Pentateuch. They may have been an early Jewish-Christian group, like the Ebionites, or else, as some scholars

---

the Pseudo-Clementine Homilies," in *Heresy and Identity in Late Antiquity*, ed. Eduard Iricinschi and Holger M. Zellentin (Tübingen: Mohr Siebeck, 2008), 273–98; and Karl Shuve, "The Pseudo-Clementine Homilies and the Antiochene Polemic Against Allegory," (Ph.D. diss., McMaster University, 2007). For the Greek text of these homilies, see Bernhard Rehm and Georg Strecker, ed., *Die Pseudoklementinen I: Homilien* (Berlin: De Gruyter, 1992).

[12] Reed, "Heresiology," 276.

[13] See, e.g., the important but dated study by Georg Strecker, *Das Judenchristentum in den Pseudoklementinen* (Berlin: Akademie Verlag, 1958).

[14] On the significance here of the oral tradition see Carlson, *Jewish-Christian Interpretation*, 111–36.

[15] Carlson, *Jewish-Christian Interpretation*, 13–50.

[16] Carlson, *Jewish-Christian Interpretation*, vii. On the notion of false pericopes, see pages 51–76.

propose, they may have been a proto-Gnostic group.[17] Although Marcion, from the mid-second century, did not deny the Mosaic origin of the Pentateuch, he did deny the Pentateuch's relevance for Christians.[18] According to a letter from Ptolemy the Gnostic preserved in Epiphanius of Salamis' *Panarion,* he questioned the Mosaic origin of certain laws within the Pentateuch, although he conceded the Pentateuch's Mosaic authorship, or at least that Moses compiled the Pentateuch.[19] The Greek philosopher Celsus is sometimes put forward as a critic of the Pentateuch's Mosaic authorship, but, although he criticized the Pentateuch, he never really challenged its Mosaic origin or authorship.[20]

The most serious challenge to the Mosaic authorship of the Pentateuch from antiquity came from the Roman Neo-Platonist philosopher Porphyry. Porphyry's challenges were the most serious to date and the most direct. Unlike other critics of Judaism and Christianity of the time, Porphyry made careful study of the Bible. He gathered together all of the arguments against the Bible he could find from Gnostic, Marcionite, Manichaean, and other sources. It should come as no surprise that after 361, when the Roman Emperor Julian took control of the Roman Empire, he borrowed his major arguments against Christianity from Porphyry. One of Porphyry's main points of attack was to detail the portions of Genesis he found to be absurd. Porphyry went further than many other critics of the time in maintaining that the entire Pentateuch was composed over one thousand years after Moses by the scribe Ezra.[21]

---

[17] Edwin M. Yamauchi, *Gnostic Ethics and Mandaean Origins* (Cambridge, MA: Harvard University Press, 1970), 60; E. S. Drower, *The Secret Adam: A Study of Nasoraean Gnosis* (Oxford, UK: Oxford University Press, 1960); and Edward J. Young, *An Introduction to the Old Testament* (Grand Rapids: Eerdmans, 1989 [1949]), 111–12. Drower's classic study on Mandaean Gnosticism links Nasoraeans with an elite group (the enlightened few) of Mandaean (the more ignorant laity) Gnostics.

[18] On Marcion see especially Judith M. Lieu, *Marcion and the Making of a Heretic: God and Scripture in the Second Century* (Cambridge, UK: Cambridge University Press, 2015); Sebastian Moll, *The Arch-Heretic Marcion* (Tübingen: Mohr Siebeck, 2010); Wolfgang A. Bienert, "Marcion und der Antijudaismus," in *Marcion und seine kirchengeschichte Wirkung: Vorträge der Internationalen Fachkonferenz zu Marcion, gehalten vom 15–18. August 2001 im Mainz,* ed. Gerhard May and Katharina Greschat with Martin Meiser (Berlin: Walter de Gruyter, 2002), 191–206; and Ulrich Schmid, *Marcion und sein Apostolos: Rekonstruktion und historische Einordnung der marionitischen Paulusbriefausgabe* (Berlin: De Gruyter, 1995).

[19] Carlson, *Jewish-Christian Interpretation,* 71–73 and 78; Young, *Introduction,* 109–10; and Robert M. Grant, "Historical Criticism in the Ancient Church," *Journal of Religion* 25, no. 3 (1945): 186–87.

[20] Young, *Introduction,* 113; Grant, "Historical Criticism," 186; and Edward J. Young, "Celsus and the Old Testament," *Westminster Theological Journal* 6, no. 2 (1944): 192–93.

[21] Aryeh Kofsky, *Eusebius of Caesarea Against Paganism* (Leiden, NL: Brill, 2000), 30;

THE RISE OF ISLAM AND MUSLIM BIBLICAL SKEPTICISM

The most important and sustained criticisms leveled against the Pentateuch, including its Mosaic origin and authorship, came from the medieval Muslim world. In continuity with these earlier challenges, such criticism from within the Muslim world was also polemical in nature. Hava Lazarus-Yafeh argues in her important work, *Intertwined Worlds: Medieval Islam and Bible Criticism*, that "this Muslim Bible criticism drew heavily on pre-Islamic pagan, Christian, Gnostic, and other sources, and later may have been transmitted—through both Jewish and Christian mediators—to early modern Bible criticism."[22] The first important but neglected figure within this context was Ḥiwi al-Balkhi. It is not entirely clear whether or not Ḥiwi was Jewish or Gnostic. He came from a Jewish background originally, but his writings were summarily condemned by Jewish intellectuals within both rabbinic and Karaite traditions. Ḥiwi utilized the earlier criticisms of Marcion, Celsus, Porphyry, and Julian the Apostate, among others. Most of what we know about Ḥiwi comes from Saadia Gaon's criticism of his work in *Polemic against Ḥiwi al-Balkhi*. Ḥiwi attacked the miracle stories in the Bible, especially the Pentateuch. He became famous for pointing out inconsistencies in the Bible.[23]

Arthur J. Droge, *Homer or Moses?: Early Christian Interpretation of the History of Culture* (Tübingen: Mohr, 1989), 178; Robert L. Wilken, *The Christians as the Romans Saw Them* (New Haven, CT: Yale University Press, 1984), 137 and 143; and Edward J. Young, *The Prophecy of Daniel: A Commentary* (Grand Rapids: Eerdmans, 1949), 317–20.

[22] Hava Lazarus-Yafeh, *Intertwined Worlds: Medieval Islam and Bible Criticism* (Princeton, NJ: Princeton University Press, 1992), xi. See also her comments on pages 63–64.

[23] Regina Grundmann, "'Die Knochen Ḥiwis,' des Hündischen, sollen zermahlen warden.' Die fundamentale Traditionskritik des Ḥiwi al-Balkhi," in *Jenseits der Tradition?: Tradition und Traditionskritik in Judentum, Christentum und Islam*, ed. Regina Grundmann and Assaad Elias Kattan (Berlin: Walter de Gruyter, 2015), 32–58; David Biale, *Not in the Heavens: The Tradition of Jewish Secular Thought* (Princeton, NJ: Princeton University Press, 2011), 63; Julius Guttmann, "The Sources of Ḥiwi al-Balkhi," in *Alexander Marx Jubilee Volume*, ed. Saul Liebermann (New York: Jewish Theological Society of America, 1950), 92–102; Judah Rosenthal, *Ḥiwi al-Balkhi* (Philadelphia, PA: Dropsie College, 1949); Judah Rosenthal, "Ḥiwi al-Balkhi: A Comparative Study," *Jewish Quarterly Review* 38, no. 3 (1948): 317–42; Judah Rosenthal, "Ḥiwi al-Balkhi: A Comparative Study (Continued)," *Jewish Quarterly Review* 38, no. 4 (1948): 419–30; Judah Rosenthal, "Ḥiwi al-Balkhi: A Comparative Study (Continued)," *Jewish Quarterly Review* 39, no. 1 (1948): 79–94; Georges Vajda, "À propos de l'attitude religieuse de Hiwi al-Balkhi," *Revue des études juives* 99 (1934): 81–91; Arthur Marmorstein, "The Background of the Haggadah," *Hebrew Union College Annual* 6 (1929): 157–204; Henry Malter, *Saadia Gaon: His Life and Works* (Philadelphia, PA: Jewish Publication Society of America, 1921), 260–71; Israel Davidson, *Saadia's Polemic against Ḥiwi al-Balkhi: A Fragment Edited from a Genizah Ms* (New York: Jewish Theological Seminary of America, 1915), 11–37; Adolf Büchler, "Über

Recently, Regina Grundmann has argued that Ḥiwi's criticisms were so trenchant that they inspired Saadia's own interpretation of Jewish tradition, which became incredibly influential.[24] Saadia's work of interpretation, or reinterpretation, as Grundmann refers to it, was in large part a massive response to Ḥiwi, and it thus solidified the reception of Ḥiwi's critique of Judaism and of the Bible, especially the Pentateuch.[25] Ḥiwi's main problems in the Bible pertain to:

1. the presence of anthropomorphisms in reference to God;
2. the ways in which God is depicted as unjust, particularly in the Pentateuch (e.g., his command for Abraham to kill his son in Genesis 22);
3. God's apparent lack of omniscience, as when he asks questions;
4. God's depiction as not all-powerful (e.g., God's apparent inability to protect Abel from Cain);
5. God gets angry;
6. God is like the pagan gods demanding bloody sacrifices;
7. the Bible's insistence that other gods exist;
8. and God changes his mind.

Ḥiwi further provided naturalistic explanations for many of the alleged miracles in the Bible, argued that many of the Bible's commands were irrational, and listed what he found to be many contradictions and inconsistencies, mainly from the Pentateuch. He compiled all of these in his *Book of Two Hundred Questions*, which focused on challenging Scripture's divine inspiration.[26]

As with Porphyry's criticisms, a number of Ḥiwi's questions travel down through history and remain important foundation stones in Pentateuchal

---

die Minim von Sepphoris und Tiberias im zweiten und dritten Jahrhundert," in *Judaica: Festschrift zu Hermann Cohens siebzigstem Geburtstage*, 271–95 (Berlin: Cassirer, 1912); Richard J. H. Gottheil, "Some Early Jewish Bible Criticism: Annual Presidential Address to the Society of Biblical Literature and Exegesis," *Journal of Biblical Literature* 23, no. 1 (1904): 6–12; S. Schechter, "Geniza Specimens. The Oldest Collections of Bible Difficulties, by a Jew," *Jewish Quarterly Review* 13, no. 3 (1901): 345–74; and Jakob Guttmann, "Die Bibelkritik des Chiwi Albalchi nach Saadia's Emunoth we-deoth," *Monatsschrift für Geschichte und Wissenschaft des Judentums* 28 (1879): 260–70 and 289–300.

24 Grundmann, "Die Knochen Ḥiwis," 45–57.

25 Grundmann, "Die Knochen Ḥiwis," 45–57. See pages 36–42 for Ḥiwi's critique of the Bible.

26 Grundmann, "Die Knochen Ḥiwis," 36–42; Rosenthal, *Ḥiwi al-Balkhi*; Rosenthal, "Ḥiwi al-Balkhi," 317–42; Rosenthal, "Ḥiwi al-Balkhi," 419–30; Rosenthal, "Ḥiwi al-Balkhi," 79–94; Gottheil, "Some Early Jewish," 6–12; Schechter, "Geniza Specimens," 345–74; and Guttmann, "Die Bibelkritik," 260–70 and 289–300.

source criticism: e.g., the presence of passages which appear anthropomorphic, apparent contradictions within the text, and apparent inconsistencies in God's will evidenced in his commands and statements. Unintentionally, Saadia Gaon ensured the survival of Ḥiwi's criticisms by his inclusion of the *Book of Two Hundred Questions* in his own polemic against Ḥiwi. In fact, at present, Ḥiwi's work has only survived in Saadia's refutation of it.[27]

Another significant, but almost forgotten, intellectual from within Judaism living under Medieval Islam was Abu Ibrahim Isaac Ibn Yashush, often known as Isaac ben Jasos (or simply Yashush). He was a Jewish physician in the medieval world of Muslim Spain who engaged in many intellectual pursuits, including biblical exegesis. He became infamous for his, at the time, bold argument that Genesis 36 must have dated after the time of Moses, since it mentioned that this took place before there were any Israelite kings, implying that when the text was written, there must already have been Israelite kings.[28] It is possible that Isaac ben Yashush was the "Yitzchaki" (Isaac, or Yitzchak) against whom Abraham Ibn Ezra defended the Bible.[29] In addition to his work as a physician and his exegetical studies, Yashush was also known for his work in Hebrew grammar.[30]

IBN ḤAZM

The most important biblical critical figure from the medieval Muslim world was Ibn Ḥazm, whose work remains all too little-known among biblical scholars.[31] Ibn Ḥazm wrote on nearly every discipline of his day: grammar

---

[27] Grundmann, "Die Knochen Ḥiwis," 45–57; Rosenthal, *Hiwi al-Balkhi*; Rosenthal, "Hiwi al-Balkhi," 317–42; Rosenthal, "Hiwi al-Balkhi," 419–30; Rosenthal, "Hiwi al-Balkhi," 79–94; Gottheil, "Some Early Jewish," 6–12; and Schechter, "Geniza Specimens," 345–74.

[28] On Isaac ben Yashush, see, e.g., Travis Bruce, "The Taifa of Denia and the Jewish Networks of the Medieval Mediterranean: A Study of the Cairo Geniza and Other Documents," *Journal of Medieval Iberian Studies* 10, no. 2 (2018): 152–53; and Young, *Introduction*, 116.

[29] Isaac Kalimi, *Fighting Over the Bible: Jewish Interpretation, Sectarianism and Polemic from Temple to Talmud and Beyond* (Leiden, NL: Brill, 2017), 94–95; Ran HaCohen, *Reclaiming the Hebrew Bible: German-Jewish Reception of Biblical Criticism* (Berlin: Walter de Gruyter, 2010), 21; and Brian Arthur Brown, *Forensic Scriptures: Critical Analysis of Scripture and What the Qur'an Reveals about the Bible* (Eugene, OR: Cascade, 2009), 29–30.

[30] Judith Olszowy-Schlanger, "The Science of Language among Medieval Jews," in *Science in Medieval Jewish Cultures*, ed. Gad Freudenthal (Cambridge: Cambridge University Press, 2011), 380.

[31] Although little known to most biblical scholars, the literature on Ibn Ḥazm is voluminous. On his life and works see, e.g., José Miguel Puerta Vílchez, "Abū Muḥmmad 'Alī Ibn Ḥazm: A Biographical Sketch," in *Ibn Hazm of Cordoba: The Life and Works of a Controversial Thinker*, ed. Camilla Adang, Maribel Fierro, and Sabine Schmidtke (Leiden,

and philology, Muslim law, philosophy, Muslim theology, the theologies of Judaism and Christianity, Qur'anic interpretation, and the interpretation and criticism of the Old and New Testaments. He even wrote poetry. His works attacking Christianity and other religious traditions and versions of

---

NL: Brill, 2013), 3–24; Bruna Soravia, "A Portrait of the 'ālim as a Young Man: The Formative Years of Ibn Ḥazm, 404/1013–420/1029," in *Ibn Hazm of Cordoba*, 25–50; Alejandro García Sanjuán, "Ibn Ḥazm and the Territory of Huelva: Personal and Family Relationships," in *Ibn Hazm of Cordoba*, 51–68; David J. Wasserstein, "Ibn Ḥazm and al-Andalus," in *Ibn Hazm of Cordoba*, 69–86; Juan Pedro Monferrer Sala, "Ibn Ḥazm: Biography," in *Christian-Muslim Relations: A Bibliographical History*, vol. 3, *1050–1200*, ed. David Thomas and Alex Mallett (Leiden, NL: Brill, 2011), 137–39; Nurshif Rifʿat, "Ibn Hazm's Criticism to Rabbis and Rabbinical Writings," in *Ibn Hazm: Uluslararasi katilimli İbn Hazm sempozyumu (26–28 Ekim 2007 Bursa/Türkiye): Bildiri ve Müzakere Metinleri*, ed. Süleyman Sayar and Muhammet Tarakçi (Istanbul: Ensar Neşriyat, 2010), 491–526; Bezalel Naor, *Ma'amar al Yishma'el/Rabbi Solomon ben Abraham ibn Adret's Mitsvat Hashem Barah/An Elucidation of the Seven Noahide Commandments: With an Introduction and Notes* (Spring Valley, NY: Orot, 2008), 3–5; Aziz Al-Azmeh, *The Times of History: Universal Topics in Islamic Historiography* (Budapest: Central European University Press, 2007); Abdelilah Ljamai, *Ibn Ḥazm et la polémique islamo-chrétienne dans l'histoire de l'islam* (Leiden, NL: Brill, 2003); Jane Dammen McAuliffe, "The Genre Boundaries of Qur'ānic Commentary," in *With Reverence for the Word: Medieval Scriptural Exegesis in Judaism, Christianity, and Islam*, ed. Jane Dammen McAuliffe, Barry D. Walfish, and Joseph W. Goering (Oxford, UK: Oxford University Press, 2003), 438, 449–50, and 453; Eric Ormsby, "Ibn Ḥazm," in *The Literature of Al-Andalus*, ed. María Rosa Menocal, Raymond P. Scheindlin, and Michael Sells (Cambridge, UK: Cambridge University Press, 2000), 237–51; Iftekhar Mahmood, *Islam Beyond Terrorists and Terrorism: Biographies of the Most Influential Muslims in History* (Lanham, MD: University Press of America, 2002), 86–87; Camilla Adang, *Islam frente a Judaísmo: La polémica de Ibn Ḥazm de Córdoba* (Madrid: Aben Ezra Ediciones, 1994); Maribel Fierro, "El Islam Andalusí del s. V/XI ante el Judaísmo y el Cristianismo," in *Diálogo filosófico-religioso entre Cristianismo, Judaísmo e Islamismo durante la edad media en la península Ibérica: Actes du colloque international de San Lorenzo de El Escorial 23–26 juin 1991, organisé par la Société Internationale pour l'Étude de la Philosophie Médiévale*, ed. Horacio Santiago-Otero (Turnhout, BE: Brepols, 1994), 57; Nurshif Rifʿat, "Ibn Ḥazm on Jews and Judaism," (PhD diss., Exeter University, 1988), 37–94; Muhammad Abu Laila, "An Introduction to the Life and Work of Ibn Ḥazm 1," *Islamic Quarterly* 29, no. 2 (1985): 75–100; Muhammad Abu Laila, "An Introduction to the Life and Work of Ibn Ḥazm 2," *Islamic Quarterly* 29, no. 3 (1985): 165–71; Bernard Lewis, *The Jews of Islam* (Princeton, NJ: Princeton University Press, 1984), 87–88; A. G. Chejne, *Ibn Hazm* (Chicago: Kazi Publications, 1982); Roger Arnaldez, *Grammaire et théologie chez Ibn Hazm de Cordoue: Essai sur la structure et les conditions de la pensée musulmane* (Paris: Librairie Philosophique J. Vrin, 1956); Miguel Asín Palacios, *Abenházam de Córdoba y su historia crítica de las ideas religiosas I* (Madrid: Tipografía de la "Revista de Archivos, Bibliotecas y Museos", 1927); Miguel Asín Palacios, *Abenházam de Córdoba y su historia crítica de las ideas religiosas II* (Madrid: Tipografía de la "Revista de Archivos, Bibliotecas y Museos", 1928); and Ignaz Goldziher, *Die Ẓâhiriten: Ihr Lehrsystem und ihre Geschichte: Beitrag zur Geschichte der muhammedanischen Theologie* (Leipzig: Schulze, 1884).

Islam made a significant contribution to Muslim intellectual engagements, albeit mostly polemical, with these religious traditions.[32] His work in philosophy became well known and continued to be engaged by Muslims and non-Muslims throughout the medieval period.[33] Within the Muslim world, perhaps he was most involved in legal studies, and he showed a marked preference for literal interpretation.[34] His contributions to grammar and philology were not insignificant, and he was one of the main sources for Isaac Ibn Yashush's grammatical studies.[35] For Catholics, he is perhaps best remembered from Pope Benedict XVI's 2006 Regensburg Address, "Faith,

---

[32] See, e.g., Martin-Samuel Behloul, "The Testimony of Reason and the Historical Reality: Ibn Ḥazm's Refutation of Christianity," in *Ibn Hazm of Cordoba*, 457–84; David Thomas, "Ibn Ḥazm: Works on Christian-Muslim Relations: Kitāb iẓhār tabdīl al-Yahūd wa-l-Naṣārā li-l-Tawrāt wa-l-Injīl wa-bayān tanāquḍ mā bi-aydīhim min dhālika min mā lā yaḥtamil al-tảwīl, 'An exposure of the Jews and Christians' alteration to the Torah and Gospel, and a demonstration of the contradiction in what they possess of this that will not permit metaphorical interpretation,'" in *Christian-Muslim Relations*, 140–41; David Thomas, "Ibn Ḥazm: Works on Christian-Muslim Relations: Unknown title; Radd 'alā risālat malik al-Rūm, 'Refutation of the Byzantine emperor's letter,'" in *Christian–Muslim Relations*, 143–45; Samuel-Martin Behloul, *Ibn Hazms Evangelienkritik. Eine methodische Utersuchung* (Leiden, NL: Brill, 2002); Hava Lazarus-Yafeh, "Some Neglected Aspects of Medieval Polemics against Christianity," *Harvard Theological Review* 89, no. 1 (1996): 61–84; Camilla Adang, "Ibn Ḥazm's Criticism of Some 'Judaizing' Tendencies Among the Mâlikites," in *Medieval and Modern Perspectives on Muslim Jewish Relations*, ed. Ronald L. Nettler (Oxford, UK: Oxford Centre for Postgraduate Hebrew Studies, 1995), 1–15; Israel Friedlander, "The Heterodoxies of the Shiites in the Presentation of Ibn Ḥazm," *Journal of the American Oriental Society* 28 (1907): 1–80; and Israel Friedlander, "Zur Komposition von Ibn Ḥazm's Milal wa'n-Niḥal," in *Orientalische Studien Theodor Nöldeke zum siebzigsten Geburtstag (2. März 1906) gewidmet von Freunden und Schülern I*, ed. Carl Bezold (Gieszen: Alfred Töpelmann, 1906), 267–77.

[33] See, e.g., Sabine Schmidtke, "Ibn Ḥazm's Sources on Ash'arism and Mu'tazilism," in *Ibn Hazm of Cordoba*, 375–402; Rafael Ramón Guerrero, "Aristotle and Ibn Ḥazm. On the Logic of the Taqrīb," in *Ibn Hazm*, 403–16; Joep Lameer, "Ibn Ḥazm's Logical Pedigree," in *Ibn Hazm of Cordoba*, 417–28; and Arnaldez, *Grammaire et théologie*.

[34] See, e.g., Adam Sabra, "Ibn Ḥazm's Literalism: A Critique of Islamic Legal Theory," in *Ibn Hazm of Cordoba*, 97–160; Alfonso Carmona González, "La doctrine sur l'exercice de la justice: Un exemple du désaccord entre Ibn Ḥazm et les mālikites," in *Ibn Hazm of Cordoba*, 161–78; Delfina Serrano, "Claim (Da'wā) or Complaint (Shakwā)? Ibn Ḥazm's and Qāḍī 'Iyāḍ's Doctrines on Accusations of Rape," in *Ibn Hazm of Cordoba*, 179–205; Adam Sabra, "Ibn Ḥazm's Literalism: A Critique of Islamic Legal Theory (I)," *Al-Qanṭara* 28, no. 1 (2007): 8; McAuliffe, "Genre Boundaries," 449; Tarif Khalidi, *Arabic Historical Thought in the Classical Period* (Cambridge, UK: Cambridge University Press, 1994), 149; Rif'at, "Ibn Ḥazm," 61–65; and Abu Laila, "An Introduction," 75–100.

[35] See, e.g., Bruce, "Taifa of Denia," 161; Salvador Peña, "Which Curiosity? Ibn Ḥazm's Suspicion of Grammarians," in *Ibn Hazm of Cordoba*, 233–51; Olszowy-Schlanger, "Science of Language," 380; and Arnaldez, *Grammaire et théologie*.

Reason, and the University," where Benedict referenced Ibn Ḥazm holding a position in contrast to the Christian union of faith and reason.[36]

For our purposes, however, Ibn Ḥazm's greatest relevance lies in his biblical criticism, especially of the Old Testament, and of the Pentateuch in particular.[37]

---

[36] Pope Benedict XVI, "Faith, Reason, and the University," in *A Reason Open to God: On Universities, Education, and Culture* (Washington, DC: The Catholic University of America Press, 2013), 10, 13.

[37] On his criticism of the Old Testament, especially the Torah, as well as its relation to his critique of Judaism, see, e.g., Joshua Berman, "The Biblical Criticism of Ibn Hazm the Andalusian: A Medieval Control for Modern Diachronic Method," *Journal of Biblical Literature* 138, no. 2 (2019): 377–90; Dominique Urvoy, "Le sens de la polémique anti-biblique chez Ibn Hazm," in *Ibn Hazm of Cordoba*, 485–96; Maribel Fierro, "Ibn Ḥazm and the Jewish zindiq," in *Ibn Hazm of Cordoba*, 497–509; Camilla Adang, "Medieval Muslim Polemics Against the Jewish Scriptures," in *Muslim Perceptions of Other Religions: A Historical Survey*, ed. Jacques Waardenburg (Oxford, UK: Oxford University Press, 1999), 143–59; Theodore Pulcini, *Exegesis as Polemical Discourse: Ibn Ḥazm on Jewish and Christian Scriptures* (Atlanta, GA: Scholars Press, 1998), 57–95; Camilla Adang, *Muslim Writers on Judaism and the Hebrew Bible: from Ibn Rabban to Ibn Ḥazm* (Leiden, NL: Brill, 1996); Hava Lazarus-Yafeh, "Taḥrīf and Thirteen Scrolls of Torah," *Jerusalem Studies in Arabic and Islam* 19 (1995): 81–88; Ron Barkai, "Diálogo filosófico-religioso en el seno de las tres culturas Ibéricas," in *Diálogo filosófico-religioso*, 7; Camilla Adang, "Eléments karaïtes dans la polémique d'Ibn Ḥazm," in *Diálogo filosófico-religioso*, 419–41; Gabriel Martinez Gros, "Ibn Hazm contre les Juifs: un bouc émissaire jusq'au jugement dernier," *Atalaya* 5 (1994): 123–34; Camilla Adang, "Ibn Ḥazm de Córdoba sobre los judíos en la sociedad islámica," *Foro Hispánico* 7 (1994): 15–23; Lazarus-Yafeh, *Intertwined Worlds*, 26–29, 31–35, 39–41, 43–46, and 135–40; Maribel Fierro, "Ibn Ḥazm et le zindiq juif," *Revue du Monde Musulman et de la Mediterranee* 63–64 (1992): 81–89; Camilla Adang, "Some Hitherto Neglected Biblical Material in the Work of Ibn Ḥazm," *Al-Masaq* 5, no. 1 (1992): 17–28; Shlomo Pines, "A Parallel Between Two Iranian and Jewish Themes," in *Irano-Judaica II: Studies Relating to Jewish Contacts with Persian Culture Throughout the Ages*, ed. Shaul Shaked and Amnon Netzer (Jerusalem: Ben-Zvi Institute, 1990), 45, 49; R. David Freedman, "The Father of Modern Biblical Scholarship," *Journal of the Ancient Near Eastern Society* 19 (1989): 31–38; Rifʿat, "Ibn Ḥazm," 220–94; Camilla Adang, "Schriftvervalsing als thema in de islamitische polemiek tegen het jodendom," *Ter Herkenning* 16, no. 3 (1988): 190–202; Norman Roth, "Forgery and Abrogation of the Torah: A Theme in Muslim and Christian Polemic in Spain," *Proceedings of the American Academy for Jewish Research* 54 (1987): 203–36; David S. Powers, "Reading/Misreading One Another's Scriptures: Ibn Ḥazm's Refutation of Ibn Nagrella al-Yahūdī," in *Studies in Islamic and Judaic Traditions: Papers Presented at the Institute for Islamic-Judaic Studies*, ed. William M. Brinner and Stephen D. Ricks (Atlanta: Scholars Press, 1986), 109–21; Camilla Adang, "Ibn Ḥazm on Jews and Judaism," (PhD diss., University of Nijmegen, 1985); Emilio García Gómez, "Polémica religiosa entre Ibn Ḥazm e Ibn al-Nagrīla," *Al-Andalus* 4, no. 1 (1936): 1–28; Ernest Algermissen, "Die Pentateuchzitate Ibn Hazms. Ein beitrag zur geschichte der arabische Bibelübersetzungen," (thesis, Westfälische Wilhelms-Universität, Münster, 1933); Ignazio Di Matteo, "La pretese contraddizioni della S. Scrittura secondo Ibn Hazm," *Bessarione* 27 (1923): 77–127;

He did this most thoroughly in his work, *Kitab al-Fiṣal*.[38] Very few translations of this Arabic work exist; one of the most complete is the four-volume Spanish translation by Miguel Asín Palacios published between 1927 and 1932.[39] Only a very small portion has been translated into English, and that is found in the appendix to Nurshif Rifʿat's 1988 doctoral dissertation.[40] According to Miguel Asín Palacios, *Kitab al-Fiṣal* is "the primary work that best reflects his system."[41] It is with Ibn Ḥazm that we first and most clearly begin to see the role of politics enter the realm of biblical criticism.

Ibn Ḥazm was born Abū Muḥammad ʿAlī ibn Aḥmad ibn Saʿīd ibn Ḥazm in 994, in Cordoba, Spain, which was under Muslim rule at the time. Scholars now believe that he was likely the direct descendant of a Muslim convert from Christianity. Ibn Ḥazm's family was wealthy and very politically involved in the Muslim caliphate. His father was a vizier in the Umayyad Caliphate. His father's high political position afforded Ibn Ḥazm the finest formal education imaginable. Ibn Ḥazm would follow his father's footsteps and likewise become a vizier. This time period, however, was somewhat tumultuous, and Ibn Ḥazm was bypassed for a high office for Shmuel Ibn

---

and Hartwig Hirschfeld, "Mohammedan Criticism of the Bible," *Jewish Quarterly Review* 13, no. 2 (1901): 222–40.

[38] On his important *Kitab al-Fiṣal*, see, e.g., Berman, "Biblical Criticism," 383–87; Urvoy, "Le sens de la polémique," 485–96; Juan Pedro Monferrer Sala, "Ibn Ḥazm: Works on Christian-Muslim Relations: *Kitāb al-fiṣal fī l-milal wa-l-ahwāʾ wa-l-niḥal*, 'Judgement regarding the confessions, inclinations and sects,'" in *Christian-Muslim Relations*, 141–43; Pulcini, *Exegesis as Polemical Discourse*; Adang, *Muslim Writers*, 192–248; Lazarus-Yafeh, "Taḥrīf," 81–88; Ghulam Haider Aasi, "Muslim understanding of other religions: an analytical study of Ibn Ḥazm's Kitab al-Fasl," (Ph.D. disseratation, Temple University, 1986); Algermissen, "Die Pentateuchzitate"; Asín Palacios, *Abenházam I*; Asín Palacios, *Abenházam II*; Miguel Asín Palacios, *Abenházam de Córdoba y su historia crítica de las ideas religiosas III* (Madrid: Tipografía de la "Revista de Archivos, Bibliotecas y Museos," 1929); Miguel Asín Palacios, *Abenházam de Córdoba y su historia crítica de las ideas religiosas IV* (Madrid: Tipografía de la "Revista de Archivos, Bibliotecas y Museos", 1929); Miguel Asín Palacios, *Abenházam de Córdoba y su historia crítica de las ideas religiosas V* (Madrid: Tipografía de la "Revista de Archivos, Bibliotecas y Museos", 1932); and Di Matteo, "La pretese contraddizioni," 77–127. Ljamai, *Ibn Ḥazm*, contains important information about the various Arabic manuscripts of *Kitab al-Fiṣal*, including textual differences.

[39] Asín Palacios, *Abenházam I*; Asín Palacios, *Abenházam II*; Asín Palacios, *Abenházam III*; Asín Palacios, *Abenházam IV*; and Asín Palacios, *Abenházam V*. The first volume does not contain his translation, but is an introduction to Ibn Ḥazm and his thought. The second volume continues the introduction, but also begins the translation, which is continued in the remaining volumes. Some of our quotations from Ibn Ḥazm's *Kitab al-Fiṣal* will be our own English translations of Asín Palacios' Spanish translation.

[40] Rifʿat, "Ibn Ḥazm," 435–88. Some of our references to Ibn Ḥazm's *Kitab al-Fiṣal* will be to Rifʿat's English translation.

[41] Asín Palacios, *Abenházam I*, 7, our translation.

Nagrela (Shmuel Ha Naggid), an important Jewish intellectual, whom we will discuss further below. Ibn Ḥazm also suffered imprisonment twice at the hand of the Berbers. His main controversies in the Muslim world were on account of his literalistic legal interpretive works as the most prominent member, and eventual head, of the Zahiri school, which was both theological and juridical.[42]

The reason Ibn Ḥazm is so important for our discussion is on account of his thorough critique of the Pentateuch (in addition to the rest of the Bible, both Old and New Testaments), especially in his *Kitab al-Fiṣal*.[43] Indeed, Lazarus-Yafeh makes the point that he "was the first Muslim author to use a systematic scholarly approach to the Bible to prove in detail this Qur'anic charge [that Jews and Christians had falsified their own Scriptures], perhaps because he was one of the first Muslim authors to have real knowledge of the biblical text, especially the Pentateuch."[44] When Ibn Ḥazm turns to the Pentateuch he argues that it is so riddled with contradictions, errors, and even blasphemies that it cannot be the same revealed text that was from the time of Moses, whom Muslims revere as a prophet. His assertions are quite substantial and thorough. His invective against Judaism, however, can cause modern readers to be distracted from his arguments—particularly from his careful philological work and textual comparisons. Perhaps no one has shown the similarities between Ibn Ḥazm's criticisms and modern biblical criticism as well as Joshua Berman.[45] Lazarus-Yafeh notes that "While his arguments against the Torah (and the New Testament) are expressed in polemical, almost anti-Semitic terms, replete with ridicule of and revulsion for the Jews, his level of argumentation and systematic critical approach to the text often equals the standard of modern Bible criticism."[46]

Rif'at summarizes Ibn Ḥazm's arguments as follows:

---

[42] Puerta Vílchez, "Abū Muḥmmad 'Alī Ibn Ḥazm," 3–24; Monferrer Sala, "Ibn Ḥazm," 137–39; Ljamai, *Ibn Ḥazm*, 13, 30, 32–33, and 40; Mahmood, *Islam*, 86; Ormsby, "Ibn Ḥazm," 237–38; Adang, *Islam frente*, 13, 25; Khalidi, *Arabic Historical Thought*, 149; Adang, "Éléments," 423; Pines, "Parallel Between," 43; Rif'at, "Ibn Ḥazm," 37–94; Abu Laila, "An Introduction 1," 75–100; Abu Laila, "An Introduction 2," 165–71; Chejne, *Ibn Ḥazm*, vi, 1, 20–25; Arnaldez, *Grammaire et théologie*, 19, 49n1, 77–73, 309; Asín Palacios, *Abenházam I*, 64, 67, 76–77, 81, 86–88; and Goldziher, *Die Ẓâhiriten*.

[43] The most important studies on Ibn Ḥazm's biblical criticism in his *Kitab al-Fiṣal* remain Berman, "Biblical Criticism," 382–90; Pulcini, *Exegesis as Polemical Discourse*, 57–95; Rif'at, "Ibn Ḥazm," 220–94; Powers, "Reading/Misreading," 109–21; Algermissen, "Die Pentateuchzitate"; and Di Matteo, "La pretese contraddizioni," 77–127.

[44] Lazarus-Yafeh, *Intertwined Worlds*, 26. See also her comments on page 66.

[45] Berman, "Biblical Criticism," 377–90.

[46] Lazarus-Yafeh, *Intertwined Worlds*, 66. See also the comments in Sidney H. Griffith, *The Bible in Arabic: The Scriptures of the "People of the Book" in the Language of Islam* (Princeton, NJ: Princeton University Press, 2013), 198–99.

For Ibn Ḥazm the Torah contains instances of anthropomorphism and blasphemy, geographical and historical impossibilities, contradictions, particularly in the chronology of the patriarchs, cases of obscenity in which even the prophets' own families are involved, adultery, lies and deception, the faulty location of certain sites, mathematically and numerically erroneous accounts and events post-dated to the authors of these books. The reference to the death of Moses in Deuteronomy 34:5–6, is a clear example. These views supply Ibn Ḥazm with ample support for his belief that the text of the Torah had been corrupted.[47]

Ibn Ḥazm's arguments are extensive: he spends more than a hundred pages detailing the evidence of corruption in the Old Testament, representing, as Berman observes, "a far more comprehensive critique of the Hebrew Scriptures than anything that would be penned prior to the eighteenth century in Europe."[48] Many of the challenges Ibn Ḥazm levels against the Old Testament will return in the later criticisms of seventeenth- and eighteenth-century European scholars. He attacks apparent absurdities, like an aged Sarai attracting other suitors. He also points to the immorality of the patriarchs and their children, especially the cases of adultery. He especially focuses on apparent contradictions, with numbers or with various other examples, as when the plagues mentioned all the water was turned to blood. Ibn Ḥazm wonders how there remained water for the Egyptian magicians to turn it likewise into blood.[49]

As Rifʿat provides an important example of Ibn Ḥazm's critique:

Ibn Ḥazm doubts the accuracy of the numbers of the Israelites in the wilderness, given as 600,000. He examines this number against the political and social position of the Jews in Egypt, the way in which they lived, the source of their income, their places of residence. All of these make it difficult to believe that the number involved in the exodus reached this figure. He says, for example, that in their Torah it is stated that the Israelites had all lived in Goshen [Ex. 9:26] and nowhere else in Egypt, and had worked as brickmakers. In his view 600,000 brickmakers are too many for one country, particularly if concentrated in one place, Goshen.[50]

---

[47] Rifʿat, "Ibn Ḥazm," 408.

[48] Berman, "Biblical Criticism," 381.

[49] See, e.g., the helpful analyses in Berman, "Biblical Criticism," 386–90; and Rifʿat, "Ibn Ḥazm," 227, 229, 234, 242, 246, 281–82, 403, and 407–8.

[50] Rifʿat, "Ibn Ḥazm," 242. In response to Ibn Ḥazm's comments here, Rifʿat mentions on the same page that, "Here Ibn Ḥazm seems partly to ignore the evidence of Exodus

The key passage, of course, for Ibn Ḥazm, as for later biblical interpreters, is the death of Moses mentioned in Deuteronomy, as Rifʿat mentions:

> Ibn Ḥazm concludes his critical examination of the Pentateuch by referring to Deuteronomy 34:5–6, where it is mentioned that Moses died and was buried and nobody knew where his grave was. Ibn Ḥazm finds that this passage provides evidence to support his argument against the Bible, that it is history written by human agents, not a revelation from God. It is impossible that such a passage was revealed to Moses during his lifetime. It might be justified as a foretelling, were it not that the whole passage is in the past tense.[51]

These positions are all consistent with the Muslim tradition that the Jewish and Christian Scriptures had been corrupted, accounting for their differences with the Qurʾan, when Muslims acknowledge many of the key biblical figures such as Abraham, Moses, and Jesus as authentic prophets. He thus concedes that Moses received an authentic revelation from God, but maintains—and bolsters through his voluminous arguments—that the Torah, and the rest of Jewish and Christian Scriptures, have been corrupted.[52] What scholars will sometimes miss or downplay, however, in part due to Ibn Ḥazm's vicious polemics, is the careful way in which he makes use both of Hebrew textual traditions as well as those of the Septuagint, and is clear he is also aware of the Samaritan version, even though he concedes he has been unable to examine the Samaritan text.[53] As Rifʿat points out, he thus "criticized the Jewish books from an historical angle, emphasizing how it lacked uninterrupted transmission."[54]

Ibn Ḥazm concludes his *Kitab al-Fiṣal* with:

---

concerning the profession of Jews while they were in Egypt. He seems to base his argument on Exodus 5:6ff, according to which Pharaoh gave orders to his officials and taskmasters not to provide the Israelite people with the straw that they used in making the bricks. The author of *al-Fiṣal* interprets this as indicating that all the Jews worked at making bricks, although in Exodus 1:11–14 it is stated that they were also builders and farmworkers."

51 Rifʿat, "Ibn Ḥazm," 246.
52 See, e.g., Adang, "Medieval Muslim Polemics," 143–59; Pulcini, *Exegesis as Polemical Discourse*, 57–95; Lazarus-Yafeh, "Taḥrīf," 81–88; Rifʿat, "Ibn Ḥazm," 281–82, 403, 407; Adang, "Schriftvervalsing," 190–202; and Roth, "Forgery," 203–36.
53 See, e.g., Rifʿat, "Ibn Ḥazm," 407–8 and Ibn Ḥazm's own discussion of this on pages 480–88. For scholarly conjecture as to what Arabic versions of the Bible Ibn Ḥazm may have had access to, see, e.g., Griffith, *Bible in Arabic*, 21, 199; Adang, *Muslim Writers on Judaism*, 133–38; Lazarus-Yafeh, *Intertwined Worlds*, 122, 136; and Algermissen, "Die Pentateuchzitate," 60, 83.
54 Rifʿat, "Ibn Ḥazm," 407.

The contradictions between the Torah[s] [of each of the two groups, Jews and Christians] and such falsehood cannot possibly stem from Allah the Almighty and Exalted, nor from the utterances of a prophet, nor even from the utterances of a truthful scholar from among the masses of the people. It becomes null and void, without doubt, because of this, the claim that the Torah and these books have been transmitted and passed down in a way that obliges us to believe in their authenticity. On the contrary, the transmission is corrupt, interrupted and unsound.[55]

So much of his criticism is theological in nature, but Berman points out how similar his philological and critical analyses, searching out fissures in the text, are to modern scholarly critical works. Berman underscores differences as well. He writes:

But Ibn Hazm's most intriguing and significant observation about inconsistency in Genesis stems from his approach to the conflicting uses of the names "Jacob" and "Israel" in the Torah as appellations for the third patriarch. This, of course, has long been a staple of modern diachronic scholarship as well, but Ibn Hazm frames the question in a way that reveals a deep divide between his poetics and those employed and expected by modern expositors. Modern diachronic scholars assume that a cohesive narrative can rename Jacob Israel only once. Thus, the presence of two such accounts (Gen 32:27–28 and 35:9–10) must be explained diachronically. For Ibn Hazm, however, the renaming of "Jacob" as "Israel" at the Jabbok River (Gen 32:27–28) is rendered problematic not by the similar renaming by YHWH at Bethel (35:9–10) but rather by a much later verse—Exod 19:3: "Thus you shall say to the House of Jacob, and proclaim to the Children of Israel." For Ibn Hazm, there is a contradiction in the text of the Torah when these two passages are considered because of the conflicting fashion in which *God* is portrayed; representing God, the angel tells Jacob in Gen 32:28 that he shall no longer be called Jacob. And yet in Exod 19:3, it is God who employs that very name, Jacob. Strikingly missing from Ibn Hazm's comments on this issue is any indication that he is bothered by the doublet created by the two naming accounts of Gen 32:27–28 and Gen 35:9–10.[56]

---

[55] English translation from Rifʿat, "Ibn Ḥazm," 485.
[56] Berman, "Biblical Criticism," 386.

Thus, although Ibn Ḥazm's criticisms against the literary unity of Genesis, or the rest of the Pentateuch, are quite similar to those of modern scholars, in stark contrast to modern scholars Ibn Ḥazm has no issue with doublets, even when it comes to the account of creation in Genesis;[57] "Indeed, Ibn Hazm never points to any repetition in the Torah as a sign of fissure in the text."[58] Berman elaborates on this point, underscoring its significance:

> It is clear that Ibn Hazm engages in a close reading of the text of Genesis and attends to details that evade the reader at first glance. For example, only a careful reading of Gen 46:8–27 reveals that there are but sixty-nine names listed in that genealogy, whereas the total of descendants of Jacob is listed as seventy. The only way to notice that there is a discrepancy concerning the age of Shem at the birth of his son is by very carefully reading the genealogy of Gen 5 in tandem with the flood account of Gen 6–9 and also the geneal- ogy of Gen 10. If Ibn Hazm has trained his eye to detect even subtle contradictions in the text of Genesis, it is curious—nay, conspicu- ous—that he fails to notice the proverbial low-hanging fruit—the doublets that are so often noted by diachronic scholars as among the most obvious signs of diachronic composition.[59]

But why did Ibn Ḥazm endeavor to make such a careful study of the Bible in the first place? In order to answer that question, we need to turn to a con- troversy that erupted during his life, namely his conflict with Ibn Nagrela.

IBN ḤAZM VS. IBN NAGRELA: THE POLITICAL CONTEXT TO IBN ḤAZM'S BIBLICAL CRITICISM

Samuel Ibn Nagrela was an important Jewish writer and political author- ity during Ibn Ḥazm's time.[60] Travis Bruce identifies Ibn Nagrela as "the

---

57 For the importance of "doublets" in modern biblical criticism see Aulikki Nahkola, *Double Narratives in the Old Testament: The Foundations of Method in Biblical Criticism* (Berlin: Walter de Gruyter, 2001).

58 Berman, "Biblical Criticism," 386.

59 Berman, "Biblical Criticism," 387.

60 Bruce, "Taifa of Denia," 152–53, 155, and 161; Ormsby, "Ibn Ḥazm," 238; Mark R. Cohen, *Under Crescent and Cross: The Jews in the Middle Ages* (Princeton, NJ: Prince- ton University Press, 1994), xv, 66, 165–66, 180–81; David J. Wasserstein, "Samuel Ibn Naghrīla ha-Nagid and Islamic Historiography in Al-Andalus," *Al-Qantara* 14, no. 1 (1993): 109–25; Angeles Navarro Peiró, "Semel Ibn Nagrella y Moshe Ibn 'Ezra: La vida, la muerte y el tiempo," *Boletín de la Institución Libre de Enseñanza* 11 (1991): 59–72; Amelia

greatest Jewish figure of his day."[61] It is difficult to overestimate the political stature of Ibn Nagrela, more often referred to in Jewish literature as Samuel Ha-Nagid, and how it angered Ibn Ḥazm. Under Islam, although Jews could fare well, they were not ordinarily permitted to lead Muslims, and particularly not in military contexts.[62] Ibn Nagrela, however, rose to the height of military power and also became the vizier of Granada. David Wasserstein explains the significance of this:

> The Nagid is the first Jew since the Bar Kokhba revolt against the Romans in the second century AD . . . to lead armies. . . . More significantly . . . the armies which he led were non-Jewish; and more significantly still, they were Muslim. . . . What is at issue here, in the case of the Nagid, is, however, precisely this: a case of a *dhimmī* serving as a soldier in a Muslim army; and a case of a non-Muslim

---

Ramón Guerrero, "Samuel ibn Nagrella y su hijo José en la 'memorias' de 'Abd Allāh, último rey Zīrī de Granada," *Miscelánea de estudios Árabes y Hebraicos* 37–38 (1988–1989): 431–37; Powers, "Reading/Misreading," 109–21; Hava Lazarus-Yafeh, "Tajdīd al-Dīn: A Reconsideration of Its Meaning, Roots, and Influence in Islam," in *Studies in Islamic and Judaic Traditions: Papers Presented at the Institute for Islamic-Judaic Studies*, ed. William M. Brinner and Stephen D. Ricks, (Atlanta: Scholars Press, 1986), 102; Angel Saenz-Badillos, "Yiṣḥaq ibn Jalfun y Šěmu'el ibn Nagrella ha-Nagid," *Miscelánea de estudios Árabes y Hebraicos* 33 (1984): 21–43; Lewis, *Jews of Islam*, 87; Roger Arnaldez, "Controverse d'Ibn Hazm contre Ibn Nagrila le juif," *Revue de mondes musulmans et de la Méditerranée* 13–14 (1973): 41–48; David Gonzalo Maeso, "Una oda de Yehudá Ha-Leví en honor del visir Ibn Nagrella," *Miscelánea de estudios Árabes y Hebraicos* 6 (1957): 193–95; and García Gómez, "Polémica religiosa," 1–28.

61 Bruce, "Taifa of Denia," 161.

62 Cohen, *Under Crescent*, shows how well Jews could fare under Muslim rule, as does the evidence amassed in S. D. Goitein, *A Mediterranean Society: The Jewish Communities of the Arab World as Portrayed in the Documents of the Cairo Genizah*, vol. 1, *Economic Foundations* (Berkeley, CA: University of California Press, 1967); S. D. Goitein, *A Mediterranean Society: The Jewish Communities of the Arab World as Portrayed in the Documents of the Cairo Genizah*, vol. 2, *The Community* (Berkeley, CA: University of California Press, 1971); S. D. Goitein, *A Mediterranean Society: The Jewish Communities of the Arab World as Portrayed in the Documents of the Cairo Genizah*, vol. 3, *The Family* (Berkeley, CA: University of California Press, 1978); S. D. Goitein, *A Mediterranean Society: The Jewish Communities of the Arab World as Portrayed in the Documents of the Cairo Genizah*, vol. 4, *Daily Life* (Berkeley, CA: University of California Press, 1983); and S. D. Goitein, *A Mediterranean Society: The Jewish Communities of the Arab World as Portrayed in the Documents of the Cairo Genizah*, vol. 5, *The Individual* (Berkeley, CA: University of California Press, 1988). The final volume, S. D. Goitein, *A Mediterranean Society: The Jewish Communities of the Arab World as Portrayed in the Documents of the Cairo Genizah*, vol. 6, *Cumulative Indices* (Berkeley, CA: University of California Press, 1992), is, as its subtitle indicates, a series of indices for the entire multi-volume work.

acting as commander of a Muslim army, possessing and wielding authority over Muslims, in the one sphere above all others that was exclusively reserved to true believers in the faith of Muhammad.[63]

Ibn Nagrela, like Ibn Ḥazm, opposed the Berbers, but Ibn Nagrela rose to a higher status in the caliphate as Ibn Ḥazm was lowered; Ibn Nagrela moved first from a lowly tax collector to a secretarial position, to that of the vizier's assistant, to becoming the vizier, the position Ibn Ḥazm wanted and thought he should have, having already served as a vizier. In this position, it seems, Ibn Ḥazm understood Ibn Nagrela actually to have criticized the Qur'an, although most scholars seem to doubt the authenticity of the tract in question and doubt it originated from Ibn Nagrela.[64]

David Powers mentions, "Clearly, it was a desire to undermine the authority of the Torah that led Ibn Ḥazm to the study of the Jewish sacred writings."[65] The conflict between Ibn Ḥazm and Ibn Nagrela helps place this in context, as R. David Freedom maintains, "The vituperation of Ibn Hazm's attack can be understood from its personal context: Ibn Hazm had not been appointed vizier of Granada—his place had been taken by that upstart Jew, Shemuel ibn Nagrela, known to the Jews as Shemuel HaNaggid."[66] This explains the fact that, in contrast to virtually all other medieval Muslim critiques of Judaism and Christianity, Ibn Ḥazm spends far more time criticizing Judaism (and the Old Testament) than he does criticizing Christianity (and the New Testament). This is the exact opposite of other Muslim thinkers engaged in religious discourses.[67]

We can see the harshness of Ibn Ḥazm's critique of Judaism throughout. His anti-Jewish polemic, which often resorts to the basest of ad hominems, is often distracting, and can cause readers to miss the care with which he attends to the texts he is critiquing. To give just two brief examples: in referring to the author of the Pentateuch, Ibn Ḥazm writes, "the ox is more discrete, and the donkey is more informed than he"; and in writing of the Jewish people, he refers to them as "the most dirty, disgusting, and repugnant race on earth."[68]

---

[63] Wasserstein, "Samuel Ibn Naghrīla," 114–15 and 117. He makes the caveat, "with the exceptions of the Jewish ruler Yūsuf Dhū Nuwās in Yemen a century before the rise of Islam and of the Khazars in the Caucasus two or three centuries later" (114–15).

[64] See, e.g., Powers, "Reading/Misreading," 110; Arnaldez, "Controverse d'Ibn Hazm," 41–48; and García Gómez, "Polémica religiosa," 1–28.

[65] Powers, "Reading/Misreading," 115.

[66] Freedman, "Father of Modern Biblical Scholarship," 35.

[67] See, e.g., Ljamai, Ibn Ḥazm, 42; and Lewis, Jews of Islam, 87.

[68] As quoted in Asín Palacios, Abenházam I, 193. Our own English translation from the Spanish.

Thus, although Ibn Ḥazm paid careful attention to the Pentateuch, and to the rest of the Old Testament, as well as the Gospels in the New Testament, it was not an attempt at simply understanding the texts that drove his criticism. As with all prior challenges to the traditional views of Pentateuchal composition, Ibn Ḥazm's work was clearly that of polemic rather than historical or exegetical interest. Unlike what came before, however—with the possible exception of Ḥiwi al-Balkhi—Ibn Ḥazm paid very careful attention to the texts themselves, and even to different textual traditions and translations, like the Septuagint. Ibn Ḥazm went far beyond even Ḥiwi al-Balkhi in his thoroughgoing challenge to the Pentateuch and the rest of the Scriptures. Also, in contrast to what had come before, with Ibn Ḥazm we find the first clearly *political* influence in his biblical criticism. This political undertone will be something that blossoms in the early modern period and remains with Pentateuchal source criticism, and historical criticism more broadly speaking, into the seventeenth, eighteenth, and nineteenth centuries.[69]

Medieval Jewish and Christian Antecedents to Modern Pentateuchal Source Criticism: The Potential Reception of Ibn Ḥazm's and Other Muslim Biblical Criticism

After Ibn Ḥazm, there is not much discussion of any challenges to the Mosaic authorship of the Pentateuch in the medieval period; such challenges would have to wait to the seventeenth century to build steam. Ibn Ḥazm's work, however, was sufficiently important in its time that it could not but have an influence.[70] Ibn Ḥazm was clearly important in the medieval Muslim world, where he was challenged or followed by many different Muslim writers.[71] His reception among Jewish sages, e.g., Judah Halevi and Maimonides, is more contested and difficult to discern, particularly because

---

[69] See, e.g., Scott W. Hahn and Benjamin Wiker, *Politicizing the Bible: The Roots of Historical Criticism and the Secularization of Scripture 1300–1700* (New York: Herder & Herder, 2013); and Scott W. Hahn and Jeffrey L. Morrow, *Modern Biblical Criticism as a Tool of Statecraft (1700–1900)* (Steubenville, OH: Emmaus Academic, 2020).

[70] On the reception of Ibn Ḥazm see, e.g., Ljamai, *Ibn Ḥazm*, 145–96; Camilla Adang, "A Jewish Reply to Ibn Ḥazm: Solomon b. Adret's Polemic against Islam," in *Judios y musulmanes en al-Andalus y el Magreb: Contactos Intelectuales*, ed. Maribel Fierro (Madrid: Casa de Velázquez, 2002), 179–209; Lazarus-Yafeh, *Intertwined Worlds*; and Asín Palacios, *Abenházam II*, 74–76.

[71] Muhammad Abu Laylah, "Ibn Hazm al-Andalusī," in *Ibn Hazm of Cordoba*, 77; and Ljamai, *Ibn Ḥazm of Cordoba*, 145–96.

they did not refer to him explicitly.[72] An exception to this is Solomon ben Adret, who explicitly wrote against Ibn Ḥazm and his *Kitab al-Fiṣal*, which raises the possibility of Hebrew translations of his works, since ben Adret did not know Arabic.[73]

It seems likely that Abraham Ibn Ezra was aware of Ibn Ḥazm's work and may have even referred to it.[74] The Jewish convert to Christianity Peter Alfonsi also was influenced by Ibn Ḥazm's work, and may have aided in mediating some of his arguments to the greater Christian Latin West.[75] Most important is Peter Abelard, who may have had knowledge of Ibn Ḥazm's work through Peter of Toledo; this is far from clear, although we do believe it is highly probable.[76] There has even been the suggestion of a possible link between Ibn Ḥazm and the later voluntarism associated with Duns Scotus and William of Ockham.[77] Regardless of whether or not Ibn Ḥazm influenced these figures and was mediated to the Latin Christian world, as Lazarus-Yafeh thinks likely,[78] there are two final figures we need to discuss more in depth before moving to the early modern period in the next chapter: Ibn Ezra and Peter Abelard.

ABRAHAM IBN EZRA'S SO-CALLED DENIAL OF THE MOSAIC AUTHORSHIP OF THE PENTATEUCH

When biblical scholars look to the pre-modern roots of any challenge to the Pentateuch's Mosaic authorship, they invariably turn to Abraham Ibn Ezra and typically ignore the figures we have mentioned thus far in this chapter, with the occasional exception of Porphyry.[79] Indeed, although Ibn Ḥazm's work has been well known to scholars of Jewish and Muslim studies

---

72 Rifʿat, "Ibn Hazm's Criticism," 492; Adang, "Jewish Reply," 179–209; and Lazarus–Yafeh, *Intertwined Worlds*, 73–74.

73 Adang, "Jewish Reply," 179–209.

74 Lazarus-Yafeh, *Intertwined Worlds*, 73–74.

75 Lazarus-Yafeh, *Intertwined Worlds*, 136, 140; and Moisés Orfali, "Anthropomorphism in the Christian Reproach of the Jews in Spain (12th–15th century)," *Immanuel* 19 (1984–1985): 60–73. On Alfonsi see especially John Tolan, "Petrus Alfonsi," in *Christian-Muslim Relations*, 356–62; Joaquín Lomba Fuentes, "El marco cultural de Pedro Alfonso," in *Estudios sobre Pedro Alfonso de Huesca*, ed. María Jesús Lacarra Ducay (Huesca, ES: Instituto de Estudios Altoaragoneses, 1996), 181–230; John Tolan, *Petrus Alfonsi and His Medieval Readers* (Gainesville, FL: University Press of Florida, 1993); and María Jesús Lacarra Ducay, *Pedro Alfonso* (Zaragoza, ES: Diputación General de Aragón, 1991).

76 Lazarus-Yafeh, *Intertwined Worlds*, 136; and Asín Palacios, *Abenházam II*, 74.

77 Asín Palacios, *Abenházam II*, 76.

78 See Lazarus-Yafeh, *Intertwined Worlds*, 73–74, 136, 140.

79 See, e.g., John J. Collins, *Introduction to the Hebrew Bible and Deutero-Canonical Books*,

for more than a century, in the world of contemporary English-speaking biblical scholarship, it seems to be one source that has brought his work to the attention of the academy. R. David Freedman's groundbreaking 1989 study on Ibn Ḥazm, "The Father of Modern Biblical Scholarship,"[80] contends that Spinoza directly relied upon Ibn Ḥazm's *Kitab al-Fiṣal* despite never mentioning him.[81] We would argue that this interpretation stretches the evidence and is reliant upon Spinoza's interpretation and use of Ibn Ezra, which we will discuss in the next chapter.

Ibn Ezra was one of the most important Jewish exegetes in the medieval period.[82] In his famous commentary on the Torah, he comments on Genesis 12:6, when it mentions the Canaanites as being in the land at that point in time, containing some great secret or mystery, namely that the text is subtly indicating some author other than Moses. Since the time of Spinoza, this has been interpreted as evidence that Ibn Ezra did not believe the Torah came from Moses's time, or else why mention that the Canaanites were then in the land, as if they were not at the time of its writing? This argument would, in fact, be used to deny its Mosaic authorship during Spinoza's time.

Interestingly, however, Ibn Ezra provides an argument against reading it as "then," but instead as "already," thus not implying at all that the text was written after Moses's time.[83] The ambiguity of Ibn Ezra's "secret," as it has been argued over the centuries, is that he had to be careful so as to avoid

---

3rd ed. (Minneapolis, MN: Fortress Press, 2018), 55; and Jean-Louis Ska, *Introduction to Reading the Pentateuch* (Winona Lake, IN: Eisenbrauns, 2006), 98–99.

[80] Freedman, "Father of Modern Biblical Scholarship," 31–38.

[81] See, e.g., the discussion of Ibn Ḥazm in James K. Hoffmeier, *Ancient Israel in Sinai: The Evidence for the Authenticity of the Wilderness Tradition* (Oxford, UK: Oxford University Press, 2005), 9, which clearly makes use of Freedman, whom he cites.

[82] On Ibn Ezra see, e.g., Uriel Simon, "Abraham Ibn Ezra," in *Hebrew Bible/Old Testament: The History of Its Interpretation*, vol. 1, *From the Beginnings to the Middle Ages (Until 1300) Part 2: The Middle Ages*, ed. Magne Sæbø (Göttingen: Vandenhoeck & Ruprecht, 2000), 377–87; Nahum M. Sarna, "Abraham Ibn Ezra as an Exegete," in *Rabbi Abraham Ibn Ezra: Studies in the Writings of a Twelfth-Century Jewish Polymath*, ed. Isadore Twersky and Jay M. Harris (Cambridge, MA: Harvard University Press, 1993), 1–27; Haim Beinart, "España y el occidente en los días de R. Abraham Ibn Ezra," in *Abraham Ibn Ezra y su tiempo: Actas del Simposio Internacional: Madrid, Tudela, Toledo, 1–8 Febrero 1989*, ed. Fernando Díaz Esteban (Madrid: Universidad Autónoma de Madrid, Asociación Española de Orientalistas, 1990), 25–38; Roland Goetschel, "The Sin of the Golden Calf in the Exegesis of Abraham Ibn Ezra," in *Abraham Ibn Ezra*, 147–54; Moisés Orfali Leví, "Abraham Ibn Ezra crítico de los exégetas de la Biblia," in *Abraham Ibn Ezra*, 225–32; and Uriel Simon, "Ibn Ezra Between Medievalism and Modernism: The Case of Isaiah XL–LXVII," in *Congress Volume Salamanca 1983*, ed. J. A. Emerton (Leiden, NL: Brill, 1985), 257–71.

[83] See the comments here in Jon D. Levenson, "The Eighth Principle of Judaism and the Literary Simultaneity of Scripture," *Journal of Religion* 68, no. 2 (1988): 209.

being charged as a heretic. In his important 1988 article "The Eighth Principle of Judaism and the Literary Simultaneity of Scripture," Jon Levenson explains how too often Ibn Ezra's comments are misread anachronistically as a wholesale rejection of the Mosaic authorship of Scripture, as if he were espousing modern critical methods.[84] In reality, what Ibn Ezra's comment and related comments from other Jewish sages reveal is that these exegetes were convinced that the Torah was from God, it was divinely inspired, and thus they were not as concerned with affirming the Mosaic authorship of every single verse. As James Kugel explains, Ibn Ezra and his contemporary medieval Jewish biblical exegetes assumed the Mosaic authorship of the bulk of the Torah.[85] Later, as we shall see, Mosaic authorship became bound up with the notion of divine inspiration, where it was defended in order to defend divine inspiration. Thus, when someone wanted to challenge the Bible's divine origin, they often went after the Pentateuch's Mosaic authorship.[86]

ABELARD AND HELOISE

The final figure to discuss before moving on to the Renaissance, Reformation, and early modern period is Peter Abelard. Abelard was clearly aware of the question of Moses as responsible for the Pentateuch, as can be revealed by his correspondence with Heloise, who raised the question. Abelard's response indicates that he thought the Torah had been destroyed by fire and that Ezra rewrote it. In her "Problem 41," from within her series of questions known as *Problemata Heloissae*,[87] Heloise wrote the following:

> We ask who added at the end of the book of Deuteronomy (33:34), which is the last of the five books of Moses, that part speaking of the death of Moses and what followed. We wonder, that is, whether

---

[84] Levenson, "Eighth Principle," 205–25.

[85] Kugel, *How to Read the Bible*, 30–31.

[86] See, e.g., Richard H. Popkin, *The History of Scepticism: From Savonarola to Bayle* (Oxford, UK: Oxford University Press, 2003), 195–96, 223; Richard H. Popkin, *The Third Force in Seventeenth-Century Thought* (Leiden, NL: Brill, 1992), 16–17, 19; and Richard H. Popkin, *Isaac La Peyrère (1596–1676): His Life, Work and Influence* (Leiden, NL: Brill, 1987), 50, 71–74.

[87] Heloise's questions to which Abelard responded are available in in English as "Heloise's Questions [Problemata Heloissae]: Forty-Two Questions Posed by Heloise and Answered by Abelard, with an Introductory Letter by Heloise," in *The Letters of Heloise and Abelard: A Translation of Their Collected Correspondence and Related Writings*, trans. and ed. Mary Martin McLaughlin with Bonnie Wheeler (New York: Palgrave Macmillan, 2009), 211–67.

Moses himself also announced this in a prophetic spirit, so that this, too, could be added to his books, or whether this was added later by someone else.[88]

Abelard's response is recorded:

As Bede recalls in his commentary on Esdras, Esdras himself re-copied not only the Law but, according to the majority opinion, the whole canon of Sacred Scripture, which was consumed by fire, just as it seemed to him was enough for the readers, so he added this, along with many other things, to the writings of the Old Testament.[89]

Abelard may have come to his knowledge of these debates from a variety of sources, perhaps even from Bede, as he mentions. He may have been aware of Muslim critique, as he seems to have been influenced by Arabic and Muslim thought. One likely source of this knowledge was from Peter the Venerable, under whom Abelard sought refuge and who was almost certainly aware of at least some of Ibn Ḥazm's polemics against the Bible, Judaism, and Christianity. Peter the Venerable was the individual responsible for orchestrating the translation team that rendered the Qur'an into Latin. He studied Islam assiduously, directly from Muslim Arabic manuscripts, and read widely in Muslim apologetical and polemical literature.[90]

As we shall see in the next two chapters, this medieval tradition gets linked with skeptical thought and begins to serve new political configurations. As with Ibn Ḥazm's conflicts with Ibn Nagrela, later figures—like Thomas Hobbes and Spinoza—will likewise have very personal stakes in their theo-political arguments. Thus, we shall see how the history of biblical scholarship solidifies the relationship between exegetical traditions that develop in a modern and critical way with politics that increasingly support

---

[88] McLaughlin, ed., *Letters of Heloise and Abelard*, 260.

[89] McLaughlin, ed., *Letters of Heloise and Abelard*, 260.

[90] Josep Hernando, "La polèmica antiislàmica i la quasi impossibilitat d'una entesa," *Anuario de Estudios Medievales* 38 (2008): 764–67; Georges C. Anawati, *Islam et christianisme. La rencontre de deux cultures en Occident au Moyen-Âge* (Cairo: Institut Dominicain d'Études Orientales, 1991), 27–31; Georges C. Anawati, O.P., "La rencontre de deux cultures, en Occident, au Moyen-Âge: Dialogue islamo-chretien et activité missionnaire," *Estudios Lulianos* 29 (1989): 161; Jean-Pierre Torrell, O.P. and Denise Bouthillier, *Pierre le Vénérable et sa vision du monde. Sa vie, son œuvre. L'homme et le demon* (Louvain, BE: Spicilegium sacrum lovaniense, 1986); James Kritzeck, *Peter the Venerable and Islam* (Princeton, NJ: Princeton University Press, 1964); and Pierre-Félix Mandonnet, "Pierre le Vénérable et son activité contre l'Islam," *Revue Thomiste* 1 (1893): 328–42.

the severing of ties with religious, ecclesial, and theological commitments. All of this takes place prior to the development of the modern disciplines of history and archaeology, and prior to the deciphering of the major ancient Near Eastern languages that form the broader cultural context in which the Bible was originally written.

CHAPTER 8

COPIES OF COPIES:

The Early Modern Foundations of the Documentary Hypothesis

Renaissance

The Renaissance was an important period for biblical scholarship. During that time, textual criticism was especially honed, wherein scholars attempted to go back to the original sources. There was a reawakening interest in learning Hebrew in the Latin West, hearkening back to St. Jerome's enthusiasm for the Old Testament's Semitic tongue. In such a context, where the authorship of books, classical and ecclesiastical, was under question, it should come as no surprise that the same began to take place with biblical books. Perhaps the most famous figure from this time period regarding the questioning of a text's commonly assumed author was Lorenzo Valla, who became well known for his argument, which won the day, that the *Donation of Constantine* was a forgery.[1] Debora Shuger explains that "What Valla does, in effect, is identify rhetorical probability with cultural rules and customs."[2]

---

[1] On Valla see, e.g., J. Cornelia Linde, "Lorenzo Valla and the Authenticity of Sacred Texts," *Humanistica Lovaniensia* 60 (2011): 35–63; Pierre Gibert, *L'invention critique de la Bible: XVe – XVIIIe siècle* (Paris: Éditions Gallimard, 2010), 39–46; Lodi Nauta, "Lorenzo Valla and the Rise of Humanistic Dialectic," in *The Cambridge Companion to Renaissance Philosophy*, ed. James Hankins (Cambridge: Cambridge University Press, 2007), 193–210; Lodi Nauta, "Lorenzo Valla and Quattrocento Scepticism," *Vivarium* 44, no. 2 (2006): 375–95; Salvatore I. Camporeale, *Lorenzo Valla: Umanesimo, Riforma e Controriforma: Studi e Testi* (Rome: Edizioni di Storia e Letteratura, 2002); and Sven Grosse, "Renaissance-Humanismus und Reformation: Lorenzo Valla und seine Relevanz für die Kontroverse über die Willensfreiheit in der Reformationszeit," *Kerygma und Dogma* 48, no. 4 (2002): 276–300.

[2] Deborah Kuller Shuger, *The Renaissance Bible: Scholarship, Sacrifice, and Subjectivity*

In his study on biblical philology in the sixteenth and seventeenth centuries, Dirk Van Miert observes that

> For centuries, humanists had fought battles over the interpretations of classical texts. . . . Having cut their teeth on these pagan texts, classical philologists found themselves on dangerous ground if they turned away from Greek and Roman antiquity and ventured to apply their sharp philological tools to antiquity's supreme book: the Bible. . . . philology eventually contributed significantly to the erosion of scriptural authority.[3]

Van Miert's comment here fits with what he earlier wrote with his coeditors:

> philological research on the Bible, even in the hands of pious and orthodox scholars, not only failed to solve the textual problems that had surfaced, but even made things worse. They had piled up ammunition for those who sought to play down the authority of the Bible as the medium of God's Word, or had at least created the conditions that made it easier to question the substance of God's Word.[4]

TOSTATUS, THE RENAISSANCE SPANISH BIBLICAL SCHOLAR

A contemporary of Valla—they were both born and died within a few years of each other—Alfonso Fernández de Madrigal was a fifteenth-century

---

(Waco, TX: Baylor University Press, 2010 [1994]), 47. She writes further, "The rhetorical construction of history is thick description, the rendering of cultural artifacts and customs rather than saints and monsters. . . . The demonstration that biblical events belong to a specific culture and are governed by its codes renders them alien, but it also makes them seem real, attaches them to the historical world of late antique bedclothes and Roman provincial government. . . . Both Valla's revolutionary essay and Renaissance biblical scholarship . . . should be viewed as an episode in the conceptual management of diversity, as a way of categorizing and analyzing the unfamiliar—rather, that is, than as a stage in the gradual secularization of Western culture" (48).

3 Dirk Van Miert, *The Emancipation of Biblical Philology in the Dutch Republic, 1590–1670* (Oxford, UK: Oxford University Press, 2018), xiv. We find something similar in Dirk Van Miert, Henk Nellen, Piet Steenbakkers, and Jetze Touber, *Scriptural Authority and Biblical Criticism in the Dutch Golden Age: God's Word Questioned*, ed. Dirk Van Miert, Henk Nellen, Piet Steenbakkers, and Jetze Touber (Oxford, UK: Oxford University Press, 2017), v, where we read, "a radical shift in the view of the Bible was due, at least in part, to philological criticism of the biblical text."

4 Van Miert, Nellen, Steenbakkers, and Touber, *Scriptural Authority*, 3.

bishop and theologian, often known simply as Tostatus (or Tostado, in Spanish).[5] He is sometimes credited as one of the early figures, after Ibn Ezra, who challenged the Mosaic authorship of the Pentateuch.[6] The most that really can be said of any of Tostatus's explicit doubting of the Pentateuch's Mosaic authorship is that he granted some post-Mosaic interpolations, like the death of Moses in Deuteronomy, which he attributed to Ezra. Noel Malcom remarks that "it is this now forgotten Spanish theologian who, more than any other Christian writer, was responsible for the eventual development of modern critical thinking about the authorship of the Pentateuch."[7]

What brought Tostatus to the attention of scholars like Malcolm was the way he raised the questions about various passages in the Pentateuch. These were not his own questions so much as those posed by others, like Ibn Ezra. He then mostly responded to how the overwhelming majority of these challenges to Mosaic authorship can be understood as authentically Mosaic.

---

[5] On Tostatus as biblical scholar see e.g., Antonio López Fonseca and José Manuel Ruiz Vila, "Alfonso Fernández de Madrigal traductor del Génesis: una interpolación en la traducción De las crónicas o tienpos de Eusebio-Jerónimo," *eHumanista* 41 (2019): 360–82; Bernd Roling, "Critics of the Critics: Johann Scheuchzer and His Followers in Defence of the Biblical Miracle," in *Scriptural Authority*, 376–78; Inmaculada Delgado Jara, "El Tostado y le exégesis bíblica," in *La primera escuela de Salamanca (1406–1516)*, ed. Cirilo Flórez Miguel, Maximiliano Hernández Marcos, and Roberto Albares Albares (Salamanca, ES: Ediciones Universidad de Salamanca, 2012), 55–74; Santiago García, "La competencia hebraica de Alfonso de Madrigal," *La corónica* 33, no. 1 (2004): 85–98; Horacio Santiago-Otero and Klaus Reinhardt, *La Biblia en la península ibérica durante la edad media (siglos XII–XV): El texto y su interpretación* (Coimbra, PT: Arquivo da Universidade de Coimbra, 2001), 131–38; Alastair J. Minnis, "Fifteenth-Century Versions of Thomistic Literalism: Girolamo Savonarola and Alfonso de Madrigal," in *Neue Richtungen in der hoch-und spätmittelalterlichen Bibelexegese*, ed. Robert E. Lerner and Elisabeth Müller-Luckner (Munich: Oldenbourg, 1996), 163–80, 170–78; Solomon Gaon, *The Influence of the Catholic Theologian Alfonso Tostado on the Pentateuch Commentary of Isaac Abravanel* (New York: KTAV, 1993); Emiliano Fernández Vallina, "Introducción al Tostado. De su vida y de su obra," *Cuadernos Salmantinos de Filosofía* 15 (1988): 153–77; and Evaristo Martín Nieto, "Los Libros Deuteronómicos del Antiguo Testamento según 'El Tostado', Alonso de Madrigal," *Estudios Abulenses* 1 (1954): 56–74.

[6] T. M. Rudavsky, "The Science of Scripture: Abraham Ibn Ezra and Spinoza on Biblical Hermeneutics," in *Spinoza and Medieval Jewish Philosophy*, ed. Steven Nadler (Cambridge: Cambridge University Press, 2014), 75–76; Miguel Ángel Tábet, *Introducción al Antiguo Testamento I. Pentateuco y Libros Históricos* (Madrid: Palabra, 2004), 40; Noel Malcolm, *Aspects of Hobbes* (Oxford, UK: Clarendon Press, 2002), 404–7; Félix García López, "Deut 34, Dtr History and the Pentateuch," in *Studies in Deuteronomy: In Honour of C.J. Labuschagne on the Occasion of His 65th Birthday*, ed. F. García Martínez, A. Hilhorst, J. T. A. G. M. van Ruiten, and A. S. van der Woude (Leiden, NL: Brill, 1994), 48.

[7] Malcolm, *Aspects of Hobbes*, 405.

Malcolm perhaps stresses the radicality and important influence of Tostatus on this matter a bit too far. He writes:

> What matters is not so much the answers he gave, as the potential questions he raised—not his particular verdict on each or any of these cases, but the way in which he alerted readers to the possibility of constructing such textual arguments for post-Mosaic additions and alterations. Indeed, his first thematic discussion at the beginning of his commentary on Deuteronomy was the "quaestio" "Who wrote the book of Deuteronomy: Moses or Ezra, or Joshua?" which began: "Doubts are raised by many people over who might have written this book." Who those "many people" were, he never said; perhaps this was nothing more than a rhetorical device. But by countering so explicitly these "many" unnamed opponents, and by explaining so openly the logic of their arguments, Tostatus ensured that the number of people considering—or even sharing—such doubts would indeed be many in the end.[8]

It is far from clear that Tostatus' raising of the questions and responding to them had this sort of effect on the history of scholarship.

REFORMATION

The Protestant Reformation took much of what had developed in the terms of textual criticism and Hebrew philology during the Renaissance and wielded those tools as weapons in their attempt to re-form Christianity into new images. Most of the Reformers, whenever the issue was broached, seemed to embrace the Mosaic authorship of the Pentateuch. Martin Luther, for example, both acknowledged that the Deuteronomic passage referencing Moses's death was written after Moses, but still maintained the essential Mosaic origin and authorship of the Pentateuch. For Luther, Mosaic authorship was not an overly important issue; he believed the Pentateuch was divinely inspired even if not from Moses, and divine inspiration was far more important.[9] John Calvin was a firm believer in the Mosaic

---

[8] Malcolm, *Aspects of Hobbes*, 407.

[9] John A. Maxfield, "Prophets and Apostles at the Professor's Lectern: Martin Luther's Lectures on Genesis (1535–1545) and the Formation of Evangelical Identity," (PhD diss., Princeton Theological Seminary, 2004), 17, 30, 52n3; Richard H. Popkin, "Spinoza and Bible Scholarship," in *The Books of Nature and Scripture: Recent Essays on Natural Philosophy, Theology, and Biblical Criticism in the Netherlands of Spinoza's Time and the British Isles of Newton's Time*, ed. James E. Force and Richard H. Popkin (Dordrecht, NL: Kluwer

authorship of the Pentateuch and made that quite explicit.[10] Calvin was intent, moreover, on defending the authenticity and historicity of Moses's work in the Pentateuch.[11]

KARLSTADT AND THE RADICAL REFORMATION

Whereas some scholars began the sort of criticism of the Pentateuch that we find in the Enlightenment much earlier with Ibn Ezra or Tostatus, Miguel Ángel Tábet identifies its beginning with Andreas Rudolph Bodenstein von Karlstadt, often known simply as Bodenstein or by the name of the place where he was from, Karlstadt.[12] Contrary to received scholarly opinion, Andreas Karlstadt[13] did not so much deny the Mosaic authorship of the Pentateuch completely as imply that it may not have been from Moses. He did this based on Deuteronomy, where it mentions Moses's death. He commented that the passage concerning Moses's death did not really fit the style of what proceeded in Deuteronomy, and thus, if this passage was not from Moses, he opined that it was possible the Pentateuch as a whole was post-Mosaic.[14] Unlike Tostatus, however, Karlstadt's work was less well known and far less influential; it does not really appear to have influenced the future discussion on this question much at all.

Academic, 1994), 4; and Roland H. Bainton, "The Bible in the Reformation," in *The Cambridge History of the Bible: The West from the Reformation to the Present Day*, ed. S. L. Greenslade (Cambridge, UK: Cambridge University Press, 1975), 7.

[10] Randall C. Zachman, "Calvin as a Commentator on Genesis," in *Calvin and the Bible*, ed. Donald K. McKim (Cambridge: Cambridge University Press, 2006), 2–3.

[11] Zachman, "Calvin as a Commentator," 3–4.

[12] Tábet, *Introducción*, 40.

[13] On Karlstadt as a biblical scholar see, e.g., Hans-Jürgen Goertz, "Scriptural Interpretation among Radical Reformers," in *Hebrew Bible/Old Testament: The History of Its Interpretation*, vol. 2, *From the Renaissance to the Enlightenment*, ed. Magne Sæbø (Göttingen: Vandenhoeck & Ruprecht, 2008), 577–81.

[14] Tábet, *Introducción*, 40; Albert de Pury and Thomas Römer, "Le Pentateuque en question. Position du problème et brève histoire de la recherche," in *Le Pentateuque en question: Les origines et la composition des cinq premiers livres de la Bible à la lumière des recherches récentes*, 3rd ed., ed. Albert de Pury and Thomas Römer (Geneva, CH: Labor et Fides, 2002), 13; Malcolm, *Aspects of Hobbes*, 407; Cees Houtman, *Der Pentateuch: Die Geschichte seiner Erforschung neben einer Auswertung* (Kampen, NL: Pharos, 1994), 31; García López, "Deut 34," 48; Popkin, "Spinoza and Bible Scholarship," 4; Bainton, "Bible in the Reformation," 7. Karlstadt was a very serious scholar of Hebrew. See, e.g., Hans Peter Rüger, "Karlstadt als Hebraist an der Universität zu Wittenberg," *Archiv für Reformationsgeschichte* 75 (1984): 297–308.

MASIUS' COMMENTARY ON THE BOOK OF JOSHUA

Another contemporary of the Reformers, Fr. Andreas Masius, a Catholic priest and philologist especially well known for his work on Syriac, contributed to this discussion as well.[15] In his commentary on Joshua, Masius includes questions concerning the Pentateuch's Mosaic authorship.[16] The first time Masius raised the issue in that commentary, he attributed the role of editor of minor additions to the Pentateuch to Ezra. He envisioned Ezra making a few scribal emendations here and there. For the later historical books, Masius saw Ezra as more of a compiler. When Masius returned to the issue of Pentateuchal composition, all of which he does in passing in his commentary on Joshua, he attributed the Pentateuch in the form in which it had come down to Ezra or someone else, making it seem that he thought the Pentateuch was post-Mosaic. He posited that the Israelites might have kept notes, journals, or diaries, which were then passed down through the generations.

---

[15] On Masius as biblical scholar see, e.g., Wim François and Albert Van Roey, "Andreas Masius (1514–73). Löwener Alumnus, Gelehrter der syrischen Studien und biblischer Humanist," in *The Quintessence of Lives: Intellectual Biographies in the Low Countries Presented to Jan Roegiers*, ed. Dries Vanysacker (Turnhout, BE: Brepols, 2010), 7–28; Wim François, "Andreas Masius (1514–1573): Humanist, Exegete and Syriac Scholar," *Journal of Eastern Christian Studies* 61 (2009): 199–244; Jared Wicks, "Catholic Old Testament Interpretation in the Reformation and Early Confessional Eras," in *Hebrew Bible/ Old Testament*, 2:641–42; Robert Wilkinson, *The Kabbalistic Scholars of the Antwerp Polyglot Bible* (Leiden, NL: Brill, 2007), 39–48; Leonard J. Greenspoon, "A Preliminary Publication of Max Leopold Margolis's Andreas Masius, together with his Discussion of Hexapla-Tetrapla," in *Origen's Hexapla and Fragments*, ed. Alison Salvesen (Tübingen: Mohr Siebeck, 1998), 39–69.

[16] Alastair Hamilton, "In Search of the Most Perfect Text: The Early Modern Printed Polyglot Bibles from Alcalá (1510–1520) to Brian Walton (1654–1658)," in *The New Cambridge History of the Bible*, vol. 3, *From 1450 to 1750*, ed. Euan Cameron (Cambridge, UK: Cambridge University Press, 2016), 144, 154; John W. Rogerson, "Early Old Testament Critics in the Roman Catholic Church—Focusing on the Pentateuch," in *Hebrew Bible/Old Testament*, 2:839; John Sandys-Wunsch, "Early Old Testament Critics on the Continent," in *Hebrew Bible/Old Testament* II:973; John Van Seters, "The Deuteronomist—Historian or Redactor? From Simon to the Present," in *Essays on Ancient Israel in Its Near Eastern Context: A Tribute to Nadav Na'aman*, ed. Yairah Amit, Ehud Ben Zvi, Israel Finkelstein, and Oded Lipschits (Winona Lake, IN: Eisenbrauns, 2006), 359–75, 360–61; De Pury and Römer, "Le Pentateuque," 13; Malcolm, *Aspects of Hobbes*, 407–9.

THE JESUIT CONTRIBUTION TO THE DISCUSSION

The Protestant Reformation that tore apart Europe was not the only reform movement in Christendom at that time. Catholic religious orders, like the Carmelites, were at the forefront of Catholic reform. The Jesuit order emerged in this era as well. Jesuits have long made contributions to education and scholarship, but two Jesuit biblical scholars in particular stand out within this history: Cornelius à Lapide and Jacques Bonfrère. These two scholars really represent the first generation after the Reformation, bringing us into the early part of the seventeenth century.

CORNELIUS À LAPIDE

Cornelius à Lapide wrote a number of important biblical commentaries, and his exegetical work became fairly well known across Europe.[17] When it came to Pentateuchal composition, he was clearly aware of the basic history of the discussion. À Lapide thought that Joshua may have compiled, or at least organized, the Pentateuch. Joshua seemed to à Lapide to be the most logical candidate. If this is the case, à Lapide suggests that perhaps Joshua utilized and based his work on Moses's very own notes, which he would have taken during his time leading the Israelites.[18] À Lapide was no skeptical scholar and was well-respected by many, and thus his views were understood as significant. In light of both the wide reach of à Lapide's works as well as the broad respect they earned, Malcolm writes, "Thanks to à Lapide, the idea that there were post-Mosaic materials in the Pentateuch became widely diffused in early seventeenth-century Europe."[19]

---

[17] On à Lapide as biblical scholar see, e.g., Luke Murray, *Jesuit Biblical Studies after Trent: Franciscus Toletus & Cornelius A Lapide* (Göttingen: Vandenhoeck & Ruprecht, 2019), 105–54; Luke Murray, "Jesuit Hebrew Studies After Trent: Cornelius a Lapide (1567–1637)," *Journal of Jesuit Studies* 4, no. 1 (2017): 76–97; Wim François, "Grace, Free Will, and Predestination in the Biblical Commentaries of Cornelius a Lapide," *Annali di storia dell'esegesi* 34, no. 1 (2017): 175–97; John S. Bergsma, "Critical and Catholic Exegesis in the Seventeenth-Century Low Countries," in *Biblical Interpretation and Doctrinal Formulation in the Reformed Tradition: Essays in Honor of James A. De Jong*, ed. Arie C. Leder and Richard A. Muller (Grand Rapids: Reformation Heritage Books, 2014), 191–208; Gilbert Dahan, "Les sources médiévales du commentaire de Cornelius a Lapide sur le Cantique des Cantiques," in *Bible, histoire et société: Mélanges offerts à Bernard Roussel*, ed. R. Gerald Hobbs and Annie Noblesse-Rocher (Turnhout, BE: Brepols, 2013) , 45–69; and Pierre Gibert, "The Catholic Counterpart and Response to the Protestant Orthodoxy," in *Hebrew Bible/Old Testament* 2:764–67.

[18] Malcolm, *Aspects of Hobbes*, 409–10.

[19] Malcolm, *Aspects of Hobbes*, 410.

JACQUES BONFRÈRE

Jacques Bonfrère was a contemporary of à Lapide.[20] Like à Lapide, Bonfrère adhered to the basic Mosaic authorship of the Pentateuch but conceded post-Mosaic additions. There were portions of the Pentateuch, similar to those that others had drawn attention to in the past, that he thought might have dated after the time of Moses.[21] In neither case, with à Lapide nor with Bonfrère, did they think that the Pentateuchal accounts were fictional musings from a later time. Not only did they view them as inspired Scripture but they understood as included in this position that the events recorded therein actually happened. Tábet views the critical work of Masius, à Lapide, and Bonfrère as legitimate attempts at faithful scholarship, "a true scientific attitude."[22] It will be later in the seventeenth century that we see a more skeptical approach to theories of Pentateuchal composition that will then be carried forward into the developing scholarly methods of analysis that at this point had not yet formed.

SEVENTEENTH CENTURY AT MIDPOINT

In his now-dated but still important study on the history of textual criticism of the Old Testament, Moshe Goshen-Gottstein identifies the seventeenth century as a pivotal time, a turning point in biblical scholarship. He specifically links three of the four figures we are about to discuss as key in this shift to what he refers to as "contents criticism."[23] The philosophical revolution of Descartes helps provide an important background context to this mid-seventeenth century transition. Van Miert explains how "Descartes's radical alternative metaphysics created intellectual space for other radical interpretations by people who likewise did not take ancient authority for granted, but who valued an empiricist approach to history."[24]

---

[20] On Bonfrère as biblical scholar see, e.g., Gibert, "Catholic Counterpart," 758–64.

[21] See, e.g., Jean-Louis Ska, "The Study of the Book of Genesis: The Beginning of Critical Reading," in *The Book of Genesis: Composition, Reception, and Interpretation*, ed. Craig A. Evans, Joel N. Lohr, and David L. Petersen (Leiden, NL: Brill, 2012), 13; Ska, *Introduction*, 101n14; Malcom, *Aspects of Hobbes*, 410–11.

[22] Tábet, *Introducción*, 40, our translation.

[23] M. H. Goshen-Gottstein, "The Textual Criticism of the Old Testament: Rise, Decline, Rebirth," *Journal of Biblical Literature* 102 (1983): 376. The three figures are Isaac La Peyrère, Spinoza, and Richard Simon. He excludes Hobbes from this discussion.

[24] Van Miert, *Emancipation of Biblical Philology*, 15. On the importance of Descartes here see especially Jeffrey L. Morrow, *Pretensions of Objectivity: Toward a Criticism of Biblical Criticism* (Eugene, OR: Pickwick, 2019), 56–59; Jeffrey L. Morrow, *Three Skeptics and the Bible: La Peyrère, Hobbes, Spinoza, and the Reception of Modern Biblical Criticism* (Eugene,

Goshen-Gottstein insightfully explains, however, that, "right up to the end of the eighteenth century it was what we would term textual criticism that formed the backbone of critical-exegetical endeavor in its entirety."[25] There are so many important philological scholars engaging in the sort of textual criticism to which Goshen-Gottstein refers that lie behind the work of the four scholars we focus on below, such as Joseph Scaliger[26] and Jean Morin.[27] But it is the four below who contribute most explicitly to what will become the Documentary Hypothesis through the ways they redeploy the philological and skeptical traditions concerning the Pentateuch.

ISAAC LA PEYRÈRE AND THE PRE-ADAMITES

Isaac La Peyrère is not a well-known name among most biblical scholars, and yet his work contributed in a very important way to modern biblical scholarship in general and the Documentary Hypothesis in particular.[28]

OR: Pickwick, 2016); and Scott W. Hahn and Benjamin Wiker, *Politicizing the Bible: The Roots of Historical Criticism and the Secularization of Scripture 1300–1700* (New York: Herder & Herder, 2013), 257–84.

[25] Goshen-Gottstein, "Textual Criticism," 376.

[26] On Scaliger's contributions here, see especially, Van Miert, *Emancipation of Biblical Philology*, 22–52; Nicholas Hardy, *Criticism and Confession: The Bible in the Seventeenth Century Republic of Letters* (Oxford, UK: Oxford University Press, 2017), 1–5, 9–12, 132–41, 182–93; Dirk Van Miert, "The Janus Face of Scaliger's Philological Heritage: The Biblical Annotations of Heinsius and Grotius," in *Scriptural Authority*, 91–96; C. Philipp E. Nothaft, "Josephus and New Testament Chronology in the Work of Joseph Scaliger," *International Journal of the Classical Tradition* 23, no. 3 (2016): 246–51; Henk Jan de Jonge, "Joseph Scaliger's Historical Criticism of the New Testament," *Novum Testamentum* 38, no. 2 (1996): 176–93; Shuger, *Renaissance Bible*, 13–16 and 22–26; Anthony T. Grafton, *Joseph Scaliger: A Study in the History of Classical Scholarship*, vol. 1, *Textual Criticism and Exegesis* (Oxford, UK: Oxford University Press, 1983); Anthony T. Grafton, *Joseph Scaliger: A Study in the History of Classical Scholarship*, vol. 2, *Historical Chronology* (Oxford, UK: Oxford University Press, 1993); and Anthony T. Grafton, "Joseph Scaliger and Historical Chronology: The Rise and Fall of a Discipline," *History and Theory* 14 (1975): 156–85.

[27] On Morin's contribution here, see especially, Hardy, *Criticism and Confession*, 249–74 and 383–89; Peter N. Miller, *Peiresc's Orient: Antiquarianism as Cultural History in the Seventeenth Century* (London: Routledge, 2012), 181–204; Dominique Barthélemy, *Studies in the Text of the Old Testament: An Introduction to the Hebrew Old Testament Project* (Winona Lake, IN: Eisenbrauns, 2012), 22–28; Gibert, *L'invention critique*, 117–27; Gibert, "Catholic Counterpart," 767–73; and Paul Auvray, "Jean Morin," *Revue biblique* 66 (1959): 396–414.

[28] The scholarly literature on La Peyrère has become especially voluminous in recent years. As a sample of some of the most important works on La Peyrère, particularly in regard to his exegetical endeavors, see, e.g., Morrow, *Pretensions*, 37–41; Morrow, *Three Skeptics*, 54–84;

Julius Wellhausen, the so-called "father" of the Documentary Hypothesis, explicitly identifies La Peyrère, using his Latinized name Peyrerius, at the very origin of what would become the Documentary Hypothesis.[29] Our work has shown, however, that both modern biblical criticism and specifically the early stages of Pentateuchal source criticism that would lead to the Documentary Hypothesis predate La Peyrère by centuries. Moreover, his work is not recognizable as modern source criticism. Indeed, as Malcolm observes, the overwhelming majority (all but one) of La Peyrère's major arguments were mentioned already in the works of à Lapide and Bonfrère.[30] And yet, his project has been described as one that "shook the foundations of traditional Christian exegesis."[31]

La Peyrère's primary importance regarding Pentateuchal criticism, and his biblical exegesis in general, lies in how widely spread his work became known, and how it inspired scholars to take what he began much further. His work was not so much a work of scholarship as it was that of an amateur relying primarily upon works which came before his. La Peyrère's name became more of a household name than any of the other figures who contributed in a major way to this history thus far. His biblical exegetical work was, moreover, connected with his other works, which made contributions to the burgeoning discipline of anthropology, geography, and even sociology as it would later develop.[32]

Van Miert, *Emancipation of Biblical Philology*, 193–212; Andreas Nikolaus Pietsch, *Isaac La Peyrère: Bibelkritik, Philosemitismus und Patronage in der Gelehrtenrepublik des 17. Jahrhunderts* (Berlin: Walter de Gruyter, 2012); Jean Bernier, *La critique du Pentateuque de Hobbes à Calmet* (Paris: Champion, 2010), 27–28, 30–32, 132–45; Gibert, *L'invention critique*, 84–87, 112–14; Élisabeth Quennehen, "«L'auteur des Préadamites», Isaac Lapeyrère. Essai biographique," in *Dissidents, excentriques et marginaux de l'Âge classique: Autour de Cyrano de Bergerac: Bouquet offert à Madeleine Alcover*, ed. Patricia Harry, Alain Mothu, and Philippe Sellier (Paris: Honoré Champion, 2006), 349–73; R. H. Popkin, "Millenarianism and Nationalism—A Case Study: Isaac La Peyrère," in *Millenarianism and Messianism in Early Modern European Culture: Continental Millenarians: Protestants, Catholics, Heretics*, ed. John Christian Laursen and Richard H. Popkin (Dordrecht, NL: Kluwer Academic, 2001), 78–82; Élisabeth Quennehen, "Lapeyrère, la Chine et la chronologie biblique," *La Lettre clandestine* 9 (2000): 243–55; Richard H. Popkin, *Isaac La Peyrère (1596-1676) His Life, Work and Influence* (Leiden, NL: Brill, 1987); Richard H. Popkin, "The Development of Religious Scepticism and the Influence of Isaac La Peyrère's Pre-Adamism and Bible Criticism," in *Classical Influences on European Culture, AD 1500-1700*, ed. Robert Ralf Bolgar (Cambridge, UK: Cambridge University Press, 1976), 271–80.

29 Julius Wellhausen, *Prolegomena zur Geschichte Israels*, 6.

30 Malcolm, *Aspects of Hobbes*, 411.

31 Henk Nellen and Piet Steenbakkers, "Biblical Philology in the Long Seventeenth Century: New Orientations," in *Scriptural Authority*, 42.

32 Much of the information that follows on La Peyrère is taken from Morrow, *Pretensions*,

La Peyrère came from a French Calvinist background, probably from a family descended from Marranos, converts from Judaism from the Iberian Peninsula.[33] For most of his career he served as the secretary for the Prince of Condé.[34] This position was more than what we might imagine a modern secretarial position to be; it also involved diplomacy and espionage activity. It afforded La Peyrère the ability to conduct his own research agenda, visiting libraries when he travelled on diplomatic missions, and brought him into the international world of the European politics of his day. His position presented him with opportunities to befriend such important figures as Queen Christina of Sweden, Descartes's patroness, who became the patroness for La Peyrère's intellectual work.[35] It is in this context that we begin to see clear political influences in the biblical exegetical and hermeneutical programs of what would become modern biblical criticism and lead to the development of source critical approaches to biblical texts, of which the Documentary Hypothesis is perhaps the greatest and most enduring example.

La Peyrère's most significant works relating to the future of Pentateuchal source criticism are his books *Prae-Adamitae* (*Pre-Adamites*, often translated as *Men Before Adam*) and his *Systema Theologicum* (*Theological System*) which, after they were published, circulated bound together.[36] Although La Peyrère only formally published these works in 1655, *Prae-Adamitae* had already been circulating in unpublished form in the 1640s and received published refutations, e.g., from Hugo Grotius.

A key to understanding La Peyrère's hermeneutic is the way in which he

---

37–41; Morrow, *Three Skeptics*, 54–84; Pietsch, *Isaac La Peyrère*; and Popkin, *Isaac La Peyrère*.

[33] The term "Marrano" describes Jews who converted to Christianity from the Iberian peninsula, or those who are descended from such converts. Some secretly retained their Jewish practices; others assimilated to their new Christian identity.

[34] See, e.g., Yvan Loskoutoff, "L'arrestation et la conversion d'Isaac de La Peyrère d'après les sources romaines (1656–1657)," *Revue de l'histoire des religions* 236, no. 3 (2019): 545–75.

[35] Queen Christina of Sweden is an important figure at the heart of the intellectual networks which formed the context for the material we are covering here. On her important place in this world of philosophy, philology, and biblical scholarship, see, e.g., Susanna Åkerman, "The Answer to the Scepticism of Queen Christina's Academy (1656)," in *Scepticism and Irreligion in the Seventeenth and Eighteenth Centuries*, ed. Richard H. Popkin and Arjo Vanderjagt (Leiden, NL: Brill, 1993), 92–101; Susanna Åkerman, *Queen Christina of Sweden and Her Circle: The Transformation of a Seventeenth-Century Philosophical Libertine* (Leiden, NL: Brill, 1991); and Susanna Åkerman, "Queen Christina of Sweden and Messianic Thought," in *Sceptics, Millenarians and Jews*, ed. David S. Katz and Jonathan I. Israel (Leiden, NL: Brill, 1990), 142–60.

[36] Isaac La Peyrère, *Prae-Adamitae. Sive Exercitatio super Versibus duodecimo, decimotertio, & decimoquarto, capitis quinti Epistolae D. Pauli ad Romanos. Quibus Inducuntur Primi Homines ante Adamum conditi* (n.p., 1655); and Isaac La Peyrère, *Systema Theologicum, ex Prae-Adamitarum Hypothesi. Pars Prima* (n.p., 1655).

used a two-pronged approach to cast doubt on traditional theological readings of Scripture. He did this in a very subtle way because what he proposed himself remained theological. As opposed to outrightly denying the veracity of the text, he created doubt as to the ways in which the Scriptures were traditionally understood. First, he cast doubt on the traditional interpretations of the opening pages of the first book of the Bible, Genesis. As opposed to Adam and Eve being understood as the parents of humanity as a whole, La Peyrère reinterpreted the texts as depicting Adam and Eve as the parents of the Jewish people alone. Thus, he posited that there were humans prior to Adam, hence his title, *Prae-Adamitae*, or, pre-Adamites. As with a very few others before him, La Peyrère began to utilize other ancient historical texts from other civilizations to aid his interpretation of the Bible. The histories in these texts, like those coming from the Americas, La Peyrère argued, told the histories of the descendants of the pre-Adamites, namely, the Gentiles.

Secondly, clearly building on the work that had come before him, La Peyrère doubted the antiquity of the Scriptures. His particular focus of attack was on the Mosaic authorship of the Pentateuch; he argued that the stories concerning Moses were from after his time. We have encountered many of his arguments before. He pointed to things like Deuteronomy's mention of "beyond the Jordan," the death of Moses in Deuteronomy, the "new" location for the "iron bed" in Deuteronomy 3:11, the repeated phrase "unto this day," Deuteronomy 2:12's mention of "as Israel did," and references to other texts, e.g., "the book of wars of the Lord." These were far from the only problems he found in the Old Testament.[37] La Peyrère concluded that "No one need wonder after this, that one reads so many things which are confused and out of order, obscure, deficient, many things omitted and misplaced; since they shall understand that they [the Scriptures] are a heap of copies confusedly taken."[38]

La Peyrère's exegetical and hermeneutical comments were intended to spark a hermeneutical revolution that would serve a decidedly political end. His arguments were ostensibly aimed at what appears to be an odd theological point—namely, that there are two Messiahs. In fact, however, this was a theological and political conclusion for La Peyrère. In reality, this "conclusion" was not the result of his exegetical labors; rather, it was his political starting point for his entire project. The Messiahs, he argued, included one for the Gentiles and a later Messiah for the Jews. This second Jewish

---

[37] For a more complete discussion of La Peyrère's critique of the Old Testament see, e.g., Morrow, *Pretensions*, 40–41; and Morrow, *Three Skeptics*, 65–75.

[38] La Peyrère, *Systema Theologicum*, 4.1.201. English translation taken from Morrow, *Pretensions*, 41, which is only slightly modified from Isaac La Peyrère, *A Theological Systeme Upon that Presupposition, That Men were before Adam. The First Part* (London: n.p., 1655).

Messiah—still to come at some point in the future—would rule the world alongside none other than the king of France. What the work of Richard Popkin has uncovered is that the king of France La Peyrère envisioned was none other than his employer, the Prince of Condé.[39]

Popkin discovered an elaborate plot hatched between the Prince of Condé, Christina of Sweden, and Oliver Cromwell to overthrow the French monarchy, place Condé on the throne, and transform France into a Protestant country with a Calvinist monarch. The plot came to nothing, apparently because no one could decide who would make the first move. Would Condé declare himself king and move with his followers against the king, or would Cromwell first send his troops to French soil? Inertia won the day, but La Peyrère was in the middle of the entire plan and perhaps aided it in his own way. His works were certainly an attempt to put these political machinations in motion. Popkin points out that "What was being proposed in La Peyrère's first work was not a pipe dream but a program of political action."[40]

Thus, at the heart of this somewhat popular attempt at challenging the traditional views concerning the origin of the Pentateuch was a clear political agenda giving shape to its narrative, hermeneutic, and exegesis. What is more, La Peyrère's work would prove highly influential in the scholarly tradition that developed in his wake, as evidenced by Wellhausen's mention of him at the beginning of his *Prolegomena zur Geschichte Israels*. Scholars may not have adopted La Peyrère's hermeneutic, nor relied upon his exegetical arguments (perhaps other than some which La Peyrère himself had inherited from others before him), and they certainly did not share his political agenda. Nevertheless, he brought these questions to the fore in such a popular form that his name was well known in intellectual circles for centuries, even if it has all but been forgotten now.

---

[39] On this political background see especially Morrow, *Pretensions*, 37–41; Morrow, *Three Skeptics*, 54–84; and Popkin, "Millenarianism and Nationalism," 78–82. On this see also Pietsch, *Isaac La Peyrère*, 127–40 and 208–20; Quennehen, "L'auteur des Préadamites," 349, 360, and 365–66; Richard H. Popkin, "The First Published Reaction to Spinoza's Tractatus: Col. J. B. Stouppe, the Condé Circle, and the Rev. Jean Lebrun," in *The Spinozistic Heresy: The Debate on the Tractatus Theologico-Politicus, 1670–1677*, ed. Paolo Christofolini (Amsterdam and Maarssen: APA-Holland University Press, 1995), 6–12; Richard H. Popkin, "Jewish-Christian Relations in the Sixteenth and Seventeenth Centuries: The Conception of the Messiah," *Jewish History* 6 (1992): 165 and 168; Åkerman, *Queen Christina*, 11, 200, 202–4, 213–15, 219; and Popkin, *Isaac La Peyrère*, 3, 8–9, 12, 40, 58–60.

[40] Popkin, "Millenarianism and Nationalism," 78.

THOMAS HOBBES ON MOSES IN HIS *LEVIATHAN*

The next significant figure within this history, Thomas Hobbes, is better known than La Peyrère, but his reputation rests on his pioneering work in political philosophy.[41] Hobbes's most famous political treatise is his 1651 *Leviathan*, which is deeply concerned with biblical interpretation, as was so much early modern political discourse.[42] Hobbes wrote the bulk of *Leviathan* while in a sort of self-imposed exile in France during the first of the English Civil Wars.[43] Like La Peyrère, Hobbes' work was inextricably bound with his politics, but unlike La Peyrère, Hobbes made no attempt to hide

---

[41] Scholarly literature on Hobbes, like so many of these other figures, is massive. For our topic the most important works include: Morrow, *Pretensions*, 42–48 and 59–62; Atsuko Fukuoka, *The Sovereign and the Prophets: Spinoza on Grotian and Hobbesian Biblical Argumentation* (Leiden, NL: Brill, 2018), 218–45; James R. Martel, "Hobbes and Spinoza on Scriptural Interpretation, the Hebrew Republic and the Deconstruction of Sovereignty," in *Spinoza's Authority*, vol. 2, *Resistance and Power in the Political Treatises*, ed. A. Kiarina Kordela and Dimitris Vardoulakis (London: Bloomsbury Academic, 2018), 70–76; Morrow, *Three Skeptics*, 85–103; Hahn and Wiker, *Politicizing the Bible*, 285–338; Bernier, *La critique du Pentateuque*, 28–29, 48, 127–33, 144–45; Justin A. I. Champion, "Hobbes and Biblical Criticism: Some Preliminary Remarks," *Bulletin Annuel Institut d'Histoire de la Réformation* 31 (2010): 53–72; Frank M. Coleman, "Thomas Hobbes and the Hebraic Bible," *History of Political Thought* 25, no. 4 (2004): 642–69; Henning Graf Reventlow, *Epochen der Bibelauslegung Band IV: Von der Aufklärung bis zum 20. Jahrhundert* (Munich: Beck, 2001), 39–57; François Tricaud, "L'Ancien Testament et le Léviathan de Hobbes: Une cohabitation difficile," *Rivista di Storia della Filosofia* 54, no. 2 (1999): 229–38; Georges Barthel, "La Bible dans le 'Leviathan,'" in *Thomas Hobbes: Critical Assessments*, ed. Preston King (London: Routledge, 1993), 231–50; Pierre-François Moreau, "L'interpretation de l'Ecriture," in *Thomas Hobbes: philosophie première, théorie de la science et politique*, ed. Yves Charles Zarka and Jean Bernhardt (Paris: Presses universitaires de France, 1990), 361–80; Michel Malherbe, "Hobbes et la Bible," in *Le Grand Siècle et la Bible*, ed. Jean-Robert Armogathe (Paris: Beauchesne, 1989), 691–99; Jean Pierre Osier, "L'herméneutique de Hobbes et de Spinoza," *Studia Spinozana* 3 (1987): 319–47; Harold W. Jones, "Thomas Hobbes and the Bible: A Preliminary Enquiry," in *Arts du spectacle et histoire des idées: Recueil offert en hommage à Jean Jacquot*, ed. *La société des amis du CESR de Tours* (Tours, FR: Centre d'études supérieures de la Renaissance, 1984), 271–85; and Henning Graf Reventlow, *Bibelautorität und Geist der Moderne: Die Bedeutung des Bibelverständnisses für die geistesgeschichtliche und politische Entwicklung in England von der Reformation bis zur Aufklärung* (Göttingen: Vandenhoeck & Ruprecht, 1980), 328–69.

[42] Much of the information that follows on Hobbes is taken from Morrow, *Pretensions*, 42–48; Morrow, *Three Skeptics*, 85–103; Hahn and Wiker, *Politicizing the Bible*, 285–338; Reventlow, *Epochen der Bibelauslegung IV*, 39–57; and Reventlow, *Bibelautorität*, 328–69.

[43] For the text of Leviathan see Noel Malcolm, ed., *Thomas Hobbes: Leviathan*, vol. 2, *The English and Latin Texts (i)* (Oxford, UK: Oxford University Press, 2012); and Noel Malcolm, ed., *Thomas Hobbes: Leviathan*, vol. 3, *The English and Latin Texts (ii)* (Oxford, UK: Oxford University Press, 2012).

this. *Leviathan*, as with his *De Cive* before it, was an explicitly political text. In both texts, but mostly in *Leviathan*, Hobbes challenged the Mosaic authorship of the majority of the Pentateuch—he conceded a few sections of Deuteronomy (11–26) as perhaps authentically Mosaic.

Hobbes included very few arguments for his position, arguing that the bulk of the Pentateuch dated from the time of Ezra. The main arguments against the Mosaic origin of the Pentateuch Hobbes leveled were few and somewhat anemic: Deuteronomy 34:6, indicating that no one remembered where Moses's tomb was to be found; Genesis 12:6, "the Canaanite was then in the land"; and Numbers 21:14's mention of nonbiblical sources— these all followed the same track as La Peyrère. Even if one were to grant that these portions of the Pentateuch were post-Mosaic, these three verses would be insufficient to support that almost the entirety of the Pentateuch was post-Mosaic. And yet, that is how Hobbes rests his case.

Hobbes' purpose in all of this is to stand traditional biblical interpretation on its head so that the authority of the text no longer rests on ecclesiastical tradition (like the Catholic Magisterium), nor on the text itself but rather on the authority of the state. For Hobbes, the sovereign ruler is the head of church and state. The authority to interpret Scripture rests in the hands of the sovereign or the court interpreters (be they in university chairs or not) that the sovereign appoints. Hobbes' theological and political position matched the status quo of the England he left for the safety of France—an England in part bequeathed to him by King Henry VIII's severing ties with Rome.[44]

It is very difficult to know from where Hobbes drew his arguments. As scholars have increasingly pointed out, Hobbes need not have been aware of La Peyrère's work in order to come up with these few arguments. He could easily have had access to Tostatus's commentaries, as well as the relevant texts by à Lapide and Bonfrère, from the library in the Minim convent housed at the Place Royale, a place Hobbes visited with some frequency during his time in Paris.[45] Scholars often point out the ostensible difficulty of Hobbes using La Peyrère's arguments in that *Prae-Adamitae* was published four years after *Leviathan* and we do not know how much of the arguments against Mosaic authorship later published in *Systema Theologicum* were present in the pre-publication manuscripts of *Prae-Adamitae* that circulated early on.

---

[44] On the importance the English Reformation had on biblical interpretation and future scholarship, see, especially, Hahn and Wiker, *Politicizing the Bible*, 221–55.

[45] Malcolm, *Aspects of Hobbes*, 413. Malcolm points out on the same page that a portion of that library's catalogue that has survived includes these texts. Hobbes did not know Hebrew very well by the writing of *Leviathan*, but evidence does indicate he at least learned a little later (Malcolm, *Aspects of Hobbes*, 413n103).

We may never know to what extent, if at all, La Peyrère's arguments influenced Hobbes. However, this knowledge is not very significant for the point we are trying to make concerning the political influences on these early hermeneutical developments leading to a completed Documentary Hypothesis in the nineteenth century. With or without La Peyrère's influence, Hobbes's politics clearly influenced his biblical exegesis and proposed hermeneutic, including his comments on Pentateuchal composition. Suffice it to say that La Peyrère's influence on Hobbes is certainly plausible if not probable.

It should be remembered that although Hobbes published *Leviathan* before La Peyrère published *Prae-Adamitae*, the latter circulated in unpublished form long before Hobbes completed his own work. It seems likely that the early versions of *Prae-Adamitae* included arguments about Pentateuchal composition in light of the published refutations. Moreover, it was very likely La Peyrère's ideas contained therein that were floated around in conversation. It must not be forgotten that La Peyrère and Hobbes travelled in the same circles when Hobbes was in Paris spending time at the palace of the Prince of Condé, for whom La Peyrère served as secretary. Although there is no evidence as of yet that the two ever met, La Peyrère and Hobbes shared many friends in common, including especially Marin Mersenne. Malcolm points out, "No one played a greater role in Hobbes's intellectual life in Paris in the 1640s than Marin Mersenne."[46] Regardless of the origin of Hobbes's thoughts, he clearly put his exegesis and his entire hermeneutic at the service of his politics.

BARUCH SPINOZA'S THEO-POLITICAL ARGUMENTATION: PARALLELS WITH IBN ḤAZM

The seventeenth-century figure most often associated with the rise of modern biblical criticism is the Jewish philosopher Baruch Spinoza.[47] Spinoza's bibli-

---

[46] Malcolm, *Aspects of Hobbes*, 420. On Mersenne's friendship with and influence on Hobbes see especially Gregorio Baldin, *Hobbes and Galileo: Method, Matter and the Science of Motion* (Cham, CH: Springer, 2020), 1–51; Armand Beaulieu, "Les relations de Hobbes et de Mersenne," in *Thomas Hobbes*, 81–90; and Quentin Skinner, "Thomas Hobbes and His Disciples in France and England," *Comparative Studies in Society and History* 8, no. 2 (1966): 154–56.

[47] Of every figure covered in our book, probably none has more written about them than Spinoza. For just a sample of the most important works on Spinoza related to our topic, see especially Morrow, "Methods of Interpreting Scripture and Nature," 157–73; Morrow, *Pretensions*, 48–54; Morrow, "Spinoza and the Theo-Political"; Jetze Touber, *Spinoza and Biblical Philology in the Dutch Republic, 1660–1710* (Oxford, UK: Oxford University

cal work relied much on what came before, and his challenge to the Mosaic authorship of the Pentateuch, far more robust than either that of La Peyrère or Hobbes, was fundamental to his project. Most often remembered as a political philosopher, like Hobbes, Spinoza's biblical exegesis was inextricably bound to his politics.[48] Unlike these other figures we have covered, Spinoza constructed a full-blown biblical hermeneutic, which he detailed in the seventh chapter of his *Tractatus theologico-politicus* (*Theological-Political Treatise*).[49] Whereas neither La Peyrère nor Hobbes were systematic in their approach, Spinoza, in the words of Dominique Barthélemey, "presents a sort of 'discourse on method' for biblical criticism in chapters seven to ten of his *Tractatus*."[50]

It is important to keep in mind that, as Van Miert points out, long before Spinoza's *Tractatus theologico-politicus*, "biblical philology was . . . [already] being translated into the vernacular and appropriated by ministers. It ceased to be a purely academic endeavour. Now, well-educated people were acquainted with the idea that the Bible was written in historical circumstances that were not necessarily applicable to the seventeenth

---

Press, 2018), 1–75; Fukuoka, *Sovereign*, 218–45; Morrow, *Theology, Politics, and Exegesis*, 16–34; Anthony Grafton, "Spinoza's Hermeneutics: Some Heretical Thoughts," in *Scriptural Authority*, 177–96; Jonathan Israel, "How Did Spinoza Declare War on Theology and Theologians?" in *Scriptural Authority*, 197–216; Morrow, *Three Skeptics*, 104–38; Hahn and Wiker, *Politicizing the Bible*, 339–93; Steven Nadler, *A Book Forged in Hell: Spinoza's Scandalous Treatise and the Birth of the Secular Age* (Princeton, NJ: Princeton University Press, 2011); Bernier, *La critique du Pentateuque*, 29, 34–35, 78–83, 89–91, 98, 107–12, 118–21, 145–67, 186–95; Gibert, *L'invention critique*, 148–75; Steven Nadler, "The Bible Hermeneutics of Baruch de Spinoza," in *Hebrew Bible/Old Testament* 2:827–36; Travis L. Frampton, *Spinoza and the Rise of Historical Criticism of the Bible* (New York: T & T Clark, 2006); Reventlow, *Epochen der Bibelauslegung IV*, 92–113; J. Samuel Preus, *Spinoza and the Irrelevance of Biblical Authority* (Cambridge, UK: Cambridge University Press, 2001); André Malet, *Le traité théologico-politique de Spinoza et la pensée biblique* (Paris: Sociéte les belles letters, 1966); and Sylvain Zac, *Spinoza et l'interprétation de l'Écriture* (Paris: Presses universitaires de France, 1965).

48 Much of the information that follows on Spinoza is taken from Morrow, *Pretensions*, 48–54; Morrow, "Spinoza and the Theo-Political," 374–87; Touber, *Spinoza and Biblical Philology*, 1–75; Morrow, *Theology, Politics, and Exegesis*, 16–34; Grafton, "Spinoza's Hermeneutics," 177–96; Morrow, *Three Skeptics*, 104–38; Hahn and Wiker, *Politicizing the Bible*, 339–93; Frampton, *Spinoza*; Reventlow, *Epochen der Bibelauslegung IV*, 92–113; Preus, *Spinoza*; and Zac, *Spinoza*.

49 The best critical edition of Spinoza's *Tractatus theologico-politicus* is Baruch Spinoza, *Œuvres III: Tractatus Theologico-Politicus/Traité théologico-politique*, 2nd ed., ed. Pierre-François Moreau, text established by Fokke Akkerman, trans. and notes by Jacqueline Lagrée and Pierre-François Moreau (Paris: Presses Universitaircs de France, 2012). For more on the detailed hermeneutic Spinoza constructs see, e.g., Morrow, *Pretensions*, 51–52; and Morrow, *Three Skeptics*, 120–31.

50 Barthélemy, *Studies in the Text*, 53.

century."[51] It has been commonplace for some time to view Spinoza as an erudite thinker who came to develop his biblical criticism through force of argument, which led to his ever more skeptical philosophy. Van Miert, however, underscores that "Spinoza was propelled to radical biblical philology not by the internal logic of textual criticism itself, no matter how efficiently he wielded its tools to discredit the authority of the Bible. It was rather his radical philosophy that acted as a framework within which biblical philology could finally manifest its most radical potential."[52]

Most of Spinoza's arguments against the Mosaic authorship of the Pentateuch are not that much different from those we have covered already: the use of the third person for Moses, the mention of "beyond the Jordan," and the mention of a time when there was not yet a king in Israel. Perhaps his one unique contribution, in terms of identifying passages, was his discussion of Exodus 16:34 and following as containing post-Mosaic narratives concerning when the Israelites would be in the promised land—after Moses had already died. What was unique with Spinoza, however, was the way this critique fit into his biblical method. Spinoza undermined the Bible in an attempt to show the necessity of a proper method of interpretation, which he claimed to provide in his *Tractatus theologico-politicus.*

Quite frequently, Spinoza has been viewed as a savant at the height of Jewish learning who was punished by the Amsterdam Jewish community by being expelled, usually described as his being excommunicated, on account of his bold arguments highlighting problems in the Old Testament. The work especially of Travis Frampton and Odette Vlessing, however, has shown that this is not likely an accurate picture of what happened.[53] Spinoza

---

[51] Van Miert, *Emancipation of Biblical Philology,* 192. See also the comment in Van Miert, Nellen, Steenbakkers, and Touber, *Scriptural Authority,* preface, v, "an originally academic debate gradually broadened into a maelstrom of public controversy."

[52] Van Miert, *Emancipation of Biblical Philology,* 245. For the way in which Spinoza fits within the philological tradition that preceded him, see Stanislaus von Dunin Borkowski, S.J., *Spinoza Band I: Der junge De Spinoza: Leben und Werdegang im Lichte der Weltphilosophie* (Münster: Aschendorff, 1933); Stanislaus von Dunin Borkowski, S.J., *Spinoza Band II: Aus den Tagen Spinozas: Geschehnisse, Gestalten, Gedankenwelt Erster Teil: Das Entscheidungsjahr 1657* (Münster: Aschendorff, 1933); Stanislaus von Dunin Borkowski, S.J., *Spinoza Band III: Aus den Tagen Spinozas: Geschehnisse, Gestalten, Gedankenwelt Zweiter Teil: Das neue Leben* (Münster: Aschendorff, 1935); Stanislaus von Dunin Borkowski, S.J., *Spinoza Band III: Aus den Tagen Spinozas: Geschehnisse, Gestalten, Gedankenwelt Dritter Teil: Das Lebenswerk* (Münster: Aschendorff, 1936).

[53] See especially, Odette Vlessing, "The Excommunication of Baruch Spinoza: The Birth of a Philosopher," in *Dutch Jewry: Its History and Secular Culture (1500–2000),* ed. Jonathan Israel and Reinier Salverda (Leiden, NL: Brill, 2002), 141–72; Frampton, *Spinoza,* 121–58; Odette Vlessing, "The Excommunication of Baruch Spinoza: A Conflict Between Jewish and Dutch Law," *Studia Spinozana* 13 (1997): 15–47; Odette Vlessing, "The Jewish Community in Transition: From Acceptance to Emancipation," *Studia Rosenthaliana* 30

was a descendant of Marranos (Iberian Jewish converts to Christianity) whose family had returned to the practice of Judaism in Amsterdam, within the Dutch Republic.[54] His Hebrew skill was significant but has been exaggerated.[55] Frampton's work has been particularly important in showing how the mythology around Spinoza developed by his disciples after his death.[56]

The historical reality, based on the archival evidence, seems to be that Spinoza ceased his formal education in Judaism at age thirteen, when Jewish boys typically make their bar mitzvah.[57] Spinoza likely developed much of his skeptical method only *after* his excommunication, even though this is contrary to how the history is normally told.[58] It is insufficient to point to the charge of heresy in the formal statement of his excommunication both because such excommunications could serve social functions apart from specific heresies, but also because the text used is from much earlier; a stylized text from Venice was adopted in Spinoza's case—the specifics of the text do not necessarily reflect the specifics of Spinoza's situation.[59] Instead, it appears the Amsterdam Jewish community felt threatened by Spinoza *not* because of some *tour de force* biblical criticism but because he threatened their status. The Sephardic Amsterdam Jewish community of Spinoza's

---

(1996): 195–211; and Odette Vlessing, "New Light on the Earliest History of the Amsterdam Portuguese Jews," in *Dutch Jewish History*, ed. Jozeph Michman (Assen, NL: Van Gorcum, 1993), 3:43–75.

[54] For the Amsterdam Jewish context of Spinoza see, e.g., David Kromhout and Irene E. Zwiep, "God's Word Confirmed: Authority, Truth, and the Text of the Early Modern Jewish Bible," in *Scriptural Authority*, 133–54; Benjamin Fisher, "God's Word Defended: Menasseh ben Israel, Biblical Chronology, and the Erosion of Biblical Authority," in *Scriptural Authority*, 155–74; Gabriel Albiac, *La sinagoga vacía: un estudio de las fuentes marranas del espinosismo* (Madrid: Hiperión, 1987).

[55] Philippe Cassuto, *Spinoza hébraïsant. L'hébreu dans le «Tractatus theologico-politicus» et le «Compendium grammatices linguae hebraeae»* (Louvain, BE: Peeters, 1999).

[56] Frampton, *Spinoza*, 76–120.

[57] Frampton, *Spinoza*, 131–32, 154; and Abraham de Mordechai Vaz Dias and Willem Gerard van der Tak, "Spinoza Merchant and Autodidact: Charters and Other Authentic Documents Relating to the Philosopher's Youth and His Relations," *Studia Rosenthaliana* 16 (1982): 103–71.

[58] See the discussion in Morrow, "Methods of Interpreting Scripture and Nature," 157–73; and Morrow, *Three Skeptics*, 110–14.

[59] H. P. Salomon, "Le vrai excommunication de Spinoza," in *Forum Literarum*, ed. H. Bots and M. Kerkhof (Amsterdam: Maarsen, 1984), 181–99; Yosef Kaplan, "The Social Functions of the *Herem* in the Portuguese Jewish Community of Amsterdam in the Seventeenth Century," in *Dutch Jewish History*, ed. Jozeph Michman and Tirtsah Levie (Jerusalem: Tel Aviv University, 1984), 1:111–55; and Israel S. Révah, "Aux origines de la rupture Spinozienne: nouveaux documents sur l'incroyance dans la communauté judéo-portugaise a Amsterdam a l'époque de l'excommunication de Spinoza," *Revue des études juives* 123 (1964): 359–431.

day enjoyed a measure of relative autonomy wherein they could even police themselves and enforce rules.[60]

How did Spinoza threaten the Amsterdam Jewish community's relative autonomy? He inherited his father's business and accrued a tremendous amount of debt he could not pay. Instead of settling it within the Jewish community, Spinoza gave them a double blow: first by defaming his father, who had been a prominent member of the Jewish community, blaming him for the debt; secondly, he requested, and was granted by the secular Amsterdam authorities, a legal guardian at the age of twenty-three, which erased his debt, including debts to members of the Jewish community.[61] Thus, Jon Levenson is correct to write of Spinoza that he "turned against the Jewish tradition and even against the Jews themselves with fury. . . . History supplied Spinoza with the coffin into which he placed the Torah."[62] It was not so much that what we find in Spinoza's *Tractatus theologico-politicus* represents his fully formed views from his time as a member of the synagogue in good standing; rather, it represents his more mature response, an "offensive weapon," to borrow the words of Yirmiyahu Yovel.[63]

Spinoza had many influences, including Machiavelli[64]—Spinoza has been numbered among his "most perceptive readers."[65] Descartes was a clear and obvious influence, as were many of Spinoza's contemporaries.[66] Fran-

---

[60] Vlessing, "New Light," 43–76; Yosef Kaplan, "The Portuguese Community in the Seventeenth-Century Amsterdam and the Ashkenazi World," in *Dutch Jewish History*, ed. Jozeph Michman (Assen, NL: Van Gorcum, 1989), 2:23–45; Jonathan I. Israel, "The Economic Contribution of Dutch Sephardim in International Trade, 1595–1713," *Tijdschrift voor geschiedenis* 96 (1983): 505–35; Yosef Kaplan, "The Portuguese Jews in Amsterdam: From Forced Conversion to a Return to Judaism," *Studia Rosenthaliana* 15 (1981): 37–51; and E. M. Koen, "The Earliest Sources Relating to the Portuguese Jews in the Municipal Archives of Amsterdam up to 1620," *Studia Rosenthaliana* 4 (1970): 25–42.

[61] See, e.g., Vlessing, "Excommunication" (*Dutch Jewry*), 141–72; Vlessing, "Excommunication" (*Studia Spinoza*), 15–47.

[62] Jon D. Levenson, *The Hebrew Bible, the Old Testament, and Historical Criticism: Jews and Christians in Biblical Studies* (Louisville, KY: Westminster/John Knox, 1993), 91 and 95.

[63] Yirmiyahu Yovel, *Spinoza and Other Heretics*, vol. 2, *The Adventures of Immanence* (Princeton, NJ: Princeton University Press, 1989), 11. Here Yovel is using the expression to describe Spinoza's biblical exegesis. Spinoza's challenge to Jewish authorities and traditions of interpretation is increasingly recognized, e.g., Eliav Grossman, "Spinoza's Critique of Maimonides in the Context of Dutch Hebraism," *Jewish Studies Quarterly* 27 (2020): 36–57.

[64] Graham Hammill, *The Mosaic Constitution: Political Theology and Imagination from Machiavelli to Milton* (Chicago: University of Chicago Press, 2012); and Carla Gallicet Calvetti, *Spinoza lettore del Machiavelli* (Milan: Università Cattolica del Sacro Cuore, 1972).

[65] Hammill, *Mosaic Constitution*, 22.

[66] Susan James, *Spinoza on Philosophy, Religion, and Politics: The Theologico-Political*

cis Bacon appears to have been another important but neglected guide.[67] Hobbes also likely had an impact on Spinoza's work; Spinoza had *De Cive* in his library. There is some question as to whether or not Spinoza had access to *Leviathan* since he did not know English. *Leviathan*, however, was published in Dutch in 1667 and in Latin in 1668, both languages Spinoza could read.[68] La Peyrère's work also seems to have influenced Spinoza.[69] He had *Prae-Adamitae* in his library. Popkin thinks it is plausible that the two may have met in person when La Peyrère made his visit to the Dutch Republic in 1655, the year *Prae-Adamitae* was finally published.[70]

R. David Freedman has argued that Spinoza was inspired by Ibn Ḥazm, but this is far from clear.[71] In fact, he isolates fourteen of twenty major arguments that he traces back to Ibn Ḥazm's *Kitab al-Fiṣal*. At present, it is impossible to know if Spinoza was familiar with Ibn Ḥazm's work. On the one hand, we do not know if Spinoza knew Arabic; there were no Arabic

---

Treatise (Oxford, UK: Oxford University Press, 2012), 9–11, 144–47; Michelle Beyssade, "Deux latinistes: Descartes et Spinoza," in *Spinoza to the Letter: Studies in Words, Texts and Books*, ed. Fokke Akkerman and Piet Steenbakkers (Leiden, NL: Brill, 2005), 55–68; Michael Della Rocca, "Mental Content and Skepticism in Descartes and Spinoza," *Studia Spinozana* 10 (1994): 19–42; Edwin Curley, *Behind the Geometrical Method: A Reading of Spinoza's Ethics* (Princeton, NJ: Princeton University Press, 1988); and Edwin Curley, "Spinoza's Geometrical Method," *Studia Spinozana* 2 (1986): 151–69. Other influences put forward include Lodewijk Meyer, Samuel Fisher, Juan de Prado, and Uriel da Costa, et al. See, e.g., Manfred Walther, "Biblische Hermeneutik und historische Erklärung: Lodewijk Meyer und Benedikt de Spinoza," *Studia Spinozana* 11 (1995): 227–300; Albiac, *La sinagoga vacía*; and Richard H. Popkin, "Spinoza and Samuel Fisher," *Philosophia* 15 (1985): 219–36.

[67] See, e.g., Morrow, "Methods of Interpreting Scripture and Nature," 157–73; Preus, *Spinoza*, 161–68; and Zac, *Spinoza*, 29–35. For a look at the reception of La Peyrère's *Prae-Adamitae* in the Dutch Republic of Spinoza's time from 1655–1659 see Eric Jorink, "Reading the Book of Nature in the Seventeenth-Century Dutch Republic," in *The Book of Nature in Early Modern and Modern History*, ed. Klaas van Berkel and Arjo Vanderjagt (Leuven, BE: Peeters, 2006), 63–65.

[68] Nadler, *A Book Forged in Hell*, 30–31, 34, 92, 94–96, 119, 188, 190, 193; Bernier, *La critique du Pentateuque*, 112, 120–21; Jon Parkin, "The Reception of Hobbes's Leviathan," in *The Cambridge Companion to Hobbes's Leviathan*, ed. Patricia Springborg (Cambridge: Cambridge University Press, 2007), 450–51; Malcolm, *Aspects of Hobbes*, 390–92; Arrigo Pacchi, "Leviathan and Spinoza's Tractatus on Revelation: Some Elements for a Comparison," *History of European Ideas* 10, no. 5 (1989): 577–93; and William Sacksteder, "How Much of Hobbes Might Spinoza Have Read?" *Southwestern Journal of Philosophy* 11 (1980): 25–39.

[69] See, e.g., Richard H. Popkin, "Spinoza and La Peyrère," *Southwestern Journal of Philosophy* 8 (1977): 172–95.

[70] Popkin, *Isaac La Peyrère*, 84–87; and Popkin, "Spinoza and La Peyrère," 172–95.

[71] R. David Freedman, "The Father of Modern Biblical Scholarship," *Journal of the Ancient Near Eastern Society* 19 (1989): 31–38.

works preserved in his library, so there is no hard evidence of his knowledge of the language. On the other hand, it was not uncommon for Jews of Sephardic ancestry to know Arabic, and he was near the University of Leiden, which he frequented, and which, as "an intellectual powerhouse of Arabic and Hebrew studies,"[72] was one of the leading centers for the study of Arabic in the Europe of Spinoza's age.[73] It is also clear that not all of the sources Spinoza read and utilized were from his personal library;[74] he utilized resources in the library of the University of Leiden, which held a copy of Ibn Ḥazm's *Kitab al-Fiṣal*.[75] Spinoza may not have known Ibn Ḥazm's work, and he may not have known Arabic, but scholars have increasingly recognized the Arabic Muslim philosophical influences on Spinoza, even if he was limited to Latin translations.[76]

If Freedman is incorrect and Spinoza never knew of Ibn Ḥazm's work, the parallels between their situations are still quite intriguing. Both set their task as deconstructing the Bible, and the Pentateuch more specifically. Both had political motivations guiding their exegetical works. Both of them were upset with members of the Jewish community—the Amsterdam Synagogue in the case of Spinoza, and Ibn Nagrela in the case of Ibn Ḥazm—and wrote their works in some sense as a partial response or backlash against the Jewish

---

[72] Van Miert, *Emancipation of Biblical Philology*, xviii.

[73] On the history of Arabic studies in the Dutch Republic see Arnoud Vrolijk, "Arabic Studies in the Netherlands and the Prerequisite of Social Impact—A Survey," in *The Teaching and Learning of Arabic in Early Modern Europe*, ed. Jan Loop, Alastair Hamilton, and Charles Burnett (Leiden, NL: Brill, 2017), 13–32; and Arnoud Vrolijk and Richard van Leeuwen, *Arabic Studies in the Netherlands: A Short History in Portraits, 1580–1950*, trans. Alastair Hamilton (Leiden, NL: Brill, 2014), 1–59 for the time period under discussion.

[74] See, e.g., Grafton, "Spinoza's Hermeneutics," 187; Yosef Kaplan, "Spanish Readings of Amsterdam's Seventeenth Century Sephardim," in *Jewish Books and Their Readers: Aspects of the Intellectual Life of Christians and Jews in Early Modern Europe*, ed. Scott Mandelbrote and Joanna Weinberg (Leiden, NL: Brill, 2016), 318–20, 325–26, 328.

[75] Jonathan Israel, "Spinoza, Radical Enlightenment, and the General Reform of the Arts in the Later Dutch Golden Age: The Aims of *Nil Volentibus Arduum*," *Intellectual History Review* 30, no. 3 (2020): 398; and Grossman, "Spinoza's Critique," 41n14.

[76] See, e.g., Youcef Djedi, "Spinoza et l'islam: un état des lieux," *Philosophiques* 37 (2010): 275–98; Carlos Fraenkel, "Spinoza on Philosophy and Religion: The Averroistic Sources," in *The Rationalists: Between Tradition and Innovation*, ed. Carlos Fraenkel, Dario Perinetti, and Justin Smith (Dordrecht, NL: Springer, 2010), 58–81; Rafael Ramón Guerrero, "Filósofos hispano-musulmanes y Spinoza: Avempace y Abentofail," in *Spinoza y España: Actas del Congreso Internacional sobre «Relaciones entre Spinoza y España» (Almagro, 5–7 noviembre 1992)*, ed. Atilano Domínguez (Almagro, ES: Ediciones de la Universidad de Castilla-La Mancha, 1994), 125–32; Roger Arnaldez, "Spinoza et la pensée arabe," *Revue de synthèse* 99 (1978): 151–74; and Henry Austryn Wolfson, *The Philosophy of Spinoza: Unfolding the Latent Process of His Reasoning: Volume I* (Cambridge, MA: Harvard University Press, 1934), 8–13, 30, 125–26, 157, 189–90, 197–99, 284.

community. Of course, their works were more than this oversimplification, but they were both guided by theo-political concerns more than an allegedly pure objective research agenda attempting to get at the truth of things.

RICHARD SIMON'S HISTORICAL CRITICISM

The final figure we come to in the seventeenth century is that of Fr. Richard Simon.[77] Richard Simon was an Oratorian priest in France, and it was among the Oratorians that he met and befriended Isaac La Peyrère, who became a lay member after converting to Catholicism under pressure.[78] La Peyrère helped enkindle Simon's interest in some of these biblical critical matters, but Simon far outshined him as a scholar. Simon used Masius's work, as well as others we have covered, and took both the work of textual and nascent historical criticism further.[79] Simon was a pioneer in the sort of historical criticism that focused on internal stylistic evidence. As Nicholas Hardy observes, "Much more than Masius, Simon drew evidence about the multiple authorship of the Pentateuch from internal evidence: particularly, the differing styles in which it narrated events."[80]

---

[77] On Simon see, e.g., John Woodbridge, "Richard Simon and the Charenton Bible Project: The Quest for 'Perfect Neutrality' in Interpreting Scripture," in *Knowledge and Profanation: Transgressing the Boundaries of Religion in Premodern Scholarship*, ed. Martin Mulsow and Asaph Ben-Tov (Leiden, NL: Brill, 2019), 253–72; Morrow, *Theology, Politics, and Exegesis*, 35–41; Roberto Bordoli, "Critica e Aufklärung. La controversia su Mosè (1685–1686): Jean Le Clerc contro Richard Simon," Archivio di storia della cultura 30 (2017): 63–77; Hardy, *Criticism and Confession*, 378–92, 398–99; Hahn and Wiker, *Politicizing the Bible*, 395–423; Barthélemy, *Studies in the Text*, 58–81; Bernier, *La critique du Pentateuque*, 29–30, 40, 44–47, 49–78, 82–96, 152–67, 172–73, 186–208; Gibert, *L'invention critique*, 176–201, 205–29, 246–69, 284–90; Antoine Fleyfel, "Richard Simon, critique de la sacralité biblique," *Revue d'histoire et de philosophie religieuses* 88 (2008): 469–92; Sascha Müller, *Richard Simon (1638–1712) Exeget, Theologe, Philosoph und Historiker* (Bamberg: Echter, 2006); Sascha Müller, *Kritik und Theologie: christliche Glaubens-und Schrifthermeneutik nach Richard Simon (1638–1712)* (St. Ottilien: EOS, 2004); Reventlow, *Epochen der Bibelauslegung IV*, 87–92; John D. Woodbridge, "Richard Simon le «père de la critique biblique»," in *Le Grand Siècle*, 193–206; Henning Graf Reventlow, "Richard Simon und seine Bedeutung für die kritische Erforschung der Bibel," in *Historische Kritik in der Theologie*, ed. Georg Schwaiger (Göttingen: Vandenhoeck & Ruprecht, 1980), 11–36.

[78] Much of the information that follows on Simon is taken from Morrow, *Theology, Politics, and Exegesis*, 35–41; Hahn and Wiker, *Politicizing the Bible*, 395–423; Müller, *Richard Simon*; Müller, *Kritik und Theologie*; Reventlow, *Epochen der Bibelauslegung IV*, 87–92; and Woodbridge, "Richard Simon," 193–206.

[79] Hardy, *Criticism and Confession*, 379–80.

[80] Hardy, *Criticism and Confession*, 380. He continues, "This new-found confidence in the power of literary and linguistic analysis to illuminate the history of a text was a recurring feature of the Histoire critique."

Simon makes explicit in his *Histoire critique du Vieux Testament* that he is responding to burgeoning skepticism, like that of Spinoza; but, as a careful reading of Simon's work shows, he relied on Spinoza's very method (without mentioning it), and, in fact, took Spinoza much further, greatly multiplying the problems with Scripture.[81] Simon ostensibly used the notion of Catholic tradition as a means of defending Scripture, but, as Hardy comments, "Simon put very little flesh on the bones of his argument for tradition."[82] In effect, Simon basically highlighted what he took to be evidence of corruption, contradictions, etc., and showed, to those Calvinists who trusted Scripture but distrusted Catholic tradition, that the Bible is nothing but a book riddled with errors that can only be inspired if Catholic tradition is inspired, since the tradition affirms the Bible as the inspired word of God. Key to Simon's argument was the denial of the Mosaic authorship of the Pentateuch. Malcolm provides a helpful chart isolating the arguments against the Mosaic origin and authorship of the Pentateuch, from Ibn Ezra through Spinoza, which Simon may have relied upon:[83]

1) Deuteronomy 31:9 uses the third person for Moses
   Argued by: Ibn Ezra and Spinoza
2) Deuteronomy 1:1 mentions "beyond the Jordan"
   Argued by: Ibn Ezra, à Lapide, La Peyrère, and Spinoza
3) Deuteronomy 34 mentions Moses's death
   Argued by: Ibn Ezra, à Lapide, Bonfrère, La Peyrère, and Spinoza
4) Deuteronomy 3:11 mentions an "iron bed"
   Argued by: Ibn Ezra, à Lapide, Bonfrère, La Peyrère, and Spinoza
5) Genesis 12:6 mentions that the Canaanites were "then" in the land (Gen 12:6)
   Argued by: Ibn Ezra, Hobbes, and Spinoza
6) Genesis 22:14 identifies Mt. Moriah as "of God"
   Argued by: Ibn Ezra and Spinoza

---

[81] Barthélemy, *Studies in the Text*, 58–65 and 80–81; F. Saverio Mirri, *Richard Simon e il metodo storico-critico di B. Spinoza. Storia di un libro e di una polemica sulla sfondo delle lotte politico–religiose della Francia di Luigi XIV* (Florence: Felice Le Monnier, 1972); Paul Auvray, "Richard Simon et Spinoza," in *Religion, érudition et critique à la fin du XVIIe siècle et au début du XVIIIe*, ed. Baudouin de Gaiffier, et al. (Paris: Presses universitaires de France, 1968), 201–14.

[82] Hardy, *Criticism and Confession*, 382. On Simon's understanding and use of tradition, as well as how others understood him, see also Jean Bernier, "Le problème de la tradition chez Richard Simon et Jean Le Clerc," *Revue des sciences religieuses* 82, no. 2 (2008): 199–223.

[83] Malcolm, *Aspects of Hobbes*, 412.

7) Deuteronomy 34:6 (and elsewhere) includes the phrase "unto this day"
     Argued by: Tostatus, à Lapide, Bonfrère, La Peyrère, Hobbes, and Spinoza
8) Deuteronomy 1:1 uses "spoke" as opposed to "wrote"
     Argued by: Tostatus
9) Numbers 12:3 praises Moses
     Argued by Tostatus, à Lapide, Bonfrère, and Spinoza
10) Genesis 48:7 mentions Bethlehem
     Argued by: Tostatus
11) Deuteronomy 2:12 uses the phrase "as Israel did"
     Argued by: Tostatus, Bonfrère, La Peyrère (maybe), and Spinoza
12) Genesis 36:31 mentions before there was a king in Israel
     Argued by: Tostatus, à Lapide, and Spinoza
13) Genesis 13:18 (and elsewhere) mentions Hebron
     Argued by: Masius and Bonfrère
14) Numbers 21:14 mentions the Book of Wars of the Lord
     Argued by: Masius, à Lapide, Bonfrère, La Peyrère, Hobbes, and Spinoza
15) Genesis 14:14 and elsewhere mentions Dan
     Argued by Masius, à Lapide, Bonfrère, and Spinoza
16) Exodus 16:34 and elsewhere includes a narrative about the time after Moses
     Argued by: Spinoza

The point we have been trying to make is not that these arguments are incorrect; rather, in tracing this history we can see how the arguments did not develop simply as the result of an objective quest for truth. They instead developed over time for a series of interrelated theological, philosophical, and political reasons, leading to a burgeoning skepticism in the seventeenth century. We shall see in the next and final chapter how this skeptical foundation was built upon in the eighteenth and nineteenth centuries, leading to the flowering of the classic Documentary Hypothesis at the hands of Julius Wellhausen just before the dawn of the twentieth century.

CHAPTER 9

PENTATEUCHAL CRITICISM THROUGH WELLHAUSEN:

The Eighteenth and Nineteenth Centuries

Enlightenment Context

In the eighteenth century, scholars built upon the work that had come before them. Virtually all biblical scholars built upon the careful textual critical work that preceded them, but they also built upon the more skeptical foundations Isaac La Peyrère, Thomas Hobbes, Baruch Spinoza, and Richard Simon constructed. In a very few instances, these scholars did so consciously and explicitly. For many, however, their work remained indebted to these figures despite their attempts to counter their criticism. The sort of critique these early modern interpreters advanced became intertwined in the system. A significant shift occurred, though, in the patronage for such scholarship. Whereas in the past much of the patronage had been by individuals—as in the case of Christina of Sweden and La Peyrère—or individual audiences, like Spinoza and his circle of friends, now states and the university systems they supported became the primary patrons of biblical scholarship.[1]

In the Germanic realms, universities like Halle were reconstituted to become Enlightenment universities, and universities like Göttingen—and later Berlin—were created to advance Enlightenment ideals.[2] These insti-

---

[1]   See Scott W. Hahn and Jeffrey L. Morrow, *Modern Biblical Criticism as a Tool of Statecraft (1700–1900)* (Steubenville, OH: Emmaus Academic, 2020), 27–34.

[2]   See, e.g., Michael C. Legaspi, *The Death of Scripture and the Rise of Biblical Studies* (Oxford, UK: Oxford University Press, 2010), 37–38, 40–41; Thomas Albert Howard, *Protestant Theology and the Making of the Modern German University* (Oxford, UK: Oxford University Press, 2006), 112–13; George S. Williamson, *The Longing for Myth in Germany: Religion and Aesthetic Culture from Romanticism to Nietzsche* (Chicago: University of

tutions were intent on forming competent civil students of the crown, and then the state. The various disciplines were coordinated in such a way as to achieve this end. In the past, the Enlightenment was viewed monolithically as a purely secular anti-religious and theological endeavor. The reality is far more complex, wherein we might speak of several enlightenments, some of which were theological.[3]

RISE OF BIBLICAL STUDIES

In his book *The Death of Scripture and the Rise of Biblical Studies*, Michael Legaspi shows how the academic study of the Bible within the university context—the very modern discipline of biblical studies as autonomous from theology—was born during the eighteenth century in the time we have come to know as the Enlightenment. Legaspi does this especially by highlighting the work of Johann David Michaelis at the University of Göttingen.[4] Legaspi's important study underscores the way in which Michaelis transformed the study of the Bible from a primarily theological enterprise into a primarily historical, philological, and cultural endeavor in order to preserve a place for this newly transformed discipline at the Enlightenment university.[5] The study of Scripture had already been secularized in the work of Johann Salomo Semler, a contemporary of Michaelis at the University of Halle; Semler had been influenced by Spinoza and Simon, among others.[6] Halle proved less influential, however, than Göttingen, which proved

---

Chicago Press, 2004), 37; and Charles E. McClelland, *State, Society, and University in Germany 1700–1914* (Cambridge, UK: Cambridge University Press, 1980), 34–98.

[3] See, e.g., Ulrich L. Lehner, *The Catholic Enlightenment: The Forgotten History of a Global Movement* (Oxford, UK: Oxford University Press, 2016); and David Sorkin, *The Religious Enlightenment: Protestants, Jews, and Catholics from London to Vienna* (Princeton, NJ: Princeton University Press, 2008).

[4] Legaspi, *Death of Scripture*, 27–51 (on the importance of Göttingen), and especially 79–104 and 129–53 (on Michaelis).

[5] On Michaelis here see also Hahn and Morrow, *Modern Biblical Criticism*, 71–95; Rudolf Smend, *From Astruc to Zimmerli: Old Testament Scholarship in Three Centuries* (Tübingen: Mohr Siebeck, 2007), 30–42; Jonathan Sheehan, *The Enlightenment Bible: Translation, Scholarship, Culture* (Princeton, NJ: Princeton University Press, 2005), 184–92 and 199–220; J. C. O'Neill, *The Bible's Authority: A Portrait Gallery of Thinkers from Lessing to Bultmann* (Edinburgh: T&T Clark, 1991), 28–38; Anna-Ruth Löwenbrück, "Johann David Michaelis et les débuts de la critique biblique," in *Le siècle des Lumières et la Bible*, ed. Yvon Belaval and Dominique Bourel (Paris: Beauchesne, 1986), 113–28; and Hans-Joachim Kraus, *Geschichte der historisch-kritischen Erforschung des Alten Testaments von der Reformation bis zur Gegenwart* (Neukirchen: Erziehungsvereins, 1956), 97–103.

[6] On Semler here see Hahn and Morrow, *Modern Biblical Criticism*, 60–69; Marianne

to be a model for later universities including Berlin.[7] What Michaelis did, according to Legaspi's study, and what ensured the Bible's survival at the Enlightenment university, was place distance between the Bible and the reader so as to make the Bible foreign as an ancient artifact that may then be mined for civic virtues. This allowed the Bible to be redeployed as a political tool in an enlightened German context. Michaelis's model was classical studies. As his classics professors and peers transformed that discipline, so he too would do the same for the study of the Bible.[8]

CONNECTION WITH CRITICISM IN CLASSICAL STUDIES

This connection with classical studies is even more germane to the development of the Documentary Hypothesis than it is to the transformation of biblical studies in general. If we walk through the history of the development of source criticism in Homeric studies, we see that it mirrors developments in Pentateuchal source criticism at every step of the way.[9] What is of particular interest is how French and German scholars in these respective fields appeared to follow each other methodologically such that as one field developed its methods in one direction, the other followed suit, up until the parting of ways after Wellhausen.

We can begin with the classical Homeric criticism put forth by François Hédelin, more commonly known by his later title the Abbé d'Aubignac,

---

Schröter, *Aufklärung durch Historisierung: Johann Salomo Semlers Hermeneutik des Christentums* (Berlin: Walter de Gruyter, 2012); Roberto Bordoli, *L'illuminismo di Dio: Alle origini della "mentalità liberale": Religione teologia filosofia e storia in Johann Salomo Semler (1725–1791): Contributo per lo studio delle fonti teologische, cartesiane e spinoziane dell' «Aufklärung»* (Florence: Olschki, 2004); Henning Graf Reventlow, *Epochen der Bibelauslegung Band IV: Von der Aufklärung bis zum 20. Jahrhundert* (Munich: Beck, 2001), 175–89; O'Neill, *Bible's Authority*, 39–53; and Kraus, *Geschichte der historisch-kritischen Erforschung*, 103–13.

[7] See, e.g., Legaspi, *Death of Scripture*, 5–6; Howard, *Protestant Theology*, 88, 112–13, and 119; Williamson, *Longing for Myth*, 37; and McClelland, *State, Society, and University*, 34–98.

[8] On this connection see Hahn and Morrow, *Modern Biblical Criticism*, 42–49, 76–77; and Legaspi, *Death of Scripture*, 53–78.

[9] On this parallel, see, e.g., Hahn and Morrow, *Modern Biblical Criticism*, 106–15; John Van Seters, *The Edited Bible: The Curious History of the "Editor" in Biblical Criticism* (Winona Lake, IN: Eisenbrauns, 2006), 133–243; Guy G. Stroumsa, "Homeros Hebraios: Homère et la Bible aux origines de la culture européenne (17e–18e siècles)," in *L'Orient dans l'histoire religieuse de l'Europe: L'invention des origines*, ed. Mohammad Ali Amir-Moezzi and John Scheid (Turnhout, BE: Brepols, 2000), 87–100; and Umberto Cassuto, *The Documentary Hypothesis and the Composition of the Pentateuch: Eight Lectures* (Jerusalem: Shalem Press, 2006 [1941]), 11–14.

who was only an amateur and not a formally trained classical scholar—he apparently knew little to no Greek, and worked on Homer in Latin translation.[10] After his death, d'Aubignac's earlier written work on Homeric composition, entitled *Conjectures académiques ou Dissertation sur l'Iliade*, was published anonymously. It appeared in print in 1715. D'Aubignac hypothesized that there were earlier poems lying behind the Homeric texts as we had them. He argued that Homer never existed and that an editor pieced together a number of earlier sources forming what we find in the Homeric corpus.

The role d'Aubignac played in Homeric criticism was mirrored by Jean Astruc, also an amateur, in Pentateuchal criticism.[11] Astruc, the surgeon for King Louis XV of France, published anonymously his 1753 book on the composition of Genesis, with the title beginning as had d'Aubignac's with the phrase "*Conjectures.*" Astruc's title was lengthier: *Conjectures sur les memoires originaux dont il paroit que Moyse s'est servi pour composer le Livre de la Genèse.*[12] Unlike d'Aubignac, however, whose work was more polemical against those he thought had an overly high view of Homer and thus denied Homer's authorship of the Iliad and the Odyssey and even Homer's existence, Astruc did in fact argue that Moses was responsible for the Pentateuch. Astruc was well aware of the challenges to this, particularly coming from La Peyrère, Hobbes, Spinoza, and Simon, against whose views he was writing. Astruc's *Conjectures* was thus intended as an apologetic against the earlier skepticism of the seventeenth century.

Astruc was aware, however, that even in the Pentateuchal narratives themselves, Moses came long after the patriarchs and earlier history recounted in the Book of Genesis. Thus, even if Moses was responsible for the Pentateuch, as Astruc believed, he must have used other sources at least for Genesis and for the very beginning of Exodus. Astruc thought he could come up with a method, which was similar to d'Aubignac's, by which he

---

[10] On d'Aubignac see, e.g., Luigi Ferreri, *La questione omerica dal cinquecento al settecento* (Rome: Edizioni di Storia e Letteratura, 2007), 113–64; and Sir John L. Myers, *Homer and His Critics*, ed. Dorothea Gray (London: Routledge, 2014 [1958]), 47–48.

[11] On Astruc and his role in Pentateuchal source criticism see, e.g., Rudolf Smend, "Jean Astruc: A Physician as a Biblical Scholar," in *Sacred Conjectures: The Context and Legacy of Robert Lowth and Jean Astruc*, ed. John Jarick (London: T&T Clark, 2007), 157–73; Pierre Gibert, "De l'intuition a l'evidence: La multiplicite documentaire dans la Genese chez H. B. Witter et Jean Astruc," in *Sacred Conjectures*, 174–89; Jan Christian Gertz, "Jean Astruc and Source Criticism in the Book of Genesis," in *Sacred Conjectures*, 190–203; Smend, *From Astruc*, 1–14; and Ana M. Acosta, "Conjectures and Speculations: Jean Astruc, Obstetrics, and Biblical Criticism in Eighteenth-Century France," *Eighteenth-Century Studies* 35, no. 2 (2002): 256–66.

[12] A recent critical edition of Astruc's work is available as Jean Astruc, *Conjectures sur la Genèse* (Paris: Noêsis, 1999) with an introduction and notes by Pierre Gibert.

could identify these sources Moses used. His work focused on style and repetition. He identified about twelve different pre-Mosaic sources, most of which were minor sources, but which included two major sources, which Astruc labeled Source A and Source B. The main way he distinguished these two primary sources was based on whether Elohim or Yahweh was used for God's name. Thus, we find the beginning of what would eventually become the Documentary Hypothesis. This is important because the notion of double narratives, or doublets, use of different names, etc., became the cornerstone of the entire source critical enterprise, even outside of Pentateuchal criticism.[13] Astruc had a precursor with regard to doublets in the Pentateuch: Bernhard Henning Witter. Witter had published his work in 1711, but apparently failed to have much of a readership and did not influence many people, and no one directly within the history we are tracing.[14] The parallel between classical and biblical studies would continue, as we shall see with the next figures we discuss.[15]

JOHANN GOTTFRIED EICHHORN AT THE HEART OF THE EARLY DOCUMENTARY HYPOTHESIS

Johann David Michaelis's most important student at Göttingen would prove to be Johann Gottfried Eichhorn.[16] What is most significant for our

---

[13] See, e.g., Aulikki Nahkola, "The Memoires of Moses and the Genesis of Method in Biblical Criticism: Astruc's Contribution," in Jarick, ed., *Sacred Conjectures*, 204–19; and Nahkola, *Double Narratives in the Old Testament*.

[14] On Witter see, e.g., Gibert, "De l'intuition," 174–89; and Hans Bardtke, "Henning Bernhard Witter. Zur 250. Wiederkehr seiner Promotion zum Philosophiae Doctor am 6. November 1704 zu Helmstedt," *Zeitschrift für die alttestamentliche Wissenschaft* 66 (1954): 153–81.

[15] Long ago, Edwin Yamauchi wrote about these parallels, both as they positively affected one another, and also as they more negatively did, in his work *Composition and Corroboration in Classical and Biblical Studies*.

[16] On Eichhorn here see, e.g., Hahn and Morrow, *Modern Biblical Criticism*, 97–106 and 112–20; Van Seters, *Edited Bible*, 191–96; Reventlow, *Epochen der Bibelauslegung IV*, 209–26; Giuseppe D'Alessandro, *L'illuminismo dimenticato: Johann Gottfried Eichhorn (1752–1827) e il suo tempo* (Naples, IT: Liguori, 2000); O'Neill, *Bible's Authority*, 78–94; Rudolf Smend, *Deutsche Alttestamentler in drei Jahrhunderten* (Göttingen: Vandenhoeck & Ruprecht, 1989), 25–37; Rudolf Smend, "Johann David Michaelis und Johann Gottfried Eichhorn—zwei Orientalisten am Rande der Theologie," in *Theologie in Göttingen: Eine Vorlesungsreihe*, ed. Bernd Moeller (Göttingen: Vandenhoeck & Ruprecht, 1987), 58–81; Fauto Parente, "La Urgeschichte di J. G. Eichhorn e l'applicazione del concetto di «mito» al Vecchio Testamento," *Annali della Scuola Normale Superiore di Pisa* 16, no. 2 (1986): 535–67; and Kraus, *Geschichte der historisch-kritischen Erforschung*, 120–43.

purposes is the way that Michaelis inadvertently mediated the earlier Pentateuchal source criticism to Eichhorn, who would then take it further and pave the way for what would become the Documentary Hypothesis.[17] Michaelis, like Astruc, was a firm adherent to the Mosaic authorship of the Pentateuch—Michaelis even went so far as to defend the Talmudic notion of Moses as the author of the Book of Job. Michaelis, however, was upset with Astruc's arguments because he found them both somewhat arbitrary and also a potential threat for the future. Rather than a robust response to the skepticism of La Peyrère, Hobbes, Spinoza, and Simon, Michaelis understood Astruc's methodology as a ticking time bomb that could be used to deconstruct the rest of the Pentateuch and the Bible. If such arbitrary literary and stylistic differences could be used to discover discrete hypothetical sources Moses may have used, what is to stop more skeptical scholars from applying the same criteria to the rest of the Pentateuch (and elsewhere), rendering Moses as the author superfluous at best? That is, of course, what did happen.

Fausto Parente argued that Eichhorn came up with his approach independently from Astruc, but Eichhorn freely admits his indebtedness to Astruc.[18] When he first wrote his highly influential *Einleitung ins Alte Testament*, he conceded Mosaic authorship even as he laid the groundwork for developing the Documentary Hypothesis by taking Astruc's method further into the other books of the Pentateuch. But by the fourth edition of his *Einleitung*, he abandoned his defense of Mosaic authorship, instead including many of the major challenges against this position. In his work, Eichhorn helped create what has been called the "mythic school" of biblical studies, based on Christian Gottlob Heyne's notion of myth as applied to classical studies.[19] As myth, stories like Genesis 1–3 were not necessarily fiction, but neither were they ordinary history.

It was not only in the realm of Pentateuchal source criticism and biblical criticism in general that Eichhorn was influential but also in classical Homeric criticism. Despite John Van Seters's arguments,[20] Eichhorn seems to have influenced the work of classical scholar Friedrich August Wolf in

---

[17] See, e.g., Hahn and Morrow, *Modern Biblical Criticism*, 209–120; Van Seters, *Edited Bible*, 192; and Nahkola, *Double Narratives*, 9.

[18] See Parente, "La Urgeschichte," 542 and 544.

[19] See, e.g., Hahn and Morrow, *Modern Biblical Criticism*, 102–6; Henning Graf Reventlow, "Towards the End of the 'Century of Enlightenment': Established Shift from Sacra Scriptura to Literary Documents and Religion of the People of Israel," in *Hebrew Bible/Old Testament*, 2:1051–57; Williamson, *Longing for Myth*, 32–33 and 152–53; and Christian Hartlich and Walter Sachs, *Der Ursprung des Mythosbegriffes in der Modernen Bibelwissenschaft* (Tübingen: Mohr, 1952), 20–38.

[20] Van Seters, *Edited Bible*, 194–95.

dissecting Homer much as Eichhorn had the Pentateuch.[21] As Anthony Grafton points out—and Van Seters insufficiently addresses—"Eichhorn provided both formulations and solutions for technical problems that the scholia posed Wolf."[22] Van Seters's main point is that because Wolf, who certainly knew d'Aubignac's work, studied under Heyne as well as Semler and Michaelis, like Eichhorn, it is more likely Heyne and Michaelis influenced Wolf in ways *similar to* the ways they shaped Eichhorn's work rather than Eichhorn having a *direct influence* on Wolf's work.

This is unlikely because, in part, one of Michaelis's primary influences on Eichhorn with regard to source criticism was his mediation of Astruc through exposing Eichhorn to his (Michaelis's) arguments against Astruc, which was unique because of Eichhorn's close relationship with Michaelis. Furthermore, Van Seters's view does not account for the close similarities between Wolf's *Prolegomena* and Eichhorn's *Einleitung*. As Hahn and Morrow explain in a footnote, Van Seters's view is insufficient to explain "the precise manner in which" Eichhorn's *Einleitung* seems to be a blueprint for Wolf's source criticism: "This is something inexplicable by the sole acknowledgement that Wolf studied with Heyne, Semler, and Michaelis, all of whom also influenced Eichhorn. Shared influence is insufficient here, when Eichhorn provides the precise solutions for Wolf, coupled with Wolf's explicit citation and use of Eichhorn in his work."[23]

To recap at this point, what we have near the beginning of the nineteenth century is a development building upon the centuries of mainly polemical philological work, but which now has included a literary component. At first, the Mosaic authorship of certain passages was challenged. Some, like Ibn Ḥazm and the earlier anti-Jewish and anti-Christian polemicists, used these challenges to distance the Pentateuch from Moses and thus relativize or outright deny the link between the Torah and God giving the Law on Mount Sinai. This was one means of striking at the foundation of Christianity by means of striking at the heart of Judaism. Other sages and exegetes within the Jewish and Christian traditions raised some of these same questions, but they did so in order to better understand the history behind the revelation they had before them, which they considered inspired by God.

By the seventeenth century, however, more skeptical intellectuals—La Peyrère, Hobbes, Spinoza, and Simon—used these arguments, and Spinoza

---

[21] See especially Anthony Grafton, "Prolegomena to Friedrich August Wolf," *Journal of the Warburg and Courtauld Institutes* 44 (1981): 101–29.

[22] Grafton, "Prolegomena," 121. See also pages 123–25 for more precise arguments Wolf almost certainly borrowed from Eichhorn.

[23] Hahn and Morrow, *Modern Biblical Criticism*, 114n74.

and Simon at least built upon them in order to return to the earlier skepticism and cast doubt upon traditional religious authority structures. As they did this, they utilized, knowingly (likely in the case of Hobbes and Spinoza) or unknowingly (perhaps in the case of La Peyrère and Simon), philosophical naturalism as the background assumption, ensuring its secure footing in the biblical criticism that would follow. Brad Gregory's words are helpful here:

> Any adequate assessment of the history of modern biblical criticism, from Hobbes and Spinoza in the seventeenth century through Protestant and Catholic exegesis up to the present, must be aware of the extent to which not only the empirical findings of science have been conflated with metaphysical naturalism, but also the extent to which historical-critical textual criticism has uncritically assumed naturalism as a *dogma* rather than as a merely abstractive methodological assumption of scientific inquiry.[24]

Astruc was in a different position here. If Simon's apologetic was more dissembling than sincere—and this is a matter of debate—Astruc's intent was clearly defensive, even if he lacked the philological and textual critical skills of Simon. Eichhorn, however, proves pivotal because he begins by the end of his career to hearken back to a more skeptical position, with regard to the authenticity of the texts, to that of Spinoza and Simon, rather than Astruc (to whom he is methodologically more indebted than to the former two) or to his own mentor Michaelis. He takes this work further with all the skills he has developed and honed from both biblical studies and classical studies, under the tutoring of Michaelis and Heyne respectively. We return to Gregory again, who insightfully points out the philosophical background implicit in the shift that was going on within biblical studies, where he makes explicit reference to Semler, Michaelis, and Eichhorn. Gregory discerns in this work "an ideological commitment to the construction of a black-hole historicism of the biblical past. Scholars would be the arbiters of what would be permitted to escape, and on whose terms . . . No one would be permitted to cross the chasm between modern present and ancient past except on the terms of the guardians of the science of antiquity."[25]

With Eichhorn, moreover, now there was a sense that combined the

---

[24] Brad S. Gregory, *The Unintended Reformation: How a Religious Revolution Secularized Society* (Cambridge, MA: Harvard University Press, 2012), 413n116.

[25] Gregory, *Unintended Reformation*, 345. He continues, "Functionally, this was just what Spinoza had sought to accomplish in his *Tractatus Theologico-Politicus* (1670), only by different means."

approaches of the past. Like Spinoza, Simon, et al., scholars could understand that the Pentateuch came from after the time of Moses. In addition,
whereas Astruc provided a literary method for identifying hypothetical
sources lying behind Genesis, so too, now with Eichhorn, those same type
of sources could be isolated for the entire Pentateuch. The stage was now
set for the Documentary Hypothesis. Politically, this methodology, and its
assumptions about the necessity of (state-run) university-trained scholars as
intellectual gate-keepers—rather than an ecclesial body like the Magisterium
or a Lutheran body—fit well in the broader political climate of Enlightenment Germany.

THE LONG NINETEENTH CENTURY

It is really in the nineteenth century that Germany would dominate modern
historical biblical critical scholarship. In the eighteenth century, scholars like
Michaelis and Semler gained much from English scholarship, like that of
Robert Lowth, and the English Deists especially.[26] It is also in this period
that the Documentary Hypothesis would develop into its classical expression at the hands of Wellhausen. The nineteenth century, with its focus on
rationalism and historicism, would give shape to the future of historical
criticism to the present. In some ways, the source critical approach to the
Pentateuch affected source critical approaches to other portions of the Bible
as well.

It is also in the nineteenth century that we can see how the politics that
formed the background to the intellectual work of the exegetes we examine left its mark on their work. The same can clearly be said for Hobbes,
Spinoza, and others. And yet, apart from perhaps Spinoza's methodological
outline of his biblical hermeneutic in the seventh chapter of his *Tractatus theologico-politicus*, scholars do not routinely use the methods of these
other figures as they had laid them down. Bible textbooks do not review
La Peyrère's exegesis from his *Prae-Adamitae*. When the rare Bible textbooks bothers to review Simon's contributions, they go no further than
review; they do not then proceed to use Simon and apply him to portions
of Scripture. With Wellhausen, however, not only do most Bible textbooks
summarize his version of the Documentary Hypothesis but they often

---

[26] See, e.g., Hahn and Morrow, *Modern Biblical Criticism*, 28–34, 61–62, and 86–89;
Legaspi, *Death of Scripture*, 115–21; Sheehan, *Enlightenment Bible*, 241–57; and John
Rogerson, *Old Testament Criticism in the Nineteenth Century: England and Germany*
(Philadelphia, PA: Fortress Press, 1984), 7, 9–10.

apply it to their discussion later on of the Pentateuch and invite students to do the same.

WILHELM MARTIN LEBERECHT DE WETTE: DISMISSING THE EVIDENCE OF THE SAMARITAN PENTATEUCH AND THE DATING OF DEUTERONOMY

Wilhelm Martin Leberecht de Wette is the next important figure we encounter after Eichhorn.[27] Few doctoral dissertations on Scripture have had the effect on the discipline that de Wette's had, to the point where the impact can still be felt today more than two hundred years later! What is even more remarkable is that the most enduring point was not so much the overall argument of the dissertation, but an aside in a single footnote. De Wette's 1805 dissertation argued that Deuteronomy was from its own literary source, distinct from the rest of the sources that composed the Pentateuch. His momentous footnote argues that Deuteronomy is likely the book mentioned in 2 Kings 22 that was discovered during King Josiah's reign.

He continued this work elsewhere and argued that Deuteronomy dated long after Moses's time to the period of Josiah when either it was discovered after not having been very influential or widely known, or, as de Wette seemed to think was more likely, it may have actually been composed then, during the Josianic reforms. Important internal evidence for de Wette that the Pentateuch in general was late is the absence of references to it in the Prophets. He modified Eichhorn's documentary approach with the notion that much of the Pentateuch also incorporated more disparate fragmentary sources. Sometimes scholars overstate the case in identifying de Wette's views on Pentateuchal composition as completely fragmentary, as in a Fragmentary Hypothesis—which may be an accurate understanding of one of de Wette's early positions—but by the end, de Wette incorporated much larger hypothetical documentary sources with a host of hypothetical fragmentary

---

[27] On de Wette here see, e.g., Hahn and Morrow, *Modern Biblical Criticism*, 126–42; Smend, *From Astruc*, 43–56; Van Seters, *Edited Bible*, 205–15; Christoph Bultmann, "Philosophie und Exegese bei W. M. L. de Wette. Der Pentateuch als Nationalepos Israels," in *Wilhelm Martin Leberecht de Wette. Ein Universaltheologe des 19. Jahrhunderts*, ed. Hans-Peter Mathys and Klaus Seybold (Basel, CH: Schwabe, 2001), 44–61; Reventlow, *Epochen der Bibelauslegung IV*, 227–40; Thomas Albert Howard, *Religion and the Rise of Historicism: W. M. L. de Wette, Jacob Burckhardt, and the Theological Origins of Nineteenth-Century Historical Consciousness* (Cambridge, UK: Cambridge University Press, 2000), 23–80, 86–100, 104–12, and 117–25; John W. Rogerson, *W. M. L. de Wette, Founder of Modern Biblical Criticism: An Intellectual Biography* (Sheffield, UK: Journal for the Study of the Old Testament Press, 1992); and Rogerson, *Old Testament Criticism*, 28–49.

sources, approaching what would later be identified as a Supplementary Hypothesis, with Deuteronomy as the last of the sources. De Wette also had an aversion to ritual that went hand-in-hand with an anti-Jewish[28] and anti-Catholic bias against such distinctively Jewish and Catholic notions about sacrifice. This anti-cult position would continue through scholarship in the nineteenth century and is even prevalent today.

De Wette was influenced by Kant's rationalism as well as Scheller's romanticism. The primary philosophical influence on de Wette was the lesser-known Jakob Friedrich Fries, who mediated to de Wette a sort of rationalist romanticism. Such rationalism could be seen, for example, in his mythologizing, or de-historicizing, of the biblical stories. The romanticism can be evidenced in de Wette's appreciation for such biblical mythology, wherein he thought he was able to redeem the biblical stories precisely as myths. Like Eichhorn, he used the category of myth, but he did not relegate it to Genesis or the Pentateuch but used it to describe all the historical books of the Old Testament. Such narratives told us more about what the authors and editors thought about reality, about their views, rather than what actually happened in history.

De Wette set in motion the idea that the real history of Israel was something other than what is found in the Old Testament. This will prove important for later figures like Wellhausen, who will attempt to understand the true history of Israel apart from the Pentateuch, which he will date in its final form to after the time of the Prophets. De Wette was already moving in this direction with his late dating of Deuteronomy.

De Wette recognized that the one major obstacle for his late dating of Pentateuchal material like Deuteronomy was the evidence from the Samaritan Pentateuch. If the Samaritans are descendants of the northern Israelites who split from the South, and yet Deuteronomy dates from long after the splintering of Israel into North and South, say, from the time of Josiah, then why would the Samaritan Pentateuch include Deuteronomy? Of course, as we saw earlier with J. Iverach Munro's criticisms, this would prove even more problematic for later forms of the Documentary Hypothesis that date much of the Pentateuch (P-material as well as Deuteronomy) to the Babylonian Exile and after the Exile.[29]

What de Wette did was rather ingenious. He created a story wherein

---

[28] We are making a distinction here between "anti-Jewish" and "anti-Semitic." We are labelling as "anti-Jewish," scholarly tendencies that assume Judaism (including its rituals) are a corruption or degeneration. This is distinct from racial "anti-Semitism," which is opposed to the Jewish people and in favor of anti-Semitic laws. Many of the scholars who might have held (implicitly or explicitly) anti-Jewish biases in fact opposed anti-Semitic legislations.

[29] J. Iverach Munro, *The Samaritan Pentateuch and Modern Criticism* (London: James Nisbet & Co., 1911).

North and South were continually in touch with one another and sufficiently congenial that the Northerners continued to borrow material in an uninterrupted fashion, and thus adopted Deuteronomy as the South did. In so doing, he removed the Samaritan Pentateuch's near identical contents to the Jewish Torah with one hypothetical story, and it remained unproblematic until Munro and others decided to look more carefully into the text and history of the Samaritan Pentateuch. By that time, however, more than a century later, the Documentary Hypothesis was firmly established in the minds of biblical scholars and would not receive major widespread challenges until after World War II as the archaeological record began to provide evidence for the antiquity of places, practices, and various data in the biblical texts that Wellhausen, et al. considered to be later fictions.

What makes de Wette even more important in the broader history of biblical scholarship, and in fact of Enlightenment scholarship coming out of Germany in general, was his prominent role at the very foundation of the University of Berlin when he was counted among its first professors in 1810. This would solidify his scholarship, which was becoming increasingly anti-Jewish.[30] Judaism, for de Wette, was "a degenerate, petrified Hebraism."[31] This is highly significant because, as James Pasto points out, "de Wette was the *first* to use the term 'Judaism' . . . as the specific designation for a post-exilic society *in contrast to* a pre-exilic Israel/Hebraism. De Wette, in fact, was the first to designate the Babylonian exile as the dividing line between pre- and post-exilic religions/societies."[32]

---

[30] On the anti-Judaism in de Wette's work see especially Anders Gerdmar, *Roots of Theological Anti-Semitism: German Biblical Interpretation and the Jews, from Herder and Semler to Kittel and Bultmann* (Leiden, NL: Brill, 2008), 77–94; James Pasto, "W. M. L. de Wette and the Invention of Post-Exilic Judaism: Political Historiography and Christian Allegory in Nineteenth-Century German Biblical Scholarship," in *Jews, Antiquity, and the Nineteenth-Century Imagination*, ed. Hayim Lapin and Dale Marin (Bethesda, MD: University Press of Maryland, 2003), 33–52; Ekkehard Stegemann, "«Die Halbierung der ‹hebräischen› Religion». De Wettes Konstruktion von «Hebraismus» und «Judentum» zum Zwecke christlicher Aneignung des Alten Testaments," in *Wilhelm Martin Leberecht de Wette*, 79–95; James Pasto, "'Strange Secret Sharers': Orientalism, Judaism, and the Jewish Question," *Comparative Studies in Society and History* 40, no. 3 (1998): 442–45; and James Pasto, "When the End is the Beginning? Or When the Biblical Past is the Political Present: Some Thoughts on Ancient Israel, 'Post-Exilic Judaism,' and the Politics of Biblical Scholarship," *Scandinavian Journal of the Old Testament* 12, no. 2 (1998): 161–80.

[31] Pasto's translation in "Strange Secret Sharers," 443.

[32] Pasto, "When the End," 161. He continues, "Previous scholars had, of course, used the term 'Judaism' in their work, and some had seen the Babylonian exile as a time of differentiation (and decline). However, none that I have been able to discover used the term 'Judaism' to mean both 'post-exilic' and 'different' (i.e., different from the pre-exilic religion)."

We do well here to keep in mind Stanley Hauerwas's insightful observation that

> Catholics understood they often became for Protestants the Jews, that is, Catholics had been surpassed. Nowhere was this more apparent than in the scholarly guilds surrounding the study of scripture in which Second Temple Judaism became the dead priest-ridden religion that the charismatic Christianity of the New Testament replaced. Protestant biblical scholarship simply reproduced that story with their triumph in the Reformation.[33]

In Germany—and this becomes even more important when we consider Wellhausen below—anti-Judaism (or, later, anti-Semitism) and anti-Catholicism often went hand-in-hand, and a critique of Judaism in biblical scholarship was often an attack on present-day (or historical) Catholicism. There were political factors at work here beyond simply theological views.

In the context of de Wette, Pasto makes some of the most important points linking de Wette's scholarly views directly with his political context. One of Pasto's main conclusions is that "de Wette was writing his Biblical past as a metaphor for his German Protestant present, and . . . he thus transformed a unified Israelite-Judean past into *dualistic Hebraic and Judaic pasts* in order to inscribe and authorize his German Protestant present."[34] The key linking the denigration of Judaism, in light of the ever-present "Jewish Question" in Germany, with Catholicism was the long drive for a unified Germany, which would happen in Wellhausen's lifetime. These were important political concerns for de Wette. De Wette was staunchly in favor of a smaller unified German state, with a Prussian head, rather than the larger German conglomeration of states that would include Catholic Austria. He feared Catholic influence would undermine the German state.

Pasto thus explains how de Wette's rereading of Israel's past maps onto his then-present political concerns:

> the German states of 1813 were in fact a kind of post-exilic (post-conquest) society caught between tendencies of particularism versus universalism, dogmatism versus freedom, i.e., the particularism of local German states versus the "universalism" of a united Germany . . . De Wette's preference for a universalistic and

---

[33] Stanley Hauerwas, *The State of the University: Academic Knowledges and the Knowledge of God* (Oxford, UK: Blackwell, 2007), 73n46.
[34] Pasto, "When the End," 165.

free "Hebraism" over a particularistic and dogmatic "Judaism" was a metaphor for his "negative" Germany and his Biblical past was a field of representation on which he sought to inscribe his German political present.[35]

What did this mean concretely in the realm of politics for de Wette? Pasto clarifies, "explicitly or not, de Wette was linking his critical 'knowledge' to institutional 'power' in the form of a history that validated the need to incorporate Jews in Germany *via* their corporate dissolution."[36]

We need to make one further point concerning politics before continuing with the history of how the Documentary Hypothesis developed. The political situation with regard to scholars was rather complex. On the one hand, the sort of dissolution of the traditional understanding of biblical history and of the composition of biblical texts supported the politics modern European states were advancing. After all, what modern state, or state ruler, could fail to be envious of the sovereign in Hobbes's *Leviathan*? Traditional views on biblical inspiration, biblical authorship, biblical history, etc., supported the traditions of interpretation that made resistance to the state, like martyrdom, possible. Such theological positions on Scripture were witnesses to the fact that those who held them held to an authority outside of the competence of any modern state. This was in no case more evident than with the Catholic Church, which represented a transnational authority.

Hahn and Morrow compare the developing modern nation states with the Catholic Church in its unifying role in medieval Christendom:

> the emerging modern states became the unifying principle of their society. Each state became its own "catholic" church, as it were.

---

[35] Pasto, "When the End," 171. Pasto continues: "foreign contact in the form of French occupation had . . . brought about a change in German culture and identity so that the people who emerged . . . were in many ways a different one with a different world view. Political unification in the form of a nation state required further changes. These included the development of a common German identity . . . De Wette offered an 'Hebraizing' alternative . . . a Hebrew past in which spontaneity, freedom, and morality had served as the basis of social life; and a Hebrew past that had been completed by Jesus and restored by Luther. This 'Hebraic' past thus gave Germans a past that was Biblical, Christian, Protestant and German in one single genealogy. However, and this was crucial, it did so in a way that completely severed Jews and Judaism from contemporary German identity" (172).

[36] Pasto, "When the End," 176. In explaining how this played out in de Wette's thought, with regard to the "Jewish Question," Pasto clarifies on the same page: "what others were claiming as a political premise de Wette was claiming as an 'historical' truth, i.e., that Judaism really was separate from and a degeneration of an earlier Mosaic religion. As 'proof' of this de Wette could offer his seemingly critical examination of the 'Old Testament,' which he claimed indicated the later decline of early Hebraism into a particularistic Judaism."

Politicians, and academics at the university, too, became the new clergy. Politicians, kings, presidents, prime ministers, and the like became the new kings, bishops, and popes when it came to matters of the common good and temporal policies. Academic professional Bible scholars became the new Magisterium when it came to matters of biblical interpretation. . . . Even the sacraments . . . were . . . replaced by civil symbols and actions: *Citizenship* became the new Baptism. *Nationalism* fed citizens the way the Eucharist fed the faithful. Modern *war* became the new Eucharistic sacrifice of the state in which all the faithful "baptized" citizens participated (at least in principle). *Voting* or other duties that complete citizenship emerged as a new form of Confirmation. The *civil courtroom* replaced the tribunal of the confessional. Modern *prisons* and other forms of legal sentences became the new penance. . . . The progress of *science* and *medicine* prolonged life instead of Anointing of the Sick preparing for death. *Professional positions* of political office, lawyer, physician, law enforcement, military, business, or academic became the new Holy Orders. Finally, *marriage* became merely a civil thing.[37]

Thus, even though scholars and intellectuals such as Eichhorn, de Wette, and Wellhausen had their own unique and distinct political positions, the sort of biblical scholarship they practiced served the broader needs of modern European nation states—even when it did not serve the exact needs of their particular state in a given moment. At times, as with de Wette (and later Heinrich Ewald and Wellhausen), who was eventually removed from teaching at the University of Berlin, scholars fall out of favor politically with the rulers of the day. Sometimes this was because their particular politics clashed with their leaders. At other times, however, they pushed the boundaries of the orthodoxy of the day too far.

Through the eighteenth and nineteenth centuries, although theologically corrosive Enlightenment biblical criticism would be a useful political tool for modern states, if it pushed too far positions considered too radical or too heterodox by the ordinary citizens, it overreached its political utility and became a political liability as opposed to a political asset. As Hahn and Morrow clarify:

---

[37] Hahn and Morrow, *Modern Biblical Criticism*, 32–33. This account is inspired by Andrew Willard Jones, *Before Church and State: A Study of Social Order in the Sacramental Kingdom of St. Louis IX* (Steubenville, OH: Emmaus Academic, 2017).

In ages past, as in the seventeenth century, intellectuals were often at the mercy of patrons who funded their work. In the eighteenth and nineteenth centuries, the necessary money and related resources that had been provided from individual patrons was transferred to the universities that served particular political and cultural needs. The ambiguities involved the shifting of political power from those who desired more skeptical and rationalist criticism to those who wanted more traditional theological work, especially among the Lutheran pietists. This theo-political ebb and flow made the lives and careers of modern critical scholars in the eighteenth and nineteenth centuries somewhat precarious. In general, their critical work tacitly supported the emerging nation-states at whose universities they served. At the same time, their rationalism sometimes clashed with the new power structures that desired theological uniformity.[38]

Filling in the Missing Pieces: The Work of Karl David Ilgen, Alexander Geddes, Johannes Severin Vater, and Hermann Hupfeld[39]

Continuing with our genealogy of the Documentary Hypothesis, Karl David Ilgen, who was older than de Wette, was an important figure in this history.[40] Ilgen was an intellectual disciple of Eichhorn when it came to the discussion of the composition and origin of the Pentateuch. When Eichhorn left the University of Jena for the University of Göttingen, Ilgen replaced him at Jena. Eichhorn had taken some of Astruc's divisions, mainly based on the different names the Pentateuch employed for God, and developed Astruc's thesis further. So with Eichhorn we have the use of a single source that Ilgen will identify as Elohistic, E. Eichhorn isolated what later becomes divided into E and P (the Priestly Source) as a single source. Ilgen is important within this history because he was the first to examine Eichhorn's source and argue that there were in fact two distinct documentary sources

---

[38] Hahn and Morrow, *Modern Biblical Criticism*, 151.

[39] A very brief but helpful and nuanced summary of the stages in development of the documentary and fragmentary hypotheses including these figures below, stretching from Astruc through Wellhausen is in Ernest Nicholson, *The Pentateuch in the Twentieth Century: The Legacy of Julius Wellhausen* (Oxford, UK: Oxford University Press, 1998), 3–11.

[40] On Ilgen see, e.g., Van Seters, *Edited Bible*, 196–99; and Bodo Seidel, *Karl David Ilgen und die Pentateuchforschung im Umkreis der sogenannten Älteren Urkundenhypothese: Studien zur Geschichte der exegetischen Hermeneutik in der Späten Aufklärung* (Berlin: Walter de Gruyter, 1993).

lying behind what Eichhorn identified as one source; that is, there were two E sources. Ilgen, moreover, introduced the nomenclature that would be preserved in the Documentary Hypothesis as the Elohist and the Jehovist (or Yahwist), for E and J sources.[41] Ilgen, however, failed to get any real scholarly recognition for his division of Eichhorn's source into two different E sources. Whereas the nomenclature he employed for E and J would be echoed, no one was convinced that E represented multiple sources.

The Scottish Catholic priest and contemporary of de Wette and Ilgen, Fr. Alexander Geddes, developed his own hypothesis concerning the composition of the Pentateuch that, although related to these earlier views, was distinct.[42] As with their characterizations of de Wette, scholars often identify Geddes' approach as a Fragmentary Hypothesis, even though Geddes never used the language of "fragments." Geddes was far more comfortable, like Astruc, in assigning some sources for Genesis to a period prior to Moses. Geddes is not as important as these other figures for the specifics of his compositional theory; he never really came up with a concrete theory of Pentateuchal composition beyond the fact that the Pentateuch was composed of numerous written sources predating its final form. What makes Geddes important is the influential role he played on the development of a full-blown Fragmentary Hypothesis.

The first scholar who articulated a fully formed Fragmentary Hypothesis that was in contrast to the documentary approach assuming major sources like J, E, and D, was Johann Severin Vater.[43] As Michaelis and Semler had earlier brought in the work of English scholars to Germany, so too Vater translated Geddes into German because he thought it represented

---

[41] Jean-Louis Ska, "The Study of the Book of Genesis: The Beginning of Critical Reading," in *The Book of Genesis: Composition, Reception, and Interpretation*, ed. Craig A. Evans, Joel N. Lohr, and David L. Petersen (Leiden, NL: Brill, 2012), 21.

[42] On Geddes see Mark Goldie, "Alexander Geddes at the Limits of the Catholic Enlightenment," *Historical Journal* 53, no. 1 (2010): 61–86; Charles Conroy, "The Biblical Work of Alexander Geddes against the Background of Contemporary Catholic Biblical Scholarship in Continental Europe," in *The Bible and the Enlightenment: A Case Study—Dr. Alexander Geddes (1737–1802): The Proceedings of the Bicentenary Geddes Conference held at the University of Aberdeen, 1–4 April 2002*, ed. William Johnstone (London: T&T Clark, 2004), 135–56; Reginald C. Fuller, *Alexander Geddes: 1737–1802: A Pioneer of Biblical Criticism* (Sheffield: Almond Press, 1984); and Rogerson, *Old Testament Criticism*, 154–57.

[43] On Vater see Thomas Römer, "'Higher Criticism': The Historical and Literary-Critical Approach—with Special Reference to the Pentateuch," in *Hebrew Bible/Old Testament: The History of Its Interpretation*, vol. 3, *From Modernism to Post-Modernism (The Nineteenth and Twentieth Centuries)*, part 1, *The Nineteenth Century—A Century of Modernism and Historicism*, ed. Magne Sæbø (Göttingen: Vandenhoeck & Ruprecht, 2013), 397–98; Van Seters, *Edited Bible*, 203–5; and Fuller, *Alexander Geddes*, 105–8.

such an important approach to Pentateuchal composition, over and against the approach of Eichhorn and Ilgen. Vater took it upon himself to expand and concretize, in his own way, what Geddes had made more suggestive and tentative. Vater thereby created a Fragmentary Hypothesis wherein he envisioned the Pentateuch as being put together over time from various documentary fragments, as opposed to larger sources and narratives. He claimed this even for the Joseph narratives which, even for de Wette (and by most scholars today), were understood to be a primarily unified narrative.

The next most significant figure in this genealogical history is Hermann Hupfeld, another contemporary of these last four individuals.[44] Hupfeld, although never having studied with de Wette, declared himself his intellectual disciple, and was certainly highly influenced by de Wette's biblical scholarship. Scholars typically identify Hupfeld as "discovering" the so-called Priestly Source, even though Hupfeld never gave it that name, nor did he attribute it to a priestly community or author. Hupfeld's contribution was unique not so much for his conclusion that Eichhorn's source later identified as E was composed of two sources—Ilgen had already argued that—but rather because his arguments for this position won the day where Ilgen's had not. Thus, after Hupfeld, a Documentary Hypothesis composed of four distinct sources, E1, E2, J, and D, was firmly set in place among a wide following of biblical scholars in the German-speaking world.

We are at an important transitional phase here. What all of these figures have in common is a commitment to the sort of specialized *Wissenschaft* (scholarship) that supported (and was supported by) German Enlightenment universities with an ever-increasing number of areas of concentration.

Up to this point in time, English biblical scholarship had exerted a tremendous influence on German biblical scholarship. That would change as English biblical scholars made less "new" developments with even less influential reach as the nineteenth century continued on, and as, at the very same time, German biblical scholars began to expand their biblical scholarly projects and developments. As English biblical scholarship remained wedded to theological commitments, German biblical scholarship—ever since Semler and Michaelis—became increasingly severed from them. Moreover, whereas the sheer number of academic chairs in biblical scholarship remained fairly static in nineteenth-century England, they greatly increased in number in German universities.[45] When Wellhausen publishes his scholarly works, the

---

[44] On Hupfeld see Otto Kaiser, "An Heir of Astruc in a Remote German University: Hermann Hupfeld and the 'New Documentary Hypothesis,'" in *Sacred Conjectures*, 220–48; Van Seters, *Edited Bible*, 221–23; Otto Kaiser, *Zwischen Reaktion und Revolution: Hermann Hupfeld (1796–1866)—ein deutsches Professorenleben* (Göttingen: Vandenhoeck & Ruprecht, 2005); and Rogerson, *Old Testament Criticism*, 130–34.

[45] Hahn and Morrow, *Modern Biblical Criticism*, 27–34; and the table of university chairs

tide of influence will shift so that German biblical scholarship begins to influence the biblical scholarship throughout the English-speaking world.[46]

SUPPLEMENTS AND LATE DATING OF P:
HEINRICH EWALD AND ÉDOUARD GUILLAUME EUGÈNE REUSS

Building on the work that came before, one of Eichhorn's own students from Göttingen, Heinrich Ewald, came up with a Supplementary Hypothesis for Pentateuchal composition. Ewald would later join the faculty of Göttingen, where he would become Wellhausen's teacher.[47] Ewald agreed with the Fragmentarians that some of the sources Documentarians like Eichhorn and Ilgen identified could not have been full-scale documents but must have been much smaller in size. Yet, against the Fragmentarians, Ewald thought his mentor Eichhorn was correct about at least one major documentary source. Ewald thus argued that the Pentateuch was composed of a single primary document, which he identified as E, the Elohist, and was supplemented by various editorial additions or layers. As opposed to multiple source documents, or smaller disparate fragments, Ewald claimed that the editorial layers were too interrelated for such diverse sources. He thus posited that a single editor was responsible for repeated revisions of the primary

---

in the Bible in England and Germany and attendant commentary in Rogerson, *Old Testament Criticism*, 138–44.

[46] Part of this German influence in the English-speaking world will be because of William Robertson Smith and the *Encyclopaedia Britannica* and part will be due to the influence of the discipline of history as practiced and taught in Germany spreading as English-speaking scholars flock to Germany to learn these studies and bring them home. See respectively Hahn and Morrow, *Modern Biblical Criticism*, 217–25; and Peter Novick, *That Noble Dream: The "Objectivity Question" and the American Historical Profession* (Cambridge, UK: Cambridge University Press, 1988). This was the same for the discipline of ancient Near Eastern Studies in the United States where the majority of the first major professors in the field at the premier universities, were taken from Germany. See, e.g., Jeffrey L. Morrow, *Alfred Loisy and Modern Biblical Studies* (Washington, DC: The Catholic University of America Press, 2019), 33–34; and C. Wade Meade, *Road to Babylon: Development of U.S. Assyriology* (Leiden, NL: Brill, 1974), 32–37.

[47] On Ewald see Suzanne L. Marchand, *German Orientalism in the Age of Empire: Religion, Race, and Scholarship* (Cambridge, UK: Cambridge University Press, 2009), 106–8; Van Seters, *Edited Bible*, 215–20; Reventlow, *Epochen der Bibelauslegung IV*, 290–95; Michael Haasler, *Heinrich Ewald und seine Auseinandersetzung mit Ernst Meier und Ferdinand Christian Baur* (Munich: GRIN, 1996), 21–103; O'Neill, *Bible's Authority*, 135–49; Rogerson, *Old Testament Criticism*, 91–103; and Rudolf Smend, "Heinrich Ewalds Biblische Theologie. Hinweis auf ein vergessenes Buch," in *Theologie und Wirklichkeit. Festschrift für Wolfgang Trillhaas zum 70. Geburtstag*, ed. Hans Walter Schütte and Friedrich Wintzer (Göttingen: Vandenhoeck & Ruprecht, 1974), 176–91.

document, adding successive layers. Ewald did not completely abandon the notion of other sources—he kept J, the Yawhist—but he believed the editor utilized J material in making revisions.

Another former student of Eichhorn, Édouard Guillaume Eugène Reuss at the University of Strasbourg, would make an important contribution to the development of the Documentary Hypothesis but would do so indirectly through one of his students.[48] Building on the scholarship that came before him, what Hupfeld had called E1 Reuss argued was actually the last of the documentary sources to have been incorporated into the Pentateuch. This was significant because up to that time scholars like Eichhorn, Hupfeld, and others assumed that it was the earliest source (along with Hupfeld's E2, which Eichhorn understood to be one unified source). Reuss did not publish this finding; rather, he reserved it for a lecture. He had already shared his argument, prior to his public lecture, with Karl Heinrich Graf, who at the time (1833) had been Reuss's student. Thus, as opposed to E1, E2, J, and D, Reuss's formulation was something like E2, J, D, and E1. We are now rapidly approaching Wellhausen's classic formulation.

PENULTIMATE STAGES: ABRAHAM KUENEN AND KARL HEINRICH GRAF

Abraham Kuenen at the University of Leiden in the Netherlands was the scholar who made the connection between the priestly material in Hupfeld's E1 from Exodus through Numbers with material he identified as similar in Genesis. Similar to, but clearly independently from, Reuss, Kuenen dated this material later than E2 and J.[49] This is significant because Kuenen's arguments contributed to convincing Graf both of the unity of E1, the priestly

---

[48] On Reuss see Jean Marcel Vincent, "Le «rationalisme mystique» d'Edouard Reuss et ses incidences sur «La Bible»," *Revue d'histoire et de philosophie religieuses* 74, no. 1 (1994): 43–66; Jean-Georges Heintz, "Édouard Reuss, Karl Heinrich Graf et le Pentateuque," *Revue d'histoire et de philosophie religieuses* 71, no. 4 (1991): 443–57; E. Jacob, "Edouard Reuss, un théologien independent," *Revue d'histoire et de philosophie religieuses* 71, no. 4 (1991): 427–33; and Jean Marcel Vincent, *Leben und Werk des frühen Eduard Reuss: ein Beitrag zu den geistesgeschichtlichen Voraussetzungen der Bibelkritik im zweiten Viertel des 19. Jahrhunderts* (Munich: Kaiser, 1990).

[49] On Kuenen see Rudolf Smend, "The Work of Abraham Kuenen and Julius Wellhausen," in *Hebrew Bible/Old Testament*, 3.1:424–36; Smend, *From Astruc*, 76–90; M. J. Mulder, "Abraham Kuenen (1828–1891)," in *Abraham Kuenen (1828–1891): His Major Contributions to the Study of the Old Testament: A Collection of Old Testament Studies Published on the Occasion of the Centenary of Abraham Kuenen's Death (10 December 1991)*, ed. P. B. Dirksen and A. Van Der Kooij (Leiden, NL: Brill, 1993), 1–7; A. Rofé, "Abraham Kuenen's Contribution to the Study of the Pentateuch: A View from Israel," in *Abraham Kuenen,*

material, as well as its relatively late dating—that it was the latest of Pentateuchal sources.

Karl Heinrich Graf, who would greatly influence Wellhausen, had learned from his mentor Reuss that the Priestly Source was the latest of the Pentateuchal sources.[50] Kuenen reinforced this with his arguments and helped convince Graf that, in fact, Reuss had been correct. Moreover, Kuenen persuaded Graf of the link between the priestly material in Genesis and that of the rest of the Pentateuch. Graf would then publish this prior to Kuenen, who would publish the same argument a few years later, and thus made the argument more widely known. This would be how Wellhausen first learned that the priestly material was late, after the Babylonian Exile. The famous Protestant theologian Albrecht Ritschl related to Wellhausen that Graf dated P, and thus the final form of the Pentateuch, after the Prophets. Wellhausen accepted the late dating and Graf's arguments. He proceeded to develop and hone the theory Kuenen and Graf had erected based on the prior work of scholars like Reuss, Hupfeld, de Wette, et al.

JULIUS WELLHAUSEN AND CLASSIC FORMULATION OF THE DOCUMENTARY HYPOTHESIS

No name is more associated with the Documentary Hypothesis, or with Pentateuchal source criticism in general, than that of Julius Wellhausen.[51]

105–12; and Simon J. De Vries, "The Hexateuchal Criticism of Abraham Kuenen," *Journal of Biblical Literature* 82, no. 1 (1963): 31–57.

[50] On Graf see Römer, "Higher Criticism," 420–23; and Joachim Conrad, *Karl Heinrich Grafs Arbeit am Alten Testament: Studien zu einer wissenschaftlichen Biographie* (Berlin: Walter de Gruyter, 2011).

[51] Quite a lot of scholarship exists on Wellhausen. For a small sample of key studies on Wellhausen in the context of our present discussion, see, e.g., Hahn and Morrow, *Modern Biblical Criticism*, 196–212; Paul Michael Kurtz, "Waiting at Nemi: Wellhausen, Gunkel, and the World Behind Their Work," *Harvard Theological Review* 109, no. 4 (2016): 567–85; Paul Michael Kurtz, "The Way of War: Wellhausen, Israel, and Bellicose Reiche," *Zeitschrift für die alttestamentliche Wissenschaft* 127, no. 1 (2015): 1–19; Reinhard G. Kratz, "Eyes and Spectacles: Wellhausen's Method of Higher Criticism," *Journal of Theological Studies* 60, no. 2 (2009): 381–402; Smend, *From Astruc*, 91–102; Rudolf Smend, *Julius Wellhausen. Ein Bahnbrecher in drei Disziplinen* (Munich: Carl Friedrich von Siemens Stiftung, 2006); Reventlow, *Epochen der Bibelauslegung IV*, 302–16; John Barton, "Wellhausen's Prolegomena to the History of Israel: Influences and Effects," in *Text and Experience: Towards a Cultural Exegesis of the Bible*, ed. Daniel Smith-Christopher (Sheffield, UK: Sheffield Academic Press, 1995), 316–29; O'Neill, *Bible's Authority*, 198–213; Rudolf Smend, "Julius Wellhausen and His Prolegomena to the History of Israel," *Semeia* 25 (1982): 1–20; and John H. Hayes, "Wellhausen as a Historian of Israel," *Semeia* 25 (1982): 37–67.

Wellhausen was a student of Ewald at the University of Göttingen, where he himself would later teach. Ewald's work inspired Wellhausen to further study Hebrew and begin studying other Semitic languages. Wellhausen's unwavering pro-Prussian political sympathies later created a rift between the two; Ewald was politically opposed to Bismarck's attempt at German unification, whereas Wellhausen would remain a diehard Bismarck supporter his entire life. While teaching Old Testament at the University of Greifswald, Wellhausen became intimate friends with the famous classical scholar Ulrich von Wilamowitz-Moellendorff, who had dominated Homeric studies (and Classical Studies in general). Wilamowitz came to be recognized for the very same documentary-type source criticism of the Homeric corpus that Wellhausen would be known for with regard to the Pentateuch. Although he knew Akkadian and even considered pursuing a full-time career in Assyriology, Wellhausen completely ignored Assyriological findings in archaeology and language in his own Old Testament studies, preferring the purely internal literary methods of source criticism—studying the Bible in a vacuum, as it were.[52]

While still at Greifswald, Wellhausen began publishing journal articles that dealt with the Documentary Hypothesis.[53] Although not as influential as his later *Prolegomena zur Geschichte Israels*, it was in these articles that he first articulated his classic formulation of the Documentary Hypothesis. He maintained that J was the earliest of the four major sources. After J came E, the Elohist (Hupfeld's E2). For Wellhausen, the Yahwist was the redactor responsible for combining J and E into a more unified JE source, which made them more difficult to untangle into original discrete sources. Even prior to this editorial composition, however, Wellhausen understood both J and E to have undergone their own development and growth, and thus prior to JE, there were J1, J2, and J3, as well as E1, E2, and E3 developmental stages. The Deuteronomist, D, wrote Deuteronomy, and some time after the Yahwistic editorial work producing a combined JE, D was added to JE, producing JED. Finally, there was what scholars refer to as P, the Priestly Source, which Wellhausen referred to as Q, *Quatuor foederum liber* (Book of Four Covenants). Wellhausen followed Reuss, Kuenen, and Graf in dating Q (P) as the last of the sources. In Wellhausen's scheme, Q was further developed prior to being added to JED; he specifically saw Leviticus

---

[52] Peter Machinist, "The Road Not Taken: Wellhausen and Assyriology," in *Homeland and Exile: Biblical and Ancient Near Eastern Studies in Honour of Bustenay Oded*, ed. Gershon Galil, Mark Geller, and Alan Millard (Leiden, NL: Brill, 2009), 469–531.

[53] J. Wellhausen, "Die Composition des Hexateuchs," *Jahrbücher für Deutsche Theologie* 21 (1876): 392–450; J. Wellhausen, "Die Composition des Hexateuchs II," *Jahrbücher für Deutsche Theologie* 21 (1876): 531–602; and J. Wellhausen, "Die Composition des Hexateuchs III," *Jahrbücher für Deutsche Theologie* 22 (1877): 407–79.

17–26 as a later addition to Q, an addition that would come to be identified (already in Wellhausen's lifetime but by another scholar) as H, the Holiness Code. Wellhausen's views were clearly more complicated than the average textbook oversimplifications of his position.

This final form, J, E, D, and P, articulated by Wellhausen, became how the Documentary Hypothesis was taught around the globe. It survives to the present day in classroom lectures and textbook summaries. Other contemporaries of Wellhausen, and later scholars as well, continued to advance other formulations. Today, virtually no source critical scholar follows Wellhausen's exact formulation. And yet, it is Wellhausen's exact formulation—minus the complex developmental history he posited—that every student of the Bible has to memorize.

How the Development of the Documentary Hypothesis Ties In with Its Historical and Political Context

Wellhausen's expression of the Documentary Hypothesis is not without its political influences giving it shape and weight. For Wellhausen, the Documentary Hypothesis expresses a clear view of the development not only of the literal *text* of the Pentateuch but, more importantly, of the very *history* of ancient Israel. The warring theo-political communities Wellhausen imagined lying behind the documentary sources of the Pentateuchal text—e.g., J and the southern Kingdom of Judah versus E and the northern Kingdom of Israel—matched his own experience of political tension in Germany and his political desires for German unification and expansive colonization under Bismarck. It is impossible to understand Wellhausen and his theory adequately apart from the context of Bismarck's *Kulturkampf*.[54]

From 1871–1876, Bismarck waged his infamous *Kulturkampf*, or "cultural struggle," which targeted the Catholic Church in particular, in his successful attempt at German unification. These were the birth pangs of German entrance into the world of unified modern nation states at a time when other nation states like England and France, with which Germany was striving to be a worthy competitor, were near the height of their colonial powers. In many ways, the anti-Catholicism of the *Kulturkampf* was the final culmination of nearly a century of anti-Catholic sentiment and measures in Germany. Michael Gross claims in fact that the *Kulturkampf*'s

---

[54] On the importance of the *Kulturkampf* for our discussion see, e.g., Hahn and Morrow, *Modern Biblical Criticism*, 189–96; and Michael B. Gross, *The War Against Catholicism: Liberalism and the Anti-Catholic Imagination in Nineteenth-Century Germany* (Ann Arbor, MI: University of Michigan Press, 2004).

point was nothing other than "to break the influence of the Roman Catholic Church and the religious, social, and political power of Catholicism."[55] Thus we find the expulsion of religious orders and a host of anti-Catholic legislation erected and enforced.

Catholicism became viewed as the enemy, in part, because the Catholic Church represented the paradigmatic transnational authority, and members of religious orders not only circumvented the state-appointed bishops' authorities but were also often composed of foreigners. Thus, the majority Protestant Prussia viewed the nationalism of Catholics skeptically. As in England after the Protestant Reformation, so too in late-nineteenth-century Germany the loyalty of Catholics was suspect, and Catholics were viewed as potential enemies of the state. This provided the immediate socio-political context for other areas in biblical scholarship beyond Wellhausen's Documentary Hypothesis.[56]

Wellhausen and his work fit neatly into this political context.[57] It is no mere accident that Wellhausen's developmental theory seems to match a Hegelian evolutionary philosophy—and not merely because of Hegel's influence. Wellhausen's theory set Judaism, and Catholicism (its symbolic representation), in the worst light as a corruption of a purer, pristine religion of the heart. He preferred the religion of the Prophets, but his view of the Prophets was inextricably bound to post-Enlightenment Protestant understandings both of Paul and of the Prophets; that is, Paul and Prophets shorn of any resemblance to cultic and priestly vestiges of Judaism and Catholicism. His history of Israel, not by coincidence, developed along the exact same lines as Jacob Grimm's (of the Brothers Grimm, whom Wellhausen long admired) history of Germany, shaped by Enlightened Lutheran sensibilities more than by historical evidence.[58]

---

[55] Gross, *War Against Catholicism*, 1.

[56] In the context of the New Testament, Markan priority was the best example of the influence of the *Kulturkampf's* influence. See, e.g., Hahn and Morrow, *Modern Biblical Criticism*, 212–17; and William R. Farmer, "State Interesse and Markan Primacy: 1870–1914," in *Biblical Studies and the Shifting of Paradigms, 1850–1914*, ed. Henning Graf Reventlow and William Farmer (Sheffield, UK: Sheffield Academic Press, 1995). David Dungan writes that Markan priority was quickly transformed into "another club with which German Protestant scholars could beat the Roman Catholic Church." See David Laird Dungan, *A History of the Synoptic Problem: The Canon, the Text, the Composition, and the Interpretation of the Gospels* (New Haven: Yale University Press, 1999), 326–27.

[57] For situating Wellhausen in this political context see, e.g., Hahn and Morrow, *Modern Biblical Criticism*, 189–212; Kurtz, "Waiting at Nemi," 567–85; Kurtz, "Way of War," 1–19; Marchand, *German Orientalism*, 178–88; O'Neill, *Bible's Authority*, 198–213; and Arnaldo Momigliano, "Religious History Without Frontiers: J. Wellhausen, U. Wilamowitz, and E. Schwartz," *History and Theory* 21, no. 4 (1982): 49–64.

[58] See Hahn and Morrow, *Modern Biblical Criticism*, 209–11.

Grimm attempted to get around Germany's pre-Reformation Catholic past by going back to its pre-Christian past. As George Williamson amply documents, Grimm and others attempted to help formulate a new mythology for Germany wherein pre-Christian pagan roots would be mined for civic and cultural virtues apart from Jewish and even Christian traditions.[59] Grimm's pre-Christian Germany resembles Wellhausen's patriarchal Hebrew culture, and both appear remarkably the way liberal Lutheran Protestantism looked in Grimm's and Wellhausen's post-Enlightenment Germany. The corruption of Israel's cultic and priestly infrastructure (the Torah) maps onto this history the way legalistic and overly ritualized Catholicism corrupted Europe. Finally, the prophetic return to a family religion and religion of the heart, of morality and faith, is akin to the Protestant Reformation's liberation of Germany from the vile clutches of Rome.

Finally, much as Williamson[60] points out how Grimm's history was shaped by the violent conflicts he witnessed Germany suffer, e.g., with French occupation, so too Paul Michael Kurtz[61] points to the same violent context for Wellhausen, e.g., various revolutions and armed conflicts (more than six). Wellhausen was absolutely "Consumed by an interest in statecraft."[62] This familiarity with conflict, his ever-present political reality of warring political parties, desires for the success of Bismarck's plans for German unification—all of this colored and shaped his understanding of the history of Israel reflected in his particular formulation of the history of the composition of the Pentateuch.[63] Thus, at the culmination of the method that had been developing over the centuries, we find in Wellhausen the embodiment of the politically motivated scholar shaping a narrative that fit his worldview more than it fit any external historical evidence. Wellhausen's historical critical theories remained literary and internal, as had those of his predecessors. Unlike them, however, he had access to material from the ancient Near East with which to compare the Bible, as some of his peers (for example, Hermann Gunkel) were doing, but in which he had no interest at all. Far from

---

[59] For how Grimm fits into this history see Williamson, *Longing for Myth*, 2, 14, 74, 76, 81–84, 88–91, 98–102, 104–12, 114–15, 119–20, 187–89, 297.

[60] Williamson, *Longing for Myth*, 110.

[61] Kurtz, "Way of War," 1–19. Kurtz points out that, "Wellhausen lived through tumultuous times . . . he saw the revolutions of 1848, the First (1848–1851) and Second (1864) Schleswig Wars, the Austro-Prussian War (1866), the North German Confederation (1867–1871), the Franco-Prussian War (1870–1871), and German unification all before starting his first academic post, at Greifswald in 1871. He died . . . ten months prior to the Great War's end and the dawn of the Weimer Republic" (2).

[62] Kurtz, "Way of War," 10.

[63] In addition to the work of Kurtz see especially also Momigliano, "Religious History," 49–64.

an unbiased attempt at a pure historical enterprise, Wellhausen's work, like many of those who came before him, fit what he hoped to find, as he basically confessed at the outset of his famous *Prolegomena*:

> In the beginning of my studies, I was attracted by the tales about Saul and David, about Elijah and Ahab, and I was taken by the speeches of Amos and Isaiah; I read into the prophetic and historical books of the Old Testament. . . . but had a bad conscience, as if I were starting at the roof instead of at the foundation; for I did not know the law of which I am told is the basis and presupposition of the rest of the literature. At last I took courage and worked my way through Exodus, Leviticus and Numbers. . . . But in vain I waited for the light which was to be poured out from this source upon the historical and prophetic books. Rather, the law spoiled the enjoyment of these writings for me; it did not bring them closer to me, but penetrated only in a disturbing manner, like a ghost, which is heard, but not visible, and not effective. . . . In the summer of 1867, I learned that Karl Heinrich Graf placed the law after the prophets and almost without knowing the reason for his hypothesis, I was won over: I allowed myself to confess that Hebraic antiquity could be understood without the book of the Torah.[64]

What far too often remains unrecognized by scholars is the degree to which Wellhausen's work is grounded in his anti-Catholicism. In fact, often what passes for anti-Judaism in Wellhausen's corpus is in fact anti-Catholicism masquerading as anti-Judaism. Even towering critics of Wellhausen, like Moshe Weinfeld, miss this salient point. Weinfeld, for example, explains how "Wellhausen continues extolling the church and denigrating Judaism."[65] Compare this with the comments of Frank Moore Cross, who sees Wellhausen's work on the Documentary Hypothesis as an example of "often unconsciously held traditions of Christian apologetics in biblical scholarship."[66] When we turn to Wellhausen's *Prolegomena*, however, we find him articulating a staunchly anti-Church position. His positive language regarding Jesus, much like Spinoza's before him, when combined with his negative evaluation of contemporary and ancient Judaism, might mislead scholars

---

[64] Wellhausen, *Prolegomena zur Geschichte Israels*, 3–4 (translation taken from Hahn and Morrow, *Modern Biblical Criticism*, 202–3).

[65] Moshe Weinfeld, *The Place of the Law in the Religion of Ancient Israel* (Leiden: Brill, 2004), 5.

[66] Frank Moore Cross, *From Epic to Canon: History and Literature in Ancient Israel* (Baltimore: Johns Hopkins University Press, 1998), 16.

into thinking Wellhausen was engaging in Christian apologetics or anti-Jewish polemics, but the reality is far different.

Instead, Wellhausen's Jesus never had the intention of founding a Church, which Wellhausen considers to be a horrible artificial human institution.[67] Wellhausen opposes modern nation states, which he considers to be good and natural, with churches, which pose unfortunate challenges to nations. Consider Wellhausen's comment: "Now we must acknowledge that the nation is more certainly created by God than the Church, and that God works more powerfully in the history of the nations than in Church history."[68] To see how Wellhausen connects Judaism and Catholicism in his not-so-subtle critique of Catholicism, one need only read the following:

> The Mosaic theocracy, the residuum of a ruined state, is itself not a state at all, but an unpolitical artificial product created in spite of unfavourable circumstances by the impulse of an ever-memorable energy: and foreign rule is its necessary counterpart. In its nature it is intimately allied to the old Catholic church, which was in fact its child. As a matter of taste it may be objectionable to speak of the Jewish church, but as a matter of history it is not inaccurate, and the name is perhaps preferable to that of theocracy, which shelters such confusion of ideas.[69]

More work needs to be done exploring the contours of Wellhausen's anti-Catholicism and how his anti-Catholic sensibilities give shape to his biblical scholarship. What we have seen in this brief survey, however, shows how the very artificially reconstructed history in which Wellhausen situates the Documentary Hypothesis is not the result of some objective and neutral scientific or scholarly endeavor; rather, it is driven by a theology, an anti-Church theology at the service of increasingly secular modern nation states. The history of scholarship we have recounted here calls for a complete rethinking of method in Pentateuchal criticism. What is needed is a fruitful path forward that is not slavishly tied to the anti-Catholic and other related ideological biases of the past. Only thus will Pentateuchal scholarship progress in coming to a better understanding of the origins of the Pentateuch, which lies at the foundation of Jewish and Christian revelation.

---

[67] See the extensive comments in Julius Wellhausen, *Prolegomena to the History of Israel with a Reprint of the Article Israel from the "Encyclopaedia Britannica,"* trans. J. Sutherland Black and Allan Menzies (Edinburgh: Adam & Charles Black, 1885), 512.

[68] Wellhausen, *Prolegomena*, 512.

[69] Wellhausen, *Prolegomena*, 422.

WORKS CITED

Aasi, Ghulam Haider. "Muslim understanding of other religions: an analytical study of Ibn Ḥazm's *Kitab al-Fasl.*" Ph.D. diss., Temple University, 1986.

Abegg, Martin G., Jr., ed. *Qumran Non-biblical Manuscripts.* Electronic version 3.2, 1999–2009.

Abegg, Martin, Peter Flint, and Eugene Ulrich. *The Dead Sea Scrolls Bible.* San Francisco: Harper, 1999.

Abu Laylah, Muhammad. "Ibn Hazm al-Andalusī as a Thinker and Critic." In *İbn Hazm: Uluslararasi katilimli İbn Hazm sempozyumu (26–28 Ekim 2007 Bursa/Türkiye): Bildiri ve Müzakere Metinleri,* edited by Süleyman Sayar and Muhammet Tarakçi, 59–80. Istanbul: Ensar Neşriyat, 2010.

———. "An Introduction to the Life and Work of Ibn Ḥazm 1." *Islamic Quarterly* 29, no. 2 (1985): 75–100.

———. "An Introduction to the Life and Work of Ibn Ḥazm 2." *Islamic Quarterly* 29, no. 3 (1985): 165–71.

Acosta, Ana M. "Conjectures and Speculations: Jean Astruc, Obstetrics, and Biblical Criticism in Eighteenth-Century France." *Eighteenth-Century Studies* 35, no. 2 (2002): 256–66.

Adang, Camilla. "Eléments karaïtes dans la polémique d'Ibn Ḥazm." In *Diálogo filosófico-religioso entre cristianismo, judaísmo e islamismo durante la Edad Media en la Península Ibérica. Actes du colloque international de San Lorenzo de El Escorial 23–26 juin 1991 organisé par la Société Internationale pour l'Études de la Philosophie Médiévale,* edited by Horacio Santiago-Otero, 419–41. Turnhout, BE: Brepols, 1994.

———. "Ibn Ḥazm de Córdoba sobre los judíos en la sociedad islámica." *Foro Hispánico* 7 (1994): 15–23.

———. "Ibn Ḥazm on Jews and Judaism." Diss., University of Nijmegen, 1985.

———. "Ibn Ḥazm's Criticism of Some 'Judaizing' Tendencies Among the Mâlikites." In *Medieval and Modern Perspectives on Muslim Jewish Relations,* edited by Ronald L. Nettler, 1–15. Oxford, UK: Oxford Center for Postgraduate Hebrew Studies, 1995.

———. *Islam frente a Judaísmo: La polémica de Ibn Ḥazm de Córdoba.* Madrid: Aben Ezra Ediciones, 1994.

——. "A Jewish Reply to Ibn Ḥazm: Solomon b. Adret's Polemic against Islam." In *Judios y musulmanes en al-Andalus y el Magreb: Contactos Intelectuales*, edited by Maribel Fierro, 179–209. Madrid: Casa de Velázquez, 2002.

——. "Medieval Muslim Polemics Against the Jewish Scriptures." In *Muslim Perceptions of Other Religions: A Historical Survey*, edited by Jacques Waardenburg, 143–59. Oxford, UK: Oxford University Press, 1999.

——. *Muslim Writers on Judaism and the Hebrew Bible: from Ibn Rabban to Ibn Ḥazm.* Leiden, NL: Brill, 1996.

——. "Schriftvervalsing als thema in de islamitische polemiek tegen het jodendom." *Ter Herkenning* 16, no. 3 (1988): 190–202.

——. "Some Hitherto Neglected Biblical Material in the Work of Ibn Ḥazm." *Al-Masaq* 5, no. 1 (1992): 17–28.

Åkerman, Susanna. "The Answer to the Scepticism of Queen Christina's Academy (1656)." In *Scepticism and Irreligion in the Seventeenth and Eighteenth Centuries*, edited by Richard H. Popkin and Arjo Vanderjagt, 92–101. Leiden, NL: Brill, 1993.

——. *Queen Christina of Sweden and Her Circle: The Transformation of a Seventeenth-Century Philosophical Libertine.* Leiden, NL: Brill, 1991.

——. "Queen Christina of Sweden and Messianic Thought." In *Sceptics, Millenarians and Jews*, edited by David S. Katz and Jonathan I. Israel, 142–60. Leiden, NL: Brill, 1990.

Al-Azmeh, Aziz. *The Times of History: Universal Topics in Islamic Historiography.* Budapest: Central European University Press, 2007.

Albiac, Gabriel. *La sinagoga vacía: un estudio de las fuentes marranas del espinosismo.* Madrid: Hiperión, 1987.

Albright, W. F. "The Ancient Near East and the Religion of Israel." *Journal of Biblical Literature* 59, no. 2 (1940): 85–112.

——. *Archaeology, Historical Analogy, and Early Biblical Tradition.* Baton Rouge, LA: Louisiana State University Press, 1966.

——. *The Archaeology of Palestine.* New York: Penguin, 1949.

——. *Archaeology and the Religion of Israel.* Louisville, KY: Westminster John Knox Press, 2006 (1942).

——. *The Biblical Period from Abraham to Ezra.* San Francisco: Harper & Row, 1963 (1950).

——. *From the Stone Age to Christianity: Monotheism and the Historical Process.* Baltimore, MD: The Johns Hopkins University Press, 1946.

——. "Moses in Historical and Theological Perspective." In *Magnalia Dei: The Mighty Acts of God*, edited by Frank M. Cross, Werner F. Lemke, and Patrick D. Miller, 120–31. Garden City, NY: Doubleday, 1976.

——. "Some Oriental Glosses on the Homeric Problem." *American Journal of Archaeology* 54, no. 3 (1950): 162–76.

——. *Yahweh and the Gods of Canaan: A Historical Analysis of Two Contrasting Faiths.* Winona Lake, IN: Eisenbrauns, 1994 (1968).

Alexander, T.D. "The Composition of the Sinai Narrative in Exodus XIX I-XXIV II." *Vetus Testamentum* 49, no. 1 (1999): 2–20.

Algermissen, Ernest. "Die Pentateuchzitate Ibn Hazms. Ein beitrag zur Geschichte der arabische Bibelübersetzungen." Thesis, Westfälische Wilhelms-Universität, Münster, 1933

Alonso-Schökel, Luis, S.J. Review of *Stylistic Criteria and the Analysis of the Pentateuch*, by W.J. Martin. *Biblica* 39, no. 1 (1958): 106.

Amit, Yairah. "Shechem in Deuteronomy: A Seemingly Hidden Polemic." In *History, Memory, Hebrew Scriptures: A Festschrift for Ehud Ben Zvi*, edited by Ian Douglas Wilson and Diana V. Edelman, 3–13. Winona Lake, IN: Eisenbrauns, 2015.

Anawati, Georges C. *Islam et christianisme. La rencontre de deux cultures en Occidente au Moyen-Âge*. Cairo: Institut Dominicain d'Études Orientales, 1991.

———. "La rencontre de deux cultures, en Occident, au Moyen-Âge: Dialogue islamo-chretien et activité missionnaire." *Estudios Lulianos* 29 (1989): 155–78.

Anbar, Moshé. "La liberation des esclaves en temps de guerre: Jer 34 et ARM XXVI.363." *Zeitschrift für die alttestamentliche Wissenschaft* 111 (1999): 253–55.

Armgardt, Matthias, Benjamin Kilchör, and Markus Zehnder, ed. *Paradigm Change in Pentateuchal Research*. Wiesbaden, DE: Harrassowitz, 2019.

Arnaldez, Roger. "Controverse d'Ibn Hazm contre Ibn Nagrila le juif." *Revue de mondes musulmans et de la Méditerranée* 13–14 (1973): 41–48.

———. *Grammaire et théologie chez Ibn Hazm de Cordoue: Essai sur la structure et les conditions de la pensée musulmane*. Paris: Librairie Philosophique J. Vrin, 1956.

———. "Spinoza et la pensée arabe." *Revue de synthèse* 99 (1978): 151–74.

Asín Palacios, Miguel. *Abenházam de Córdoba y su historia crítica de las ideas religiosas I*. Madrid: Tipografía de la "Revista de Archivos, Bibliotecas y Museos," 1927.

———. *Abenházam de Córdoba y su historia crítica de las ideas religiosas II*. Madrid: Tipografía de la "Revista de Archivos, Bibliotecas y Museos," 1928.

———. *Abenházam de Córdoba y su historia crítica de las ideas religiosas III*. Madrid: Tipografía de la "Revista de Archivos, Bibliotecas y Museos," 1929.

———. *Abenházam de Córdoba y su historia crítica de las ideas religiosas IV*. Madrid: Tipografía de la "Revista de Archivos, Bibliotecas y Museos," 1929.

———. *Abenházam de Córdoba y su historia crítica de las ideas religiosas V*. Madrid: Tipografía de la "Revista de Archivos, Bibliotecas y Museos," 1932.

Astruc, Jean. *Conjectures sur la Genèse*. Introduction and notes by Pierre Gibert. Paris: Noêsis, 1999.

———. *Conjectures sur les memoires originaux dont il paroit que Moyse s'est servi pour composer le Livre de la Genèse. Avec des Remarques, qui appuient ou qui éclaircissent ces Conjectures*. Brussels [Paris]: Fricx, 1753.

Auvray, Paul. "Jean Morin." *Revue biblique* 66 (1959): 396–414.

———. "Richard Simon et Spinoza." In *Religion, érudition et critique à la fin du XVIIe siècle et au début du XVIIIe*, edited by Baudouin de Gaiffier, et al., 201–14. Paris: Presses universitaires de France, 1968.

Averbeck, Richard E. "The Cult in Deuteronomy and Its Relationship to the Book of the Covenant and the Holiness Code." In *Sepher Torath Mosheh: Studies in the Interpretation of Deuteronomy*, edited by Daniel I. Block and Richard L. Schultz, 232–60. Peabody, MA: Hendrickson, 2017.

———. "The Egyptian Sojourn and Deliverance from Slavery in the Framing and Shaping of the Mosaic Law." In *"Did I Not Bring Israel Out of Egypt?" Biblical, Archaeological, and Egyptological Perspectives on the Exodus Narratives*, edited by James K. Hoffmeier, Alan R. Millard, and Gary A. Rendsburg, 143–76. Winona Lake, IN: Eisenbrauns, 2016.

———. "Factors in Reading the Patriarchal Narratives: Literary, Historical, and Theological Dimensions." In *Giving the Sense: Understanding and Using Old Testament Historical Texts*, edited by David M. Howard, Jr. and Michael A. Grisanti, 115–37. Grand Rapids, MI: Kregel, 2003.

———. "Pentateuchal Criticism and the Priestly Torah." In *Do Historical Matters Matter to Faith? A Critical Appraisal of Modern and Postmodern Approaches to Scripture*, edited by James K. Hoffmeier and Dennis R. Magary, 151–80. Wheaton, IL: Crossway, 2012.

———. "Reading the Torah in a Better Way: Unity and Diversity in Text, Genre, and Compositional History." In *Paradigm Change in Pentateuchal Research*, edited by Matthias Armgardt, Benjamin Kilchör, and Markus Zehnder, 21–44. Wiesbaden, DE: Harrassowitz, 2019.

———. "The Sumerian Historiographic Tradition and Its Implications for Genesis 1–11." In *Faith, Tradition, and History: Old Testament Historiography in Its Near Eastern Context*, edited by A. R. Millard, James K. Hoffmeier, and David W. Baker, 79–102. Winona Lake, IN: Eisenbrauns, 1994.

Bainton, Roland H. "The Bible in the Reformation." In *The Cambridge History of the Bible: The West from the Reformation to the Present Day*, edited by S. L. Greenslade, 1–37. Cambridge, UK: Cambridge University Press, 1975.

Baker, David W. "Approaches to Genesis: A Review Article." *Ashland Theological Journal* 31 (1999): 103–7.

———. "Diversity and Unity in the Literary Structure of Genesis." In *Essays on the Patriarchal Narratives*, edited by A. R. Millard and D. J. Wiseman, 189–205. Leicester, UK: InterVarsity Press, 1980.

———. "Division Markers and the Structure of Leviticus 1–7." In *Studia Biblica 1978 I: Papers on Old Testament and Related Themes: Sixth International Congress on Biblical Studies: Oxford 3–7 April 1978*, edited by Elizabeth A. Livingstone, 9–15. Sheffield, UK: Journal for the Study of the Old Testament Press, 1979.

———. "The Mosaic Covenant Against Its Environment." *Ashland Theological Journal* 20 (1989): 9–18.

———. "The Old Testament and Criticism." *Journal of Theology for Southern Africa* 48 (1984): 13–20.

Baldin, Gregorio. *Hobbes and Galileo: Method, Matter and the Science of Motion*. Cham, CH: Springer, 2020.

Baltzer, Klaus. *Deutero-Isaiah: A Commentary on Isaiah 40–55*. Minneapolis, MN: Fortress Press, 2001.

Barclay, John M.G. *Flavius Josephus: Against Apion*. Leiden, NL: Brill, 2007.

Bardtke, Hans. "Henning Bernhard Witter. Zur 250. Wiederkehr seiner Promotion zum Philosophiae Doctor am 6. November 1704 zu Helmstedt." *Zeitschrift für die alttestamentliche Wissenschaft* 66 (1954): 153–81.

Barkai, Ron. "Diálogo filosófico-religioso en el seno de las tres culturas Ibéricas." In *Diálogo filosófico-religioso entre cristianismo, judaísmo e islamismo durante la edad media en la península Ibérica: Actes du colloque international de San Lorenzo de El Escorial 23–26 juin 1991, organisé par la Société Internationale pour l'Étude de la Philosophie Médiévale*, edited by Horacio Santiago-Otero, 1–27. Turnhout, BE: Brepols, 1994.

Barker, David G. "Voices for the Pilgrimage: A Study in the Psalms of Ascent." *The Expository Times* 116 (2005): 109–16.

Barthel, Georges. "La Bible dans le 'Leviathan.'" In *Thomas Hobbes: Critical Assessments*, edited by Preston King, 231–50. London: Routledge, 1993.

Barthélemy, Dominique. *Studies in the Text of the Old Testament: An Introductionto the Hebrew Old Testament Project*. Winona Lake, IN: Eisenbrauns, 2012.

Barton, John. "Wellhausen's *Prolegomena to the History of Israel*: Influences and Effects." In *Text and Experience: Towards a Cultural Exegesis of the Bible*, edited by Daniel Smith-Christopher, 316–29. Sheffield, UK: Sheffield Academic Press, 1995.

Bass, David Drummond. "Hosea's Use of Scripture: An Analysis of His Hermeneutics." Ph.D. diss., Southern Baptist Theological Seminary, 2009.

Batto, Bernard F. and Kathryn L. Roberts, ed. *David and Zion: Biblical Studies in Honor of J. J. M. Roberts*. Winona Lake, IN: Eisenbrauns, 2004.

Baur, Johannes B. "The Law of Manumission in Jer 34." *Biblische Zeitschrift* 15 (1971): 105–8.

Bautch, Kelley Coblentz. *"No One Has Seen What I Have Seen": A Study of the Geography of 1 Enoch 17–19*. Leiden, NL: Brill, 2003.

Bea, Augustinus. *Institutiones biblicae scholis accommodatae. Vol. 2, De Libris Veteris Testamenti. I. De Pentateucho*. Rome: Pontifical Biblical Institute, 1933 (1928).

———. *La Parola di Dio e l'umanità. La dottrina del concilio sulla rivelazione*. Assisi: Cittadella, 1967.

Beaulieu, Armand. "Les relations de Hobbes et de Mersenne." In *Thomas Hobbes: philosophie première, théorie de la science et politique*, edited by Yves Charles Zarka and Jean Bernhardt, 81–90. Paris: Presses universitaires de France, 1990.

Behloul, Samuel-Martin. *Ibn Hazms Evangelienkritik. Eine methodische Utersuchung*. Leiden, NL: Brill, 2002.

———. "The Testimony of Reason and the Historical Reality: Ibn Ḥazm's Refutation of Christianity." In *Ibn Hazm of Cordoba: The Life and Works of a Controversial Thinker*, edited by Camilla Adang, Maribel Fierro, and Sabine Schmidtke, 457–84. Leiden, NL: Brill, 2013.

Beinart, Haim. "España y el occidente en los días de R. Abraham Ibn Ezra." In *Abraham Ibn Ezra y su tiempo: Actas del Simposio Internacional: Madrid, Tudela, Toledo, 1–8 Febrero 1989*, edited by Fernando Díaz Esteban, 25–38. Madrid: Universidad Autónoma de Madrid, Asociación Española de Orientalistas, 1990.

Beitzel, Barry J. "From Harran to Imar Along the Old Babylonian Itinerary: The Evidence from the *Archives Royales de Mari*." In *Biblical and Near Eastern Studies: Essays in Honor of William Sanford LaSor*, edited by Gary A. Tuttle, 209–19. Grand Rapids, MI: Eerdmans, 1978.

Benedict XVI, Pope. *A Reason Open to God: On Universities, Education, and Culture.* Washington, DC: The Catholic University of America Press, 2013.

Bergland, Kenneth. "Jeremiah 34 Originally Composed as a Legal Blend of Leviticus 25 and Deuteronomy 15." In *Paradigm Change in Pentateuchal Research*, edited by Benjamin Kilchör and Markus Zehnder, 189–205. Wiesbaden, DE: Harrassowitz Verlag, 2019.

Bergsma, John S. "The Biblical Manumission Laws: Has the Literary Dependence of H on D been Demonstrated?" In *A Teacher for All Generations: Essays in Honor of James C. VanderKam. Vol. 1,* edited by Eric F. Mason, Samuel I. Thomas, Alison Schofield, and Eugene Ulrich, 65–89. Leiden, NL: Brill, 2012.

———. "Critical and Catholic Exegesis in the Seventeenth-Century Low Countries." In *Biblical Interpretation and Doctrinal Formulation in the Reformed Tradition: Essays in Honor of James A. De Jong*, edited by Arie C. Leder and Richard A. Muller, 185–208. Grand Rapids, MI: Reformation Heritage Books, 2014.

———. "Cultic Kingdoms in Conflict: Liturgy and Empire in the Book of Daniel." *Letter & Spirit* 5 (2009): 51–76.

———. *The Jubilee from Leviticus to Qumran: A History of Interpretation*. Leiden, NL: Brill, 2007.

———. "The Jubilee: A Post-Exilic Priestly Attempt to Reclaim Lands?" *Biblica* 84 (2003): 225–46.

———. "The Persian Period as Penitential Era: The 'Exegetical Logic' of Daniel 9.1–27." In *Exile and Restoration Revisited: Essays in Memory of Peter R. Ackroyd*, edited by Gary N. Knoppers and Lester L. Grabbe, 50–64. New York: Continuum/T & T Clark, 2009.

———. "The Relevance of Ezekiel and the Samaritans for Pentateuchal Composition: Converging Lines of Evidence." In *Exploring the Composition of the Pentateuch: Conference Papers 2016. Bulletin for Biblical Research* Supplement 27. Winona Lake, IN: Eisenbrauns, 2020.

———. "A 'Samaritan' Pentateuch? The Implications of the Pro-Northern Tendency of the Common Pentateuch." In *Paradigm Change in Pentateuchal Research*, edited by Matthias Armgardt, Benjamin Kilchör, and Markus Zehnder, 287–300. Wiesbaden, DE: Harrassowitz, 2019.

———. "The Year of Jubilee and the Ancient Israelite Economy." *Southwestern Journal of Theology* 59, no. 2 (2017): 155–64.

Bergsma, John and Brant Pitre. *A Catholic Introduction to the Bible. Volume 1, The Old Testament*. San Francisco: Ignatius Press, 2018.

Berman, Joshua. "The Biblical Criticism of Ibn Hazm the Andalusian: A Medieval Control for Modern Diachronic Method." *Journal of Biblical Literature* 138, no. 2 (2019): 377–90.

———. "CTH 133 and the Hittite Provenance of Deuteronomy 13." *Journal of Biblical Literature* 130, no. 1 (2011): 25–44.

———. *Inconsistency in the Torah: Ancient Literary Convention and the Limits of Source Criticism.* Oxford, UK: Oxford University Press, 2017.

Bernier, Jean. *La critique du Pentateuque de Hobbes à Calmet.* Paris: Champion, 2010.

———. "Le problème de la tradition chez Richard Simon et Jean Le Clerc." *Revue des sciences religieuses* 82, no. 2 (2008): 199–223.

Beyssade, Michelle. "Deux latinistes: Descartes et Spinoza." In *Spinoza to the Letter: Studies in Words, Texts and Books*, edited by Fokke Akkerman and Piet Steenbakkers, 55–68. Leiden, NL: Brill, 2005.

Biale, David. *Not in the Heavens: The Tradition of Jewish Secular Thought.* Princeton, NJ: Princeton University Press, 2011.

Bienert, Wolfgang A. "Marcion und der Antijudaismus." In *Marcion und seine kirchengeschichte Wirkung: Vorträge der Internationalen Fachkonferenz zu Marcion, gehalten vom 15–18. August 2001 im Mainz*, edited by Gerhard May and Katharina Greschat with Martin Meiser, 191–206. Berlin: Walter de Gruyter, 2002.

Bienkowski, Piotr, Christopher Mee, and Elizabeth Slater. Preface to *Writing and Ancient Near Eastern Society: Papers in Honour of Alan R. Millard.* Edited by Piotr Bienkowski, Christopher Mee, and Elizabeth Slater, 7–8. New York: T&T Clark, 2005.

Bimson, John J. "Archaeological Data and the Dating of the Patriarchs." In *Essays on the Patriarchal Narratives*, edited by A. R. Millard and D.J. Wiseman, 59–92. Leicester, UK: InterVarsity Press, 1980.

Binder, Susanne. "Joseph's Rewarding and Investiture (Genesis 41:41–43) and the Gold of Honour in New Kingdom Egypt." In *Egypt, Canaan and Israel: History, Imperialism, Ideology and Literature*, edited by S. Bar, D. Kahn, and J.J. Shirley, 44–64. Leiden, NL: Brill, 2011.

Blenkinsopp, Joseph. *The Pentateuch: An Introduction to the First Five Books of the Bible.* New Haven, CT: Yale University Press, 2000.

———. *Prophecy and Canon: A Contribution to the Study of Jewish Origins.* Notre Dame, IL: University of Notre Dame Press, 1977.

Bloch, Joshua. "Max L. Margolis' Contribution to the History and Philosophy of Judaism." In *Max Leopold Margolis: Scholar and Teacher*, edited by Robert Gordis, 45–59. New York: Bloch, 1952.

Block, Daniel I. *Beyond the River Chebar: Studies in the Kingship and Eschatology in the Book of Ezekiel.* Eugene, OR: Cascade Books, 2013.

———. *The Book of Ezekiel: Chapters 1–24.* New International Commentary on the Old Testament. Grand Rapids: Eerdmans, 1997.

———. "Transformation of Royal Ideology in Ezekiel." In *Transforming Visions: Transformations of Text, Tradition, and Theology in Ezekiel*, edited by William A. Tooman and Michael A. Lyons, 208–46. Princeton Theological Monograph Series 127. Eugene, OR: Pickwick, 2010.

———. "Zion Theology in the Book of Ezekiel." In *Beyond the River Chebar: Studies in the Kingship and Eschatology in the Book of Ezekiel*, 1–9. Eugene, OR: Cascade Books, 2013.

Block, Daniel I. and Richard L. Schultz, ed. *Sepher Torath Mosheh: Studies in the Composition and Interpretation of Deuteronomy*. Peabody, MA: Hendrickson, 2017.

Boadt, Lawrence. "Do Jeremiah and Ezekiel Share a Common View of the Exile?" Paper presented at the Annual Meeting of the Society of Biblical Literature, Atlanta, 22 November 2003.

Bordoli, Roberto. "Critica e Aufklärung. La controversia su Mosè (1685–1686): Jean Le Clerc contro Richard Simon." *Archivio di storia della cultura* 30 (2017): 63–77.

———. *L'illuminismo di Dio: Alle origini della "mentalità liberale": Religione teologia filosofia e storia in Johann Salomo Semler (1725–1791): Contributo per lo studio delle fonti teologische, cartesiane e spinoziane dell' «Aufklärung»*. Florence: Olschki, 2004.

Brown, Brian Arthur. *Forensic Scriptures: Critical Analysis of Scripture and What the Qur'an Reveals about the Bible*. Eugene, OR: Cascade, 2009.

Bruce, Travis. "The Taifa of Denia and the Jewish Networks of the Medieval Mediterranean: A Study of the Cairo Geniza and Other Documents." *Journal of Medieval Iberian Studies* 10, no. 2 (2018): 147–66.

Büchler, Adolf. "Über die Minim von Sepphoris und Tiberias im zweiten und dritten Jahrhundert." In *Judaica: Festschrift zu Hermann Cohens siebzigstem Geburtstage*, 271–95. Berlin: Cassirer, 1912.

Bultmann, Christoph. "Philosophie und Exegese bei W. M. L. de Wette. Der Pentateuch als Nationalepos Israels." In *Wilhelm Martin Leberecht de Wette. Ein Universaltheologie des 19. Jahrhunderts*, edited by Hans-Peter Mathys and Klaus Seybold, 44–61. Basel, CH: Schwabe, 2001.

Calvert, Kenneth R. "Edwin M. Yamauchi." In *The Light of Discovery: Studies in Honor of Edwin M. Yamauchi*, edited by John D. Wineland, 1–23. Eugene, OR: Pickwick, 2007.

Calvetti, Carla Gallicet. *Spinoza lettore del Machiavelli*. Milan: Università Cattolica del Sacro Cuore, 1972.

Camporeale, Salvatore I. *Lorenzo Valla: Umanesimo, Riforma e Controriforma: Studi e Testi*. Rome: Edizioni di Storia e Letteratura, 2002.

Cardellini, Innocenzo. *Die biblischen "Sklaven"-Gesetze im Lichte des keilschriftlichen Sklavenrechts: ein Beitrag zur Tradition, Überlieferung und Redaktion der alttestamentlichen Rechtstexte*. Königstein: Hanstein, 1981.

Carlson, Donald H. *Jewish-Christian Interpretation of the Pentateuch in the Pseudo-Clementine Homilies*. Minneapolis, MN: Fortress Press, 2013.

Carmona González, Alfonso. "La doctrine sur l'exercice de la justice: Un exemple du désaccord entre Ibn Ḥazm et les mālikites." In *Ibn Hazm of Cordoba: The Life and Works of a Controversial Thinker*, edited by Camilla Adang, Maribel Fierro, and Sabine Schmidtke, 161–78. Leiden, NL: Brill, 2013.

Carr, David. "Method in Determination of Direction of Dependence: An Empirical Test of Criteria Applied to Exodus 34, 11–26 and its Parallels." In *Gottes Volk am Sinai: Untersuchungen zu Ex 32–34 and Dtn 9–10*, edited by Matthias Köckert and Erhard Blum, 107–40. Gütersloh, DE: Gütersloh Verlaghaus, 2001.

Cassuto, Philippe. *Spinoza hébraïsant. L'hébreu dans le «Tractatus theologico-politicus» et le «Compendium grammatices linguae hebraeae»*. Louvain, BE: Peeters, 1999.

Cassuto, Umberto. *Biblical and Oriental Studies. Vol. 1, The Bible.* Jerusalem: Magnes Press, 1973.

———. *A Commentary on the Book of Genesis Part II: From Noah to Abraham, Genesis VI 9– XI 32, with an Appendix: A Fragment of Part III.* Jerusalem: Magnes Press, 1964 (1949).

———. *The Documentary Hypothesis and the Composition of the Pentateuch: Eight Lectures.* Jerusalem: Shalem Press, 2006 (1941).

———. "Jerusalem in the Pentateuch." In *Biblical & Oriental Studies.* Vol. 1, *Bible*, 71–78. Jerusalem: Magnes Press, The Hebrew University, 1973.

———. *La questione della Genesi.* Florence: Felice Le Monnier, 1934.

Catlett, Michael Lee. "Reversals in Hosea: A Literary Analysis." Ph.D. diss., Emory University, 1988.

———. "The Prophet Hosea and the Books of the Pentateuch." In *Biblical and Oriental Studies*, translated by Israel Abrahams, 79–100. Jerusalem: Magnes Press, 1973.

Champion, Justin A. I. "Hobbes and Biblical Criticism: Some Preliminary Remarks." *Bulletin Annuel Institut d'Histoire de la Réformation* 31 (2010): 53–72.

Charlesworth, James H. "The Discovery of an Unknown Dead Sea Scroll: The Original Text of Deuteronomy 27?" Online: http://blogs.owu.edu/magazine/ the-discovery-of-an-unknown-dead-sea-scroll-the-original-text-of-deuteronomy-27/.

———. "What is a Variant?: Announcing a Dead Sea Scrolls Fragment of Deuteronomy." *Maarav* 16 (2009): 201–12 and 273–74.

Chavalas, Mark W. and Murray R. Adamthwaite. "Archaeological Light on the Old Testament." In *The Face of Old Testament Studies*, edited by David W. Baker and Bill T. Arnold, 59–96. Grand Rapids, MI: Baker Academic, 1999.

Chavel, Simeon. "'Let My People Go!': Emancipation, Revelation, and Scribal Activity in Jeremiah 34:8–14." *Journal for the Study of the Old Testament* 76 (1997): 71–95.

Chejne, A. G. *Ibn Hazm.* Chicago: Kazi Publications, 1982.

Chen, Y. S. *The Primeval Flood Catastrophe: Origins and Early Development in Mesopotamian Traditions.* Oxford, UK: Oxford University Press, 2013.

Chirichigno, Gregory C. "The Narrative Structure of Exod. 19–24." *Biblica* 68 (1987): 457–79.

Clines, David J. A. *On the Way to the Postmodern: Old Testament Essays, 1967–1998. Vol. 2.* Sheffield, UK: Sheffield Academic Press, 1998.

Cohen, Chaim, Avi Hurvitz, and Shalom Paul. "Prof. Moshe Weinfeld: A Professional Profile." In *Sefer Moshe: The Moshe Weinfeld Jubilee Volume: Studies in the Bible and the Ancient Near East, Qumran, and Post-Biblical Judaism*, edited by Chaim Cohen, Avi M. Hurvitz, and Shalom M. Paul, ix–xi. Winona Lake, IN: Eisenbrauns, 2004.

Cohen, Mark R. *Under Crescent and Cross: The Jews in the Middle Ages*. Princeton, NJ: Princeton University Press, 1994.

Cohn, Leopoldus and Paulus Wendland, ed. *Philonis Alexandrini: Opera Quae Supersunt. Vol. 4*. Berlin: Reimer, 1902.

Coleman, Frank M. "Thomas Hobbes and the Hebraic Bible." *History of Political Thought* 25, no. 4 (2004): 642–69.

Collier, Mark and Steven Snape. Preface to *Ramesside Studies in Honour of K.A. Kitchen*. Edited by Mark Collier and Steven Snape, vii. Bolton, UK: Rutherford Press, 2011.

Collins, John J. *Introduction to the Hebrew Bible and Deutero-Canonical Books*. 3rd ed. Minneapolis, MN: Fortress Press, 2018.

Conrad, Joachim. *Karl Heinrich Grafs Arbeit am Alten Testament: Studien zu einer wissenschaftlichen Biographie*. Berlin: Walter de Gruyter, 2011.

Conroy, Charles. "The Biblical Work of Alexander Geddes against the Background of Contemporary Catholic Biblical Scholarship in Continental Europe." In *The Bible and the Enlightenment: A Case Study—Dr. Alexander Geddes (1737–1802): The Proceedings of the Bicentenary Geddes Conference held at the University of Aberdeen, 1–4 April 2002*, edited by William Johnstone, 135–56. London: T&T Clark, 2004.

Cross, Frank Moore. "The Contributions of W. F. Albright to Semitic Epigraphy and Palaeography." In *The Scholarship of William Foxwell Albright: An Appraisal: Papers Delivered at the Symposium "Homage to William Foxwell Albright," The American Friends of the Israel Exploration Society, Rockville, Maryland, 1984*, edited by Gus W. Van Beek, 17–31. Atlanta, GA: Scholars Press, 1989.

———. *From Epic to Canon: History and Literature in Ancient Israel*. Baltimore: Johns Hopkins University Press, 1998.

Curley, Edwin. *Behind the Geometrical Method: A Reading of Spinoza's Ethics*. Princeton, NJ: Princeton University Press, 1988.

———. "Spinoza's Geometrical Method." *Studia Spinozana* 2 (1986): 151–69.

Currid, John D. *Ancient Egypt and the Old Testament*. Grand Rapids, MI: Baker, 1997.

———. "An Examination of the Egyptian Background of the Genesis Cosmogony." *Biblische Zeitschrift* 35 (1991): 18–40.

Dahan, Gilbert. "Les sources médiévales du commentaire de Cornelius a Lapide sur le Cantique des Cantiques." In *Bible, histoire et société: Mélanges offerts à Bernard Roussel*, edited by R. Gerald Hobbs and Annie Noblesse-Rocher, 45–69. Turnhout, BE: Brepols, 2013.

D'Alessandro, Giuseppe. *L'illuminismo dimenticato: Johann Gottfried Eichhorn (1752–1827) e il suo tempo*. Naples, IT: Liguori, 2000.

Damgaard, Finn. *Recasting Moses: The Memory of Moses in Biographical and Autobiographical Narratives in Ancient Judaism and 4th-Century Christianity*. Frankfurt am Main, DE: Peter Lang, 2013.

Daniels, Dwight R. *Hosea and Salvation History: The Early Traditions of Israel in the Prophecy of Hosea*. Berlin: Walter de Gruyter, 1990.

David, Martin. "The Manumission of Slaves under Zedekiah." *Oudtestamentische studiën* 5 (1948): 63–79.

Davidson, Israel. *Saadia's Polemic against Hiwi al-Balkhi: A Fragment Edited from a Genizah Ms.* New York: Jewish Theological Seminary of America, 1915.

de Jonge, Henk Jan. "Joseph Scaliger's Historical Criticism of the New Testament." *Novum Testamentum* 38, no. 2 (1996): 176–93.

de Mordechai Vaz Dias, Abraham and Willem Gerard van der Tak. "Spinoza Merchant and Autodidact: Charters and Other Authentic Documents Relating to the Philosopher's Youth and His Relations." *Studia Rosenthaliana* 16 (1982): 103–71.

de Pury, Albert and Thomas Römer. "Le Pentateuque en question. Position du problème et brève histoire de la recherche." In *Le Pentateuque en question: Les origines et la composition des cinq premiers livres de la Bible à la lumière des recherches récentes*, 3rd ed., edited by Albert de Pury and Thomas Römer, 9–80. Geneva, CH: Labor et Fides, 2002.

De Vries, Simon J. "The Hexateuchal Criticism of Abraham Kuenen." *Journal of Biblical Literature* 82, no. 1 (1963): 31–57.

de Wette, Wilh. Martin Leberecht. *Beiträge zur Einleitung in das Alte Testament: Erstes Bändchen: Kritischer Versuch über die Glaubwürdigkeit der Bücher der Chronik mit Hinsicht auf die Geschichte der Mosaischen Bücher und Gesetzgebung*. Halle, DE: Schimmelpfennig, 1806.

Dekker, Jaap. *Zion's Rock-Solid Foundations: An Exegetical Study of the Zion Text in Isaiah 28:16*. Leiden, NL: Brill, 2007.

Delgado Jara, Inmaculada. "El Tostado y le exégesis bíblica." In *La primera escuela de Salamanca (1406–1516)*, edited by Cirilo Flórez Miguel, Maximiliano Hernández Marcos, and Roberto Albares Albares, 55–74. Salamanca, ES: Ediciones Universidad de Salamanca, 2012.

Della Rocca, Michael. "Mental Content and Skepticism in Descartes and Spinoza." *Studia Spinozana* 10 (1994): 19–42.

Dever, William G. "What Remains of the House That Albright Built?" *Biblical Archaeologist* 56, no. 1 (1993): 25–35.

Di Matteo, Ignazio. "La pretese contraddizioni della S. Scrittura secondo Ibn Hazm." *Bessarione* 27 (1923): 77–127.

Dillmann, August. *Die Bücher Numeri, Deuteronomium und Josue*. Leipzig, DE: Hirzel, 1886.

——. *Die Genesis*. 5th ed. Leipzig, DE: Hirzel, 1886.

Djedi, Youcef. "Spinoza et l'islam: un état des lieux." *Philosophiques* 37 (2010): 275–98.

Driver, S. R. *The Book of Genesis: With Introduction and Notes*. 6th ed. London: Methuen, 1907 (1904).

——. "On Some Alleged Linguistic Affinities of the Elohist." *Journal of Philology* 11 (1882): 201–36.

Droge, Arthur J. *Homer or Moses?: Early Christian Interpretation of the History of Culture*. Tübingen, DE: Mohr, 1989.

Drower, E.S. *The Secret Adam: A Study of Nasoraean Gnosis*. Oxford, UK: Oxford University Press, 1960.

Dungan, David Laird. *A History of the Synoptic Problem: The Canon, the Text, the Composition, and the Interpretation of the Gospels*. New Haven, CT: Yale University Press, 1999.

Farmer, William R. "State *Interesse* and Markan Primacy: 1870–1914." In *Biblical Studies and the Shifting of Paradigms, 1850–1914*, edited by Henning Graf Reventlow and William Farmer, 15–49. Sheffield, UK: Sheffield Academic Press, 1995.

Feinman, Peter Douglas. *William Foxwell Albright: And the Origins of Biblical Archaeology*. Berrien Springs, MI: Andrews University Press, 2000.

Feldman, Louis H. *Philo's Portrayal of Moses in the Context of Ancient Judaism*. Notre Dame, IL: University of Notre Dame Press, 2007.

Fellman, Jack. "Founders of Ethiopic Studies: Job Ludolf (1624–1704) and August Dillman (1823–1894)." *Ancient Near Eastern Studies* 39 (2002): 207–11.

Fernández Vallina, Emiliano. "Introducción al Tostado. De su vida y de su obra." *Cuadernos Salmantinos de Filosofía* 15 (1988): 153–77.

Ferreri, Luigi. *La questione omerica dal cinquecento al settecento*. Rome: Edizioni di Storia e Letteratura, 2007.

Fierro, Maribel. "Ibn Ḥazm and the Jewish *zindiq*." In *Ibn Hazm of Cordoba: The Life and Works of a Controversial Thinker*, edited by Camilla Adang, Maribel Fierro, and Sabine Schmidtke, 497–509. Leiden, NL: Brill, 2013.

———. "Ibn Ḥazm et le zindiq juif." *Revue du Monde Musulman et de la Mediterranee* 63–64 (1992): 81–89.

———. "El Islam Andalusí del s. V/XI ante el Judaísmo y el Cristianismo." In *Diálogo filosófico-religioso entre Cristianismo, Judaísmo e Islamismo durante la edad media en la península Ibérica: Actes du colloque international de San Lorenzo de El Escorial 23–26 juin 1991, organisé par la Société Internationale pour l'Étude de la Philosophie Médiévale*, edited by Horacio Santiago-Otero, 53–98. Turnhout, BE: Brepols, 1994.

Finkelstein, Israel. "Jerusalem and Judah 600–200 BCE: Implications for Understanding Pentateuchal Texts." In *The Fall of Jerusalem and the Rise of the Torah*, edited by Dominik Markl, Jean-Pierre Sonnet, and Peter Dubovský, 3–18. Forschungen zum Alten Testament 107. Tübingen: Mohr Siebeck, 2016.

Finn, A. H. *The Unity of the Pentateuch: An Examination of the Higher Critical Theory as to the Composite Nature of the Pentateuch*. London: Marshall Brothers, n.d.

Fishbane, Michael. *Biblical Interpretation in Ancient Israel*. Oxford, UK: Oxford University Press, 1985.

———. "Composition and Structure in the Jacob Cycle (Gen. 25:19–35:22)." *Journal of Jewish Studies* 26 (1975): 15–38.

Fisher, Benjamin. "God's Word Defended: Menasseh ben Israel, Biblical Chronology, and the Erosion of Biblical Authority." In *Scriptural Authority and Biblical Criticism in the Dutch Golden Age: God's Word Questioned*, edited by Dirk Van Miert, Henk Nellen, Piet Steenbakkers, and Jetze Touber, 155–74. Oxford, UK: Oxford University Press, 2017.

Fisher, Georg. "The Relationship of the Book of Jeremiah to the Torah." In *The Formation of the Pentateuch: Bridging the Academic Cultures of Europe, Israel, and North America*, edited by Jan C. Gertz, Bernard Levinson, Dalit Rom-Shiloni, and Konrad Schmid, 891–911. Tübingen, DE: Mohr Siebeck, 2016.

Fleyfel, Antoine. "Richard Simon, critique de la sacralité biblique." *Revue d'histoire et de philosophie religieuses* 88 (2008): 469–92.

Fraenkel, Carlos. "Spinoza on Philosophy and Religion: The Averroistic Sources." In *The Rationalists: Between Tradition and Innovation*, edited by Carlos Fraenkel, Dario Perinetti, and Justin Smith, 58–81. Dordrecht, NL: Springer, 2010.

Frampton, Travis L. *Spinoza and the Rise of Historical Criticism of the Bible*. New York: T & T Clark, 2006.

François, Wim. "Andreas Masius (1514–1573): Humanist, Exegete and Syriac Scholar." *Journal of Eastern Christian Studies* 61 (2009): 199–244.

———. "Grace, Free Will, and Predestination in the Biblical Commentaries of Cornelius a Lapide." *Annali di storia dell'esegesi* 34, no. 1 (2017): 175–97.

François, Wim and Albert Van Roey. "Andreas Masius (1514–73). Löwener Alumnus, Gelehrter der syrischen Studien und biblischer Humanist." In *The Quintessence of Lives: Intellectual Biographies in the Low Countries Presented to Jan Roegiers*, edited by Dries Vanysacker, 7–28. Turnhout, BE: Brepols, 2010.

Freedman, R. David. "The Father of Modern Biblical Scholarship." *Journal of the Ancient Near Eastern Society* 19 (1989): 31–38.

Fretheim, Terrence. "The Priestly Document: Anti-Temple?" *Vetus Testamentum* 18 (1968): 313–29.

Friedlander, Israel. "The Heterodoxies of the Shiites in the Presentation of Ibn Ḥazm." *Journal of the American Oriental Society* 28 (1907): 1–80.

———. "Zur Komposition von Ibn Ḥazm's Milal wa'n-Niḥal." In *Orientalische Studien Theodor Nöldeke zum siebzigsten Geburtstag (2. März 1906) gewidmet von Freunden und Schülern I*, edited by Carl Bezold, 267–77. Gieszen, DE: Alfred Töpelmann, 1906.

Fukuoka, Atsuko. *The Sovereign and the Prophets: Spinoza on Grotian and Hobbesian Biblical Argumentation*. Leiden, NL: Brill, 2018.

Fuller, Reginald C. *Alexander Geddes: 1737–1802: A Pioneer of Biblical Criticism*. Sheffield, UK: Almond Press, 1984.

Fumagalli, Pier Francesco. "Umberto Cassuto, *peritissimus rerum hebraicarum magister*." *La Rassegna Mensile di Israel* 82 (2016): 285–94.

Ganzel, Tova. "Transformation of Pentateuchal Descriptions of Idolatry." In *Transforming Visions: Transformations of Text, Tradition, and Theology in Ezekiel*, edited by William A. Tooman and Michael A. Lyons, 33–49. Princeton Theological Monograph Series 127. Eugene, OR: Pickwick, 2010.

Gaon, Solomon. *The Influence of the Catholic Theologian Alfonso Tostado on the Pentateuch Commentary of Isaac Abravanel*. New York: KTAV, 1993.

García, Santiago. "La competencia hebraica de Alfonso de Madrigal." *La corónica* 33, no. 1 (2004): 85–98.

García Gómez, Emilio. "Polémica religiosa entre Ibn Ḥazm e Ibn al-Nagrīla." *Al-Andalus* 4, no. 1 (1936): 1–28.

García López, Félix. "Deut 34, Dtr History and the Pentateuch." In *Studies in Deuteronomy: In Honour of C. J. Labuschagne on the Occasion of His 65th Birthday*, edited by F. García Martínez, A. Hilhorst, J. T. A. G. M. van Ruiten, and A. S. van der Woude, 47–62. Leiden, NL: Brill, 1994.

García Sanjuán, Alejandro. "Ibn Ḥazm and the Territory of Huelva: Personal and Family Relationships." In *Ibn Hazm of Cordoba: The Life and Works of a Controversial Thinker*, edited by Camilla Adang, Maribel Fierro, and Sabine Schmidtke, 51–68. Leiden, NL: Brill, 2013.

Gerdmar, Anders. *Roots of Theological Anti-Semitism: German Biblical Interpretation and the Jews, from Herder and Semler to Kittel and Bultmann*. Leiden, NL: Brill, 2008.

Gertz, Jan Christian. "Jean Astruc and Source Criticism in the Book of Genesis." In *Sacred Conjectures: The Context and Legacy of Robert Lowth and Jean Astruc*, ed. John Jarick, 190–203. London: T&T Clark, 2007.

Gertz, Jan C., Bernard Levinson, Dalit Rom-Shiloni, and Konrad Schmid, ed. *The Formation of the Pentateuch: Bridging the Academic Cultures of Europe, Israel, and North America*. Tübingen, DE: Mohr Siebeck, 2016.

Gesenii, Gulielmi. *De Pentateuchi Samaritani origine Indole et Auctoritate. Commentario-Philologica Critica*. Halle, DE: Libreria Rengerianae, 1815.

Gibert, Pierre. "The Catholic Counterpart and Response to the Protestant Orthodoxy." In *Hebrew Bible/Old Testament: The History of Its Interpretation. Vol. 2, From the Renaissance to the Enlightenment*, edited by Magne Sæbø, 758–73. Göttingen, DE: Vandenhoeck & Ruprecht, 2008.

———. "De l'intuition a l'evidence: La multiplicite documentaire dans la Genese chez H. B. Witter et Jean Astruc." In *Sacred Conjectures: The Context and Legacy of Robert Lowth and Jean Astruc*, edited by John Jarick, 174–89. London: T&T Clark, 2007.

———. *L'invention critique de la Bible: XVe – XVIIIe siècle*. Paris: Éditions Gallimard, 2010.

Gilbert, Maurice. *The Pontifical Biblical Institute: A Century of History (1909–2009)*. Rome: Pontifical Biblical Institute, 2009.

Gile, Jason. "Deuteronomic Influence on the Book of Ezekiel." Ph.D. diss, Wheaton College, 2013.

———. *Ezekiel and the World of Deuteronomy. The Library of Hebrew Bible/Old Testament Studies 703*. London: Bloomsbury/T & T Clark, 2021.

Gillingham, Susan. "The Zion Tradition and the Editing of the Hebrew Psalter." In *Temple and Worship in Biblical Israel*, edited by John Day, 308–41. London: T&T Clark, 2007.

Goertz, Hans-Jürgen. "Scriptural Interpretation among Radical Reformers." In *Hebrew Bible/Old Testament: The History of Its Interpretation. Vol. 2, From the Renaissance to the Enlightenment*, edited by Magne Sæbø, 576–601. Göttingen, DE: Vandenhoeck & Ruprecht, 2008.

Goetschel, Roland. "The Sin of the Golden Calf in the Exegesis of Abraham Ibn Ezra." In *Abraham Ibn Ezra y su tiempo: Actas del Simposio Internacional: Madrid, Tudela,*

Toledo, 1–8 Febrero 1989, edited by Fernando Díaz Esteban, 147–54. Madrid: Universidad Autónoma de Madrid, Asociación Española de Orientalistas, 1990.

Goitein, S.D. *A Mediterranean Society: The Jewish Communities of the Arab World as Portrayed in the Documents of the Cairo Genizah. Vol. 1, Economic Foundations.* Berkeley: University of California Press, 1967.

———. *A Mediterranean Society: The Jewish Communities of the Arab World as Portrayed in the Documents of the Cairo Genizah. Vol. 2, The Community.* Berkeley: University of California Press, 1971.

———. *A Mediterranean Society: The Jewish Communities of the Arab World as Portrayed in the Documents of the Cairo Genizah. Vol. 3, The Family.* Berkeley: University of California Press, 1978.

———. *A Mediterranean Society: The Jewish Communities of the Arab World as Portrayed in the Documents of the Cairo Genizah. Vol. 4, Daily Life.* Berkeley: University of California Press, 1983.

———. *A Mediterranean Society: The Jewish Communities of the Arab World as Portrayed in the Documents of the Cairo Genizah. Vol. 5, The Individual.* Berkeley: University of California Press, 1988.

———. *A Mediterranean Society: The Jewish Communities of the Arab World as Portrayed in the Documents of the Cairo Genizah. Vol. 6, Cumulative Indices.* Berkeley: University of California Press, 1992.

Goldingay, John. "The Patriarchs in Scripture and History." In *Essays on the Patriarchal Narratives,* edited by A. R. Millard and D. J. Wiseman, 11–42. Leicester, UK: InterVarsity Press, 1980.

Goldziher, Ignaz. *Die Ẓâhiriten. Ihr Lehrsystem und ihre Geschichte: Beitrag zur Geschichte der muhammedanischen Theologie.* Leipzig, DE: Schulze, 1884.

Gonzalo Maeso, David. "Una oda de Yehudá Ha-Leví en honor del visir Ibn Nagrella." *Miscelánea de estudios Árabes y Hebraicos* 6 (1957): 189–216.

Gordis, Robert. "The Life of Professor Max Leopold Margolis: An Appreciation." In *Max Leopold Margolis: Scholar and Teacher,* edited by Robert Gordis, 1–16. New York: Bloch, 1952.

Gordon, Cyrus H. "Abraham and the Merchants of Ura." *Journal of Near Eastern Studies* 17, no. 1 (1958): 28–31.

———. "Ancient Israel and Egypt." *New York University Education Quarterly* 12 (1981): 9–13.

———. "Biblical Customs and the Nuzu Tablets." *Biblical Archaeologist* 3 (1940): 1–12.

———. "Ebla and Genesis 11." In *A Spectrum of Thought: Essays in Honor of Dennis F. Kinlaw,* edited by Michael L. Peterson, 125–34. Wilmore: Asbury College Press, 1982.

———. "Higher Critics and Forbidden Fruit." *Christianity Today* 4 (23 November 1959): 3–6.

———. "Homer and the Bible: The Origin and Character of East Mediterranean Literature." *Hebrew Union College Annual* 26 (1955): 43–108.

———. *Introduction to Old Testament Times.* Ventnor: Ventnor, 1953.

———. *New Horizons in Old Testament Literature*. Ventnor: Ventnor, 1960.

———. "The Patriarchal Age." *Journal of Bible and Religion* 21 (1953): 238–43.

———. "The Patriarchal Narratives." *Journal of Near Eastern Studies* 13 (1954): 56–59.

———. *A Scholar's Odyssey*. Atlanta, GA: Society of Biblical Literature, 2000.

———. "The Story of Jacob and Laban in the Light of the Nuzi Tablets." *Bulletin of the American Schools of Oriental Research* 66 (1937): 25–27.

———. *Ugaritic Grammar*. Rome: Pontifical Biblical Institute, 1940.

———. *Ugaritic Handbooks*. Rome: Pontifical Biblical Institute, 1947.

———. *Ugaritic Literature: A Comprehensive Translation of the Poetic and Prose Texts*. Rome: Pontifical Biblical Institute, 1949.

———. *Ugaritic Manual*. Rome: Pontifical Biblical Institute, 1955.

———. *Ugaritic Textbook*. Rome: Pontifical Biblical Institute, 1965.

Goshen-Gottstein, M. H. "The Textual Criticism of the Old Testament: Rise, Decline, Rebirth." *Journal of Biblical Literature* 102 (1983): 365–99.

Gottheil, Richard J. H. 1904. "Some Early Jewish Bible Criticism: Annual Presidential Address to the Society of Biblical Literature and Exegesis." *Journal of Biblical Literature* 23, no. 1 (1904): 1–12.

Grafton, Anthony T. "Joseph Scaliger and Historical Chronology: The Rise and Fall of a Discipline." *History and Theory* 14 (1975): 156–85.

———. *Joseph Scaliger: A Study in the History of Classical Scholarship I: Textual Criticism and Exegesis*. Oxford, UK: Oxford University Press, 1983.

———. *Joseph Scaliger: A Study in the History of Classical Scholarship II: Historical Chronology*. Oxford, UK: Oxford University Press, 1993.

———. "*Prolegomena* to Friedrich August Wolf." *Journal of the Warburg and Courtauld Institutes* 44 (1981): 101–29.

———. "Spinoza's Hermeneutics: Some Heretical Thoughts." In *Scriptural Authority and Biblical Criticism in the Dutch Golden Age: God's Word Questioned*, edited by Dirk Van Miert, Henk Nellen, Piet Steenbakkers, and Jetze Touber, 177–96. Oxford, UK: Oxford University Press, 2017.

Grant, Robert M. "Historical Criticism in the Ancient Church." *Journal of Religion* 25, no. 3 (1945): 183–96.

Greenberg, Moshe. *Ezekiel 1–20*. Garden City, NY: Doubleday, 1983.

Greenspoon, Leonard. *Max Leopold Margolis: A Scholar's Scholar*. Atlanta, GA: Scholars Press, 1987.

———. "Max Leopold Margolis: A Scholar's Scholar (A BA Portrait)." *Biblical Archaeologist* 48 (1985): 103–6.

———. "On the Jewishness of Modern Jewish Biblical Scholarship: The Case of Max L. Margolis." *Judaism* 39 (1990): 82–92.

———. "A Preliminary Publication of Max Leopold Margolis's *Andreas Masius*, together with his Discussion of Hexapla-Tetrapla." In *Origen's Hexapla and Fragments*, edited by Alison Salvesen, 39–69. Tübingen, DE: Mohr Siebeck, 1998.

Gregory, Brad S. *The Unintended Reformation: How a Religious Revolution Secularized Society*. Cambridge, MA: Harvard University Press, 2012.

Griffith, Sidney H. *The Bible in Arabic: The Scriptures of the "People of the Book" in the Language of Islam*. Princeton, NJ: Princeton University Press, 2013.

Grisanti, Michael A. "Josiah and the Composition of Deuteronomy." In *Sepher Torah Mosheh: Studies in the Composition and Interpretation of Deuteronomy*, edited by Daniel I. Block and Richard L. Schultz, 110–38. Peabody, MA: Hendrickson, 2017.

Gross, Michael B. *The War Against Catholicism: Liberalism and the Anti-Catholic Imagination in Nineteenth-Century Germany*. Ann Arbor: University of Michigan Press, 2004.

Grosse, Sven. "Renaissance-Humanismus und Reformation: Lorenzo Valla und seine Relevanz für die Kontroverse über die Willensfreiheit in der Reformationszeit." *Kerygma und Dogma* 48, no. 4 (2002): 276–300.

Grossman, Eliav. "Spinoza's Critique of Maimonides in the Context of Dutch Hebraism." *Jewish Studies Quarterly* 27 (2020): 36–57.

Grundmann, Regina. ",Die Knochen Ḥiwis, des Hündischen, sollen zermahlen warden.' Die fundamentale Traditionskritik des Ḥiwi al-Balkhi." In *Jenseits der Tradition?: Tradition und Traditionskritik in Judentum, Christentum und Islam*, edited by Regina Grundmann and Assaad Elias Kattan, 32–58. Berlin: Walter de Gruyter, 2015.

Guttmann, Jakob. "Die Bibelkritik des Chiwi Albalchi nach Saadia's Emunoth we-deoth." *Monatsschrift für Geschichte und Wissenschaft des Judentums* 28 (1879): 260–70 and 289–300.

Guttmann, Julius. "The Sources of Ḥiwi al-Balkhi." In *Alexander Marx Jubilee Volume*, edited by Saul Liebermann, 92–102. New York: Jewish Theological Society of American, 1950.

Haasler, Michael. *Heinrich Ewald und seine Auseinandersetzung mit Ernst Meier und Ferdinand Christian Baur*. Munich, DE: GRIN, 1996.

HaCohen, Ran. *Reclaiming the Hebrew Bible: German-Jewish Reception of Biblical Criticism*. Berlin: Walter de Gruyter, 2010.

Hahn, Scott W. *The Kingdom of God as Liturgical Empire: A Theological Commentary on 1–2 Chronicles*. Grand Rapids, MI: Baker Academic, 2012.

Hahn, Scott W. and Benjamin Wiker. *Politicizing the Bible: The Roots of Historical Criticism and the Secularization of Scripture 1300–1700*. New York: Herder & Herder, 2013.

Hahn, Scott W. and Jeffrey L. Morrow. *Modern Biblical Criticism as a Tool of Statecraft (1700–1900)*. Steubenville: Emmaus Academic, 2020.

Hahn, Scott Walker and John Sietze Bergsma. "What Laws Were 'Not Good'?: A Canonical Approach to the Theological Problem of Ezekiel 20:25–26." *Journal of Biblical Literature* 123, no. 2 (2004): 201–18.

Hallo, William W. "Biblical History in its Near Eastern Setting: The Contextual Approach." In *Scripture in Context: Essays on the Comparative Method*, edited by Carl D. Evans, William W. Hallo, and John B. White, 1–26. Eugene, OR: Pickwick, 1980.

———. "Compare and Contrast: The Contextual Approach to Biblical Literature." In *The Bible in the Light of Cuneiform Literature*, edited by William W. Hallo, Bruce William Jones, and Gerald L. Mattingly, 1–30. Lewiston, NY: Edwin Mellen Press, 1990.

———. "The Concept of Canonicity in Cuneiform and Biblical Literature: A Comparative Appraisal." In *The Biblical Canon in Comparative Perspective*, edited by K. Lawson Younger, Jr., William W. Hallo, and Bernard Frank Batto, 1–20. Lewiston, NY: Edwin Mellen Press, 1991.

———. "Introduction: Ancient Near Eastern Texts and Their Relevance for Biblical Exegesis." In *The Context of Scripture. Vol. 1, Canonical Compositions from the Biblical World*, edited by William W. Hallo and K. Lawson Younger, Jr., xxv–xxviii. Leiden, NL: Brill, 2002.

———. "Introduction: The Bible and the Monuments." In *The Context of Scripture. Vol. 2, Monumental Inscriptions from the Biblical World*, edited by William W. Hallo and K. Lawson Younger, Jr., xxi–xxvi. Leiden, NL: Brill, 2002

———. "The Limits of Skepticism." *Journal of the American Oriental Society* 110, no. 2 (1990): 187–99.

———. "New Directions in Historiography (Mesopotamia and Israel)." In *Dubsar antamen: Studien zur Altorientalistik: Festschrift für Willem H.Ph. Römer zur Vollendung seines 70. Lebensjahres mit Beiträgen von Freunden, Schülern und Kollegen*, edited by Manfried Dietrich and Oswald Loretz, 109–28. Münster, DE: Ugarit-Verlag, 1998

———. "New Viewpoints on Cuneiform Literature." *Israel Exploration Journal* 12, no. 1 (1962): 13–26.

———. Preface to *The World's Oldest Literature: Studies in Sumerian Belles-Lettres*, by William W. Hallo, xvii–xxi. Leiden, NL: Brill, 2010.

———. "Suche nach den Ursprüngen." In *Vergegenwärtigungen des zerstörten jüdischen Erbes. Franz-Rosenzweig-Gastvorlesungen, Kassel 1987–1998*, edited by Wolfdietrich Schmied-Kowarzik, 139–46. Kassel: Kassel University Press, 1997.

———. "Sumer and the Bible: A Matter of Proportion." In *The Future of Biblical Archaeology: Reassessing Methodologies and Assumptions: The Proceedings of a Symposium, August 12–14, 2001 at Trinity International University*, edited by James K. Hoffmeier and A. R. Millard, 163–75. Grand Rapids, MI: Eerdmans, 2004.

Hamilton, Alastair. "In Search of the Most Perfect Text: The Early Modern Printed Polyglot Bibles from Alcalá (1510–1520) to Brian Walton (1654–1658)." In *The New Cambridge History of the Bible. Vol. 3, From 1450 to 1750*, edited by Euan Cameron, 138–56. Cambridge, UK: Cambridge University Press, 2016.

———. "Scaliger the Orientalist." In *"All My Books in Foreign Tongues": Scaliger's Oriental Legacy in Leiden*, edited by Arnoud Vrolijk and Kasper van Ommen, 10–17. Leiden, NL: Leiden University Library, 2009.

Hammill, Graham. *The Mosaic Constitution: Political Theology and Imagination from Machiavelli to Milton*. Chicago: University of Chicago Press, 2012.

Haran, Menahem. "Ezekiel, P, and the Priestly School." *Vetus Testamentum* 58 (2008): 211–18.

Hardy, Nicholas. *Criticism and Confession: The Bible in the Seventeenth Century Republic of Letters*. Oxford, UK: Oxford University Press, 2017.

Hartlich, Christian and Walter Sachs. *Der Ursprung des Mythosbegriffes in der Modernen Bibelwissenschaft*. Tübingen, DE: Mohr, 1952.

Hauerwas, Stanley. *The State of the University: Academic Knowledges and the Knowledge of God*. Oxford: Blackwell, 2007.

Hayes, John H. "Wellhausen as a Historian of Israel." *Semeia* 25 (1982): 37–67.

Heintz, Jean-Georges. "Édouard Reuss, Karl Heinrich Graf et le Pentateuque." *Revue d'histoire et de philosophie religieuses* 71, no. 4 (1991): 443–57.

Hernando, Josep. "La polèmica antiislàmica i la quasi impossibilitat d'una entesa." *Anuario de Estudios Medievales* 38 (2008): 764–67.

Hess, Richard S. "The Genealogies of Genesis 1–11 and Comparative Literature." *Biblica* 70, no. 2 (1989): 241–54.

———. "Genesis 1–2 in its Literary Context." *Tyndale Bulletin* 14, no. 1 (1990): 143–53.

———. "One Hundred and Fifty Years of Comparative Studies on Genesis 1–11: An Overview." In *"I Studied Inscriptions from Before the Flood": Ancient Near Eastern, Literary, and Linguistic Approaches to Genesis 1–11*, edited by Richard S. Hess and David Toshio Tsumura, 3–26. Winona Lake, IN: Eisenbrauns, 1994.

———. "Onomastics of the Exodus Generation in the Book of Exodus." In *"Did I Not Bring Israel Out of Egypt?" Biblical, Archaeological, and Egyptological Perspectives on the Exodus Narratives*, edited by James K. Hoffmeier, Alan R. Millard, and Gary A. Rendsburg, 37–48. Winona Lake, IN: Eisenbrauns, 2016.

Hillers, Delbert R. "William F. Albright as a Philologian." In *The Scholarship of William Foxwell Albright: An Appraisal: Papers Delivered at the Symposium "Homage to William Foxwell Albright," The American Friends of the Israel Exploration Society, Rockville, Maryland, 1984*, edited by Gus W. Van Beek, 45–59. Atlanta, GA: Scholars Press, 1989.

Hirschfeld, Hartwig. "Mohammedan Criticism of the Bible." *Jewish Quarterly Review* 13, no. 2 (1901): 222–40.

Hjelm, Ingrid. "Lost and Found? A Non-Jewish Israel from the Merneptah Stele to the Byzantine Period." In *History, Archeology, and the Bible Forty Years after "Historicity,"* edited by Ingrid Hjelm and Thomas Thompson, 112–29. London: Routledge, Taylor & Francis Group, 2016.

———. "Northern Perspectives in Deuteronomy and its relation to the Samaritan Pentateuch." *Hebrew Bible and Ancient Israel* 4 (2015): 184–204.

Hoffmeier, James K. *Ancient Israel in Sinai: The Evidence for the Authenticity of the Wilderness Tradition*. Oxford, UK: Oxford University Press, 2005.

———. "Egyptian Religious Influences on the Early Hebrews." In *"Did I Not Bring Israel Out of Egypt?" Biblical, Archaeological, and Egyptological Perspectives on the Exodus Narratives*, edited by James K. Hoffmeier, Alan R. Millard, and Gary A. Rendsburg, 3–36. Winona Lake, IN: Eisenbrauns, 2016.

———. "The Exodus and Wilderness Narratives." In *Ancient Israel's History: An Introduction to Issues and Sources*, edited by Bill T. Arnold and Richard S. Hess, 46–90. Grand Rapids, MI: Baker Academic, 2014.

———. *Israel in Egypt: The Evidence for the Authenticity of the Exodus Tradition*. Oxford, UK: Oxford University Press, 1996.

———. "Some Thoughts on Genesis 1 & 2 and Egyptian Cosmology." *Journal of the Ancient Near Eastern Society* 15 (1983): 39–49.

———. "The Structure of Joshua 1–11 and the Annals of Thutmose III." In *Faith, Tradition, and History: Old Testament Historiography in Its Near Eastern Context*, edited by A. R. Millard, James K. Hoffmeier, and David W. Baker, 165–79. Winona Lake, IN: Eisenbrauns, 1994.

Hoffner, Harry A., Jr., "Ancient Israel's Literary Heritage Compared with Hittite Textual Data." In *The Future of Biblical Archaeology: Reassessing Methodologies and Assumptions: The Proceedings of a Symposium, August 12–14, 2001 at Trinity International University*, edited by James K. Hoffmeier and A. R. Millard, 176–92. Grand Rapids, MI: Eerdmans, 2004.

———. "Hittite-Israelite Cultural Parallels." In *The Context of Scripture. Vol. 3, Archival Documents from the Biblical World*, edited by William W. Hallo and K. Lawson Younger, Jr., xxix–xxxiv. Leiden, NL: Brill, 2002.

———. "Hittite *Tarpiš* and Hebrew *Terāphîm*." *Journal of Near Eastern Studies* 27, no. 1 (1968): 61–68.

———. "Some Contributions of Hittitology to Old Testament Study." *Tyndale Bulletin* 20 (1969): 27–55.

Holt, Else K. *Prophesying the Past: The Use of Israel's History in the Book of Hosea*. Sheffield, UK: Sheffield Academic Press, 1995.

Homan, Michael M. "How Moses Gained and Lost the reputation of Being the Torah's Author: Higher Criticism prior to Julius Wellhausen." In *Sacred History, Sacred Literature: Essays on Ancient Israel, the Bible, and Religion in Honor of R.E. Friedman on His Sixtieth Birthday*, edited by Shawna Dolansky, 111–31. Winona Lake, IN: Eisenbrauns, 2008.

Hornkohl, Aaron. *Ancient Hebrew Periodization and the Language of the Book of Jeremiah: The Case for a Sixth-Century Date of Composition*. Leiden, NL: Brill, 2014.

Houtman, Cees. *Der Pentateuch: Die Geschichte seiner Erforschung neben einer Auswertung*. Kampen: Pharos, 1994.

Howard, Thomas Albert. *Protestant Theology and the Making of the Modern German University*. Oxford, UK: Oxford University Press, 2006.

———. *Religion and the Rise of Historicism: W. M. L. de Wette, Jacob Burckhardt, and the Theological Origins of Nineteenth-Century Historical Consciousness*. Cambridge, UK: Cambridge University Press, 2000.

Hugenberger, Gordon P. *Marriage as Covenant: Biblical Law and Ethics as Developed from Malachi*. Leiden, NL: Brill, 1994.

Hurvitz, Avi. *A Linguistic Study of the Relationship between the Priestly Source and the Book of Ezekiel*. Paris: Gabalda, 1982.

Hwang, Jerry. "'I Am Yahweh Your God from the Land of Egypt': Hosea's Use of the Exodus Traditions." In *"Did I Not Bring Israel Out of Egypt?": Biblical, Archaeological, and Egyptological Perspectives on the Exodus Narratives*, edited by James K. Hoffmeier, Alan R. Millard, and Gary A. Rendsburg, 243–53. Winona Lake, IN: Eisenbrauns, 2016.

Isbell, Charles. "The Structure of Exodus 1:1–14." In *Art and Meaning: Rhetoric in Biblical Literature*, edited by David J. A. Clines, David M. Gunn, and Alan J. Hauser, 37–61. Sheffield, UK: JSOT Press, 1982.

Ishida, Tomoo. *The Royal Dynasties in Ancient Israel: A Study on the Formation and Development of Royal-Dynastic Ideology*. New York: de Gruyter, 1977.

Israel, Jonathan. "The Economic Contribution of Dutch Sephardim in International Trade, 1595–1713." *Tijdschrift voor geschiedenis* 96 (1983): 505–35.

———. "How Did Spinoza Declare War on Theology and Theologians?" In *Scriptural Authority and Biblical Criticism in the Dutch Golden Age: God's Word Questioned*, edited by Dirk Van Miert, Henk Nellen, Piet Steenbakkers, and Jetze Touber, 197–216. Oxford, UK: Oxford University Press, 2017.

———. "Spinoza, Radical Enlightenment, and the General Reform of the Arts in the Later Dutch Golden Age: The Aims of *Nil Volentibus Arduum*." *Intellectual History Review* 30, no. 3 (2020): 387–409.

Jacob, E. "Edouard Reuss, un théologien indépendant." *Revue d'histoire et de philosophie religieuses* 71, no. 4 (1991): 427–33.

James, Susan. *Spinoza on Philosophy, Religion, and Politics: The Theologico-Political Treatise*. Oxford, UK: Oxford University Press, 2012.

Jindo, Job Y. "Recontextualizing Yehezkel Kaufmann: His Empirical Conception of the Bible and Its Significance in Jewish Intellectual History." *Journal of Jewish Thought and Philosophy* 19, no. 2 (2011): 95–129.

———. "Revisiting Kaufmann: Fundamental Problems in Modern Biblical Scholarship." *Journal of the Interdisciplinary Study of Monotheistic Religions* 3 (2007): 41–77.

Jones, Andrew Willard. *Before Church and State: A Study of Social Order in the Sacramental Kingdom of St. Louis IX*. Steubenville: Emmaus Academic, 2017.

Jones, Harold W. "Thomas Hobbes and the Bible: A Preliminary Enquiry." In *Arts du spectacle et histoire des idées: Recueil offert en hommage à Jean Jacquot*, edited by La société des amis du CESR de Tours, 271–85. Tours: Centre d'études supérieures de la Renaissance, 1984.

Jorink, Eric. "Reading the Book of Nature in the Seventeenth-Century Dutch Republic." In *The Book of Nature in Early Modern and Modern History*, edited by Klaas van Berkel and Arjo Vanderjagt, 45–68. Leuven: Peeters, 2006.

Kaiser, Otto. "An Heir of Astruc in a Remote German University: Hermann Hupfeld and the 'New Documentary Hypothesis.'" In *Sacred Conjectures: The Context and Legacy of Robert Lowth and Jean Astruc*, edited by John Jarick, 220–48. London: T&T Clark, 2007.

———. *Zwischen Reaktion und Revolution: Hermann Hupfeld (1796–1866)—ein deutsches Professorenleben*. Göttingen, DE: Vandenhoeck & Ruprecht, 2005.

Kaiser, Walter C., Jr. "The Literary Form of Genesis 1–11." In *New Perspectives on the Old Testament*, edited by Barton Payne, 48–65. Waco, TX: Word Books, 1970.

———. *The Old Testament Documents: Are They Reliable and Relevant?* Downers Grove, IL: InterVarsity Press, 2001.

Kalimi, Isaac. *Fighting Over the Bible: Jewish Interpretation, Sectarianism and Polemic from Temple to Talmud and Beyond*. Leiden, NL: Brill, 2017.

Kaplan, Yosef. "The Portuguese Community in the Seventeenth-Century Amsterdam and the Ashkenazi World." In *Dutch Jewish History. Vol. 2,* edited by Jozeph Michman, 23–45. Assen, NL: Van Gorcum, 1989.

———. "The Portuguese Jews in Amsterdam: From Forced Conversion to a Return to Judaism." *Studia Rosenthaliana* 15 (1981): 37–51.

———. "The Social Functions of the *Herem* in the Portuguese Jewish Community of Amsterdam in the Seventeenth Century." In *Dutch Jewish History. Vol. 1,* edited by Jozeph Michman and Tirtsah Levie, 111–55. Jerusalem: Tel Aviv University, 1984.

———. "Spanish Readings of Amsterdam's Seventeenth Century Sephardim." In *Jewish Books and Their Readers: Aspects of the Intellectual Life of Christians and Jews in Early Modern Europe*, edited by Scott Mandelbrote and Joanna Weinberg, 312–41. Leiden, NL: Brill, 2016.

Kartveit, Magnar. "The Samaritan Temple and Rewritten Bible." In *Holy Places and Cult*, edited by Erkki Koskenniemi and J. Cornelis de Vos, 85–99. Studies in the Reception History of the Bible 5. Winona Lake, IN: Eisenbrauns, 2014.

Kaufmann, Yehezkel. *The Religion of Israel: From Its Beginnings to the Babylonian Exile*. Translated and abridged by Moshe Greenberg. Chicago: University of Chicago Press, 1960.

Kebede, Messay. "Eurocentrism and Ethiopian Historiography: Deconstructing Semitization." *International Journal of Ethiopian Studies* 1, no. 1 (2003): 1–19.

Keown, Gerald L., Pamela J. Scalise, and Thomas G. Smothers. *Jeremiah 26–52*. World Biblical Commentary 27. Grand Rapids: Zondervan, 1995.

Khalidi, Tarif. *Arabic Historical Thought in the Classical Period*. Cambridge, UK: Cambridge University Press, 1994.

Kikawada, Isaac M. "The Double Creation of Mankind in *Enki and Ninmah, Atrahasis* I 1–351, and *Genesis* 1–2." *Iraq* 45, no. 1 (1983): 43–45.

———. "Genesis on Three Levels." *Annual of the Japanese Biblical Institute* 7 (1981): 3–15.

———. "Literary Convention of the Primaeval History." *Annual of the Japanese Biblical Institute* 1 (1975): 3–21.

———. "Literary Conventions Connected with Antediluvian Historiography in the Ancient Near East." Ph.D. diss., University of California, Berkeley, 1979.

———. "A Quantitative Analysis of the 'Adam and Eve,' 'Cain and Abel,' and 'Noah' Stories." In *Perspectives on Language and Text: Essays and Poems in Honor of Francis I.*

Andersen's Sixtieth Birthday July 28, 1985, edited by Edgar W. Conrad and Edward G. Newing, 195–203. Winona Lake, IN: Eisenbrauns, 1987.

———. "The Shape of Genesis 11:1–9." In *Rhetorical Criticism: Essays in Honor of James Muilenburg*, edited by Jared J. Jackson and Martin Kessler, 18–32. Pittsburgh: Pickwick Press, 1974.

———. "The Unity of Genesis 12:1–9." In *Proceedings of the Sixth World Congress of Jewish Studies, held at the Hebrew University of Jerusalem 13–19 August 1973, under the auspices of the Israel Academy of Sciences and Humanities. Vol. 1,* edited by Avigdor Shinan, 229–35. Jerusalem: World Union of Jewish Studies, 1977.

Kikawada, Isaac M. and Arthur Quinn. *Before Abraham Was: The Unity of Genesis 1–11.* Nashville, TN: Abingdon Press, 1985.

Kilchör, Benjamin. "Did H Influence D on an Early or a Late Stage of the Redaction of D?" *Old Testament Essays* 29, no. 3 (2016): 502–12.

———. "The Direction of Dependence between the Laws of the Pentateuch: The Priority of a Literary Approach." *Ephemerides Theologicae Lovanienses* 89, no. 1 (2013): 1–14.

———. "Frei aber arm? Soziale Sicherheit als Schüssel zum Verhältnis der Sklavenfreilassungsgesetze im Pentateuch." *Vetus Testamentum* 62, no. 3 (2012): 381–97.

———. "Levirate Marriage in Deuteronomy 25:5–10 and Its Precursors in Leviticus and Numbers: A Test Case for the Relationship between P/H and D." *Catholic Biblical Quarterly* 77 (2015): 429–40.

———. "Sacred and Profane Space: The Priestly Character of Exodus 20:24–26 and Its Reception in Deuteronomy 12." *Bulletin for Biblical Research* 29, no. 4 (2019): 455–67.

———. "Überlegungen zum Verhältnis zwischen Levitikus 26 und Ezechiel und die tempeltheologische Relevanz der Abhängigkeitsrichtung." *Zeitschrift für altorientalisch und biblische Rechtsgeschichte* 24 (2018): 295–306.

———. "Wellhausen's Five Pillars for the Priestly Priority of D over P/H: Can They Still Be Maintained." In *Paradigm Change in Pentateuchal Research*, edited by Matthias Armgardt, Benjamin Kilchör, and Markus Zehnder, 101–11. Wiesbaden, DE: Harrassowitz, 2019.

———. *Wieder-Hergestellter Gottesdienst: Eine Deutung der zweiten Tempelvision Ezechiels (Ez 40–48) am Beispiel der Aufgaben der Priester und Leviten.* Herders Biblische Studien 95. Freiburg: Herder, 2020.

Kitchen, Kenneth A. "Ancient Egypt and the Old Testament." *Bulletin of the Anglo-Israel Archaeological Society* 11 (1991–1992): 48–51.

———. "Ancient Near Eastern Studies: Egypt." In *The Oxford Handbook of Biblical Studies*, edited by Judith M. Lieu and J.W. Rogerson, 89–98. Oxford, UK: Oxford University Press, 2006.

———. *Ancient Orient and Old Testament.* London: InterVarsity Press, 1966.

———. *The Bible in its World: The Bible and Archaeology Today.* Exeter: Paternoster Press, 1977.

———. "The Desert Tabernacle: Pure Fiction or Plausible Account?" *Bible Review* 16, no. 6 (2000): 14–21.

———. "From the Brickfields of Egypt." *Tyndale Bulletin* 27 (1976): 137–47.

———. "Genesis 12–50 in the Near Eastern World." In *He Swore an Oath: Biblical Themes from Genesis 12–50*, edited by Richard S. Hess, Gordon J. Wenham, and Philip E. Satterhwaite, 67–92. Grand Rapids, MI: Baker, 1994.

———. "The Hebrew Bible and its Critics—A Verdict from the Ancient Near East." *Bulletin of the Anglo-Israel Archaeological Society* 26 (2008): 149–50.

———. "Historical Method and Early Hebrew Tradition." *Tyndale Bulletin* 17 (1966): 63–97.

———. *In Sunshine and Shadow: An Autobiographical Sketch in a Family Context*. Liverpool: Abercromby Press, 2016.

———. "Moses: A More Realistic View." *Christianity Today* 12 (21 June 1968): 8–10.

———. "New Directions in Biblical Archaeology: Historical and Biblical Aspects." In *Biblical Archaeology Today, 1990: Proceedings of the Second International Congress on Biblical Archaeology: Jerusalem, June-July 1990*, 34–52. Jerusalem: Israel Exploration Society, 1993.

———. "The Old Testament in its Context 1: From the Origins to the Eve of the Exodus." *Theological Students' Fellowship Bulletin* 59 (1971): 2–10.

———. "The Old Testament in its Context 2: From Egypt to the Jordan." *Theological Students' Fellowship Bulletin* 60 (1971): 3–11.

———. "The Old Testament in its Context 6." *Theological Students' Fellowship Bulletin* 64 (1972): 2–10.

———. *On the Reliability of the Old Testament*. Grand Rapids, MI: Eerdmans, 2003.

———. "The Patriarchal Age: Myth or History?" *Biblical Archaeology Review* 21, no. 2 (1995): 48–57, 88, 90–92, and 94–95.

———. *Pentateuchal Criticism and Interpretation: Notes of Three Lectures Given at the Annual Conference of the Theological Students' Fellowship, held at The Hayes, Swanwick, Derbyshire from December 27 to 31, 1965*. Leicester: Theological Students' Fellowship, 1965.

———. "A Recently Published Egyptian Papyrus and its Bearing on the Joseph Story." *Tyndale Bulletin* 2 (1956–1957): 1–2.

———. Review of *Ancient Israel: A Short History from Abraham to the Roman Destruction of the Temple*, ed. Hershel Shanks. *Themelios* 15, no. 1 (1989): 25–28.

———. Review of *Joseph en Égypte. Genèse chap. 37–50 à la lumière des études égyptologiques récentes*, by Jozef Vergote. *Journal of Egyptian Archaeology* 47 (1961): 158–64.

———. Review of *A Study of the Biblical Story of Joseph*, by Donald B. Redford. *Oriens antiquus* 12 (1973): 233–42.

———. "Some Egyptian Background to the Old Testament," *Tyndale Bulletin* 5–6 (1960): 4–18.

———. "The Tabernacle—A Bronze Age Artifact," *Eretz-Israel* 24 (1993): 119–29.

Kitchen, Kenneth A. and Paul J.N. Lawrence. *Treaty, Law and Covenant in the Ancient Near East Part 1: The Texts*. Wiesbaden, DE: Harrassowitz, 2012.

———. *Treaty, Law and Covenant in the Ancient Near East Part 2: Text, Notes and Chromograms*. Wiesbaden, DE: Harrassowitz, 2012.

———. *Treaty, Law and Covenant in the Ancient Near East Part 3: Overall Historical Survey*. Wiesbaden, DE: Harrassowitz, 2012.

Knibb, Michael A. "Temple and Cult in Apocryphal and Pseudepigraphal Writings from Before the Common Era." In *Temple and Worship in Biblical Israel*, edited by John Day, 401–16. London: T&T Clark, 2007.

Knoppers, Gary. *Jews and Samaritans: The Origins and History of their Early Relations*. New York: Oxford University Press, 2013.

———. "Mt. Gerizim and Mt. Zion: A Study in the Early History of the Samaritans and Jews." *Studies in Religion* 34 (2005): 309–38.

———. "When the Foreign Monarch Speaks about the Israelite Tabernacle." In *History, Memory, Hebrew Scriptures: A Festschrift for Ehud Ben Zvi*, edited by Ian Douglas Wilson and Diana V. Edelman, 49–63. Winona Lake, IN: Eisenbrauns, 2015.

Koen, E.M. "The Earliest Sources Relating to the Portuguese Jews in the Municipal Archives of Amsterdam up to 1620." *Studia Rosenthaliana* 4 (1970): 25–42.

Kofsky, Aryeh. *Eusebius of Caesarea Against Paganism*. Leiden, NL: Brill, 2000.

Konkel, Michael. *Architektonik des Heiligen: Studien zur zweiten Tempelvision Ezekchiels (Ez. 40–48). Bonner Biblische Beiträge 129*. Berlin: Philo, 2001.

———. "Ezekiel 40–48 and P: Questions and Perspectives." Paper given at the Sociey of Biblical Literature Annual Meeting, San Diego, Nov. 22, 2014.

———. Review of *The Book of Ezekiel: Chapters 25–48*, by Daniel I. Block. *Biblische Zeitschrift* 44 (2000): 296–98.

Krapf, Thomas M. "Yehezkel Koifman: An Outline of his Life and Work." In *Yehezkel Kaufmann and the Reinvention of Jewish Biblical Scholarship*, edited by Job Y. Jindo, Benjamin D. Sommer, and Thomas Staubli, 3–44. Fribourg: Academic Press; Göttingen, DE: Vandenhoeck & Ruprecht, 2017.

Kratz, Reinhard G. "Eyes and Spectacles: Wellhausen's Method of Higher Criticism." *Journal of Theological Studies* 60, no. 2 (2009): 381–402.

Kraus, Hans-Joachim. *Geschichte der historisch-kritischen Erforschung des Alten Testaments von der Reformation bis zur Gegenwart*. NeukircheCn: Erziehungsvereins, 1956.

———. *The Theology of the Psalms*. Translated by Keith Crim. Minneapolis, MN: Fortress Press, 1992.

Kritzeck, James. *Peter the Venerable and Islam*. Princeton, NJ: Princeton University Press, 1964.

Kromhout, David and Irene E. Zwiep. "God's Word Confirmed: Authority, Truth, and the Text of the Early Modern Jewish Bible." In *Scriptural Authority and Biblical Criticism in the Dutch Golden Age: God's Word Questioned*, edited by Dirk Van Miert, Henk Nellen, Piet Steenbakkers, and Jetze Touber, 133–54. Oxford, UK: Oxford University Press, 2017.

Kugel, James L. *How to Read the Bible: A Guide to Scripture, Then and Now*. New York: Free Press, 2007.

Kuhn, Thomas S. *The Structure of Scientific Revolutions*. Chicago: University of Chicago Press, 1962.

Kurtz, Paul Michael. "Waiting at Nemi: Wellhausen, Gunkel, and the World Behind Their Work." *Harvard Theological Review* 109, no. 4 (2016): 567–85.

———. "The Way of War: Wellhausen, Israel, and Bellicose *Reiche*." *Zeitschrift für die alttestamentliche Wissenschaft* 127, no. 1 (2015): 1–19.

Kuyvenhoven, Rosalie. "Jeremiah 23:1–8: Shepherds in Diachronic Perspective." In *Paratext and Megatext as Channels of Jewish and Christian Traditions: The Textual Markers of Contextualization*, edited by A.A. den Hollander, U.B. Schmid, and W. F. Smelik, 1–24. Leiden, NL: Brill, 2003.

Kwon, JiSeong James. "Re-Examining the Torah in the Book of Isaiah." *Revue biblique* 126 (2019): 547–64.

La Peyrère, Isaac. *Prae-Adamitae. Sive Exercitatio super Versibus duodecimo, decimotertio, & decimoquarto, capitis quinti Epistolae D. Pauli ad Romanos. Quibus Inducuntur Primi Homines ante Adamum conditi*. n.p., 1655.

———. *Systema Theologicum, ex Prae–Adamitarum Hypothesi. Pars Prima*. n.p., 1655.

———. *A Theological Systeme Upon that Presupposition, That Men were before Adam. The First Part*. London: n.p., 1655.

Laato, Antti. "The Cult Site on Mount Ebal: A Biblical Tradition Rewritten and Reinterpreted." In *Holy Places and Cult*, edited by Erkki Koskenniemi and J. Cornelis de Vos, 51–84. Studies in the Reception History of the Bible 5. Winona Lake, IN: Abo Akademi University/Eisenbrauns, 2014.

Labow, Dagmar. *Flavius Josephus, Contra Apionem, Buch I: Einleitung, Text, Textkritischer Apparat, Übersetzung und Kommentar*. Stuttgart: Kohlhammer, 2005.

Lacarra Ducay, María Jesús. *Pedro Alfonso*. Zaragoza: Diputación General de Aragón, 1991.

Lameer, Joep. "Ibn Ḥazm's Logical Pedigree." In *Ibn Hazm of Cordoba: The Life and Works of a Controversial Thinker*, edited by Camilla Adang, Maribel Fierro, and Sabine Schmidtke, 417–28. Leiden, NL: Brill, 2013.

Lazarus-Yafeh, Hava. *Intertwined Worlds: Medieval Islam and Bible Criticism*. Princeton, NJ: Princeton University Press, 1992.

———. "Some Neglected Aspects of Medieval Polemics against Christianity." *Harvard Theological Review* 89, no. 1 (1996): 61–84.

———. "Taḥrīf and Thirteen Scrolls of Torah." *Jerusalem Studies in Arabic and Islam* 19 (1995): 81–88.

———. "*Tajdīd al-Dīn*: A Reconsideration of Its Meaning, Roots, and Influence in Islam." In *Studies in Islamic and Judaic Traditions: Papers Presented at the Institute for Islamic-Judaic Studies*, edited by William M. Brinner and Stephen D. Ricks, 99–108. Atlanta, GA: Scholars Press, 1986.

Leathes, Stanely. *The Law in the Prophets*. London: Eyre and Spottiswoode, 1891.

Legaspi, Michael C. *The Death of Scripture and the Rise of Biblical Studies*. Oxford, UK: Oxford University Press, 2010.

Lehner, Ulrich L. *The Catholic Enlightenment: The Forgotten History of a Global Movement.* Oxford, UK: Oxford University Press, 2016.

Lemche, Niels Peter "The Manumission of Slaves—The Fallow Year—The Sabbatical Year—The Jobel Year." *Vetus Testamentum* 26 (1976): 38–59.

Lemoine, Michel. "Abélard et les juifs." *Revue des études juives* 153 (1994): 253–67.

Lenzi, Alan. "Scribal Revision and Textual Variation in Akkadian *Šuila*-Prayers: Two Case Studies in Ritual Adaptation." In *Empirical Models Challenging Biblical Criticism*, ed. Raymond F. Person, Jr. and Robert Rezetko, 63–108. Atlanta, GA: SBL Press, 2016.

Levenson, Jon D. "The Eighth Principle of Judaism and the Literary Simultaneity of Scripture." *Journal of Religion* 68, no. 2 (1988): 205–25.

———. *The Hebrew Bible, the Old Testament, and Historical Criticism: Jews and Christians in Biblical Studies.* Louisville, KY: Westminster/John Knox, 1993.

———. "Response." In *The State of Jewish Studies*, ed. Shaye J.D. Cohen and Edward L. Greenstein, 47–54. Wayne State University Press, 1990.

———. *Sinai & Zion: An Entry into the Jewish Bible.* San Francisco: Harper One, 1985.

———. *Theology of the Program of Restoration of Ezekiel 40–48.* Missoula: Scholars Press, 1976.

Levine, Baruch. *Numbers 1–20: A New Translation with Introduction and Commentary.* New York: Doubleday, 1993.

Levinson, Bernard M. "Zedekiah's Release of Slaves as the Babylonians Besiege Jerusalem: Jeremiah 34 and the Formation of the Pentateuch." In *The Fall of Jerusalem and the Rise of the Torah*, edited by Dominik Markl, Jean-Pierre Sonnet, and Peter Dubovský, 315–27. Tübingen, DE: Mohr Siebeck, 2016.

Levitt Kohn, Risa. *A New Heart and a New Soul: Ezekiel, the Exile, and the Torah.* Sheffield, UK: Sheffield Academic Press, 2002.

———. "A Prophet Like Moses? Rethinking Ezekiel's Relationship to the Torah." *Zeitschrift für die alttestamentliche Wissenschaft* 114 (2002): 236–54.

Lewis, Bernard. *The Jews of Islam.* Princeton, NJ: Princeton University Press, 1984.

Liebeschutz, Hans. "The Significance of Judaism in Peter Abelard's Dialogue." *Journal of Jewish Studies* 12 (1961): 1–18.

Lieu, Judith M. *Marcion and the Making of a Heretic: God and Scripture in the Second Century.* Cambridge, UK: Cambridge University Press, 2015.

Linde, J. Cornelia. "Lorenzo Valla and the Authenticity of Sacred Texts." *Humanistica Lovaniensia* 60 (2011): 35–63.

Lipschits, Oded. "Ramat Rachel between Jerusalem and Mizpah." Paper presented at the Society of Biblical Literature Annual Meeting, Boston, MA, Nov. 11, 2017.

Ljamai, Abdelilah. *Ibn Ḥazm et la polémique islamo-chrétienne dans l'histoire de l'islam.* Leiden, NL: Brill, 2003.

Lomba Fuentes, Joaquín. "El marco cultural de Pedro Alfonso." In *Estudios sobre Pedro Alfonso de Huesca*, edited by María Jesús Lacarra Ducay, 181–230. Huesca: Instituto de Estudios Altoaragoneses, 1996.

Long, Burke O. "Mythic Trope in the Autobiography of William Foxwell Albright." *Biblical Archaeologist* 56, no. 1 (1993): 36–45.

López Fonseca, Antonio and José Manuel Ruiz Vila. "Alfonso Fernández de Madrigal traductor del Génesis: una interpolación en la traducción *De las crónicas o tienpos* de Eusebio-Jerónimo." *eHumanista* 41 (2019): 360–82.

Loskoutoff, Yvan. "L'arrestation et la conversion d'Isaac de La Peyrère d'après les sources romaines (1656–1657)." *Revue de l'histoire des religions* 236, no. 3 (2019): 545–75.

Low, Maggie. *Mother Zion in Deutero-Isaiah*. New York: Peter Lang, 2013.

Löwenbrück, Anna-Ruth. "Johann David Michaelis et les débuts de la critique biblique." In *Le siècle des Lumières et la Bible*, edited by Yvon Belaval and Dominique Bourel, 113–28. Paris: Beauchesne, 1986.

Lubetski, Meir and Claire Gottlieb. "'Forever Gordon': Portrait of a Master Scholar with a Global Perspective." *Biblical Archaeologist* 59, no. 1 (1996): 2–12.

Lyons, Michael A. *From Law to Prophecy: Ezekiel's Use of the Holiness Code*. New York: T & T Clark, 2009.

———. *An Introduction to the Study of Ezekiel*. London: Bloomsbury T&T Clark, 2015.

Machinist, Peter. "The Road Not Taken: Wellhausen and Assyriology." In *Homeland and Exile: Biblical and Ancient Near Eastern Studies in Honour of Bustenay Oded*, edited by Gershon Galil, Mark Geller, and Alan Millard, 469–531. Leiden, NL: Brill, 2009.

———. "William Foxwell Albright: The Man and His Work." In *The Study of the Ancient Near East in the Twenty-First Century: The William Foxwell Albright Centennial Conference*, edited by Jerrold S. Cooper and Glenn M. Schwartz, 385–403. Winona Lake, IN: Eisenbrauns, 1996.

Machinist, Peter and Piotr Michalowski. "Introduction: William Hallo and Assyriological, Biblical, and Jewish Studies." In *The World's Oldest Literature: Studies in Sumerian Belles-Lettres*, by William W. Hallo, xxiii–xxxii. Leiden, NL: Brill, 2010.

Maier, Johann. *The Temple Scrolls: An Introduction, Translation & Commentary. Journal for the Study of the Old Testament* Supplement 34. Sheffield: JSOT Press, 1985.

Maier, Paul L. Foreword to *The Light of Discovery: Studies in Honor of Edwin M. Yamauchi*, edited by John D. Wineland, xi–xiv. Eugene, OR: Pickwick, 2007.

Malcolm, Noel. *Aspects of Hobbes*. Oxford: Clarendon Press, 2002.

———. ed. *Thomas Hobbes: Leviathan. Vol. 2, The English and Latin Texts (i)*. Oxford, UK: Oxford University Press, 2012.

———. ed. *Thomas Hobbes: Leviathan. Vol. 3, The English and Latin Texts (ii)*. Oxford, UK: Oxford University Press, 2012.

Malet, André. *Le traité théologico-politique de Spinoza et la pensée biblique*. Paris: Société les belles lettres, 1966.

Malherbe, Michel. "Hobbes et la Bible." In *Le Grand Siècle et la Bible*, edited by Jean-Robert Armogathe, 691–99. Paris: Beauchesne, 1989.

Malter, Henry. *Saadia Gaon: His Life and Works*. Philadelphia, PA: Jewish Publication Society of America, 1921.

Mandelbrote, Scott. "The Old Testament and Its Ancient Versions in Manuscript and Print in the West, from *c.* 1480 to *c.* 1780." In *The New Cambridge History of the Bible. Vol. 3, From 1450 to 1750*, edited by Euan Cameron, 82–109. Cambridge, UK: Cambridge University Press, 2016.

Mandonnet, Pierre-Félix. "Pierre le Vénérable et son activité contre l'Islam." *Revue Thomiste* 1 (1893): 328–42.

Marblestone, Howard. "A 'Mediterranean Synthesis': Professor Cyrus H. Gordon's Contributions to the Classics." *Biblical Archaeologist* 59, no. 1 (1996): 22–30.

Marchand, Suzanne L. *German Orientalism in the Age of Empire: Religion, Race, and Scholarship*. Cambridge, UK: Cambridge University Press, 2009.

Marmorstein, Arthur. "The Background of the Haggadah." *Hebrew Union College Annual* 6 (1929): 141–204.

Marsden, George M. *Fundamentalism and American Culture*. New ed. Oxford, UK: Oxford University Press, 2006.

Martel, James R. "Hobbes and Spinoza on Scriptural Interpretation, the Hebrew Republic and the Deconstruction of Sovereignty." In *Spinoza's Authority. Vol. 2, Resistance and Power in the Political Treatises*, edited by A. Kiarina Kordela and Dimitris Vardoulakis, 67–100. London: Bloomsbury Academic, 2018.

Martin, W.J. *Stylistic Criteria and the Analysis of the Pentateuch*. London: Tyndale House, 1955.

Martín Nieto, Evaristo. "Los Libros Deuteronómicos del Antiguo Testamento según 'El Tostado', Alonso de Madrigal." *Estudios Abulenses* 1 (1954): 56–74.

Martinez Gros, Gabriel. "Ibn Hazm contre les Juifs: un bouc émissaire jusq'au jugement dernier." *Atalaya* 5 (1994): 123–34.

Maxfield, John A. "Prophets and Apostles at the Professor's Lectern: Martin Luther's Lectures on Genesis (1535–1545) and the Formation of Evangelical Identity." Ph.D. diss., Princeton Theological Seminary, 2004.

McAuliffe, Jane Dammen. "The Genre Boundaries of Qur'anic Commentary." In *With Reverence for the Word: Medieval Scriptural Exegesis in Judaism, Christianity, and Islam*, edited by Jane Dammen McAuliffe, Barry D. Walfish, and Joseph W. Goering, 445–61. Oxford, UK: Oxford University Press, 2003.

McClelland, Charles E. *State, Society, and University in Germany 1700–1914*. Cambridge, UK: Cambridge University Press, 1980.

McConville, J. Gordon. *Grace in the End: A Study in Deuteronomic Theology*. Grand Rapids: Zondervan, 1993.

McKenzie, Steven L. *1–2 Chronicles*. Nashville, TN: Abingdon, 2004.

McLaughlin, Mary Martin, ed. *The Letters of Heloise and Abelard: A Translation of Their Collected Correspondence and Related Writings*. Translated by Mary Martin McLaughlin. With Bonnie Wheeler. New York: Palgrave Macmillan, 2009.

Meade, C. Wade. *Road to Babylon: Development of U.S. Assyriology*. Leiden, NL: Brill, 1974.

Mews, Constant J. "Abelard and Heloise on Jews and *hebraica veritas.*" *Christian Attitudes Toward the Jews in the Middle Ages: A Casebook*, edited by Michael Frassetto, 83–108. London: Routledge, 2007.

———. "Peter Abelard and the Enigma of Dialogue." *Beyond the Persecuting Society: Religious Toleration Before the Enlightenment*, edited by John Christian Laursen and Cary Nederman, 25–52. Philadelphia, PA: University of Pennsylvania Press, 1998.

Mews, Constant J. and Micha J. Perry. "Peter Abelard, Heloise and Jewish Biblical Exegesis in the Twelfth Century." *Journal of Ecclesiastical History* 62, no. 1 (2011): 3–19.

Milgrom, Jacob. *Leviticus 17–22: A New Translation with Introduction and Commentary.* New York: Doubleday, 2000.

———. "Leviticus 26 and Ezekiel." In *The Quest for Context and Meaning: Studies in Biblical Intertextuality in Honor of James A. Sanders*, edited by Craig A. Evans and Shemaryahu Talmon, 57–62. Leiden, NL: Brill, 1997.

———. *Numbers.* JPS Torah Commentary. Philadelphia: Jewish Publication Society, 1990.

Millard, Alan R. "Archaeology." In *Dictionary for Theological Interpretation of the Bible*, edited by Kevin J. Vanhoozer, Craig G. Bartholomew, Daniel J. Treier, and N.T. Wright, 60–63. Grand Rapids, MI: Baker Academic, 2005.

———. "Archaeology and Ancient Israel." *Faith and Thought* 108 (1981): 53–62.

———. "Archaeology and the Reliability of the Bible." *Evangel* (Summer 1991): 22–25.

———. *The Bible BC: What Can Archaeology Prove?* Leicester, UK: InterVarsity Press, 1977.

———. "Books in the Late Bronze Age in the Levant." *Israel Oriental Studies* 18 (1998): 171–81.

———. "Deuteronomy and Ancient Hebrew History Writing in Light of Ancient Chronicles and Treaties." In *For Our Good Always: Studies on the Message and Influence of Deuteronomy in Honor of Daniel I. Block*, edited by Jason S. DeRouchie, Jason Gile, and Kenneth J. Turner, 3–15. Winona Lake, IN: Eisenbrauns, 2013.

———. *Discoveries from Bible Times: Archaeological Treasures Throw Light on the Bible.* Oxford: Lion, 1985.

———. "Donald John Wiseman 1918–2010." *Proceedings of the British Academy* 172 (2011): 379–93.

———. "Die Geschichte Israels auf dem Hintergrund der Religionsgeschichte des alten Vorderen Orients." In *Israel in Geschichte und Gegenwart*, edited by Gerhard Maier, 25–42. Wuppertal: R. Brockhaus; Giessen & Basel, CH: Brunnen, 1996.

———. "How Can Archaeology Contribute to the Study of the Bible?" *Evangel* (Spring 1991): 9–12.

———. "How Reliable is Exodus?" *Biblical Archaeology Review* 26, no. 4 (2000): 50–57.

———. "Methods of Studying the Patriarchal Narratives as Ancient Texts." In *Essays on the Patriarchal Narratives*, edited by A. R. Millard and D.J. Wiseman, 43–58. Leicester, UK: InterVarsity Press, 1980.

———. "A New Babylonian 'Genesis' Story." *Tyndale Bulletin* 18 (1967): 3–18.

———. "On Giving the Bible a Fair Go." *Buried History* 35, no. 4 (1999): 5–12.

——. "Ramesses Was Here . . . And Others Too!" In *Ramesside Studies in Honour of K.A. Kitchen*, edited by Mark Collier and Steven Snape, 305–12. Bolton, UK: Rutherford Press, 2011.

——. "The Tablets in the Ark." In *Reading the Law: Studies in Honour of Gordon J. Wenham*, edited by J. G. McConville and Karl Möller, 254–66. New York: T&T Clark, 2007.

——. "The Text of the Old Testament." In *A Bible Commentary for Today*, edited by G. C. D. Howley, F. F. Bruce, and H. L. Ellison, 27–39. London: Pickering & Inglis, 1979.

——. "Were the Israelites Really Canaanites?" In *Israel—Ancient Kingdom or Late Invention?*, edited by Daniel I. Block, 156–68. Nashville, TN: B&H Academic, 2008.

——. "Where Was Abraham's Ur: The Case for the Babylonian City." *Biblical Archaeology Review* 27, no. 3 (2001): 52–53, 57.

Millard, A. R. and D.J. Wiseman, ed. *Essays on the Patriarchal Narratives*. Leicester, UK: InterVarsity Press, 1980.

Miller, Patrick D. "Sin and Judgment in Jeremiah 34:17–19." *Journal of Biblical Literature* 103 (1984): 611–23.

Miller, Peter N. *Peiresc's Orient: Antiquarianism as Cultural History in the Seventeenth Century*. London: Routledge, 2012.

Milstein, Sara J. "Outsourcing Gilgamesh." In *Empirical Models Challenging Biblical Criticism*, edited by Raymond F. Person, Jr. and Robert Rezetko, 37–62. Atlanta, GA: SBL Press, 2016.

Minnis, Alastair J. "Fifteenth-Century Versions of Thomistic Literalism: Girolamo Savonarola and Alfonso de Madrigal." In *Neue Richtungen in der hoch-und spätmittelalterlichen Bibelexegese*, edited by Robert E. Lerner and Elisabeth Müller-Luckner, 163–80. Munich, DE: Oldenbourg, 1996.

Mirri, F. Saverio. *Richard Simon e il metodo storico-critico di B. Spinoza. Storia di un libro e di una polemica sulla sfondo delle lotte politico–religiose della Francia di Luigi XIV*. Florence: Felice Le Monnier, 1972.

Mitchell, T. C. "Archaeology and Genesis i–xi." *Faith and Thought* 91 (1959): 28–49.

——. *Biblical Archaeology: Documents from the British Museum*. Cambridge, UK: Cambridge University Press, 1988.

Moll, Sebastian. *The Arch-Heretic Marcion*. Tübingen, DE: Mohr Siebeck, 2010.

Momigliano, Arnaldo. "Religious History Without Frontiers: J. Wellhausen, U. Wilamowitz, and E. Schwartz." *History and Theory* 21, no. 4 (1982): 49–64.

Monferrer Sala, Juan Pedro. "Ibn Ḥazm: Biography." In *Christian-Muslim Relations: A Bibliographical History. Vol. 3, (1050–1200)*, edited by David Thomas and Alex Mallett, 137–39. Leiden, NL: Brill, 2011.

——. "Ibn Ḥazm: Works on Christian-Muslim Relations: *Kitāb al-fiṣal fī l-milal wa-l-ahwā' wa-l-niḥal*, 'Judgement regarding the confessions, inclinations and sects.'" In *Christian-Muslim Relations: A Bibliographical History. Vol. 3, (1050–1200)*, edited by David Thomas and Alex Mallett, 141–43. Leiden, NL: Brill, 2011.

Moreau, Pierre-François. "L'interpretation de l'Ecriture." In *Thomas Hobbes: philosophie première, théorie de la science et politique,* edited by Yves Charles Zarka and Jean Bernhardt, 361–80. Paris: Presses universitaires de France, 1990.

Morrison, Martha A. "A Continuing Adventure: Cyrus Gordon and Mesopotamia." *Biblical Archaeologist* 59, no. 1 (1996): 31–35.

Morrow, Jeffrey L. *Alfred Loisy and Modern Biblical Studies.* Washington, DC: The Catholic University of America Press, 2019.

———. "Bea, Augustin Cardinal (1881–1968)." In *The Encyclopedia of Christian Civilization. Vol. 1,* edited by George Thomas Kurian, 217–18. Oxford: Wiley-Blackwell, 2011.

———. "Faith, Reason and History in Early Modern Catholic Biblical Interpretation: Fr. Richard Simon and St. Thomas More." *New Blackfriars* 96 (2015): 658–73.

———. "French Apocalyptic Messianism: Isaac La Peyrère and Political Biblical Criticism in the Seventeenth Century." *Toronto Journal of Theology* 27, no. 2 (2011): 203–13.

———. *Liturgy and Sacrament, Mystagogy and Martyrdom: Essays in Theological Exegesis.* Eugene, OR: Pickwick, 2020.

———. "Methods of Interpreting Scripture and Nature: The Influence of the Baconian Method on Spinoza's Bible Criticism." In *Studies in the History of Exegesis,* edited by Mark W. Elliott, Raleigh C. Heth, and Angela Zautcke, 157–73. Tübingen: Mohr Siebeck, 2022.

———. *Pretensions of Objectivity: Toward a Criticism of Biblical Criticism.* Eugene, OR: Pickwick, 2019.

———. "Spinoza and the Theo-Political Implications of his Freedom to Philosophize." *New Blackfriars* 99 (2018): 374–87.

———. *Theology, Politics, and Exegesis: Essays on the History of Modern Biblical Criticism.* Eugene, OR: Pickwick, 2017.

———. *Three Skeptics and the Bible: La Peyrère, Hobbes, Spinoza, and the Reception of Modern Biblical Criticism.* Eugene, OR: Pickwick, 2016.

———. "Yamauchi, Edwin Masao (b. 1937)." In *The Encyclopedia of Christian Civilization. Vol. 4,* edited by George Thomas Kurian, 2549–50. Oxford: Wiley-Blackwell, 2011.

Mulder, M.J. "Abraham Kuenen (1828–1891)." In *Abraham Kuenen (1828–1891): His Major Contributions to the Study of the Old Testament: A Collection of Old Testament Studies Published on the Occasion of the Centenary of Abraham Kuenen's Death (10 December 1991),* edited by P.B. Dirksen and A. Van Der Kooij, 1–7. Leiden, NL: Brill, 1993.

Müller, Sascha. *Kritik und Theologie: christliche Glaubens-und Schrifthermeneutik nach Richard Simon (1638–1712).* St. Ottilien: EOS, 2004.

———. *Richard Simon (1638–1712) Exeget, Theologe, Philosoph und Historiker.* Bamberg: Echter, 2006.

Munro, J. Iverach. *The Samaritan Pentateuch and Modern Criticism.* London: James Nisbet & Co., 1911.

Murphy-O'Connor, Jerome. "The Teacher of Righteousness." In *The Anchor Bible Dictionary. Vol. 6,* edited by David Noel Freedman, 340–41. New York: Doubleday, 1992.

Murray, Luke. *Jesuit Biblical Studies after Trent: Franciscus Toletus & Cornelius A Lapide.* Göttingen, DE: Vandenhoeck & Ruprecht, 2019.

———. "Jesuit Hebrew Studies After Trent: Cornelius a Lapide (1567–1637)." *Journal of Jesuit Studies* 4, no. 1 (2017): 76–97.

Myers, Jacob M. *1 Chronicles.* New York: Doubleday, 1965.

Myers, Sir John L. *Homer and His Critics.* Ed. Dorothea Gray. London: Routledge, 2014 (1958).

Nadler, Steven. "The Bible Hermeneutics of Baruch de Spinoza." In *Hebrew Bible/ Old Testament: The History of Its Interpretation. Vol.2, From the Renaissance to the Enlightenment,* edited by Magne Sæbø, 827–36. Göttingen, DE: Vandenhoeck & Ruprecht, 2008.

———. *A Book Forged in Hell: Spinoza's Scandalous Treatise and the Birth of the Secular Age.* Princeton, NJ: Princeton University Press, 2011.

Nahkola, Aulikki. *Double Narratives in the Old Testament: The Foundations of Method in Biblical Criticism.* Berlin: Walter de Gruyter, 2001.

———. "The *Memoires* of Moses and the Genesis of Method in Biblical Criticism: Astruc's Contribution." In *Sacred Conjectures: The Context and Legacy of Robert Lowth and Jean Astruc,* edited by John Jarick, 204–19. London: T&T Clark, 2007.

Naor, Bezalel. *Ma'amar al Yishma'el/Rabbi Solomon ben Abraham ibn Adret's Mitsvat Hashem Barah/An Elucidation of the Seven Noahide Commandments: With an Introduction and Notes.* Spring Valley: Orot, 2008.

Nauta, Lodi. "Lorenzo Valla and Quattrocento Scepticism." *Vivarium* 44, no. 2 (2006): 375–95.

———. "Lorenzo Valla and the Rise of Humanistic Dialectic." In *The Cambridge Companion to Renaissance Philosophy,* edited by James Hankins, 193–210. Cambridge, UK: Cambridge University Press, 2007.

Navarro Peiró, Angeles. "Semel Ibn Nagrella y Moshe Ibn 'Ezra: La vida, la muerte y el tiempo." *Boletín de la Institución Libre de Enseñanza* 11 (1991): 59–72.

Neef, Heinz-Dieter. *Die Heilstraditionen Israels in der Verkündigung des Propheten Hosea.* Berlin: Walter de Gruyter, 1987.

Nellen, Henk and Piet Steenbakkers. "Biblical Philology in the Long Seventeenth Century: New Orientations." In *Scriptural Authority and Biblical Criticism in the Dutch Golden Age: God's Word Questioned,* edited by Dirk Van Miert, Henk Nellen, Piet Steenbakkers, and Jetze Touber, 16–57. Oxford, UK: Oxford University Press, 2017.

Nicholson, Ernest. *The Pentateuch in the Twentieth Century: The Legacy of Julius Wellhausen.* Oxford, UK: Oxford University Press, 1998.

Nihan, Christophe. "Cult Centralization and the Torah Traditions in Chronicles." In *The Fall of Jerusalem and the Rise of Torah,* edited by Peter Dubovský, Dominik Markl, and Jean-Pierre Sonnet, 253–88. Forschungen zum Alten Testament 107. Tübingen, DE: Mohr Siebeck, 2016.

———. *From Priestly Torah to Pentateuch: A Study in the Composition of the Book of Leviticus.* Tübingen, DE: Mohr Siebeck, 2007.

———. "The Torah between Samaria and Judah: Shechem and Gerizim in Deuteronomy and Joshua." In *The Pentateuch as Torah: New Models for Understanding Its Promulgation and Acceptance,* edited by Gary N. Knoppers and Bernard M. Levinson, 187–223. Winona Lake, IN: Eisenbrauns, 2007.

Niskanen, Paul V. *Isaiah 56–66.* Collegeville, MN: Liturgical Press, 2014.

Nodet, Etienne. "Israelites, Samaritans, Temples, Jews." In *Samaria, Samarians, Samaritans: Studies on Bible, History and Linguistics,* edited by József Zsengellér, 121–71. Studia Judaica 66. Studia Samaritana 6. Berlin: De Gruyter, 2011.

———. *A Search for the Origins of Judaism: From Joshua to the Mishnah.* Translated by Ed Crowley. Sheffield, UK: Sheffield Academic Press, 1997.

Nöldeke, Theodor. *Untersuchungen zur Kritik des Alten Testaments.* Kiel: Schwers, 1869.

Noonan, Benjamin J. "Egyptian Loanwords as Evidence for the Authenticity of the Exodus and Wilderness Traditions." In *"Did I Not Bring Israel Out of Egypt?" Biblical, Archaeological, and Egyptological Perspectives on the Exodus Narratives,* edited by James K. Hoffmeier, Alan R. Millard, and Gary A. Rendsburg, 49–68. Winona Lake, IN: Eisenbrauns, 2016.

Noth, Martin. *Überlieferungsgeschichtliche Studien: Die sammelnden und bearbeitenden Geschichtswerke im Alten Testament.* Tübingen: M. Niemeyer, 1957. In English: *The Deuteronomistic History.* Journal for the Study of the Old Testament Supplement 15. Sheffield: University of Sheffield, 1981.

Nothaft, C. Philipp E. "Josephus and New Testament Chronology in the Work of Joseph Scaliger." *International Journal of the Classical Tradition* 23, no. 3 (2016): 246–51.

Novick, Peter. *That Noble Dream: The "Objectivity Question" and the American Historical Profession.* Cambridge, UK: Cambridge University Press, 1988.

Olszowy-Schlanger, Judith. "The Science of Language among Medieval Jews." In *Science in Medieval Jewish Cultures,* edited by Gad Freudenthal, 359–424. Cambridge, UK: Cambridge University Press, 2011.

O'Neill, J. C. *The Bible's Authority: A Portrait Gallery of Thinkers from Lessing to Bultmann.* Edinburgh: T&T Clark, 1991.

Orfali Leví, Moisés. "Abraham Ibn Ezra crítico de los exégetas de la Biblia." In *Abraham Ibn Ezra y su tiempo: Actas del Simposio Internacional: Madrid, Tudela, Toledo, 1–8 Febrero 1989,* edited by Fernando Díaz Esteban, 225–32. Madrid: Universidad Autónoma de Madrid, Asociación Española de Orientalistas, 1990.

———. "Anthropomorphism in the Christian Reproach of the Jews in Spain (12th–15th century)." *Immanuel* 19 (1984–1985): 60–73.

Orlinsky, Harry M. "Margolis' Work in the Septuagint." In *Max Leopold Margolis: Scholar and Teacher,* edited by Robert Gordis, 35–44. New York: Bloch, 1952.

Ormsby, Eric. "Ibn Ḥazm." In *The Literature of Al-Andalus,* edited by María Rosa Menocal, Raymond P. Scheindlin, and Michael Sells, 237–51. Cambridge, UK: Cambridge University Press, 2000.

Oropeza, B. J., and Steve Moyise, eds. *Exploring Intertextuality: Diverse Strategies for New Testament Interpretation of Texts*. Eugene, OR: Wipf & Stock, 2016.

Osier, Jean Pierre. "L'herméneutique de Hobbes et de Spinoza." *Studia Spinozana* 3 (1987): 319–47.

Pacchi, Arrigo. "*Leviathan* and Spinoza's *Tractatus* on Revelation: Some Elements for a Comparison." *History of European Ideas* 10, no. 5 (1989): 577–93.

Parente, Fausto. "La *Urgeschichte* di J. G. Eichhorn e l'applicazione del concetto di «mito» al Vecchio Testamento." *Annali della Scuola Normale Superiore di Pisa* 16, no. 2 (1986): 535–67.

Parkin, Jon. "The Reception of Hobbes's *Leviathan*." In *The Cambridge Companion to Hobbes's Leviathan*, edited by Patricia Springborg, 441–59. Cambridge, UK: Cambridge University Press, 2007.

Pasto, James. "'Strange Secret Sharers': Orientalism, Judaism, and the Jewish Question." *Comparative Studies in Society and History* 40, no. 3 (1998): 437–74.

———. "When the End is the Beginning? Or When the Biblical Past is the Political Present: Some Thoughts on Ancient Israel, 'Post-Exilic Judaism,' and the Politics of Biblical Scholarship." *Scandinavian Journal of the Old Testament* 12, no. 2 (1998): 157–202.

———. "W. M. L. de Wette and the Invention of Post-Exilic Judaism: Political Historiography and Christian Allegory in Nineteenth-Century German Biblical Scholarship." In *Jews, Antiquity, and the Nineteenth-Century Imagination*, edited by Hayim Lapin and Dale Marin, 33–52. Bethesda, MD: University Press of Maryland, 2003.

Patrick, D. "The Covenant Code Structure." *Vetus Testamentum* 27 (1977): 145–57.

Patton, Corrine. "'I Myself Gave Them Laws That Were Not Good': Ezekiel 20 and the Exodus Traditions.'" *Journal for the Study of the Old Testament* 69 (1996): 74–75.

Pelikan, Jaroslav. *The Christian Tradition: A History of the Development of Doctrine. Vol. 3, The Growth of Medieval Theology (600–1300)*. Chicago: University of Chicago Press, 1978.

Peña, Salvador. "Which Curiosity? Ibn Ḥazm's Suspicion of Grammarians." In *Ibn Hazm of Cordoba: The Life and Works of a Controversial Thinker*, edited by Camilla Adang, Maribel Fierro, and Sabine Schmidtke, 233–51. Leiden, NL: Brill, 2013.

Person, Raymond F., Jr. and Robert Rezetko. "Introduction: The Importance of Empirical Models to Assess the Efficacy of Source and Redaction Criticism." In *Empirical Models Challenging Biblical Criticism*, edited by Raymond F. Person, Jr. and Robert Rezetko, 1–35. Atlanta, GA: SBL Press, 2016.

Peterson, Lina. "The Linguistic Profile of the Priestly Narrative of the Pentateuch." In *Paradigm Change in Pentateuchal Research*, edited by Matthias Armgardt, Benjamin Kilchör, and Markus Zehnder, 243–64. Wiesbaden: Harrassowitz, 2019.

Philo. *The Works of Philo: Complete and Unabridged*. Translated by Charles Duke Yonge. Peabody, MA: Hendrickson, 1993.

Piattelli, Angelo M. "Umberto Cassuto: dalla formazione al Collegio Rabbinico Italiano alla polemica con Alfonso Pacifici." *La Rassegna Mensile di Israel* 82 (2016): 27–89.

Pietsch, Andreas Nikolaus. *Isaac La Peyrère: Bibelkritik, Philosemitismus und Patronage in der Gelehrtenrepublik des 17. Jahrhunderts.* Berlin: Walter de Gruyter, 2012.

Pines, Shlomo. "A Parallel Between Two Iranian and Jewish Themes." In *Irano-Judaica II: Studies Relating to Jewish Contacts with Persian Culture Throughout the Ages,* edited by Shaul Shaked and Amnon Netzer, 41–51. Jerusalem: Ben-Zvi Institute, 1990.

Pitkänen, Pekka. "Reconstructing the Social Contexts of the Priestly and Deuteronomic Materials in a Non-Wellhausian Setting." In *Paradigm Change in Pentateuchal Research,* edited by Matthias Armgardt, Benjamin Kilchör, and Markus Zehnder, 323–38. Wiesbaden, DE: Harrassowitz, 2019.

Pontifical Biblical Commission. "De mosaica authentia Pentateuchi." *Acta Sanctae Sedis* 39 (1906): 377–78.

Popkin, Richard H. "The Development of Religious Scepticism and the Influence of Isaac La Peyrère's Pre-Adamism and Bible Criticism." In *Classical Influences on European Culture, AD 1500–1700,* edited by Robert Ralf Bolgar, 271–80. Cambridge, UK: Cambridge University Press, 1976.

———. "The First Published Reaction to Spinoza's *Tractatus*: Col. J. B. Stouppe, the Condé Circle, and the Rev. Jean Lebrun." In *The Spinozistic Heresy: The Debate on the Tractatus Theologico-Politicus, 1670–1677,* edited by Paolo Christofolini, 6–12. Amsterdam and Maarssen: APA-Holland University Press, 1995.

———. *The History of Scepticism: From Savonarola to Bayle.* Oxford, UK: Oxford University Press, 2003.

———. *Isaac La Peyrère (1596–1676): His Life, Work and Influence.* Leiden, NL: Brill, 1987.

———. "Jewish-Christian Relations in the Sixteenth and Seventeenth Centuries: The Conception of the Messiah." *Jewish History* 6 (1992) 163–77.

———. "Millenarianism and Nationalism—A Case Study: Isaac La Peyrère." In *Millenarianism and Messianism in Early Modern European Culture: Continental Millenarians: Protestants, Catholics, Heretics,* edited by John Christian Laursen and Richard H. Popkin, 78–82. Dordrecht, NL: Kluwer Academic, 2001.

———. "Spinoza and Bible Scholarship." In *The Books of Nature and Scripture: Recent Essays on Natural Philosophy, Theology, and Biblical Criticism in the Netherlands of Spinoza's Time and the British Isles of Newton's Time,* edited by James E. Force and Richard H. Popkin, 1–20. Dordrecht, NL: Kluwer Academic, 1994.

———. "Spinoza and La Peyrère." *Southwestern Journal of Philosophy* 8 (1977): 172–95.

———. "Spinoza and Samuel Fisher." *Philosophia* 15 (1985): 219–36.

———. *The Third Force in Seventeenth-Century Thought.* Leiden, NL: Brill, 1992.

Portier, William L. "Fundamentalism in North America: A Modern Anti-Modernism." *Communio* 28, no. 3 (2001): 581–98.

Powers, David S. "Reading/Misreading One Another's Scriptures: Ibn Ḥazm's Refutation of Ibn Nagrella al-Yahū d ī." In *Studies in Islamic and Judaic Traditions: Papers Presented at the Institute for Islamic-Judaic Studies,* edited by William M. Brinner and Stephen D. Ricks, 109–21. Atlanta, GA: Scholars Press, 1986.

Preus, J. Samuel. *Spinoza and the Irrelevance of Biblical Authority*. Cambridge, UK: Cambridge University Press, 2001.

Puerta Vílchez, José Miguel. "Abū Muḥmmad ʿAlī Ibn Ḥazm: A Biographical Sketch." In *Ibn Hazm of Cordoba: The Life and Works of a Controversial Thinker*, edited by Camilla Adang, Maribel Fierro, and Sabine Schmidtke, 3–24. Leiden, NL: Brill, 2013.

Pulcini, Theodore. *Exegesis as Polemical Discourse: Ibn Ḥazm on Jewish and Christian Scriptures*. Atlanta, GA: Scholars Press, 1998.

Pummer, Reinhard. "The Samaritans and Their Pentateuch." In *The Pentateuch as Torah: New Models for Understanding Its Promulgation and Acceptance, edited by* Gary N. Knoppers and Bernard M. Levinson, 237–69. Winona Lake, IN: Eisenbrauns, 2007.

Quennehen, Élisabeth. "«L'auteur des *Préadamites*», Isaac Lapeyrère. Essai biographique." In *Dissidents, excentriques et marginaux de l'Âge classique: Autour de Cyrano de Bergerac: Bouquet offert à Madeleine Alcover*, edited by Patricia Harry, Alain Mothu, and Philippe Sellier, 349–73. Paris: Honoré Champion, 2006.

———. "Lapeyrère, la Chine et la chronologie biblique." *La Lettre clandestine* 9 (2000): 243–55.

Ramón Guerrero, Amelia. "Samuel ibn Nagrella y su hijo José en la 'memorias' de ʿAbd Allāh, último rey Zīrī de Granada." *Miscelánea de estudios Árabes y Hebraicos* 37–38 (1988–1989): 431–37.

Ramón Guerrero, Rafael. "Aristotle and Ibn Ḥazm. On the Logic of the *Taqrīb*." In *Ibn Hazm of Cordoba: The Life and Works of a Controversial Thinker*, edited by Camilla Adang, Maribel Fierro, and Sabine Schmidtke, 403–16. Leiden, NL: Brill, 2013.

———. "Filósofos hispano-musulmanes y Spinoza: Avempace y Abentofail." In *Spinoza y España: Actas del Congreso Internacional sobre «Relaciones entre Spinoza y España» (Almagro, 5–7 noviembre 1992)*, edited by Atilano Domínguez, 125–32. Almagro: Ediciones de la Universidad de Castilla-La Mancha, 1994.

Reed, Annette Yoshiko. "Heresiology and the (Jewish-) Christian Novel: Narrativized Polemics in the Pseudo-Clementine *Homilies*." In *Heresy and Identity in Late Antiquity*, edited by Eduard Iricinschi and Holger M. Zellentin, 273–98. Tübingen, DE: Mohr Siebeck, 2008.

Rehm, Bernhard and Georg Strecker, ed. *Die Pseudoklementinen I: Homilien*. Berlin: De Gruyter, 1992.

Rendsburg, Gary A. "Cyrus H. Gordon (1908–2001): A Giant Among Scholars." *Jewish Quarterly Review* 92 (2001): 137–43.

———. "The Genesis of the Bible." The Blanche and Irving Laurie Chair in Jewish History Investiture Address, October 14, 2004, and Inaugural Lecture, October 28, 2004. New Brunswick, NJ: Rutgers University, 2004

———. "The Literary Unity of the Exodus Narrative." In *"Did I Not Bring Israel Out of Egypt?" Biblical, Archaeological, and Egyptological Perspectives on the Exodus Narratives*, edited by James K. Hoffmeier, Alan R. Millard, and Gary A. Rendsburg, 113–32. Winona Lake, IN: Eisenbrauns, 2016.

———. *The Redaction of Genesis*. Winona Lake, IN: Eisenbrauns, 1986.

Rendtorff, Rolf. *The Old Testament: An Introduction*. Translated by John Bowden. Philadelphia, PA: Fortress Press, 1986.

Renz, Thomas. "The Use of the Zion Tradition in the Book of Ezekiel." In *Zion, City of Our God*, edited by Richard S. Hess and Gordon J. Wenham, 77–103. Grand Rapids, MI: Eerdmans, 1999.

Révah, Israel S. "Aux origines de la rupture Spinozienne: nouveaux documents sur l'incroyance dans la communauté judéo-portugaise a Amsterdam a l'époque de l'excommunication de Spinzoa." *Revue des études juives* 123 (1964): 359–431.

Reventlow, Henning Graf. *Bibelautorität und Geist der Moderne: Die Bedeutung des Bibelverständnisses für die geistesgeschichtliche und politische Entwicklung in England von der Reformation bis zur Aufklärung*. Göttingen, DE: Vandenhoeck & Ruprecht, 1980.

———. *Epochen der Bibelauslegung Band IV: Von der Aufklärung bis zum 20. Jahrhundert*. Munich, DE: Beck, 2001.

———. "Richard Simon und seine Bedeutung für die kritische Erforschung der Bibel." In *Historische Kritik in der Theologie*, edited by Georg Schwaiger, 11–36. Göttingen, DE: Vandenhoeck & Ruprecht, 1980.

———. "Towards the End of the 'Century of Enlightenment': Established Shift from *Sacra Scriptura* to Literary Documents and Religion of the People of Israel." In *Hebrew Bible/Old Testament: The History of Its Interpretation. Vol. 2, From the Renaissance to the Enlightenment*, edited by Magne Sæbø, 1024–63. Göttingen, DE: Vandenhoeck & Ruprecht, 2008.

Richelle, Matthieu. "Elusive Scrolls: Could Any Hebrew Literature Have Been Written Prior to the Eighth Century BCE?," *Vetus Testamentum* 66 (2016): 556–94.

———. "When Did Literacy Emerge in Judah?" *Biblical Archeology Review* 46, no. 2 (Spring, 2020): 58, 60–61.

Richter, Sandra. "The Archaeology of Mt. Ebal and Mt. Gerizim and Why It Matters to Deuteronomy." In *Sepher Torath Mosheh: Studies in the Composition and Interpretation of Deuteronomy*, edited by Daniel I. Block and Richard L. Schultz, 304–37. Peabody, MA: Hendrickson, 2017.

———. "What's Money Got to Do with It? Economics and the Question of the Provenance of Deuteronomy in the Neo-Babylonian and Persian Periods." In *Paradigm Change in Pentateuchal Research*, edited by Matthias Armgardt, Benjamin Kilchör, and Markus Zehnder, 301–21. Wiesbaden, DE: Harrassowitz, 2019.

Rif'at, Nurshif. "Ibn Ḥazm on Jews and Judaism." Diss., Exeter University, 1988.

———. "Ibn Hazm's Criticism to Rabbis and Rabbinical Writings." In *İbn Hazm: Uluslararasi katilimli İbn Hazm sempozyumu (26–28 Ekim 2007 Bursa/Türkiye): Bildiri ve Müzakere Metinleri*, edited by Süleyman Sayar and Muhammet Tarakçi, 491–526. Istanbul: Ensar Neşriyat, 2010.

Rigano, Gabriele. "Umberto Cassuto all'Università di Roma." *La Rassegna Mensile di Israel* 82 (2016): 117–36.

Roberts, J. J. M. *The Bible and the Ancient Near East: Collected Essays*. Winona Lake, IN: Eisenbrauns, 2000.

———. "The Davidic Origin of the Zion Tradition." *Journal of Biblical Literature* 92 (1973): 329–44.

———. "The Historicity of David's Imperial Conquests." *Theology Today* 70 (2013): 109–18.

Rofé, A. "Abraham Kuenen's Contribution to the Study of the Pentateuch: A View from Israel." In *Abraham Kuenen (1828–1891): His Major Contributions to the Study of the Old Testament: A Collection of Old Testament Studies Published on the Occasion of the Centenary of Abraham Kuenen's Death (10 December 1991)*, edited by P.B. Dirksen and A. Van Der Kooij, 105–12. Leiden, NL: Brill, 1993.

Rogerson, John W. "Early Old Testament Critics in the Roman Catholic Church—Focusing on the Pentateuch." In *Hebrew Bible/Old Testament: The History of Its Interpretation. Vol. 2, From the Renaissance to the Enlightenment*, edited by Magne Sæbø, 837–50. Göttingen, DE: Vandenhoeck & Ruprecht, 2008.

———. *Old Testament Criticism in the Nineteenth Century: England and Germany.* Philadelphia, PA: Fortress Press, 1984.

———. *W. M. L. de Wette Founder of Modern Biblical Criticism: An Intellectual Biography.* Sheffield, UK: Journal for the Study of the Old Testament Press, 1992.

Roling, Bernd. "Critics of the Critics: Johann Scheuchzer and His Followers in Defence of the Biblical Miracle." In *Scriptural Authority and Biblical Criticism in the Dutch Golden Age: God's Word Questioned*, edited by Dirk Van Miert, Henk Nellen, Piet Steenbakkers, and Jetze Touber, 374–91. Oxford, UK: Oxford University Press, 2017.

Römer, Thomas. "'Higher Criticism': The Historical and Literary-Critical Approach—with Special Reference to the Pentateuch." In *Hebrew Bible/Old Testament: The History of Its Interpretation. Vol. 3, From Modernism to Post-Modernism (The Nineteenth and Twentieth Centuries) Part 1: The Nineteenth Century—A Century of Modernism and Historicism*, edited by Magne Sæbø, 393–423. Göttingen, DE: Vandenhoeck & Ruprecht, 2013.

Rom-Shiloni, Dalit. *Exclusive Inclusivity: Identity Conflicts between the Exiles and the People Who Remained (6th–5th Centuries BCE).* Library of Hebrew Bible/Old Testament Studies 543. New York: T&T Clark, 2013.

———. "'How can you say, "I am not defiled . . ."?' (Jeremiah 2:20–25): Allusions to Priestly Legal Traditions in the Poetry of Jeremiah." *Journal of Biblical Literature* 133 (2014): 757–75.

———. *Voices from the Ruins: Theodicy and the Fall of Jerusalem in the Hebrew Bible.* Grand Rapids, MI: Eerdmans, 2021.

Rooker, Mark F. *Biblical Hebrew in Transition: The Language of the Book of Ezekiel.* Sheffield, UK: JSOT Press, 1990.

———. "The Use of the Old Testament in the Book of Hosea." *Criswell Theological Review* 7 (1993): 51–66.

Rosenthal, Judah. *Hiwi al-Balkhi.* Philadelphia, PA: Dropsie College, 1949.

———. "Hiwi al-Balkhi: A Comparative Study." *Jewish Quarterly Review* 38, no. 3 (1948): 317–42.

———. "Hiwi al-Balkhi: A Comparative Study (Continued)." *Jewish Quarterly Review* 38, no. 4 (1948): 419–30.

———. "Hiwi al-Balkhi: A Comparative Study (Continued)." *Jewish Quarterly Review* 39, no. 1 (1948): 79–94.

Roth, Norman. "Forgery and Abrogation of the Torah: A Theme in Muslim and Christian Polemic in Spain." *Proceedings of the American Academy for Jewish Research* 54 (1987): 203–36.

Rudavsky, T.M. "The Science of Scripture: Abraham Ibn Ezra and Spinoza on Biblical Hermeneutics." In *Spinoza and Medieval Jewish Philosophy*, edited by Steven Nadler, 59–78. Cambridge, UK: Cambridge University Press, 2014.

Rüger, Hans Peter. "Karlstadt als Hebraist an der Universität zu Wittenberg." *Archiv für Reformationsgeschichte* 75 (1984): 297–308.

Running, Leona Glidden and David Noel Freedman. *William Foxwell Albright: A Twentieth-Century Genius*. New York: Morgan Press, 1975.

Sabra, Adam. "Ibn Ḥazm's Literalism: A Critique of Islamic Legal Theory." In *Ibn Hazm of Cordoba: The Life and Works of a Controversial Thinker*, edited by Camilla Adang, Maribel Fierro, and Sabine Schmidtke, 97–160. Leiden, NL: Brill, 2013.

———. "Ibn Ḥazm's Literalism: A Critique of Islamic Legal Theory (I)." *Al-Qanṭara* 28, no. 1 (2007): 7–40.

Sacksteder, William. "How Much of Hobbes Might Spinoza Have Read?" *Southwestern Journal of Philosophy* 11 (1980): 25–39.

Saenz-Badillos, Angel. "Yiṣḥaq ibn Jalfun y Šěmu'el ibn Nagrella ha-Nagid." *Miscelánea de estudios Árabes y Hebraicos* 33 (1984): 21–43.

Salomon, H.P. "Le vrai excommunication de Spinoza." In *Forum Literarum*, edited by H. Bots and M. Kerkhof, 181–99. Amsterdam: Maarsen, 1984.

Sandys-Wunsch, John. "Early Old Testament Critics on the Continent." In *Hebrew Bible/Old Testament: The History of Its Interpretation. Vol. 2, From the Renaissance to the Enlightenment*, edited by Magne Sæbø, 971–84. Göttingen, DE: Vandenhoeck & Ruprecht, 2008.

Santiago-Otero, Horacio and Klaus Reinhardt. *La Biblia en la península ibérica durante la edad media (siglos XII–XV): El texto y su interpretación*. Coimbra: Arquivo da Universidade de Coimbra, 2001.

Sarna, Nahum M. "Abraham Ibn Ezra as an Exegete." In *Rabbi Abraham Ibn Ezra: Studies in the Writings of a Twelfth-Century Jewish Polymath*, edited by Isadore Twersky and Jay M. Harris, 1–27. Cambridge, MA: Harvard University Press, 1993.

———. *The JPS Torah Commentary: Genesis*. Philadelphia, PA: Jewish Publication Society, 1989.

———. "Zedekiah's Emancipation of Slaves and the Sabbatical Year." In *Occident and Orient: Essays Presented to Cyrus H. Gordon on the Occasion of his Sixty-fifth Birthday*, edited by Harry A. Hoffner, Jr., 143–49. Neukirchen-Vluyn: Neukirchener Verlag, 1973.

Sasson, Jack M. "Albright as an Orientalist." *Biblical Archaeologist* 56, no. 1 (1993): 3–7.

———. "The 'Tower of Babel' as a Clue to the Redactional Structuring of the Primeval History (Gen. 1–11:9)." In *The Bible World: Essays in Honor of Cyrus H. Gordon*, edited by Gary A. Rendsburg, Ruth Adler, Milton Arfa, and Nathan H. Winter, 211–19. New York: KTAV, 1980.

Satterthwaite, Philip E. "Zion in the Songs of Ascent." In *Zion, City of Our God*, edited by Richard S. Hess and Gordon J. Wenham, 105–28. Grand Rapids, MI: Eerdmans, 1999.

Schechter, S. "Geniza Specimens. The Oldest Collections of Bible Difficulties, by a Jew." *Jewish Quarterly Review* 13, no. 3 (1901): 345–74.

———. "Higher Criticism—Higher Anti-Semitism." In *Seminary Address and Other Papers*, by Solomon Schechter, 35–39. Cincinnati, OH: Ark Publishers, 1915.

Schmid, Konrad. "The Prophets after the Law or the Law after the Prophets?— Terminological, Biblical, and Historical Perspectives." In *The Formation of the Pentateuch: Bridging the Academic Cultures of Europe, Israel, and North America*, edited by Jan C. Gertz, Bernard M. Levinson, Dalit Rom-Shiloni, and Konrad Schmid, 841–50. Tübingen: Mohr Siebeck, 2016.

Schmid, Ulrich. *Marcion und sein Apostolos: Rekonstruktion und historische Einordnung der marionitischen Paulusbriefausgabe.* Berlin: De Gruyter, 1995.

Schmidt, Stjepan. *Augustin Bea: The Cardinal of Unity.* New Rochelle, NY: New City Press, 1992.

Schmidtke, Sabine. "Ibn Ḥazm's Sources on Ashʿarism and Muʿtazilism." In *Ibn Hazm of Cordoba: The Life and Works of a Controversial Thinker*, edited by Camilla Adang, Maribel Fierro, and Sabine Schmidtke, 375–402. Leiden, NL: Brill, 2013.

Schniedewind, William. "Linguistic Dating, Writing Systems, and the Pentateuchal Sources." In *The Formation of the Pentateuch: Bridging the Academic Cultures of Europe, Israel, and North America*, edited by Jan C. Gertz, Bernard M. Levinson, Dalit Rom-Shiloni, and Konrad Schmid, 345–55. Tübingen, DE: Mohr Siebeck, 2016.

Schröter, Marianne. *Aufklärung durch Historisierung: Johann Salomo Semlers Hermeneutik des Christentums.* Berlin: Walter de Gruyter, 2012.

Schulman, Alan R. "On the Egyptian Name of Joseph: A New Approach." *Studien zur Altägyptischen Kultur* 2 (1975): 235–43.

Seely, David Rolph. "The Raised Hand of God as an Oath Gesture." In *Fortunate the Eyes that See: Essays in Honor of David Noel Freedman*, edited by Astrid B. Beck et al., 411–21. Grand Rapids: Eerdmans, 1995.

Segal, M. H. "El, Elohim, and Yhwh in the Bible." *Jewish Quarterly Review* 46, no. 2 (1955): 89–115.

Seidel, Bodo. *Karl David Ilgen und die Pentateuchforschung im Umkreis der sogenannten Älteren Urkundenhypothese: Studien zur Geschichte der exegetischen Hermeneutik in der Späten Aufklärung.* Berlin: Walter de Gruyter, 1993.

Selman, Martin J. "Comparative Customs and the Patriarchal Age." In *Essays on the Patriarchal Narratives*, edited by A. R. Millard and D. J. Wiseman, 93–138. Leicester, UK: InterVarsity Press, 1980.

——. "Published and Unpublished Fifteenth Century BC Cuneiform Documents and Their Bearing on the Patriarchal Narratives of the Old Testament." Ph.D. diss., University of Wales, 1975.

——. "Social Environment of the Patriarchs." *Tyndale Bulletin* 27 (1976): 114–36.

Serrano, Delfina. "Claim (Daʿwā) or Complaint (Shakwā)? Ibn Ḥazm's and Qāḍī ʿIyāḍ's Doctrines on Accusations of Rape." In *Ibn Hazm of Cordoba: The Life and Works of a Controversial Thinker*, edited by Camilla Adang, Maribel Fierro, and Sabine Schmidtke, 179–205. Leiden, NL: Brill, 2013.

Sheehan, Jonathan. *The Enlightenment Bible: Translation, Scholarship, Culture*. Princeton, NJ: Princeton University Press, 2005.

Shuger, Deborah Kuller. *The Renaissance Bible: Scholarship, Sacrifice, and Subjectivity*. Waco, TX: Baylor University Press, 2010 (1994).

Shuve, Karl. "The Pseudo-Clementine Homilies and the Antiochene Polemic against Allegory." Ph.D. diss., McMaster University, 2007.

Simon, Uriel. "Abraham Ibn Ezra." In *Hebrew Bible/Old Testament: The History of Its Interpretation. Vol. 1, From the Beginnings to the Middle Ages (Until 1300). Part 2, The Middle Ages*, edited by Magne Sæbø, 377–87. Göttingen, DE: Vandenhoeck & Ruprecht, 2000.

——. "Ibn Ezra Between Medievalism and Modernism: The Case of Isaiah XL–LXVII." In *Congress Volume Salamanca 1983*, edited by J. A. Emerton, 257–71. Leiden, NL: Brill, 1985.

Ska, Jean-Louis. "L'Institut Biblique et l'hypothèse documentaire: un dialogue difficile. À propos du Pentateuque." In *Biblical Exegesis in Progress: Old and New Testament Essays*, edited by J.N. Aletti and J.L. Ska, 1–32. Rome: Editrice Pontificio Istituto Biblico, 2009.

——. *Introduction to Reading the Pentateuch*. Winona Lake, IN: Eisenbrauns, 2006.

——. "The Study of the Book of Genesis: The Beginning of Critical Reading." In *The Book of Genesis: Composition, Reception, and Interpretation*, edited by Craig A. Evans, Joel N. Lohr, and David L. Petersen, 1–26. Leiden, NL: Brill, 2012.

——. "Why Does the Pentateuch Speak so Much of Torah and so Little of Jerusalem?" In *The Fall of Jerusalem and the Rise of the Torah*, edited by Peter Dubovský, Dominik Markl, and Jean-Pierre Sonnet, 113–28. Tübingen, DE: Mohr Siebeck, 2016.

——. "The Yahwist, a Hero with a Thousand Faces: A Chapter in the History of Modern Exegesis." In *Abschied vom Jahwisten: Die Komposition des Hexateuch in der jüngsten Diskussion*, edited by Jan Christian Gertz, Konrad Schmid, and Markus Witte, 1–23. Berlin: Walter de Gruyter, 2002.

Skinner, Quentin. "Thomas Hobbes and His Disciples in France and England." *Comparative Studies in Society and History* 8, no. 2 (1966): 153–67.

Smend, Rudolf. *Deutsche Alttestamentler in drei Jahrhunderten*. Göttingen, DE: Vandenhoeck & Ruprecht, 1989.

——. "Jean Astruc: A Physician as a Biblical Scholar." In *Sacred Conjectures: The Context and Legacy of Robert Lowth and Jean Astruc*, edited by John Jarick, 157–73. London: T&T Clark, 2007.

———. *Julius Wellhausen. Ein Bahnbrecher in drei Disziplinen*. Munich, DE: Carl Friedrich von Siemens Stiftung, 2006.

———. "Julius Wellhausen and His *Prolegomena to the History of Israel*." *Semeia* 25 (1982): 1–20.

———. *From Astruc to Zimmerli: Old Testament Scholarship in Three Centuries*. Tübingen, DE: Mohr Siebeck, 2007.

———. "Johann David Michaelis und Johann Gottfried Eichhorn—zwei Orientalisten am Rande der Theologie." In *Theologie in Göttingen: Eine Vorlesungsreihe*, edited by Bernd Moeller, 58–81. Göttingen, DE: Vandenhoeck & Ruprecht, 1987.

———. "The Work of Abraham Kuenen and Julius Wellhausen." In *Hebrew Bible/Old Testament: The History of Its Interpretation. Vol. 3, From Modernism to Post-Modernism (The Nineteenth and Twentieth Centuries) Part 1: The Nineteenth Century—A Century of Modernism and Historicism*, edited by Magne Sæbø, 424–53. Göttingen, DE: Vandenhoeck & Ruprecht, 2013.

Smith, Mark S. *Untold Stories: The Bible and Ugaritic Studies in the Twentieth Century*. Peabody, MA: Hendrickson, 2001.

———. "W. F. Albright and His 'Household': The Cases of C. H. Gordon, M. H. Pope, and F. M. Cross." In *"A Wise and Discerning Mind": Essays in Honor of Burke O. Long*, edited by Saul M. Olyan and Robert C. Culley, 221–44. Providence, RI: Brown University Press, 2000.

Sommer, Benjamin. *A Prophet Reads Scripture: Allusion in Isaiah 40–66*. Stanford, CA: Stanford University Press, 1997.

Soravia, Bruna. "A Portrait of the *ʿālim* as a Young Man: The Formative Years of Ibn Ḥazm, 404/1013–420/1029." In *Ibn Hazm of Cordoba: The Life and Works of a Controversial Thinker*, edited by Camilla Adang, Maribel Fierro, and Sabine Schmidtke, 25–50. Leiden, NL: Brill, 2013.

Sorkin, David. *The Religious Enlightenment: Protestants, Jews, and Catholics from London to Vienna*. Princeton, NJ: Princeton University Press, 2008.

Speiser, Ephraim A. "The Contribution of Max Leopold Margolis to Semitic Linguistics." In *Max Leopold Margolis: Scholar and Teacher*, edited by Robert Gordis, 27–33. New York: Bloch, 1952.

Spinoza, Baruch. *Œuvres III: Tractatus Theologico-Politicus/Traité théologico-politique*. 2nd ed. Ed. Pierre-François Moreau. Text established by Fokke Akkerman. Translated and notes by Jacqueline Lagrée and Pierre-François Moreau. Paris: Presses universitaires de France, 2012.

Stegemann, Ekkehard. "«Die Halbierung der ‹hebräischen› Religion». De Wettes Konstruktion von «Hebraismus» und «Judentum» zum Zwecke christlicher Aneignung des Alten Testaments." In *Wilhelm Martin Leberecht de Wette. Ein Universaltheologie des 19. Jahrhunderts*, edited by Hans-Peter Mathys and Klaus Seybold, 79–95. Basel, CH: Schwabe, 2001.

Strecker, Georg. *Das Judenchristentum in den Pseudoklementinen*. Berlin: Akademie Verlag, 1958.

Stroumsa, Guy G. "*Homeros Hebraios*: Homère et la Bible aux origines de la culture européenne (17e–18e siècles)." In *L'Orient dans l'histoire religieuse de l'Europe: L'invention des origines*, edited by Mohammad Ali Amir-Moezzi and John Scheid, 87–100. Turnhout, BE: Brepols, 2000.

Sweeney, Marvin. "Hosea's Reading of Pentateuchal Narratives: A Window for a Foundational E Stratum." In *The Formation of the Pentateuch: Bridging the Academic Cultures of Europe, Israel, and North America*, edited by Jan C. Gertz, Bernard M. Levinson, Dalit Rom-Shiloni, and Konrad Schmid, 851–71. Tübingen, DE: Mohr Siebeck, 2016.

———. *The Twelve Prophets. Vol. 1, Hosea, Joel, Amos, Obadiah, Jonah*. Collegeville, MN: The Liturgical Press, 2000.

Tábet, Miguel Ángel. *Introducción al Antiguo Testamento I. Pentateuco y Libros Históricos*. Madrid: Palabra, 2004.

Thomas, David. "Ibn Ḥazm: Works on Christian-Muslim Relations: *Kitāb iẓhār tabdīl al-Yahūd wa-l-Naṣārā li-l-Tawrāt wa-l-Injīl wa-bayān tanāquḍ mā bi-aydīhim min dhālika min mā lā yaḥtamil al-tâwīl*, 'An exposure of the Jews and Christians' alteration to the Torah and Gospel, and a demonstration of the contradiction in what they possess of this that will not permit metaphorical interpretation." In *Christian-Muslim Relations: A Bibliographical History. Vol. 3, (1050–1200)*, edited by David Thomas and Alex Mallett, 140–41. Leiden, NL: Brill, 2011.

———. "Ibn Ḥazm: Works on Christian-Muslim Relations: Unknown title; *Radd 'alā risālat malik al-Rūm*, 'Refutation of the Byzantine emperor's letter.'" In *Christian-Muslim Relations: A Bibliographical History. Vol. 3, (1050–1200)*, edited by David Thomas and Alex Mallett, 143–45. Leiden, NL: Brill, 2011.

Thompson, Thomas L. *The Historicity of the Patriarchal Narratives: The Quest for the Historical Abraham*. Berlin: Walter de Gruyter, 1974.

Tiemeyer, Lena-Sofia. *For the Comfort of Zion: The Geographical and Theological Location of Isaiah 40–55*. Leiden, NL: Brill, 2011.

Tolan, John. "Petrus Alfonsi." In *Christian-Muslim Relations: A Bibliographical History. Vol. 3, (1050–1200)*, edited by David Thomas and Alex Mallett, 356–62. Leiden, NL: Brill, 2011.

———. *Petrus Alfonsi and His Medieval Readers*. Gainesville, FL: University Press of Florida, 1993.

Torrell, Jean-Pierre, O.P. and Denise Bouthillier. *Pierre le Vénérable et sa vision du monde. Sa vie, son œuvre. L'homme et le demon*. Louvain, BE: Spicilegium sacrum lovaniense, 1986.

Touber, Jetze. *Spinoza and Biblical Philology in the Dutch Republic, 1660–1710*. Oxford, UK: Oxford University Press, 2018.

Tov, Emanuel. "The Literary History of the Book of Jeremiah in the Light of its Textual History." In *Empirical Models for Biblical Criticism*, edited by Jeffrey H. Tigay, 211–37. Philadelphia, PA: University of Pennsylvania Press, 1985.

Tricaud, François. "L'Ancien Testament et le *Léviathan* de Hobbes: Une cohabitation difficile." *Rivista di Storia della Filosofia* 54, no. 2 (1999): 229–38.

Tsumura, David Toshio. "The Father of Ugaritic Studies." *Biblical Archaeologist* 59, no. 1 (1996): 44–50.

———. "Genesis and Ancient Stories of Creation and Flood: An Introduction." In *"I Studied Inscriptions from Before the Flood": Ancient Near Eastern, Literary, and Linguistic Approaches to Genesis 1–11*, edited by Richard S. Hess and David Toshio Tsumura, 27–57. Winona Lake, IN: Eisenbrauns, 1994.

Ulrich, Dean R. "The Framing Function of the Narratives about Zelophehad's Daughters." *Journal of the Evangelical Theological Society* 41 (1998): 529–38.

Ulrich, Eugene. "4QJosha." In *Qumran Cave 4: IX: Deuteronomy, Joshua, Judges, Kings*, edited by Eugene Ulrich, Frank Moore Cross, Sidnie White Crawford, Julie Ann Duncan, Patrick W. Skehan, Emanuel Tov, Julio Trebolle Barrera, 145–46. Oxford, UK: Clarendon Press, 1995.

Urvoy, Dominique. "Le sens de la polémique anti-biblique chez Ibn Hazm." In *Ibn Hazm of Cordoba: The Life and Works of a Controversial Thinker*, edited by Camilla Adang, Maribel Fierro, and Sabine Schmidtke, 485–96. Leiden, NL: Brill, 2013.

Vajda, Georges. "À propos de l'attitude religieuse de Hiwi al-Balkhi." *Revue des études juives* 99 (1934): 81–91.

Van Beek, Gus W. "W. F. Albright's Contribution to Archaeology." In *The Scholarship of William Foxwell Albright: An Appraisal: Papers Delivered at the Symposium "Homage to William Foxwell Albright," The American Friends of the Israel Exploration Society, Rockville, Maryland, 1984*, edited by Gus W. Van Beek, 61–73. Atlanta, GA: Scholars Press, 1989.

Van Miert, Dirk. *The Emancipation of Biblical Philology in the Dutch Republic, 1590–1670*. Oxford, UK: Oxford University Press, 2018.

———. "The Janus Face of Scaliger's Philological Heritage: The Biblical Annotations of Heinsius and Grotius." In *Scriptural Authority and Biblical Criticism in the Dutch Golden Age: God's Word Questioned*, edited by Dirk Van Miert, Henk Nellen, Piet Steenbakkers, and Jetze Touber, 91–108. Oxford, UK: Oxford University Press, 2017.

Van Miert, Dirk, Henk Nellen, Piet Steenbakkers, and Jetze Touber. Editors' Introduction to *Scriptural Authority and Biblical Criticism in the Dutch Golden Age: God's Word Questioned*, edited by Dirk Van Miert, Henk Nellen, Piet Steenbakkers, and Jetze Touber, 1–15. Oxford, UK: Oxford University Press, 2017.

———. Preface to *Scriptural Authority and Biblical Criticism in the Dutch Golden Age: God's Word Questioned*, edited by Dirk Van Miert, Henk Nellen, Piet Steenbakkers, and Jetze Touber, v–vi. Oxford, UK: Oxford University Press, 2017.

Van Seters, John. *Abraham in History and Tradition*. New Haven, CT: Yale University Press, 1975.

———. *The Edited Bible: The Curious History of the "Editor" in Biblical Criticism*. Winona Lake, IN: Eisenbrauns, 2006.

———. "The Deuteronomist—Historian or Redactor? From Simon to the Present." In *Essays on Ancient Israel in Its Near Eastern Context: A Tribute to Nadav Na'aman*, edited by Yairah Amit, Ehud Ben Zvi, Israel Finkelstein, and Oded Lipschits, 359–75. Winona Lake, IN: Eisenbrauns, 2006.

VanderKam, James C. *The Book of Jubilees*. Sheffield, UK: Sheffield Academic Press, 2001.

Vang, Carsten. "When a Prophet Quotes Moses: On the Relationship Between the Book of Hosea and Deuteronomy." In *Sepher Torath Mosheh: Studies in the Composition and Interpretation of Deuteronomy*, edited by Daniel I. Block and Richard L. Schultz, 277–30. Peabody, MA: Hendrickson, 2017.

Vereb, Jerome-Michael Vereb. *"Because He Was a German!": Cardinal Bea and the Origins of Roman Catholic Engagement in the Ecumenical Movement*. Grand Rapids, MI: Eerdmans, 2006.

Vincent, Jean Marcel. *Leben und Werk des frühen Eduard Reuss: ein Beitrag zu den geistesgeschichtlichen Voraussetzungen der Bibelkritik im zweiten Viertel des 19. Jahrhunderts*. Munich, DE: Kaiser, 1990.

———. "Le «rationalisme mystique» d'Edouard Reuss et ses incidences sur «La Bible»." *Revue d'histoire et de philosophie religieuses* 74, no. 1 (1994): 43–66.

Viterbo, Ariel. "'Maestro di Bibbia nel paese della Bibbia': Umberto Cassuto in Eretz Israel." *La Rassegna Mensile di Israel* 82 (2016): 137–62.

Vlessing, Odette. "The Excommunication of Baruch Spinoza: The Birth of a Philosopher." In *Dutch Jewry: Its History and Secular Culture (1500–2000)*, edited by Jonathan Israel and Reinier Salverda, 141–72. Leiden, NL: Brill, 2002.

———. "The Excommunication of Baruch Spinoza: A Conflict Between Jewish and Dutch Law." *Studia Spinozana* 13 (1997): 15–47.

———. "The Jewish Community in Transition: From Acceptance to Emancipation." *Studia Rosenthaliana* 30 (1996) 195–211.

———. "New Light on the Earliest History of the Amsterdam Portuguese Jews." In *Dutch Jewish History. Vol. 3,* edited by Jozeph Michman, 43–75. Assen, NL: Van Gorcum, 1993.

Vogt, Peter T. "'These Are the Words Moses Spoke': Implied Audience and a Case for a Pre-Monarchic Dating of Deuteronomy." In *For Our Good Always: Studies on the Message and Influence of Deuteronomy in Honor of Daniel I. Block*, edited by Jason S. DeRouchie, Jason Gile, and Kenneth J. Turner, 61–80. Winona Lake, IN: Eisenbrauns, 2013.

von Dunin Borkowski, Stanislaus, S.J. *Spinoza Band I: Der junge De Spinoza: Leben und Werdegang im Lichte der Weltphilosophie*. Münster, DE: Aschendorff, 1933.

———. *Spinoza Band II: Aus den Tagen Spinozas: Geschehnisse, Gestalten, Gedankenwelt Erster Teil: Das Entscheidungsjahr 1657*. Münster, DE: Aschendorff, 1933.

———. *Spinoza Band III: Aus den Tagen Spinozas: Geschehnisse, Gestalten, Gedankenwelt Zweiter Teil: Das neue Leben*. Münster, DE: Aschendorff, 1935.

———. *Spinoza Band III: Aus den Tagen Spinozas: Geschehnisse, Gestalten, Gedankenwelt Dritter Teil: Das Lebenswerk*. Münster, DE: Aschendorff, 1936.

von Moos, Peter. "Les *Collationes* d'Abélard et la 'question juive' au xiie siècle." *Journal des savants* 2 (1999): 449–89.

von Rad, Gerhard. *Old Testament Theology. Vol. 2, The Theology of Israel's Prophetic Traditions*. Translated by D. M. G. Stalker. San Francisco: Harper and Row, 1965.

von Wilamowitz-Moellendorff, Ulrich. *Erinnerungen, 1814–1914*. 2nd ed. Leipzig, DE: Koehler, 1928.

———. *The Preserved Letters of Ulrich von Wilamowitz-Moellendorff to Eduard Schwartz*. Edited by William M. Calder III and Robert L. Fowler. Munich, DE: Verlag der Bayerischen Akademie der Wissenschaften, 1986.

Vrolijk, Arnoud. "Arabic Studies in the Netherlands and the Prerequisite of Social Impact—A Survey." In *The Teaching and Learning of Arabic in Early Modern Europe*, edited by Jan Loop, Alastair Hamilton, and Charles Burnett, 13–32. Leiden, NL: Brill, 2017.

Vrolijk, Arnoud and Richard van Leeuwen. *Arabic Studies in the Netherlands: A Short History in Portraits, 1580–1950*. Translated by Alastair Hamilton. Leiden, NL: Brill, 2014.

Walther, Manfred. "Biblische Hermeneutik und historische Erklärung: Lodewijk Meyer und Benedikt de Spinoza." *Studia Spinozana* 11 (1995): 227–300.

Wasserstein, David J. "Ibn Ḥazm and al-Andalus." In *Ibn Hazm of Cordoba: The Life and Works of a Controversial Thinker*, edited by Camilla Adang, Maribel Fierro, and Sabine Schmidtke, 69–86. Leiden, NL: Brill, 2013.

———. "Samuel Ibn Naghrīla ha-Nagid and Islamic Historiography in Al-Andalus." *Al-Qantara* 14, no. 1 (1993): 109–25.

Weinfeld, Moshe. *Deuteronomy and the Deuteronomic School*. Oxford: Clarendon Press, 1972.

———. *Getting at the Roots of Wellhausen's Understanding of the Law of Israel on the 100th Anniversary of the Prolegomena*. Jerusalem: Institute for Advanced Studies, Hebrew University, 1979.

———. *Normative and Sectarian Judaism in the Second Temple Period*. London: T & T Clark, 2005.

———. *The Place of the Law in the Religion of Ancient Israel*. Leiden: Brill, 2004.

Weisberg, David B. "William W. Hallo: An Appreciation." In *The Tablet and the Scroll: Near Eastern Studies in Honor of William W. Hallo*, edited by Mark E. Cohen, Daniel C. Snell, and David B. Weisberg, ix–xvi. Bethesda, MD: CDL, 1993.

Weisman, Zeev. "Prof. Moshe Weinfeld's Contribution to Biblical Scholarship: An Appreciation." In *Sefer Moshe: The Moshe Weinfeld Jubilee Volume: Studies in the Bible and the Ancient Near East, Qumran, and Post-Biblical Judaism*, edited by Chaim Cohen, Avi M. Hurvitz, and Shalom M. Paul, xii–xviii. Winona Lake, IN: Eisenbrauns, 2004.

Wellhausen, Julius. "Die Composition des Hexateuchs." *Jahrbücher für Deutsche Theologie* 21 (1876): 392–450.

———. "Die Composition des Hexateuchs II." *Jahrbücher für Deutsche Theologie* 21 (1876): 531–602.

———. "Die Composition des Hexateuchs III." *Jahrbücher für Deutsche Theologie* 22 (1877): 407–79.

———. *Die Pharisäer und die Sadducäer. Eine Untersuchung zur innern jüdischen Geschichte*. Greifswald, DE: Bamberg, 1874.

———. *Prolegomena zur Geschichte Israels*. 5th ed. Berlin: Reimer, 1899.

———. *Prolegomena to the History of Israel with a Reprint of the Article Israel from the "Encyclopaedia Britannica."* Translated by J. Sutherland Black and Allan Menzies. Edinburgh: Adam & Charles Black, 1885.

Wenham, Gordon J. "The Coherence of the Flood Narrative." *Vetus Testamentum* 28, no. 3 (1978): 336–48.

———. "The Date of Deuteronomy: Linch-Pin of Old Testament Criticism: Part One." *Themelios* 10, no. 3 (1985): 15–20.

———. "The Date of Deuteronomy: Linch-Pin of Old Testament Criticism: Part Two." *Themelios* 11, no. 1 (1985): 15–18.

———. "The Religion of the Patriarchs." In *Essays on the Patriarchal Narratives*, edited by A. R. Millard and D.J. Wiseman, 157–88. Leicester, UK: InterVarsity Press, 1980.

———. "Sanctuary Symbolism in the Garden of Eden Story." In *Proceedings of the Ninth World Congress of Jewish Studies, Jerusalem, August 4–12, 1985*, 19–25. Jerusalem: World Union of Jewish Studies, 1986.

Wessels, W. "Zion, Beautiful City of God – Zion Theology in the Book of Jeremiah." *Verbum et Ecclesia* 27 (2006): 729–48.

Whybray, R.N. *The Making of the Pentateuch: A Methodological Study*. Sheffield, UK: Journal for the Study of the Old Testament Press, 1987.

Wicks, Jared. "Catholic Old Testament Interpretation in the Reformation and Early Confessional Eras." In *Hebrew Bible/Old Testament: The History of Its Interpretation. Vol. 2, From the Renaissance to the Enlightenment*, edited by Magne Sæbø, 617–48. Göttingen, DE: Vandenhoeck & Ruprecht, 2008.

Wilken, Robert L. *The Christians as the Romans Saw Them*. New Haven, CT: Yale University Press, 1984.

Wilkinson, Robert. *The Kabbalistic Scholars of the Antwerp Polyglot Bible*. Leiden, NL: Brill, 2007.

Williamson, George S. *The Longing for Myth in Germany: Religion and Aesthetic Culture from Romanticism to Nietzsche*. Chicago: University of Chicago Press, 2004.

Williamson, H. G. M. *The Book Called Isaiah: Deutero-Isaiah's Role in Composition and Redaction*. Oxford, UK: Oxford University Press, 1994.

Wilson, Gerald H. *The Editing of the Hebrew Psalter*. Chico, CA: Scholars Press, 1985.

Wilson, Robert Dick. "Scientific Biblical Criticism." *Princeton Theological Review* 17 (1919): 190–240.

———. *A Scientific Investigation of the Old Testament*. Philadelphia, PA: The Sunday School Times Company, 1926.

———. "The Use of 'God' and 'Lord' in the Koran." *Princeton Theological Review* 17 (1919): 644–50.

Wineland, John D. Preface to *The Light of Discovery: Studies in Honor of Edwin M. Yamauchi*, edited by John D. Wineland, xv–xvii. Eugene, OR: Pickwick, 2007.

Wintermute, O. S. "Jubilees." In *The Old Testament Pseudepigrapha*, edited by James H. Charlesworth, 2:35–142. Anchor Bible Reference Library. New York: Doubleday, 1985.

Wiseman, Donald J. "Abraham in History and Tradition Part I: Abraham the Hebrew."
Bibliotheca Sacra 134 (1977): 123–30.

———. "Abraham in History and Tradition Part II: Abraham the Prince." *Bibliotheca Sacra*
135 (1977): 228–37.

———. "Abraham Reassessed." In *Essays on the Patriarchal Narratives*, edited by A. R.
Millard and D.J. Wiseman, 139–56. Leicester, UK: InterVarsity Press, 1980.

———. "Annual Address: The Place and Progress of Biblical Archaeology." *Journal of the
Transactions of the Victoria Institute* 88 (1956): 117–28.

———. "Archaeological Confirmation of the Old Testament." In *Revelation and the Bible:
Contemporary Evangelical Thought*, edited by Carl F. H. Henry, 301–16. Grand Rapids,
MI: Baker, 1958.

———. "Archaeology and Scripture." *Westminster Theological Journal* 33, no. 2 (1971):
133–52.

———. "Genesis 10: Some Archaeological Considerations." *Journal of the Transactions of the
Victoria Institute* 87 (1955): 13–24.

———. "Law and Order in Old Testament Times." *Vox Evangelica* 8 (1973): 5–21.

———. *Life Above and Below: Memoirs*. N.p.: privately published, 2003.

———. "Secular Records in Confirmation of the Scriptures." *Journal of the Transactions of
the Victoria Institute* 87 (1955): 25–36.

———. "Some Recent Trends in Biblical Archaeology." *Journal of the Transactions of the
Victoria Institute* 82 (1950): 1–18.

———. "They Lived in Tents." In *Biblical and Near Eastern Studies: Essays in Honor
of William Sanford LaSor*, edited by Gary A. Tuttle, 195–200. Grand Rapids, MI:
Eerdmans, 1978.

Wiseman, Donald J. and Edwin Yamauchi. *Archaeology and the Bible: An Introductory Study*.
Grand Rapids, MI: Zondervan, 1979.

Wiseman, P.J. *Ancient Records and the Structure of Genesis: A Case for Literary Unity*.
Nashville, TN: Thomas Nelson, 1985 (1936).

Witter, Henning Bernhard. *Jura israelitarum in Palaestinam Terram Chananaeam
Commentatione in Genesin Perpetua sic demonstrate ut idiomatis authentici nativus sensus
fideliter detegatur, Mosis autoris primaeva intentio sollicite desiniatur, adeoque corpus
doctrinae et juris Cum antiquissimum, tum consumatissimum tandem eruatur; accedit in
paginarum fronte ipse textus Hebraeus cum versione Latina*. Hildesheim, DE: Schröder,
1711.

Wolfson, Henry Austryn. *The Philosophy of Spinoza: Unfolding the Latent Process of His
Reasoning. Vol. 1*. Cambridge, MA: Harvard University Press, 1934.

Woodbridge, John. "Richard Simon and the Charenton Bible Project: The Quest for 'Perfect
Neutrality' in Interpreting Scripture." In *Knowledge and Profanation: Transgressing the
Boundaries of Religion in Premodern Scholarship*, edited by Martin Mulsow and Asaph
Ben-Tov, 253–72. Leiden, NL: Brill, 2019.

———. "Richard Simon le «père de la critique biblique»." In *Le Grand Siècle et la Bible*,
edited by Jean-Robert Armogathe, 193–206. Paris: Beauchesne, 1989.

Yamauchi, Edwin M. "Abraham and Archaeology: Anachronisms or Adaptations?" In *Perspectives on Our Father Abraham: Essays in Honor of Marvin R. Wilson*, edited by Steven A. Hunt, 15–32. Grand Rapids, MI: Eerdmans, 2010.

———. "Abraham and Mesopotamia." *The Way* (September 1965): 1–5.

———. "The Achaemenid Capitals." *Near Eastern Archaeological Society Bulletin* 8 (1976): 5–81.

———. "Additional Notes on Tammuz." *Journal of Semitic Studies* 11 (1966): 10–15.

———. *Africa and the Bible*. Grand Rapids, MI: Baker Academic, 2004.

———. "Akhenaten, Moses, and Monotheism." *Near Eastern Archaeological Society Bulletin* 55 (2010): 1–15.

———. "An Ancient Historian's View of Christianity." In *Professors Who Believe: The Spiritual Journeys of Christian Faculty*, edited by Paul M. Anderson, 192–99. Downers Grove, IL: InterVarsity Press, 1998.

———. "Aramaic Magic Bowls." *Journal of the American Oriental Society* 85 (1965): 511–23.

———. "The Archaeological Background of Daniel." *Bibliotheca Sacra* 137, no. 1 (1980): 3–16.

———. "The Archaeological Background of Esther." *Bibliotheca Sacra* 137, no. 2 (1980): 99–117.

———. "The Archaeological Background of Ezra." *Bibliotheca Sacra* 173, no. 3 (1980): 195–211.

———. "The Archaeological Confirmation of Suspect Elements in the Classical and Biblical Traditions." In *The Law and the Prophets: Old Testament Studies Prepared in Honor of Oswald Thompson Allis*, edited by John H. Skilton, Milton C. Fisher, and Leslie W. Sloat, 54–70. Nutley, NJ: Presbyterian and Reformed, 1974.

———. "Archaeology and the Bible." In *The Oxford Companion to the Bible*, edited by Bruce M. Metzger and Michael D. Coogan, 46–54. Oxford, UK: Oxford University Press, 1993.

———. "Archaeology and the Gospels: Discoveries and Publications of the Past Decade (1977–1987)." In *The Gospels Today: A Guide to Some Recent Discoveries*, edited by John H. Skilton, 1–12. Philadelphia, PA: Skilton House, 1990.

———. *The Archaeology of New Testament Cities in Western Asia Minor*. Grand Rapids, MI: Baker Book House, 1980.

———. "Archaeology and the Scriptures." *Seminary Journal* 25 (1974): 163–241.

———. "Babylon." In *Major Cities of the Biblical World*, edited by R.K. Harrison, 32–48. Nashville, TN: Thomas Nelson, 1985.

———. "Christians and the Jewish Revolts against Rome." *Fides et Historia* 23 (1991): 11–30.

———. *Composition and Corroboration in Classical and Biblical Studies*. Philadelphia, PA: Presbyterian and Reformed, 1966.

———. "The Crucifixion and Docetic Christology." *Concordia Theological Quarterly* 46, no. 1 (1982): 1–20.

———. "The Current Status of Old Testament Historiography." In *Faith, Tradition, and History: Old Testament Historiography in Its Near Eastern Context*, edited by A. R.

Millard, James K. Hoffmeier, and David W. Baker, 1–36. Winona Lake, IN: Eisenbrauns, 1994.

———. "A Decade and a Half of Archaeology in Israel and Jordan." *Journal of the American Academy of Religion* 42 (1974): 710–26.

———. "Do the Bible's Critics Use a Double Standard?" *Christianity Today* 10 (19 November 1965): 179–82.

———. "Documents from Old Testament Times." *Westminster Theological Journal* 41, no. 1 (1978): 1–32.

———. "Elchasaites, Manichaeans, and Mandaeans in Light of the Cologne Mani Codex." In *Beyond the Jordan: Studies in Honor of W. Harold Mare*, edited by Glenn A. Carnagey, Sr., Glenn Carnagey, Jr., and Keith N. Schoville, 49–60. Eugene, OR: Wipf & Stock, 2005.

———. "The Episode of the Magi." In *Chronos, Kairos, and Christos: Nativity and Chronological Studies Presented to Jack Finegan*, edited by Jerry Vardaman and Edwin M. Yamauchi, 15–39. Winona Lake, IN: Eisenbrauns, 1989.

———. "Erasmus' Contribution to New Testament Scholarship." *Fides et Historia* 19, no. 3 (1987): 6–24.

———. *Foes from the Northern Frontier: Invading Hordes from the Russian Steppes*. Grand Rapids, MI: Baker Book House, 1982.

———. *Gnostic Ethics and Mandaean Origins*. Cambridge, MA: Harvard University Press, 1970.

———. *Greece and Babylon: Early Contacts between the Aegean and the Near East*. Grand Rapids, MI: Baker Book House, 1967.

———. "The Greek Words in Daniel in the Light of Greek Influence in the Near East." In *New Perspectives on the Old Testament*, edited by J. Barton Payne, 170–200. Waco, TX: Word Books, 1970.

———.. "Herodotus—Historian or Liar." In *Crossing Boundaries and Linking Horizons: Studies in Honor of Michael C. Astour*, edited by Gordon D. Young, Mark W. Chavalas, and Richard E. Averbeck, 599–614. Bethesda, MD: CDL Press, 1997.

———. "History and Hermeneutics." *Evangelical Journal* 5, no. 2 (1987): 55–66.

———. "Homer and Archaeology: Minimalists and Maximalists in Classical Context." In *The Future of Biblical Archaeology: Reassessing Methodologies and Assumptions: The Proceedings of a Symposium, August 12–14, 2001 at Trinity International University*, edited by James K. Hoffmeier and A. R. Millard, 69–90. Grand Rapids, MI: Eerdmans, 2004.

———. "Homer, History, and Archaeology." *Near Eastern Archaeological Society Bulletin* 3 (1973): 21–42.

———. "Jesus Outside the New Testament: What Is the Evidence?" In *Jesus Under Fire*, edited by Michael J. Wilkins and J. P. Moreland, 207–29. Grand Rapids, MI: Zondervan, 1995.

———. "Joseph in Egypt." *The Way* (September 1965): 28–36.

———. "Magic Bowls: Cyrus H. Gordon and the Ubiquity of Magic in the Pre-Modern World." *Biblical Archaeologist* 59, no. 1 (1996): 51–55.

———. "Magic or Miracle? Demons, Diseases and Exorcisms." In *Gospel Perspectives. Vol. 6, The Miracles of Jesus*, edited by David Wenham and Craig Blomberg, 89–183. Sheffield, UK: Journal for the Study of the Old Testament Press, 1986.

———. *Mandaic Incantation Texts*. New Haven, CT: American Oriental Society, 1967.

———. "Mordecai, the Persepolis Tablets, and the Susa Excavations." *Vetus Testamentum* 42 (1992): 272–75.

———. "Obelisks and Pyramids." *Near Eastern Archaeological Society Bulletin* 24 (1985): 111–15.

———. "The Patriarchal Age." In *Wycliffe Bible Encyclopedia*, edited by Charles F. Pfeiffer, Howard F. Vos, and John Rhea, 1287–91. Chicago: Moody Press, 1975.

———. *Persia and the Bible*. Grand Rapids, MI: Baker Book House, 1990.

———. "Persians." In *Peoples of the Old Testament*, edited by Alfred J. Hoerth, Gerald L. Mattingly, and Edwin M. Yamauchi, 107–24. Grand Rapids, MI: Baker Academic, 1994.

———. "Pre-Christian Gnosticism in the Nag Hammadi Texts?" *Church History* 48 (1979): 129–41.

———. *Pre-Christian Gnosticism? A Survey of the Proposed Evidence*. London: Tyndale, 1973.

———. "The Present Status of Mandaean Studies." *Journal of Near Eastern Studies* 25 (1966): 88–96.

———. "The Proofs, Problems and Promises of Biblical Archaeology." *Evangelical Review of Theology* 9, no. 1 (1985): 117–38.

———. "The Proofs, Problems and Promises of Biblical Archaeology." *Journal of the American Scientific Affiliation* 36, no. 3 (1984): 129–38.

———. Review of *Before Abraham Was*, by Isaac M. Kikawada and Arthur Quinn. *Journal of the American Oriental Society* 108, no. 2 (1988): 310–11.

———. Review of *The Documentary Hypothesis and the Composition of the Pentateuch*, by Umberto Cassuto. *Journal of the American Oriental Society* 85, no. 4 (1965): 582–83.

———. *The Scriptures and Archaeology: Abraham to Daniel*. Portland, OR: Western Conservative Baptist Seminary, 1980.

———. "The Scythians: Invading Hordes from the Russian Steppes." *Biblical Archaeologist* 46, no. 2 (1983): 90–99.

———. "The Scythians—Who Were They? And Why Did Paul Include Them in Colossians 3:11?" *Priscilla Papers* 21, no. 4 (2007): 13–18.

———. "Stones, Scripts, and Scholars." *Christianity Today* 13 (14 February 1969): 432–34 and 436–37.

———. *The Stones and the Scriptures: An Introduction to Biblical Archaeology*. Philadelphia, PA: Lippincott, 1972.

———. "Tammuz and the Bible." *Journal of Biblical Literature* 81 (1965): 283–90.

———. "Was Nehemiah the Cupbearer a Eunuch?" *Zeitschrift für die alttestamentliche Wissenschaft* 92, no. 1 (1980): 132–42.

Yamauchi, Edwin M., with contributions from Paul J. N. Lawrence and Daniel I. Block "In Praise of a Venerable Scribe: A Bibliographic Tribute to Alan R. Millard." In *Write That They May Read: Studies in Literacy and Textualization in the Ancient Near East and in the Hebrew Scriptures: Essays in Honour of Professor Alan R. Millard*, edited by Daniel I. Block, David C. Deuel, C. John Collins, and Paul J.N. Lawrence, 392–415. Eugene, OR: Pickwick, 2020.

Young, Edward J. "Celsus and the Old Testament." *Westminster Theological Journal* 6, no. 2 (1944): 166–97.

———. *An Introduction to the Old Testament*. Grand Rapids, MI: Eerdmans, 1989 (1949).

———. *The Prophecy of Daniel: A Commentary*. Grand Rapids, MI: Eerdmans, 1949.

Younger, K. Lawson, Jr. *Ancient Conquest Accounts: A Study in Ancient Near Eastern and Biblical History Writing*. Sheffield, UK: Journal for the Study of the Old Testament Press, 1990.

———. "The 'Contextual Method': Some West Semitic Reflections." In *The Context of Scripture. Vol. 3, Archival Documents from the Biblical World*, edited by William W. Hallo and K. Lawson Younger, Jr., xxxv–xlii. Leiden, NL: Brill, 2002.

Yovel, Yirmiyahu. *Spinoza and Other Heretics. Vol. 2, The Adventures of Immanence*. Princeton, NJ: Princeton University Press, 1989.

Zac, Sylvain. *Spinoza et l'interprétation de l'Écriture*. Paris: Presses universitaires de France, 1965.

Zahn, Molly M. "New Voices, Ancient Words: The *Temple Scroll's* Reuse of the Bible." In *Temple and Worship in Biblical Israel*, edited by John Day, 435–58. London: T&T Clark, 2007.

Zammit, Abigail R. "To Read, or Not to Read: The Question of Literacy in Lachish 3." In *To Gaul, to Greece and into Noah's Ark: Essays in Honour of Kevin J. Cathcart on the Occasion of His Eightieth Birthday*, edited by Laura Quick, Ekaterina E. Kozlova, Sona Noll, and Philip Y. Yoo, 111–22. Oxford, UK: University of Manchester/Oxford University Press, 2019.

Zehnder, Markus. "Leviticus 26 and Deuteronomy 28." In *Paradigm Change in Pentateuchal Research*, edited by Matthias Armgardt, Benjamin Kilchör, and Markus Zehnder, 115–78. Wiesbaden: Harrassowitz, 2019

Zetterholm, Karin Hedner. "Jewish Teachings for Gentiles in the Pseudo-Clementine *Homilies*: A Reception of Ideas in Paul and Acts Shaped by a Jewish Milieu?" *Journal of the Jesus Movement in its Jewish Setting* 6 (2019): 68–87.

Zimmermann, Frank. "The Contributions of M. L. Margolis to the Fields of Bible and Rabbinics." In *Max Leopold Margolis: Scholar and Teacher*, edited by Robert Gordis, 17–26. New York: Bloch, 1952.

Zevit, Ziony. "Deuteronomy and the Temple: An Exercise in Historical Imagining." In *Mishneh Todah: Studies in Deuteronomy and Its Cultural Environment in Honor of Jeffrey H. Tigay*, edited by Nili Sacher Fox, David A. Glatt-Gilad, and Michael J. Williams, 201–18. Winona Lake, IN: Eisenbrauns, 2009.

Works Cited

Zimmerli, Walther. *Ezekiel 1*. Philadelphia, PA: Fortress Press, 1969.

Ziolkowski, Jan M. "Peter Abelard as Textual Critic and Historian." *Journal of Medieval Latin* 17 (2007): 361–71.